Can
Virtue
Make Us
Happy?

Can Virtue Make Us Happy?

THE ART OF LIVING AND MORALITY

Otfried Höffe

Translated from the German by
Douglas R. McGaughey

Translation edited by Aaron Bunch

NORTHWESTERN UNIVERSITY PRESS
EVANSTON, ILLINOIS

Northwestern University Press
www.nupress.northwestern.edu

Printed in the United States of America

10 9 8 7 6 5 4 3 2 1

Library of Congress Cataloging-in-Publication Data

Höffe, Otfried.
[Lebenskunst und Moral. English]
Can virtue make us happy? : the art of living and morality / Otfried Höffe ;
translated from the German by Douglas R. McGaughey ; translation edited by
Aaron Bunch.
p. cm.
"Originally published in German by Verlag C. H. Beck oHG, Munchen
2007."—T.p. verso.
Includes bibliographical references and index.
ISBN 978-0-8101-2545-2 (cloth : alk. paper) 1. Ethics. 2. Hedonism.
3. Autonomy (Philosophy) I. McGaughey, Douglas R., 1947– II. Bunch, Aaron.
III. Title.
BJ1114.H57513 2010
170—dc22

2009040431

CONTENTS

1 Introduction

Two things above and beyond the necessities of life are essential to humanity: one's own well-being, also called happiness, and morals. At first glance, it appears that these contradict one another since well-being places the individual in the center, whereas morals protest against this self-centeredness. As an exercise in fundamental ethics, this study takes a second look and asks: Must one act contrary to morals in order to be happy, and must the individual who acknowledges morals risk his own happiness? Or is it possible to have both—to experience happiness and nevertheless live in conformity with morals?

These questions already occur in everyday life. They are not artificial questions created by philosophers but arise already in advance of philosophical inquiry and demand an answer that will stand the test of normal life. In order for what follows to be understood by those who lead everyday lives, this study avoids unnecessary erudition. It does attempt to think through the issues with necessary thoroughness. Nonetheless, there is no naive presumption that it is engaging in such a process for the first time. In the case of such questions that have forever pressed themselves upon humanity, there are rarely novel, pathbreaking answers. It would be disingenuous to suppress the abundance of stimulating suggestions—above all in the history of philosophy—to which today's discussion is indebted. What one expects for oneself, one owes to others: the recognition of the accomplishment of others without jealousy; one claims originality only where it is actually justified.

When concerned with the fundamentals of being human, we don't learn only from philosophers but also from life experience and the reflections of everyday understanding, from science and, not least, from traditions of wisdom and world literature. In the process, we learn that with respect to questions of happiness and morals there can be a consensus above and beyond all epochal, cultural, and religious boundaries:

reflection about the art of living and morals leads of itself to an intercultural discussion.

What unites humanity is not merely commitments, and the concepts and arguments used to discuss them. Doubts and difficulties are also universal. This is where the intercultural discussion begins. When it comes to simple doubt, of course, one doesn't need philosophy. Even with respect to morals, philosophy only enters into play when doubts are so fundamental that they turn into difficulties that the usual strategies of life, experience, and judgment, as well as life's wisdom, cannot resolve. One response in such a circumstance is to capitulate to the difficulties and to declare them to be an unsolvable aporia. Just as in the case of a good physician or research scientist, however, philosophy does not consist exclusively in the dramatic description of hopelessness. At the least, the aptitude for finding a way out of the difficulties is also expected. In such a case, one declares the difficulties to be a puzzle capable of solution. Thereby, curiosity is aroused, and curiosity itself calls forth the determination to insist that there must be, and surely is, a way out of the impasse. It is often even the case that, in the precise diagnosis of the situation, a solution emerges.

With respect to ethics, the difficulties don't just emerge with the relationship between happiness and morals. They begin with the prior question: just what does one mean with these concepts? If ethics begins with happiness, and conceives it purely subjectively as mere well-being, then at best happiness can only accidentally cohere with morals. However, if happiness is concerned with the quality of a successful life in the sense that one's existence is happy (Greek: *eudaimonia*), then attitudes like prudence, generosity, and justice, which doubtless have a moral dimension to them, are included, for that reason are called virtues, and allow to a great extent happiness to be compatible with morals.

According to another point of view, that of utilitarian ethics, from the beginning more is in play than merely one's own happiness. All actions have far more to do with the end (*telos*) of contributing to the welfare of all involved. A third ethical perspective begins with the concept of morals and views morals as limited neither to one's own nor to the other's happiness but as having to do with what one can call duty (*deon*), for example, the injunction against lying or the obligation to assist those in need. The principle involved in such a case is freedom in the sense of self-legislation (*auto-nomia*) by the will. Now we have a new tension. It lies no longer between happiness and morals but among three concepts of morals and their different principles. In the first case, one is concerned with a virtue morals that is oriented toward one's own happiness; in the second case with an obligatory ends- or success-morals that is concerned with collective happiness; and in the third case with a duty-morals that arises out of autonomy.

In the natural sciences, new innovations are often named after their discoverers. One speaks, for example, of Newton's laws and of Planck's constant. Analogously, (Western) philosophy turns to its discoverers, particularly the Greeks. The ethic of happiness is named according to the Greek expression eudaimonistic, the ethic of goal-orientation is named teleological, and the ethics of duty is named deontological or, in light of self-legislation, the ethics of autonomy. Insofar as philosophy refers to its classic forebears, it assigns the principle of happiness (eudaimonia) above all to a "church father" of classical philosophy, Aristotle; the principle of freedom (autonomy) to the extraordinary thinker of modernity, Immanuel Kant; and for utilitarian teleology one thinks of Jeremy Bentham and John Stuart Mill as the decisive classics.

As in other fields of study, in philosophical ethics, the reservoir of fundamental concepts and arguments is limited and also long well known. With respect to fine-tuning and mediating positions, of course, the philosophical cards have been reshuffled many times. However, the play is essentially already written with three suits: eudaimonism, teleology as utilitarianism, and deontology as autonomy. A philosophy not limited to the academic tradition speaks of a fourth suit: the critique of morals.

For a long time philosophical languages were shaped by "their" classics: the German debate was among Kant, the Kant critic Hegel, and the critic of morals, Nietzsche. In English circles utilitarianism has dominated. Only the "founding fathers" Plato and above all Aristotle are included and respected in both the Continental and the Anglo-American discussions. For quite a while now, however, we can identify a major shift. After a period of bad press, utilitarianism has gained greater weight in German philosophy, and the work of John Rawls has resulted in a breakthrough in Anglo-American moral philosophy based on his theory of justice that critiques utilitarianism from a Kantian perspective.

As in other aspects of philosophy, moral philosophy is identifiable in terms of three moments. In the quest to expose errors in its ranks and to acquire the greatest knowledge, philosophy does not make appeals but works with arguments, reflection, and an aim to be free of presuppositions. The *first* task is the clarification of concepts, since especially basic concepts tend to be ambiguous. The task is to find a measuring stick for the subject matter of these fundamental concepts—in this case: for morals and for the happy life—and to discuss their compatibility. In order to arrive at an acceptable conclusion, philosophy develops both justifications for holding a point of view as well as counterpositions and weighs them against one another.

This procedure that as a totality one calls argument is accompanied by a *second* task, that of reflection. Reflection begins with foreknowledge—in this case, a sense of what morals and happiness in life are—and distances itself from this foreknowledge in order through a new examination to clearly distinguish among its elements or moments with the goal of establishing warrants for the fundamental principles involved or, as in the case of the critique of morals, of discrediting the principles.

The standard to which one frequently appeals in philosophy is mathematics. However, in the case of mathematics, it is capable to a great degree of creating its own objects. It can constructively de-fine [de-limit] its objects and, thereby, avoid ambiguities by a complete determination and construction of its elements. Such a luxury is not available to moral philosophy. The very nature of its reflective character means that it is an application to an already known world, a world that desires happiness and morals. Since this world is found in practically all cultures and epochs, one can identify a fundamental fact of humanity and can ascertain a dual concern: on the one hand, toward happiness and morals and, on the other hand, reflection on this orientation toward happiness and morals.

Philosophy maintains as a *third* task that it is to be free from presuppositions in its argumentation and reflection, that it place nothing beyond question. Even what appears to be most self-evident must be placed in question or at least be open to criticism: radical criticism belongs essentially to philosophy. In moral philosophy there is a fourth suit, multifaceted criticism of morals, which (for example, as a form of strong relativism) recognizes no universally valid obligations. In addition, today we have a neuroscientific determinism that declares freedom and responsibility to be an illusion. This study attempts to play using all of moral philosophy's four suits in the moral game to play out their moves with the intention of softening the barriers among them, especially where their interaction has become fossilized.

According to a favorite image in antiquity, the individual is like an archer who is assisted by the moral philosopher in hitting his target. If we change our focus from an image to the medium in which philosophy functions, the concept, there emerges a self-evidence that is welcomed by the public: ethics as practical philosophy. This notion stands in contrast to theoretical philosophy but sounds, just like the notion itself, unusual, even provocative, since philosophy is already a form of theory, so that the addition of "theoretical" is taken to be unnecessary and practical philosophy, then, is taken to be contradictory. "Practical" means what serves the successful solution of concrete life problems, and it is assumed that philosophy is not concerned with such concrete life problems.

However, theory, in contrast to practical philosophy, is not a name for this relatively fundamental knowledge. What is meant is "theoretical theory" that is sought for its own sake and that makes knowledge its goal. Practical philosophy is distinguished from theoretical philosophy in a trivial sense by means of its object. Theoretical philosophy is directed toward what is independent of humanity, nature, whereas practical philosophy is concerned with praxis, which is by definition dependent on humanity. Practical philosophy becomes truly practical, however, only with a second distinction: it is concerned with understanding what matters to the concrete experience of persons, with the execution of one's existence and of one's institutions, and not with knowledge merely for its own sake. Ethics as practical philosophy seeks an existential meaning.

Nonetheless, it remains true to its profession, philosophy. It develops exclusively through concepts, arguments, and reflection. An impatient ethic that did otherwise (i.e., was eager to change the world in order to bring about personal transformation, political revolution, or counter-revolution) steps outside its competence. As a consequence, it risks pursuing an immature philosophy and a naive politics, and hence, of practicing both bad theory and bad praxis. If philosophy wishes to be practical in its sense of the term, it can do so only through understanding that is relevant to praxis.

This achievement appears to be accomplished more easily by an ethics of happiness. For that reason one eagerly vaunts such an ethic as a philosophical art of living. In fact, however, a freedom- and duty-ethic as practical philosophy can also be cultivated as a philosophical art of living. Nonetheless, it is self-evident that both forms of moral philosophy, as eudaimonistic and as autonomy-ethics, provide enlightenment and a fundamental orientation, but neither offers a simple recipe. Equally self-evident is the rejection by both of every form of authoritarian morals. Anyone who wishes to lead one's life in terms of personal responsibility will reject every recipe and every authoritarian prescription.

Eudaimonism and a morals of autonomy do not need to be distinguished when it comes to the goal of practical philosophy and the art of living. Their opposition commences at a different place, at that point we have not yet examined: in the fundamental concept of human action. It is because of human action that we can engage the two principal themes of happiness and freedom. Common to both is an interest in constructing a superlative of good with the aid of the fundamental concept "good"; however, they are different in terms of the object to which this interest is applied. If one understands action to be the approaching of a goal, as aspiration, then the superlative "good" consists in an unsurpassable and absolutely highest aim. Consistent with this understanding, what it calls "moral principle" lies in the totality of the fulfillment of all aspiring, in eudaimonistic happiness. If one, to the contrary, understands action not in terms of a goal but in terms of its origin, the superlative [good] is taken to be, with respect to this absolute origin, what philosophy calls freedom of the will or the autonomy of the will.

These reflections result in the following outline: *the first part* [of this book] develops the fundamental notion of the argumentation model "Ethics plus Theory of Action" by working through and solving a series of difficulties and methods. The catchword "ethics" refers to what the two principal themes of happiness and freedom have in common, the superlative "good" (chapter 2). Two further shared elements follow: the appropriate logic of argumentation that avoids a host of erroneous conclusions (chapter 3) and a sketch of what is often overlooked in philosophical ethics, moral anthropology (chapter 4). Only with the turn to the theory of action do we encounter the bifurcation into eudaimonistic aspiration and autonomous willing (chapter 5). The two following parts [of this book] engage the principal themes that emerge out of this bifurcation: "The Principle of Happiness: Eudaimonia" and "The Principle of Freedom: Autonomy."

The second part commences with a clarification of the concept of happiness as it applies to action as aspiration (chapter 6). On the basis of reflection concerning how a philosophical art of living would look in terms of action as aspiration (chapter 7), one follows the following steps: How are we to evaluate the widely embraced life goals of pleasure, affluence, power, and prestige in terms of happiness (chapter 8)? What does the characteristic concept of virtue mean for an ethic of happiness (chapter 9); what are its characteristic examples (chapter 10), and why does it need to be complemented by wisdom rather than by the calculation of happiness preferred by the utilitarians (chapter 11)? There then follow two critical additional questions: "Can Virtue Make Us Happy?" (chapter 12) and "Euthanasia of Morals?" (chapter 13). These two additional critical questions forge ahead to the transition from an ethic of aspiration to an ethic of willing (chapter 14).

The third part develops initially the difficult principal theme, that of the freedom of the will (chapters 15–17). Because a thorough philosophy must engage the relevant skepticism, the project turns to examine two provocations against the freedom of the will: determinism (chapter 18) and the challenge represented by cognitive science and neuroscience (chapter 19). Only after this detour can a philosophy of the freedom of the will be "constructive." It develops the criterion of the universalization of life principles (maxims) and distinguishes this criterion from two alternatives, consequentialism and discourse ethics (chapter 20). On the basis of two often discussed examples, promise and the deposit, the criterion acquires concrete significance (chapter 21). Then follows the difficult question of whether or not there is such a thing as autonomous freedom and in what sense it exists (chapter 22). After a quick look at the contrary concept to the morally good, evil, which is surprisingly often overlooked (chapter 23), we can conclude that: the art of living that one usually evaluates only in terms of the principle of happiness is anything but foreign to autonomous morals (chapters 24 and 25).

Again there are many to thank: above all attentive and critical students, then come engaged colleagues, this time Dirk Brantl and Axel Rittsteiger, and especially, however, Nico Scarano, and not least the German Research Foundation (Deutsche Forschungsgemeinschaft) for a semester with no teaching responsibilities and fewer commissions to attend. The English translation was made possible in part thanks to the generosity of a grant from the Volkswagen Foundation.

Otfried Höffe
Tübingen, October 2006

Part 1
Ethics plus Theory of Action

2 Thinking the Good Through

Ethics already encounters four major difficulties with its first task, the determination of its object. These difficulties, however, are peculiar neither to Western culture nor to the present "moral situation": both the object and the discourse of the discipline are characterized by ambiguity (chapter 2.1); the fundamental concept "good" resists every attempt at definition according to the so-called naturalistic fallacy (chapter 2.2); the usual presupposition of ethics, universal obligation, is questioned by relativism (chapter 2.3); and, according to a popular theory of modernism, morality is supposed to have lost its function (chapter 2.4).

2.1 Three Objects, Three Discourses

Whereas others like to engage the object of their reflections quickly, philosophy asks, first, just what is the object? Philosophy's subject matter is so rich and its concepts so loaded with overtones of meaning that its concepts themselves require clarification. As is generally the case, in ethics the ambiguity is grounded less in a lack of clear thought or the vagueness of speaking than in the multiple layers of its object.

Western moral philosophy begins with the Greeks; it becomes a separate discipline with Aristotle under the title *ta êthika*. The term's root includes the three meanings of *ethos*, all of which philosophers have treated, understandably, though with varying degrees of emphasis.

The first meaning, Ethos 1, the lived location of an organism, already has a role in the prehuman sphere. As water is for fish and the air is for birds, so the space under dead tree bark is the appropriate habitat for bark beetles. Domestic animals already have more than one single life space: cattle, sheep, and horses find themselves at home in the field as well as in stalls created for them by humans. However, it is the domesticators themselves who can function in many places and with technical help practically anywhere: on, under, or over the earth, in caves, tents, simple houses or high-rises, in poverty or in luxurious palaces. What in animals is largely predetermined by biology depends in the case of human beings to a great extent on interest and technical skill, which in turn are shaped culturally: the biological species in this case generously leaves tremendous power to culture. Liberal cultures expand this generosity and provide great latitude for the individual. Both cultural and individual latitude confront us with questions of value and orientation, which in turn call philosophical ethics onto the scene.

The difference between cultural and individual degrees of freedom indicates an additional feature of humanity: its ethos is developed in two ways. On the one hand, a social ethos or Ethos 2 (Greek *ethos* with a short *e;* Latin *mores*) is quintessential normalcy and force of habit that extends from mere convention (e.g., right- or left-lane traffic) over etiquette and what is proper to lifestyles and institutions (e.g., marriage and family, schools, universities, civic law and the state). On the other hand, we can speak of a personal ethos (Ethos 3), namely, the manner in which someone conducts his own life within a social ethos. This more or less personal life strategy or form of living has as its subjective condition the character of an individual's mindset and sensitivity. To one's personal ethos belongs, as well, the acceptance or rejection felt by the subject in his social context (e.g., personal praise or reprimand; respect or scorn). As a consequence of this feature, ethics develops in two additional areas. On the one hand, social ethics investigates community morals and institutions; on the other hand, personal ethics investigates individual ways of living and character.

Moral philosophy alone, of course, is by no means responsible for these objects. Social and personal ethos can be examined in terms of three epistemological interests.

(1) In the broadest framework of *empirical ethics,* (1.1) a *descriptive ethics* is concerned with the factually present, dominant ethos, *positive morality,* and involves a diversity but also simultaneously a commonality. (1.2) Scientifically more rigorous, *explanatory ethics* seeks to explain the origin and function of positive morals and to generalize this explanation to a theory of human conduct. Empirical discourse insists upon diligent neutrality: one abstains from every form of judgment with respect to value or non-value, from good or bad; one maintains a normative neutrality.

In the case of descriptive and explanatory questions, other sciences are primarily responsible. However, even in this case philosophy is not entirely incompetent. Philosophy can introduce new perspectives for research (e.g., the often overlooked question of whether despite many differences there might not also be tremendous agreements in morality among cultures). In contrast to a strenuous relativism, an open-minded view encounters in fact a great number of commonalities, so many that morals may claim the status of a common heritage of humanity (see chapter 2.3).

(2) Most importantly, philosophical ethics concerns itself with the second, *normative task* which is itself divided into two parts. The first part, *evaluative ethics*, determines whether or not the given ethos conforms to an appropriately valid ethos (i.e., in terms of *critical morals*), which often is called simply "moral." Here one is taking morals in a broad sense as a concept that encompasses four competing principles: eudaimonism, autonomy, collective well-being, and the various criticisms of morality. In the case of a positive evaluation, one speaks of the good, and of what is correct, and, in the case of the opposite conclusion, of the bad, false, or of evil.

The second part, *prescriptive ethics*, extends *evaluative ethics*. Because we humans do not always do what is positive and reject what is negative, moral judgments take on the character of a *should* that, in the case of a well-founded, justified *should*, is called an "imperative." Philosophical ethics does not take an imperative to be the command of a superior power that demands uncritical obedience. Rather, by imperatives are meant only those demands that of course can acknowledge opposing, contrary interests but, nonetheless, establish their priority on the basis of carefully argued reasons. Their obligation is not authoritarian but authoritative.

Many moral philosophers maintain that rationally grounded *shoulds* or imperatives are a characteristic of ethics of duty. In fact, the alternatives to ethics of duty require imperatives as well. Eudaimonistic virtue ethics, for example, demands at least tacitly that virtues should be acquired and applied. Furthermore, the demands for a good life are imperatives that are justified on the basis of personal well-being. As a prescriptive theory, ethics establishes what is positively valued and rejects what is negatively valued on the basis of well-founded reasons. A positive imperative has the form of a command ("you *should* . . ."); a negative imperative has the form of a prohibition ("you *should* not . . ."; better: "you *may* not . . .").

A creative but also easily adaptive language such as German translates *ethos* with "*Sitte* [custom]" and constructs the expressions "*sittlich* [moral]" and "*Sittlichkeit* [morality/cultural mores]" on this basis. Nevertheless, German preserves in foreign words not only the Greek expression "*Ethik* [ethic]" and "*ethisch* [ethical]" but also their Latin equivalents "*Moral* [morals]" and "*moralisch* [morally]." The consequence is the confusing situation that three expressions have somewhat the same meaning. One can, on the one hand, [1] refer to "*ethisch* [ethically]" in the sense of classical antiquity and, on the other hand, [2] refer to "*moralisch* [morally]" in the modern sense (above all in the Kantian sense). The forerunners of modernity extend, however, over the Middle Ages back to late antiquity. In any event, the current meaning of "*ethisch* [ethically]" corresponds only to a limited degree to the understanding of classical antiquity. [3] In the case of Hegel, he wants to replace Kant's concept of *Moralität* [morality] with the expression *Sittlichkeit* [cultural mores]— but Kant uses this expression, too.

Given this confusing situation, it is advisable to use the term "ethics [*Ethik*]" for the scientific discipline, the theory of morals and customs, and to use the terms "morals [*Moral*]" and "custom [*Sitten*]" for the object of this discipline. Positive morals and custom is, then, the object of descriptive and empirical ethics; in contrast, critical morals, or simply morals, is the object of normative ethics that also is called moral philosophy.

In both forms of ethics (i.e., valuing and prescriptive ethics), philosophy is not primarily interested in concrete evaluations. The latter is the task of moral discourses in which philosophy at best aids in a subsidiary, supporting manner. More important for philosophy is a second-level discourse, ethical discourse, that along with other tasks seeks a general standard, a "moralometer," for morals that structurally will prove to be much more complicated than a thermometer.

(3) To the degree that imperatives contain principles that already establish standards, moral philosophy seeks a standard for standards; in other words, it seeks a moral standard at a second level. To accomplish this goal, moral philosophy clarifies, first, the crucial concepts and the logical structure of a moral foundation, which consists of a third level of discourse and constitutes "meta-ethics." This expression is admittedly confusing because the meta-discourse of philosophical ethics necessarily belongs to such a meta-ethics. The classical works of philosophical ethics, for example, Aristotle's *Nicomachean Ethics* and Kant's *Groundwork of the Metaphysic of Morals*, refrain from moralizing discourse but

in contrast emphasize—as in the case of this project—the other two, the ethical and the meta-ethical discourses.

2.2 (The) Moral Good

According to the influential claim of the British philosopher G. E. Moore (1903), the fundamental word in moral philosophy, "good," is an absolutely simple object. As a consequence, the concept defies definition and is accessible only by mental intuition. By no means boastfully, Moore seeks to discredit the entirety of philosophical ethics with this argument. Philosophical ethics has erroneously equated "good" with other objects, especially with natural qualities like "useful" (utilitarianism), "passionate" (hedonism), or "valuable for life" (evolutionism), which is why Moore speaks of a naturalistic fallacy. He charges metaphysical ethics with having made a similar mistake, so he claims that there is a metaphysical fallacy as well. (See the detailed discussion of Moore in Höffe 1988, 25ff.)

Moore offers no conclusive evidence in support of his claim that "good" is incapable of definition. Rather, he offers a direct and an indirect argument. The direct argument ("good" cannot be broken down into further constitutive elements) is circular. Namely, it presupposes as proved what is yet to be proved: that it cannot be broken down into elements, from which follows the simplicity of "good." According to the indirect argument (the "open question" argument), whenever one equates "good" in some sense with "useful" or "pleasurable," it remains an open question whether the useful, the pleasurable, and so on is in all cases good. In fact, one can call a dishonest promise useful or the tortures of a sadist pleasurable and, nonetheless, question whether or not either is good. However, this argument is also not completely evident because there may be concealed synonyms. Where the identity of meaning is not immediately obvious, for example, by brunch [*Brunch*] and tiffin [*Gabelfrühstück*], the question, "This is A (brunch); is it also B (tiffin)?" is not meaningless.

As long as the open question argument is not more strenuously developed, the assertion of a naturalistic fallacy remains the dry affirmation of a contrary position: where Moore wishes to "see" two different qualities in "good" and "useful" ("valuable for life" . . .), his opponents "see" only one. Moore can charge the naturalists (and the metaphysicians) with only a kind of color blindness; namely, an inadequate capacity to distinguish, whereas his opponents blame him for a kind of hallucination: supposed but not actual perception of different qualities, as in the case of "useful," and so on.

According to Moore, to the present day moral philosophy has not come "to its object," the concept of the good. In response to this claim that this deficit is only imagined, one can invoke a new kind of constructive semantics. This rejoinder identifies three meanings of the normative foundational concept "good," maintains that the three meanings build on one another in a ranked order, and suggests that for all practical purposes one equates perhaps already the second level, and in any case the third level, with "morally good."

On the lowest level one evaluates the suitability of the ways and means for arbitrary intentions or goals. For example, whoever desires affluence needs far more income than expenditures. However, the question of whether or not it is good to become affluent remains an open one. This "good for something (or other)" includes everything technical, tactical, or strategic as well as everything instrumental and even what is functionally good; it can be in the widest sense of the term "technically good," and also "factually good." If one takes the appraisal to be a well-founded demand, it takes on the form of a technical imperative—a "*should*" that follows from a technical demand.

In light of its binding character, a technical imperative (in the widest sense) possesses a relative or conditional ("hypothetical") character: "*If* I want *x, then* I must do *y.*" In this case, *y,* as the embodiment of the ways and means, can be something simple or difficult and/or can consist in a rich mixture of options. For example, one can achieve affluence either by limiting one's expenditures or through increasing one's income, which in turn can occur through more lucrative work, creating inventions, writing a bestseller, winning the lottery, or receiving an inheritance. Some even attempt to improve their standard of living by robbing banks.

According to emotivism, a widely shared point of view during the first half of the twentieth century (e.g., Stevenson 1944), "good" designates neither natural nor nonnatural properties because the expression possesses only a feeling- (emotional-)meaning. If someone says "*a* is good," he expresses merely a personal attitude, his private taste, which, to be sure, is combined with an attempt to move others to share that attitude or taste.

If this view were correct, then all valuing, including moral judgments, would be eliminated from the sphere of the knowable (the cognitive).

Ethics would be possible only as noncognitive—as the theory of differing tastes; and, consequently, as a mere moment of consensus about the lack of consensus. At least for this first, technical level of appraisal, the view is unconvincing. In the case of assertions about a technical good, the pre-given goal "Z" establishes the standard in respect to which the correctness of the claim "*a* is good for Z" is objectively measured. Consequently, the conviction expresses neither a merely personal feeling nor a merely subjective taste; it maintains an objective, in any event cognitive, claim.

Of course, this does not mean that a technical benchmark is a standard description or claim, not even that it is a description with something added, a "description plus *x*." In the case of a technical benchmark, something is not claimed "about" something; rather, something is appraised "in light of" something, for example, an action as leading to the goal. The appraisal can be reformulated into a generic claim. Someone who says "*a* is good for Z" claims: "with respect to accomplishing Z, *a* assists in reaching the goal."

One could defend emotivism by explaining that the means may have an objective character, but the decisive goal is subjective, so that the entire claim has a subjective character. This plea misses the essence of a technical good, which is a benchmark limited to the means-goal relationship. Only in another respect can one concede the subjective claim to be correct: one who engages in only technical evaluations misses the bulk of the opportunities for objective appraisal.

The technical good, or imperative, corresponds to technical rationality, which also is called "technical reason." In turn, both expressions are intended in the widest sense to encompass tactical, strategic, instrumental, and functional rationality or reason. Because they are concerned not with knowledge but with action, one also speaks of practical, more correctly, technical-practical reason and means the capacity to follow a technical-practical rationale in order to accomplish an end.

At the *second* level of valuation, which one merely presupposes at the lowest level, one evaluates the goal itself. The valuation is accomplished with respect to a goal of the second level, with respect to a leading intention, one's own welfare, which—as we will see—one naturally desires. Whether concerned with a natural or a juridical individual (i.e., a school, a business, or a state)—at this second level one asks whether or not the natural or juridical individual's welfare is promoted. Contained here in the "good for something" is the "good for everyone," and to the technical level of rationality is added pragmatic rationality which includes a pragmatic imperative. In this case two partial levels can be distinguished: one concerned merely with the individual, the individually pragmatic, and one concerned with the group, the socially pragmatic.

As in the case of technical assessments, pragmatic assessments are only relative (i.e., hypothetically binding) because welfare is, to be sure, a natural but not a necessary goal. Above all, the appropriate assessment is valid only under the presupposition of this goal: "*If* one pursues one's own (individual or social) well-being, *then y* is good or necessary." There is no question that pragmatic assessments have an objective element. Just how far they are objective will be examined in part 2. Here it is sufficient to indicate that, once again, something is assessed "in light of" something. In this respect, the decisive goal, well-being, is exceedingly ambitious with respect to theoretical knowledge because it is extremely difficult to translate it into well-defined ways and means. In Julian Barnes's novel *The Porcupine,* the long-standing dictator, Stojo Petkanow, defends himself in court not only technically brilliantly but also to a great extent pragmatically successfully. He couldn't prevent his conviction, of course, because that was obvious from the beginning. Nonetheless, he enjoyed an important element of success: the satisfaction of outdoing his ambitious opponent, the Attorney General, so that not only did the Attorney General lose the love of his wife but also, as a consequence of his miserable performance, he lost her respect, as well. At the end of the proceedings, the victorious Attorney General was more devastatingly beaten than the inferior dictator.

From the perspective of the great defenders of an ethic of happiness (eudaimonism), the goal of happiness involves not only virtues that, like prudence, belong to the second level of obligation [as pragmatic imperatives], but also a virtue of the third level [of moral imperatives], justice. Already in this respect, humanity's desire for happiness reaches into the region of morality in the strict sense, and eudaimonism is to be taken seriously as a true moral philosophy.

Utilitarianism is a social pragmatics whose starting point is the well-being of all concerned. Our normative-ethical evaluation of it can wait. Here, in meta-ethics, we already have a possible preliminary appraisal: *if* utilitarianism already semantically equates the "morally good" (i.e., without any normative argument) with "good for all concerned," it makes too limited a normative claim because it is satisfied with a hypothetical obligation—although this obligation leaves the normative, irrefutable, and simultaneously higher-level question open: why should one pursue the well-being of all? One who serves the well-being of strangers must at least occasionally restrict one's own well-being, which leads to the question: in the case of a conflict situation, why would one subordinate one's own well-being to that of the other?

Because this question remains unanswered, the possibilities of assessment are not exhausted. They can be complete only where one encounters something that is good in itself, absolutely good in the sense of "straightforwardly" good—without any additions or assumptions. Only in the case of this *third* level of assessment are all hypothetical conditions eliminated, and one is entirely free of any preestablished conditions and has reached an unqualified good. One calls this the morally good in the narrow and strict sense. As with the technical good and the pragmatic good, the morally good has a corresponding rationally justified *should*. However, since any hypothetical accountability is eliminated, one is no longer concerned with a merely hypothetical imperative. The corollary to such a hypothetical imperative in this case is moral rationality and moral reason. The hierarchy of assessment is completed only here, since the assessment itself extends to the ultimate goal: one's own well-being and/or collective well-being.

Considered merely conceptually, morals signify the highest demand one can make on one's personal and communal world and, at the same time, a fundamental basis of justification for this demand. To the extent that it would be arbitrary to terminate prematurely the question about what in a certain case is good, authentic, or critical, morals constitute an irrefutable necessity. Nevertheless, because other values remain important, this necessity would be only a foremost perspective, superior to the others but, nonetheless, capable of being compromised by them. For example, moral weakness could be compensated for by extraordinary scientific, artistic, or political accomplishment. However, according to well-considered conviction, not even a genius has the right to deceive, steal, or murder.

If this is acknowledged, then morals possess a characteristic that many philosophers all too quickly shove aside as absurd: with respect to obligation, morals obtain the rank of an unconditionally valid claim. With respect to the determination of value, morals are equivalent to a trump that ranks over all other cards, or they are the equivalent of the first letter of a word in terms of its listing in a dictionary, whose lexical priority by no means can be ignored. The corresponding imperative, known since Kant as a categorical imperative, is first and foremost no standard for morals in addition to which there could possibly be alternative standards. Rather, it establishes what morals are and is valid absolutely: in the case of morals, the obligation does not have the character of a "*provided*, one wants to do *x*, one *should* do *y*." Rather, it is without precondition, pure as such and for itself, and therefore unqualified, that is, categorically valid. From the point of view of morals, whether that of individuals or of institutions, praxis is not limited to playing the role of a function for something else; morals are their own role and are an unqualified good.

Obviously, this claim is not limited to a specific region or aspect of life—whether to sexuality or to some unusual limit situation—nor is it limited to natural persons. Not only Ethos 3, the personal side, but also Ethos 2, the social and political side of praxis, is subordinate to the highest, moral valuation. Morality includes not only specific actions inclusive of limit situations and relevant character traits but also the structures and constitutional principles of a community.

Here at the third level, one can discern two subordinate levels. The bottom level, *civic morality*, also called (political) justice, consists in obligations whose recognition is expected from everyone so that their violation brings a reaction of outrage. Included at this level are respect for the life and limb of the other and for other religious convictions. The more demanding second level of *moral virtue* deservingly consists of more. For someone who offers aid in a situation where he is partly responsible for the need for the aid, political justice suffices. However, someone who offers such aid gratuitously fulfills a duty of virtue. The standard is love of neighbor which, by the way, is highly valued not merely in Christian culture (see Höffe 2007b, no. 5 for ancient Egyptian, no. 31 for Confucianism, and no. 39 for Islam). The love of neighbor is wreathed by other duties of virtue: concern for the well-being of others, sympathy, and empathy, perhaps also gratitude.

A more recent moral philosopher, Bernard Williams (1985), defends an anti-foundationalist and anti-reductionist ethic. Anti-foundationalism here means that no collection of moral categories constitutes the foundation for all praxis; anti-reductionist here means no method exists that would lead all moral thought back to such a list of categories. The concept of an absolute good introduces an alternative. Contrary to usual expectations, however, the absolute good turns out to be far more formal than most people would expect. Since we have yet to develop this formal account, we could for the moment loftily say: we are not thinking about the origin of morals thoroughly enough. Their origin consists neither in the principle of happiness in Aristotle's *Nicomachean Ethics* nor in Kant's principle of the good will but in a superlative common to both: the idea of the absolutely good.

Philosophical ethics benefits from the fact that its primary object, the morally good, stands at the highest level of valuation. In contrast to Moore's influential thesis that the concept of the good resists all definition because it is absolutely foundational, one can maintain: first, that it provides no formal definition; "good" means what one values positively. Second, in ethics one is concerned not with the good generally but only with the morally good, so that one does not have to stop with the definition of the generic term "good." Moral philosophers who limit themselves to the generic term are not more fundamental; rather, they overlook what is at stake, namely, not some kind of good but the morally good. For the morally good there is a formal definition: "morally good" means what one absolutely, positively values according to the structurally highest level of assessment.

This definition has the additional benefit of openness and neutrality in contrast to other alternatives. In particular, it avoids taking a side in meta-ethics with respect to two controversies. On the one hand, the question remains open whether or not the principle of happiness is capable of establishing morals in a strict sense. On the other hand, morals are not restricted from the beginning to the social dimension. It remains thinkable that, in addition to moral obligations to others, there are also obligations to oneself. There may be good reasons for not thinking so. However, one should present those reasons rather than hold morals distinct from personal obligations by means of a prior semantic decision. To some extent, at least the thought of a primary duty to oneself, namely self-respect on moral grounds, is not "obviously absurd."

2.3 Relativism

Fundamental moral philosophy argues against relevant kinds of skepticism. One form of skepticism surfaces very early and ubiquitously in history: by means of economic and cultural exchange, later as a consequence of sociological and cultural studies, and in the meantime through personal experience in one's own pluralistic society, one becomes acquainted with an almost unlimited, often conflicting variety of customs and laws. The practical consequences are obvious: whoever desires to be moral is confused by a lack of orientation with respect to how one should conduct one's life.

Some react with dogmatic self-justification to this personal existential problem of orientation; they declare their own customs and laws for the best. Not infrequently this dogmatism takes the form of a missionary proclamation: others would be better off were they to embrace this better system of obligations. Anyone with a minimum of openness encounters such dogmatic self-justification in many places, and it raises the question: "Who is right, then, and why?"

An initial cultural relativism (e.g., Herskovits 1972) answered: "everyone"; a second, ethical relativism (examined by Ladd 1985 and Rippe 1993) answered: "no one." Cultural relativism does not deny that moral norms are binding but rejects the assumption of transcultural obligations.

Likewise, ethical relativism views the various obligations as equally valid. On the basis of merely culturally relative validity, it infers the absence of universal validity and maintains that the latter isn't even possible. In this case, the problem of personal existential orientation turns into an ethical problem of legitimation. Because it is characterized by such great dissimilarity and capriciousness in its principles, all that presents itself as morals appears to be merely a human construction and arbitrary assertion. In such circumstances, what is missing is precisely what is necessary for morals: the moment of unequivocal obligation. In this fashion, ethical relativism escalates to a demoralizing in the literal sense: a comprehensive distancing from all morals that one can call in part amorality, in part (ethical) nihilism.

A fundamental philosophy questions even further. Itself skeptical of moral skepticism, it calls attention, first of all, to both an unrecognized and undesired consequence. Whoever acknowledges only cultural obligations represents something that can be dangerous within a pluralistic culture and, at a global level, even deadly. Whoever declares all moral obligation to be only culturally relative takes all conversation about the foundations of a peaceful coexistence and interaction of cultures to be impossible. Furthermore, because one takes the obligations of property ownership and special rights exclusively from one's own culture, one promotes a new kind of "cultural chauvinism."

In a second step, philosophy examines the extent of relativism: pluralism in moral norms is easy to see. Already Herodotus (*Histories*, book 3, chapter 38) reported differences in burial rituals and the assumption that one took one's own to be the best; so, for example, just as the Greeks would not think to eat their dead for any price, so would the Callatians from India not incinerate their dead for any fee.

> Darius, after he had got the kingdom, called into his presence certain Greeks who were at hand, and asked, "What should he pay them to eat the bodies of their fathers when they died?" To which they answered, that there was no sum that would tempt them to do such a thing. He then sent for certain Indians, of the race called Callatians, men who eat their fathers, and asked them, while the Greeks stood by, and knew by the help of an interpreter all that was said, "What should he give them to burn the bodies of their fathers at their decease?" The Indians exclaimed aloud, and bade him forebear from such language.

However, in the presence of many cultural differences, one can also observe scores of commonalities. Whoever ignores them is proceeding on the basis of prejudice. Almost all cultures highly value reciprocity combined with generosity; they recognize the prohibition of incest even when the criterion for incest is not always the same; and they reject sexual libertinism. Generally one finds the prohibition of lying and deception, a respect for elders, the care for children, and a general compassion for one another; in addition, one finds the recognition of considerateness, cooperativeness, and courage, including civic courage. Fundamental legal rights such as the right to life and limb, property ownership, and honor are legally protected everywhere. In addition, one finds conventions concerned with ensuring justice in contracts and agreements of exchange.

Thus, an unprejudiced and open view discovers a list of widely recognized obligations that is surprisingly long, contrary to a prevailing perception that sees only differences. A partial cultural relativism deceives one into thinking that it extends to a total ethical relativism. Nevertheless, someone who views the richness of cultural diversity impartially can discern the prejudicial limitedness of ethical relativism. Intercultural studies demonstrate generally that: what is usually proscribed in one's society will be found in most other societies to be proscribed; and what one values highly at home is most everywhere equally highly valued. (Insight into various but not always different moral perspectives can be found in the *Lesebuch* [Höffe 2007b].)

A further illusion: the remaining differences are usually concerned foremost with relatively concrete "superficial norms" that arise from the application of common principles to diverse ancillary conditions. Such ancillary conditions include the society's characteristic geographical, meteorological, and economic factors, as well as convictions concerning the consequences of actions. As long as one is convinced, for example, that nature is governed by the gods, whose anger can be appeased through animal or human sacrifice, one doesn't hesitate in the face of a successful harvest or a natural catastrophe to provide the appropriate sacrifice. However, as soon as one views nature as governed by anonymous powers, one ceases to make sacrifices and in place of them seeks to discern the natural powers themselves in order to obtain sovereignty over them for one's own ends.

Even the already mentioned burial rituals contain to be sure a conventional and at the same time differentiating element. The very enthusiasm with which one defends the superiority of one's own ritual, however, illuminates an essential commonality: the high respect for the dead. When this respect is openly violated, for example, when the King of Troy's son, Hector, decapitates the dead Patroclus and drags the headless cadaver over the battlefield only to throw it to the dogs to be devoured (see Homer's *Iliad*, 17.125–27; 18.170–80), or when one hears today that soldiers mutilate the bodies of their dead enemies only to dance over them, the reaction of outrage is felt not only by the victim's nearest relatives but worldwide.

The decisive fundamental commonalities among obligations can be discovered only by one who has filtered out the culturally specific ancillary conditions from the concrete customs so that the normatively fundamental emerges. As soon as one recognizes the observed obligations as the culturally specific manifestation of general principles, the differences are no longer surprising but actually necessary. The first, relative interpretation of cultural diversity turns out to be an illusion of perspective that is exaggerated to the degree that one suppresses the elements held in common among cultures.

This is the point at which moral philosophy applies the differences among the three levels of discourse and sets an empirical over against a normative-ethical and both over against a (in fact rarely defended) meta-ethical relativism. Within empirical relativism, moral philosophy separates descriptive cultural relativism which is limited to observed norms from a culturally principled relativism which in turn maintains that moral principles are merely culturally relative. The evidence in support of the claim, however, is usually not provided. In any event, not every difference in norms or change in values amounts to a moral difference or change. With this clarifying orientation, philosophical ethics demonstrates how its claim to truly practical philosophy is legitimate: frequently, it is not the fundamental principles but merely the times, namely the ancillary conditions, that change. If one nevertheless clings to these concrete norms, one betrays the presence of universal determining moral principles.

In the end there are differences at the level of principles. For example, one can respond to an offense with revenge or generosity. However, normative-principled relativism does not follow from the observation of differences of principles, as ethical relativism maintains. Whoever turns conflicting principles into a conflict between equally valid principles in fact makes an error in logical reasoning, as we shall see.

2.4 Morality: Functionless?

Cultural relativism limits the validity of moral principles to a specific culture although, to be sure, it acknowledges that within the culture itself moral principles have validity. Someone who challenges this validity defends an ethical nihilism. Viewed historically, ethical nihilism is relatively late and occurs rather infrequently—usually as the consequence of the devaluation of all highest principles that up to then were viewed as the meaning to life and death. The feeling of emptiness and meaninglessness that comes with such devaluation leads some people to embrace a measureless, perhaps even criminal, self-interest; with others it leads to an apathetic languor or, because one is weary of life, to suicide. For the individual involved, this devaluation is in any event frequently an existential catastrophe, such as that in Fyodor Dostoevsky's *Brothers Karamazov*. Philosophically, it is above all Nietzsche who diagnosed for his day a European (now seen in part to be worldwide) nihilism for which he proposed a new morality: the morality of the sovereign individual.

Nihilism surfaces today in a less lofty form, although its consequences are more far-reaching, in sociological systems theory. With reference to John Milton's famous epic *Paradise Lost*, Niklas Luhmann (1988) declared morality to be the lost paradigm for modern society (for a criticism, see Höffe 1995b, section 3.1). Contemporary society consists of relatively independent functional systems. Each one (for example, the economy, the sciences, politics, etc.) is subject to its own functionally specific normativity. The sciences, for example, are concerned with truth and falsity; democratic politics with the cooperation and conflict between the governing party and opposition. Morality as a functionally specific normative system has no role to play in a society divided into multiple functional systems.

Once again, philosophy investigates. First of all, it remembers that long before our contemporary world there were regionally specific ideas of normativity: for philosophy and the sciences, as always, it was truth; and for the economy a certain material surplus. Following this initial critique of oversimplification, philosophy proceeds with its concept of morals. Philosophy contradicts neither Luhmann's concern with an empirically useful concept of morals nor his proposal that we approach morals as "a special kind of communication," which brings with it an "indication of respect or disrespect." The additional claim that morals are not concerned with good and bad in a functionally specific sense but with the entire person raises two concerns. First, morals are not directed only at individuals but also at institutions and social structures. Second, the alternative "function-specific and/or function-unspecific" involves an irrelevant simplification because a function-unspecific normativity can, nonetheless, be applied functionally in specific respects.

Scientists who further their career by fabricating data, as well as politicians or judges who are guilty of corruption, put their personal integrity into question in a functionally specific respect. In his private life, a scientist can be dishonest: in order for research "to function," however, dishonesty is forbidden. In like manner, the political and justice systems function only when here, the politician, and there, the judge, are not corrupt. With the negative formulation, "neither dishonest nor corrupt," a peculiarity of functionally specific morality emerges: it occurs in the form of a veto. Someone who falsifies data disqualifies himself as a scientist; someone who is careless must permit external examination of the quality of his research.

According to the first, sociohistorical argument against Luhmann, modernity is not all that new. According to the second, socially theoretical argument, modernity, namely with its functional differentiation, cannot function without the moral perspective. According to a third argument that is both an ethical as well as a social theoretical argument, modern society is at least in one respect (that is, with respect to personal morals) to a limited extent free from morals. From another perspective, one doesn't begin to see a hint of such freedom. With politics, for instance, the question arises as to why it is formally structured as the cooperation and conflict between a governing party and an opposition party and in addition why it should recognize material principles such as basic and human rights.

This question is concerned with the moral foundation of a political system and is hardly touched by functionally specific normativity. Once again, Luhmann's morally nihilistic thesis proves to be too hasty. Instead of constituting a solid argument for a radical moral skepticism, it demonstrates in two respects that the moral perspective is nonnegotiable. On the one hand, a society's functional system could not work without functionally specific personal morals. On the other hand, only institutional morals provide the legitimating conditions without which the system, lacking the disposition to seek agreement among the participants, is threatened by dysfunctionality, perhaps even the danger of dissolution. In this respect, it is advisable to turn to Milton's less well-known epic *Paradise Regained* to discover morals as a recovered paradigm. For a second time, philosophical ethics places a fundamental orientation under examination: in the process, it demonstrates that in contrast to popular skepticism with respect to them, morals are hardly dispensable.

3 Fallacious Conclusions

Often philosophers trust formal logic to solve many of our problems. Aristotle, the founder of moral logic, was more restrained, and developments in recent moral philosophy properly recognize that he was right. That is to say, for quite some time one expected that nearly all traditional moral philosophy could be unmasked as erroneous by pointing out *a single* logical error, the is-ought fallacy, in combination with the previously mentioned naturalistic fallacy. In fact, though, the logical fallacy resided in the expectation itself. Both fallacies—the is-ought fallacy and the naturalistic fallacy—together with a third fallacy, moralization, have a didactic argumentative significance. This is exposed by a method familiar to philosophy, that of determinate negation: whoever sees through the error will grasp the proper logic of argumentation for ethics. It is not the case that the decisive arguments of moral philosophy succumb to the is-ought fallacy.

3.1 The Is-Ought Fallacy

This first fallacy violates a semantic distinction between expressions of "is" and "ought." Of course, the distinction is so obvious that it is not only recognized but embraced by countless philosophers. For example, Kant distinguished the region of the laws of nature ("is") from laws of freedom ("ought") that like the laws of nature also show themselves to be imperatives. Mediated through neo-Kantianism, the distinction continues to function as the separation of facts, about which one can make true or false judgments, from values, which determine good and bad. Philosophers like Hegel, to be sure, cultivate a certain skepticism with respect to *should*-claims. However, even they do not eliminate—as we will see—the distinction between a world of true/false judgments and a world of good/bad judgments.

Whoever, nevertheless, accuses an ethic of violating the distinction between "is" and "ought" immediately appeals to David Hume's dense passage from *A Treatise of Human Nature* (book 3, part 1, section 1). According to the usual interpretation, called Hume's law, it is logically impossible to derive ought-claims from mere is-claims. No elaborate logical, in this case deontologically oriented (i.e., concerned with duties or "shoulds") calculus is required to prove the validity of Hume's law. Two simple elements suffice. The first consists of an insight into what formal logic can accomplish. As a principle of validity, what is deduced (the conclusion) may not include more than is contained in the former statements (the premises). If one accepts in addition the semantic presupposition of a language that distinguishes between being- and should-expressions, one requires at least one should-premise to arrive at a should-conclusion.

Nonetheless, in order to show that the is-ought inference is not an actual but only an apparent fallacy, philosophical dissidents look for a counterexample. Instead of following the example of one of the greats, Aristotle or Hegel or Kant's thesis of a fact of pure practical, that is, moral, reason (see chapter 22.2), these dissidents make an attempt to expose the illusion on the basis of logical-semantic ingenuity that in the end, nonetheless, fails: according to Searle (1969, chapter 8), a special kind of being-expression, the descriptive but at the same time performative statement "A promises to do x," implies the should-expression "A should do x." The proof, however, is based on the unarticulated should-premise that one should keep one's promises. One can understand promises to be personal commitments to which one is obligated (compare chapter 21.1). If so, *with Searle* one can derive the commitment to do what is promised; *in contrast to Searle,* however, one must understand the major premise to already be a normative-laden claim. "A promises to do x" is, namely, equal to "A commits himself to do x." However, someone who neither holds that the commitment is included in the promise nor recognizes it as an added premise cannot arrive at Searle's conclusion. In short: either the alleged being-premise already contains the moment of should, or the alleged should-conclusion is in truth only a being-expression.

Even philosophers who do not accept the separation of natural facts and ideal norms (or moral values) indirectly confirm the error of the transition from is to ought. Hegel is a good example. In the preface to his *Philosophy of Right* he provocatively declares: "What is rational is actual; and what is actual is rational." Of course, Hegel equates reason with Plato's concept of the idea—thus, according to our understanding today, with an ought—so that the claim, the actual ("is") is rational ("ought"), appears to succumb straightaway to an extreme is-ought fallacy. In fact, he does not derive an ought from a naturalistic actuality. He is not so silly as to declare that everything that occurs in the social world is rational. On the contrary, he introduces "the power of the just and moral" (section 258, note) and denounces the "slavery of Roman children" as one of the "most tainted of institutions" (section 175).

What at only first glance is so shocking in Hegel's thesis is actually the result of a special understanding of (practical) philosophy. In place of a moral philosophical question, "What should I do?"—with the apparent danger that the "ideal should" will never be actualized—one finds a speculative ontology that avoids the usual distinction between expressions of is and ought. The actual includes the presence of reason because only the rational counts as truly actual. In this case "rationality" and "actuality" are concepts of degree. To the extent that social relationships do not measure up to the standard of reason, they are both irrational and non-actual. In the background is the historical-philosophical expectation that clearly irrational social relationships will in time crumble because they contradict the idea of right (on Hegel, see chapter 22.6).

3.2 Moralization

An ethic that is transfixed by the accusation of the is-ought fallacy overlooks the equally great danger that philosophy move exclusively in the world of shoulds. Where all reference to reality and experience is absent, one also abdicates all *instruction* and becomes incapable of obtaining meaningful *obligations* from it. Obviously, concrete oughts cannot be derived exclusively from *should*-claims. In order to concretely satisfy the *technical* imperative that leads to prosperity—"take in much more than you spend"—one needs specific economic expertise and an overview of one's own circumstances as well as experience and sound judgment. In the case of a *pragmatic* imperative (for example, concern for one's health), we find a similar situation, and not least a similar situation with some *moral* principles (for example, the obligation to help the needy). In order to assist someone in need, one must know (or correctly estimate) three things: the concrete need, the means for eliminating the need, and one's own access to those means.

Anyone who believes one can do without such knowledge and estimates succumbs to an illogical and indefensible normativism. In the case of morals, this takes the form of moralization. The fallacy of moralization consists in the adoption of the position diametrically opposed to those concerned to prove the error of the is-ought inference. The moralization fallacy is the belief that specific or even concrete commitments can be derived exclusively from moral presuppositions. In fact, pure moral reflections lead only to general principles of judgment, which cannot justify concrete obligations without the mediation of actual life-conditions.

With the expression "mediation" one avoids, by the way, the misleading "ontology" that accompanies the more frequently employed expression "application." "Application" encourages one to think of two existing entities (morals and experience) and, in addition, of a privileging of the moral above experience. In fact, however, a conclusive moral argument establishes a relationship between our two kinds of assertion, is and ought; it arbitrates between them. This arbitration knows nothing of a morals that exists alone for itself and knows nothing of a likewise independent natural reality. In addition, it does *not* believe that an initial "pure morals" is supplemented by, or perhaps even "contaminated" by, a subordinate empirical element.

The task of mediation does not commence merely with the concretization of moral principles but, rather, already with their justification. The command to help the needy, for example, focuses morals on a fundamental condition of humanity, that is, on an anthropological element: the possibility of destitution and the requirement of assistance. We can witness the same pattern of argumentation on several levels: one can arrive at valid conclusions only when one avoids both fallacies—the is-ought fallacy and the moralization fallacy.

By means of originally moral premises, those of logically independent morals, philosophy is free in the other, descriptive step to take into consideration empirical knowledge derived from the richness of human experience and the scientific study of humanity. In fact, a critique of moralization encourages these considerations. *General obligations* require general insights into the *conditio humana;* whereas *specific commands and prohibitions* need a knowledge grounded in historical and social experience. Finally, for concrete obligations, "*la minutie du savoir*" is required—that detailed, particular, necessarily nuanced and careful knowledge that Michel Foucault (1971, 145) attributes to one of his sources of inspiration, Nietzsche. Only such a detailed knowledge can overcome the distance between the generalization of principles and the particularization of life. One who balks at such an effort has no right to judge the concrete circumstances of the social world. Such an individual is no "pure soul" in an otherwise contaminated world, but, rather, a "corrupt soul"; namely, too comfortable to study the world with its discipline-specific laws, functional processes, and limit-conditions.

This logic of argumentation has consequences for political debates. Because both normative and descriptive elements are included in concrete moral judgments, it is usually hasty in a controversy to charge one's opponent in a moralizing way with a failure of moral engagement, or to accuse him in a purely technocratic way of too little knowledge of the issue. Before adopting such a highly rhetorical if often successful model of criticism, one should examine whether between the opponents not a similar encounter with the situation but another analysis of it is involved; or whether there is a comparable technical knowledge but a divergent moral appraisal.

3.3 Interpreting Moral Consciousness

The clear distinction between moral and empirical premises is to be understood as logical, not substantial. In experience, there are innumerable "overlapping interests [Gemengelagen]" so that one can extract moral principles by means of an interpretation of reality, namely moral consciousness. A special kind of hermeneutics is responsible for obtaining moral principles. Usually, one understands hermeneutics to be concerned only with the interpretation of art and texts. In an expanded sense, hermeneutics applies not only to works of art and music, but also to habits and customs as well as legal and other institutions. It extends also to myths, primordial symbols, and the unconscious, even the subconscious; in short: to all cultural productions. Among these belongs moral consciousness. The hermeneutics of consciousness has two sides, namely, a content side ("What is obligatory?") and a formal side ("In what way is it obligatory?"), so that the hermeneutic of moral consciousness has two objects, which means that there are two methods to be employed.

If one is concerned with content, one proceeds like John Rawls (1972, sections 9 and 87), for example, on the basis of well-considered moral judgments (that is, from well-thought-out judgments, rather than hesitant ones accompanied by confusion and anxiety) and on the basis of judgments that are not influenced by one's personal advantage or disadvantage. With such judgments as one's starting point, one seeks out principles, which allow both sides (the well-thought-out initial judgments and the fundamental principles) to be brought together without contradiction. In the event that one has found such a combination, one has reached the goal of reflective equilibrium. Without doubt this hermeneutic accomplishes clarification about morals. In addition, it allows for a moderate moral critique. There are definite moral questions about which one is still uncertain (for example, the question of whether one in a certain desperate situation is permitted to lie) that can eventually be decided with the help of such well-thought-out principles. There is no certainty about this possibility, however. Furthermore, in order to be successful, the procedure must fulfill two conditions. First, there must be a sufficient number of persons who agree concerning the well-thought-out judgment; and second, the different themes about which one formulates judgments may not turn out to be so varied that they make a contradiction-free combination impossible.

The critical potential of such an ethic is limited for yet another reason. Satisfied with a noncontradictory combination, with coherence, one is committed to demands of content and, ultimately, one is dependent upon the background consensus of a culture. Coherence requires that one undertake certain corrections, since the different moral convictions in an individual and still more in a culture are hardly free of contradiction. The coherence that is eventually achieved remains tightly bound to the convictions of the respective culture. The hermeneutic of moral consciousness does not eliminate cultural relativism. What today in the West is taken to be coherent does not mean that it was so understood in the past, much less taken to be so in non-Western cultures. As a consequence, two overlapping tasks of a moral philosophy are missing: intercultural discourse and a claim to universality. Even if one appeals to a highly developed morals, one is concerned in the end only with a *positive*, not with a *critical*, morals. The expectation of coherence is not even sufficient for the respective culture to say what direction should be taken to remedy a possible incoherence. To the extent that one can address a given incoherence in different ways, there is no unequivocal outcome.

Someone who does not yield to the limits of the coherence method begins at a deeper level. Whether in the present or the past, whether Western or non-Western, he *brackets all contents* with respect to moral consciousness. Even with respect to the controversies in ethics, such as the conflict between duty ethics (deontology) and goal-oriented ethics (teleology or utilitarianism), on the one side, and the conflict between eudaimonistic and autonomous morals, on the other, he maintains his neutrality. His only concern is the kind of obligation (the *form*) involved.

Even if one brackets all content of moral consciousness and remains indifferent to the question of whether moral consciousness is deontological, teleological, eudaimonistic, or autonomous, there remains one enduring certainty: one is conscious of an obligation that can no longer be relativized by a still higher obligation—an absolutely highest imperative. In this case, constructive semantics provides a certain proof: there is actually present in moral consciousness the thought of a highest-ranking good and a highest-level imperative.

Our reference to great moral philosophers might lead to the misunderstanding that morals are a concern only for professionals—even to the misconception that they are accessible only to extraordinary thinkers. In truth—and this is demonstrated by the hermeneutic of moral consciousness—morals are familiar to just about every human being beginning at a certain age. Philosophy only elucidates that with which everyone is familiar; it deals with the self-reflection of moral consciousness. Whether or not the moral actuality that thereby comes to light includes a "should" is something that will be addressed later (chapters 9 and 22). Already here, however, we can see that the separation between is and ought is too simplistic. The semantics of separation is to be sublated [*aufheben*] in a Hegelian sense: namely, preserved and simultaneously surmounted.

3.4 The Critique of Morals as Genealogy

A moralist who indirectly says about himself: "They all speak of me" (*Zarathustra*, "The Bedwarfing Virtue," 2); a moral theoretician and language artist who, with his Dionysian poison and spiritual dynamite, mesmerizes intellectual and artistically inclined youths; a critic of European civilization to whom Heidegger, Camus, and Foucault appeal; an epistemological and social critic whom Freud and the Frankfurt school esteem; a philosopher who as an anti-philosopher at least wants to be at once "critic and skeptic and dogmatizer and historian and beyond even these poet, collector, and traveler," but above all a "free spirit" (*Beyond Good and Evil*, no. 211) and who, nevertheless, is esteemed by analytic philosophers

and pragmatists, by deconstructionists, postmodernists, and feminists—
this intellectual artist, shaman, and seducer, Friedrich Nietzsche, leads
the Western critique of morals to a philosophical apogee. Many engage in moral criticism in a bonsai format; however, Nietzsche is over-
dimensionally radical and fundamental at the same time.

However, argumentative logic is interested solely in his methodology.
In order not to situate this logic incorrectly, it maintains with respect to
the content of his critique of morals, the revaluation of all values, only
this much: revaluation does not mean devaluation; rather, values are established on a new foundation. In place of the (presumed) attempt to
seek the meaning of life only in values and truths of a life hereafter, one
encounters a this-worldly justification of meaning. To be sure, this logic
dismisses some traditional values, but it compensates by elevating other
values (e.g., justice and honesty) to a higher position.

Now the this-worldly justification serves only the method of a debunking genealogy. Radical in a literal sense, the strategy digs out the
roots of morals in order to shake the foundations of their traditional
justification. One can already find valuable examples of this procedure
in antiquity. For example, one sees the roots of a religiously established
morals in the jealousy of the gods, or declares justice to be either the
egocentricity of rulers (Thrasymachus in Plato's *Republic* 338c) or by
contrast the resentment of the weak (Callicles in Plato's *Gorgias* 492a-e).
Modernity took up this pattern of moral criticism. We find the model
of Thrasymachus in Karl Marx and of Callicles in Friedrich Nietzsche.
Another debunking genealogy exposes the hidden self-interest behind
the alleged selfless impulse of sympathy—as the fear of one's own future
suffering (Hobbes) or as "clever foresight with respect to misfortunes
that could happen to us" (La Rochefoucauld). Others explain conscience
as the misplaced internal voice of an other (Sigmund Freud). In the case
of all these forms, a debunking genealogy seeks a source for morals that
erodes the justification for present morals.

A mere logic of argumentation has no interest in the question of
whether and to what extent the alleged past origin is right. It asks only
whether a genealogy is capable of deciding the legitimacy of morals:
literally, by means of the history of its development. Semantically, language concerned with development possesses an "is"-character; legitimation language, in contrast, possesses an "ought"-character. To be sure, a
debunking history of the development of morals is not inconsequential
for its legitimacy; for there is a shaking of the traditional legitimation-

foundation. However, it remains open whether or not there is some other, not yet discovered, legitimation. Anyone who explicitly or implicitly denies this open possibility commits an "is"-"ought" fallacy, a genealogical fallacy, which distinguishes itself from other forms of the "is"-"ought" fallacy only by its subtlety.

The genealogical fallacy has two forms. In its affirmative variation, it maintains that a positively appraised origin for morals would be a vindication. The stronger, more prevalent, critical variation maintains that a negative appraisal of its origin would eliminate any possible vindication of morals. However, the fact of a positive or a negative appraisal of an origin does not mean that the outcome itself is to be positively or negatively appraised. What is more, in the course of development the valuation can change; there can even be a reversal of value polarity. Additionally, many genealogies are selective; they limit themselves to a few factors and suppress those that disturb the aimed at, desired interpretation.

In the case of Nietzsche: if his thesis is correct that Jewish-Christian morals arise from the jealousy of the weak and the interest in dominance on the part of priests, then one must place a powerful question mark after the morals of compassion and love of neighbor. The question mark demands that the task of justification be taken more seriously if one is to weaken Nietzsche's objections. However, genealogy cannot eliminate all legitimacy for a morals of compassion.

According to Nietzsche, however, one must never forget the goal of revaluation. Whereas others practice only a destructive critique of morals, Nietzsche's critique is in the end positive. Precisely the concept of revaluation shows that the debunking genealogy serves as the path to a better foundation for morals. It is not a nihilism that denies all obligation and takes the place of a morals based on otherworldly values, but rather a self-affirmation and simultaneous intensification of life, an "instinct for freedom," that Nietzsche calls the will to power.

3.5 Ethics Without Metaphysics?

The philosophical spirit of our age maintains that the question of this section is superfluous—at least the question mark is unnecessary. This is because the dominant philosophers today explicitly call their thought either non- or post-metaphysical. Nonetheless, when it comes to ethics, doubts arise. The expression "metaphysics" means neither an unenlightened thought nor an intellectually extravagant philosophizing, nor does it include a grounding of ethics in religion or an ideology—both of which secular philosophers reject. According to its original meaning, metaphysics is a knowledge that is concerned with an object beyond (*meta-*) the research of nature (*physics*). Originating in Greek culture at a time when the Jewish-Christian revelation was still unknown, metaphysics is that first philosophy or fundamental philosophy which concerns itself with those basic questions that necessarily go beyond the area of competency of the research of nature.

There is no independent logic of argument common to all metaphysics. Rather, it is the history of metaphysics that ever again seeks such an independent logic. Even in the case of a praxis-oriented fundamental philosophy, practical metaphysics, the logic of argumentation is resolved only in the process of its application. According to the preceding reflections, two standpoints speak in favor of a certain metaphysical character of ethics. Since we are concerned with a foundation as presupposition-less as possible (i.e., with a fundamental ethic), ethics has precisely for this reason, as a fundamental analysis, a metaphysical status. Secondly, its object, the thought of a highest good, has a non-empirical character. Already as a value to which one does not necessarily adhere, as a *should*, this character has a non-empirical tinge. In the case of an absolutely highest good, the *should* loses, in addition, the empirical moment that always remains when one is concerned with a technical or pragmatic good or *should*. Fundamental ethics has a status that extends beyond a concern with natural experience not only from the perspective of its foundational interest but also with respect to its paramount object, the morally good. When it rejects this status and merely appeals to natural experience, it obviously commits an "is-ought" fallacy.

The question that provides the title of this section is, thereby, at least provisionally answered. Paradoxically, the history of truly fundamental (i.e., metaphysical) ethics commences for all intents and purposes without this metaphysics. The project undertaken by the important theoretician of political morals, John Rawls, as a political, not a metaphysical, theory, can be found already more than two thousand years earlier in the first treatise with the title "ethics," Aristotle's *Nicomachean Ethics*. There is a second paradox: Rawls's most important source of inspiration, Kant, is a philosopher who sharply criticized traditional metaphysics but, nevertheless, classifies his ethics as metaphysics.

In the course of the present study, it will be necessary to clarify whether this situation is accidental or whether, on the one hand, there are legitimate grounds for maintaining that the definitive ethics of eu-daimonia, Aristotle's philosophy of the art of living, is free of meta-physics, or, on the other hand, the definitive ethics of autonomy, Kant's moral philosophy, in contrast, is metaphysical. The consequences would be surprising, even unsettling: the older, ancient ethic would reject pre-cisely that which one holds against it, metaphysics; and the newer, modern ethic with its principle of autonomy would appear to need metaphysics.

With respect to our logic of argumentation, we can identify in the interim two senses in which a fundamental ethic is metaphysical, at least in a restricted sense. It is concerned with a non-empirical object, the highest good, and it conducts a very fundamental investigation of this object. Whether or not there is a more ambitious, perhaps problematic, sense in which it is metaphysical remains open at least for the moment (see chapter 22.7).

4 *Animal Morabile*

Philosophical ethics is concerned primarily with the discussion of normative questions. However, it does not ignore empirical questions; in particular, it does not ignore the question of how and to what end the *Homo sapiens sapiens* species arose in natural evolution to become, eventually, the only moral being. According to a pointed expression by the philosopher Joseph de Maistre, "human" is a fiction, the imputation of a general essence, although being human occurs only in cultural particularities: "There is no such thing as *man* in the world. In my lifetime I have seen Frenchmen, Italians, Russians, etc.; but as for *man*, I declare that I have never in my life met him" (*Considerations*, 1814/1974, 97).

When it comes to philosophical ethics' alternative, philosophical anthropology, its concern with an ethics of moral anthropology, again, is methodologically a hermeneutics of a special kind. It no longer interprets specific cultural expressions of humanity, but rather interprets the empirical data about humanity. It proceeds along two complementary paths. One path goes off into the distance and seeks out commonalities between our experience of humanity today and fellow humans from widely different spaces and times. The other path seeks out what is close by and establishes differences that distinguish humanity from other species, especially from our relatives, the primates, on other branches of evolutionary development. (On biological anthropology, see Eibl-Eibesfeldt 2004; on comparative primate research, see Paul 1998, de Waal 2005; on paleo-anthropology, see Diamond 1992; see also Illies 2006).

A methodologically informed moral anthropology does not expect to be able to replace normative philosophical ethics. The logic of argumentation stands in opposition to the occasional imperialism of some technical scientists: one can never arrive at *oughts* on the basis of only empirical observations (on the basis of "*is*"-claims). Therefore, one is satisfied with the more modest question: what biological, including neurobiological, peculiarities of humanity are responsible for its capacity for morals? The question also involves: why do morals have a general foundation in nature but, nevertheless, are culturally shaped? An additional question: why do morals have the character of a justifying ought, an imperative, without being an unconscious ought?

Although ethics today, like recent philosophy generally, has to a great extent lost interest in anthropology, a few initial comments are worthy of note: although the subject seems to be old, the word "anthropology" is surprisingly new. It appears first at the end of the sixteenth century as the "science of human nature" and still later becomes, primarily around the time of Kant, the empirical science of humanity. Kant properly observed that, methodologically, anthropology occupies a mediating position; it is a "knowledge of the world" that one can acquire neither by means of philosophy alone nor by means of the exemplary empirical science of the time, physics (*Anthropology*, 8:3ff.). Philosophical anthropology thrived in the decades of the '20s through the '40s of the last century thanks above all to three philosophers: Max Scheler, Helmut Plessner, and Arnold Gehlen.

Contrary to the fear that humanity would be defined in terms of an ahistorical essence [*Wesen*], anthropology demonstrates that there is in humanity's biological nature a dynamic that creates not only culture in the singular, not merely the organic-natural human being, but also culture in the plural, the historically distinguishable forms of societies. As a consequence, one must reject the dualistic position: here nature, there culture. Whereas humanity's natural existence is thoroughly shaped by culture, the cultural imprint is never entirely free from organic-natural constructions. Anthropology acknowledges at most a skeleton of humanity that becomes a being [*Wesen*] of "flesh and blood" only by means of cultural and, in addition, individual factors.

In the meantime, anthropology now has much more information at its disposal than it did in the late eighteenth century. However, its fundamental question as well as the two paths of inquiry and, above all, two basic claims actually reach back to antiquity: human beings as rational and linguistically endowed creatures and human beings as social, more precisely, juridical and political animals. To be sure, both apply to human beings, as individuals and as a genus—though at first they are only potential. In the absence of a certain development (evolution) that includes one's own efforts, neither reason nor the political nature of humanity reaches its actualization or eventual complete realization. This necessity of individual development also applies to morals. A human being is not immediately an *"animal morale,"* a moral being, but, rather, certainly in three respects an *"animal morabile"*: one has the capacity for morals, one is called to be moral, but one must develop one's moral capacity. In light of the necessity of personal effort, morals possess in an even more fundamental respect an "ought-"character: morals don't consist only in the form of imperatives; rather, a more fundamental imperative is at the base of their development.

Very early, even in the earliest form of rational thought, in myth, humanity is distinguished from animals by two characteristics, one a weakness, the other a strength. The weakness: in its physical and instinctual endowments, humanity has such obvious deficits that it is easy to conclude that it appears to be a mistake. However, because humanity's strength, in contrast, consists in its mind (i.e., intelligence), the conclusion one could arrive at is: weak body, strong mind. However, in reality, both sides are intertwined in such a fashion that even the weakness turns out to be a strength: in order that intelligence has room to operate, the physical and instinctual cannot be tied too closely to a particular environment. The proper diagnosis, then, is not that humanity has a physical weakness and an instinctual defect, but an openness rather than blind dependence on its environment; and that humanity possesses an indirect reflective world- and self-relation rather than a direct and immediate connection to its world and self.

In other words, what initially appears to be a weakness turns out upon closer examination to be a strength. Furthermore, one should never underestimate humanity's potential for physical achievement. Humanity cannot achieve the spurts of speed of a rabbit, cannot climb like a koala bear, swim like a fish, and cannot even rudimentarily fly like a bird. Nonetheless, humanity does possess the three capacities of running, climbing, and swimming; and, thanks to technical equipment, humanity can even fly. Our ancestors, according to the newest research, were so good at endurance running that they could hunt down many animals simply by chasing them to exhaustion. Having consumed the protein from the game captured in the chase, humanity developed a larger brain. The larger brain, in turn, aided humanity's survival because humanity belongs to those prey animals among which only the most cunning can escape from predators. As evidence: large predators such as leopards, jaguars, and pumas capture more animals with less developed brains than with more developed ones.

There are other physical respects in which humanity has a high potential for achievement. Its eyes are tremendously maneuverable and sensitive to light; with respect to pitch, some persons have not only a very acute but also an absolute sense of hearing; our tongues have the capacity to sense an object that is a fraction of a millimeter thick; and with our hands we can just as well carry heavy objects as perform the most precise tasks of a goldsmith, a surgeon, or a pianist. A human being is a generalist who is capable of almost unlimited possibilities and who has the fortune that, in respect to his physical capacities, he enjoys an openness with respect to his physical environment. This latter ability makes it possible for us to live in the most impossible regions on earth.

This many-sided openness to the world accounts for the breadth of our horizon, which opens up a wide field, but one that is not yet "concrete." In other words, a person is like a piece of land that must be cultivated. This task, of course, is one that he recognizes as shared with others in an ordered fashion over a relative duration in the form of a culture. In this respect, the individual is already from his biological condition a social and cultural being. He can develop very different cultures, some better and some worse—however, he can for all intents and purposes never live without any culture (including its positive morals).

At this point we are confronted with the question of whether or not we have allowed the "is-ought" fallacy to creep in—to the extent that we are able to ground a culture's morals purely biologically, that is, on the basis of a mere "is." In addition, we appear to have succumbed to the naturalistic fallacy, since morals are explained in terms of their benefiting life. Among those who engage in this debate, one side, the side of biological naturalism, gives a positive answer whereas their opponents, the ethical antinaturalists, give a negative answer to the question. Both sides overlook two things. One is that we are concerned here not with a normative or critical "principled morals" but solely with a valid, positive morals. There is no succumbing to the "is-ought" fallacy because one remains in the domain of the positive, the "is." The second thing that is ignored is that here positive morals remain essentially undetermined: our openness to the world requires, to be sure, some kind of positive morals; however, the specific obligations are not determined as a consequence. One can understand this "not" as a tolerance for differences among positive determinations. In fact, an indifference is exhibited that leaves open the possibility of, and in a certain respect even necessity for, other alternatives, truly moral arguments.

In an attempt to carry out the more careful grounding in a purely biological manner, one tends to work with criteria like the optimization of life possibilities. Yet even with this criterion, morals remain undetermined. There is a long way to go in order to get from here to a concrete moral program. In particular, the question remains open whether or not morals, as is apparently common in nature, should serve the survival of the species, or, as is the case among human beings, should serve the survival of a particular culture, or, finally, whether they should serve the survival of particular members, the individuals. Here there emerges an alternative (species, culture, individuals) that is difficult to resolve on the basis of biological means. Furthermore, there is another alternative that must be taken into consideration: one that is almost entirely foreign to a biological perspective. This is the alternative: merely to live (survival) or, rather, to live a good life? The second alternative consists not merely in an improvement over the former but one that can even contradict it.

Even the animal kingdom exhibits a phenomenon that one would call in human beings a heroic altruism: that an individual sacrifices itself for another—especially a mother animal for its offspring. In the case of animals, however, this behavior occurs without the additional inquiry whether or not one should make the sacrifice. In addition, this question is extended in two ways that are foreign to the animal kingdom: should I sacrifice myself for someone other than my offspring; perhaps even for non-related offspring? And: should I stand firm on the basis of a conviction (religious, political, or cultural) in the face of great sacrifice, including even the possibility of my death? Even in the case where positive morals demand sacrifice, there can be grounds, perhaps even moral grounds, either particular or general, to refuse to sacrifice oneself. Such questions cannot be answered biologically but, in the end, can be answered only by principled morals.

This state of affairs also applies to the refined naturalism proposed by the moral philosopher Philippa Foot. According to the thesis reflected in the title of her book, *Natural Goodness* (2001; translated into German under the unfortunate title *Die Natur des Guten*, 2004), "good" means generally what the members of a biological species do that is good. As in the case of all animals, even plants, so also in the case of human beings, the good consists in that which is beneficial for survival: "I . . . prefer to say that virtues play a necessary part in the life of humans as do stings in the life of bees" (2001, 35). Foot is by no means suggesting that humans are in the end nothing other than bees. She maintains only a semantic and biological commonality: in spite of other differences, for both humans and animals, "good is what the species needs in order for it to live." To be sure, in this formulation she ignores the distinction made above that in the case of animals the concern is essentially with survival. However, in the case of humanity, there is much more involved. Whereas stings aid the survival of bees, only a part of morals aids humanity in survival. Another aspect of morals aids in living a good life. Immediately a conflict arises here that is unknown to animals: should one pursue the demands of mere survival at the cost of a good life or, in contrast, the obligations of the good life at the expense of mere survival?

Let's return to our anthropological findings. To humanity's multiple biological talents belongs the psychological uniqueness of a nonspecialized surplus of energy. Its biological basis is a hormone, noradrenaline, that enables increased performance. Along with intelligence, it does not determine what specific path or goal one should follow; not even the general goal of individual or collective survival. It is this surplus of energy that makes possible extraordinary engineering and medical accomplishments as well as those in music, art and architecture, literature, science, philosophy, and, finally, heroic renunciations.

The new possibilities here are combined, however, with new kinds of dangers so that humanity can also go in the other direction, too: reversing a biological advantage into a weakness. Our energy surplus empowers us to an almost limitless more and more: gluttony, sexual excesses, ambition, dominance, and avarice in the literal sense of addiction. Not least, one can succumb to fantasies of omnipotence: the desire "to be God" is unknown to other animals, so that the individual ironically can be defined as an ape who occasionally wants to be God. Apparently, only humanity is capable of harming others and itself without constraints. For example, these human apes are not squeamish since they tear out the fingernails of their enemies, crush their testicles, or tear out their tracheas. Only humanity appears to engage in cold-blooded murder, either at the command of others or by one's own initiative, and to transform it into sadism as an end in itself. Morals raise objections to such actions and also determine the grounds for objecting to, and/or establishing criteria for the performance of, such actions. Humanity is by no means a simple monster. In contrast to apes, only humanity establishes friendly relationships with neighbors, engages in trade, and assists when catastrophes occur. Morals have a place to play even here and not merely as an aid to our survival.

An initial biological ground for morals consists in the following: in the absence of biologically programmed restraints, a human being must channel his surplus of energy and must learn to make it productive rather than destructive. In order to accomplish this goal, he must develop himself into a being who plans what is to be done and not done, as well as one who directs and develops his own life as an active agent.

Whether we call it spirit, reason, or intelligence, the responsible authority possesses, constitutively, a cultural component that is obvious from the linguistic dependence of much of intelligence. The converse holds equally true: culture is an essential accomplishment of intelligence. Properly, brain research says that humanity's far superior mental capacity over against other primates is what allows for the acquisition of culture. This conclusion includes, as well, the repercussion that culture, observed from the perspective of evolution, has made the brain a dependent variable. One may not ignore, however, that acquisition of a culture requires an enormous potential with respect to individual learning and involves considerable differences in intellectual achievement. Adult apes, in contrast, achieve at best the level of a three- to four-year-old (i.e., the level of small children).

This is not to discount the intellectual and social capabilities of certain animals (see Tomasello 1999; de Waal 1996 and 2005; Perler and Wild 2005). Already the Enlightenment scholar d'Holbach (1770/German, *System der Natur,* 1978, 629, note 50) warned against underestimating the capabilities of animals. We know today that certain animals have the capacity to categorize their world with respect to those objects and events relevant for survival. They are capable of memorizing a huge quantity of personal experience and, on the basis of this memory, of anticipating future situations to a certain degree. In the process of their domestication, cats, and even more so dogs, have learned to cultivate a wide spectrum of interaction and communication with humans—thus, with a different species. In the case of primates, we find gestures of conciliation and tactical deception in abundance. For example, in the presence of another chimpanzee, a chimpanzee is able to pretend that it doesn't notice a berry bush in order to be able to harvest the berries for itself once the competitor has moved on. Birds, for example, the plover, can feign an injured wing in order to distract a predator from its nest. A chimpanzee can conceal its erection with its hand from a dominant male, and a female can make a conciliatory gesture toward another female in order to be all the more successful in biting her.

Do such strategies of deception establish a moral capacity in chimpanzees because chimpanzees are capable of violating morals—in this case openness and honesty? What is correct is that the deception maneuvers are not merely goal-oriented but are also intentional; however, they occur only with respect to the wished-for result. One wants to avoid attracting the animosity of the dominant male; the other wants to make things easier for herself. A structural complication is missing in order for us to classify the behavior as conscious deception, as lying or cheating: not merely that the behavior actually occurs, but that it occurs *as deception.*

Lying involves one in an intentional attempt to cause another to believe something that is not true. In this respect, it involves a mental capacity that one doesn't find in the case of highly developed animals. The animal would have to combine in one and the same thought the representation of something actual (in our examples, the gesture of concealment or of self-restraint) with the representation of a possible or even an imagined situation: the dominant male is convinced that it doesn't have any sexual competitors; or the threatened female takes the gesture of its competitor for a sign of reconciliation and is thereby lulled into striking range. The ability to lie involves mental mirroring processes of the kind: "I know that you know that I know." Here: "I believe that you believe that I mean this gesture so (as a gesture of reconciliation)."

Controlled studies demonstrate that the animal behavior described above can be explained as learned acquisition of a manner of acting in a specific situation. In order to reach the expected goal, animals do not need to know that their fellow members of the species are going to act on the basis of a commensurate conviction. There is no deception here in the strictest sense of intentionally pulling the wool over someone's eyes. As a consequence, there is no adverse moral behavior in such a case. What many claim is the application of a moral capacity is in truth, to be sure, remarkable, but only a preliminary stage. The same applies to the capacity of memory. A moral subject, a person, possesses an ability that is missing even in primates: the capacity to take into account one's own past and future; a capacity that one can call one's "autobiographical memory" (see Markowitsch and Welzer 2005).

A moral anthropology grounded in experience would emphasize other morally relevant perspectives (for example, that the human being is concerned with recognition, and even struggles with the possible consequences of envy, jealousy, and resentment, of revenge, but also of forgiveness, sympathy and empathy, compassion, regret, and shame). (On the philosophy and psychology of feelings or emotions, see Solomon 2004 and Wassermann 2002; on the anthropology of facial mimicking, see Meuter 2006.) Other human innovations are indeed only indirectly relevant to morality: for example, the worlds of engineering and medicine, the worlds of work and play. These are worlds with an almost unlimited capacity for development (perfectibility) in contrast to which even the most intelligent chimpanzee population over millennia has remained as if on a treadmill.

Anthropologically considered, then, morals at this point in our investigation can be viewed in a bifocal perspective: as the capacity for morals in light of humanity's intelligence and openness to the world; and simultaneously as the need for morals in light of the dangerous potential of this surplus of drive and openness to the world. In any event, morals are not something actually realized by humanity from the very beginning either at the individual's birth or at the origin of the species. Considered from the perspective of anthropology, morals are a strange mixture of "oughts," needs, and "is." A human being, this life-form that is open to the world but also endangered, needs obligations that permit the intelligence to inquire about their goodness, and finally even about an absolute good, which to be sure is not necessary but over time cannot be ignored. Consequently, morals, first, turn out to be primed for biologically. Second, morals take on the concrete form of positive morals only within a culture, so that one, as we've already said, may not understand humanity's natural endowments and cultural formation in opposition to one another. Third, thanks to a universal human reason, positive morals are subject to critical morals, and, not infrequently, critical morals transform culture's positive morals. Biology, including humanity's neurobiological nature, establishes the basic conditions that are conducive for the development of morals and that even call forth the development of morals just for bare survival. Morals themselves, however, are something that humanity has to develop by means of its own efforts and according to its own criteria.

5 Action

An interim assessment says two things: thanks to its openness to the world, its surplus driving force, and its intelligence, humanity is capable, and in need, of personally responsible action with critical appraisal and practical reflection. Furthermore, within the framework of critical judgment, the highest level is determined to be the morally good as the absolute good. Obviously, there is no content to this morality, and we haven't arrived at a single meaningful moral principle. In order to accomplish that, two central elements require more specificity: personally responsible action and the absolute good. Both determinations—and this is something to which hardly any moral philosopher has paid attention—are closely related to each other. A meaningful moral principle is presupposed by any particular understanding of action, and, conversely, a moral principle presupposes an understanding of action—admittedly, only when in combination with the idea of an absolute good. Thus, the foundational model of argumentation here is called: ethics plus theory of action.

5.1 Conscious and Voluntary

"Action" is a basic word that we use daily, but, nevertheless, it is difficult to say what the word means. It is already a matter of controversy exactly what falls under consideration with the word. Should a train wreck occur because the signalman failed to close the crossing gate, he neglected to do something: is an omission a kind of action, or do only deeds count as actions? Some people do things aggressively, others reluctantly: is only the impetuously performed deed an action, or does action include reluctance, reflection, and delay? Further: is one acting when he twitches an eyelid, when he breathes, yawns, or sneezes; when he commits himself to something or miscalculates? It could be that these questions concern borderline cases. Let's begin with core cases: what is common to such different behaviors as eating, walking, and driving an automobile; of declaring one's love, marrying, and conceiving children; of helping an accident victim, greeting, or taking leave of someone?

Another difficulty is the ambiguity of behavior. If someone is walking down a street, he can be taking a stroll, but he can also be following someone or impatiently waiting for someone. Someone writing on a piece of paper could be writing a letter but also drawing, writing poetry, generating a seminar paper, or merely scribbling in boredom. Is "action" in the end only an unspecific, unscientific concept?

At first glance, action is a unique human phenomenon. There is a practical self-understanding that distinguishes humanity, by means of its intelligence and world-openness, from vegetative processes and animal behavior. This practical self-understanding consists of the capacity for reflection, for consultation (with oneself and with others), and for decision-making.

Already this provisional determination allows us to answer a few of our questions: to the extent that one can impute an omission to someone, it has the character of an action; to the extent that the twitching of an eyelid and breathing cannot be imputed to someone, they cannot count as actions; however, an intentional twitching and a self-conscious breathing, in contrast, are appropriately classified as actions. Two moments come together in practical, self-determined behavior: intentionality (volitional, genuinely practical) and, in relation to this intentional moment, consciousness (cognitive). Action involves one's more or less conscious awareness of one's activity. It requires a knowledge not only of the goal and intention but also of the means appropriate to the goal in a specific situation. Praxis combines knowledge of a final (i.e., a teleological) "aim" (or "end") with an instrumental element (the "means"). However, knowledge of the two elements, ends and means, is not necessarily combined in praxis. One can apply one's knowledge of means to pursue a goal that is embraced merely out of habit. Other times, one has clear goals, but they are served only by inadequate means. In another situation, both elements are self-consciously combined successfully.

The mere combination of both ends and means initially constitutes a practically oriented but not a truly practical knowledge. Such a combination is concerned with praxis, but it doesn't bring a concrete result. This is like the pianist who explains a sonata but doesn't actually perform it. Another possible perspective reduces action down to a moment of knowledge; it succumbs to a theoretical or cognitive abridgment. However, the "knowledge of" praxis is transformed into "practical knowledge" (one in which something practically occurs) only when the moment of knowledge is combined with the indispensable moment of intention. It is only where knowledge, more precisely, the adjudicative moment in the form of an explicit or silent judgment with respect to a goal and the means to achieving it, is combined with an intentional or executive moment in the form of drive and motivation that one may speak of a practical rationality (or practical reason): on the one side, that of knowledge, one selects among possible goals and means which, only in combination with the other side, that of intention, result in practical reason. What one does is, then, purposeful (intended); by the same token, what one intends is done.

Because of its ambiguity, it is advisable to avoid the term "will" for the executive side of praxis. For example, a broad definition of "will" refers to any effective wish, which is more precisely called "intentional" or "voluntary." In contrast, there is a narrow and precise definition that means "a condition initiated by the self." For that reason, it might need more than the anthropological character of reflective world-openness. In that case, "will" would not be something basically human but would presuppose a considerable cultural development, so that it could be unknown in less developed cultures and epochs. In this present study, the terms "intentional" and "voluntary" refer to the lowest level of practical reflection, whereas the strict notion of "will" is reserved for a second level.

Practical reflection provides an answer to Wittgenstein's "difficult" problem that could no longer be resolved because it is purely analytic: "What is left over when I subtract from raising my arm the fact that my arm is raised?" (*Philosophical Investigations*, no. 621). What remains is the practical self-reflection, which of course does not exist merely for itself but rather as the reflective, conscious, and voluntary structure of patterns of behavior.

It is a given that not all human behavior is conscious and voluntary. Purely physiological processes and mere automatic reflexes are by no means voluntary. Someone who misses a train, dozes off, or is hit by lightning usually is not understood to have knowingly or intentionally acted. A yawning or sneezing, a stumbling or stuttering does not always occur unintentionally, but usually it does. In contrast, there are some behaviors that are always intentional. Someone who makes a claim about something or seeks to deceive another, calculates logarithms or interprets philosophical classics, can hardly act unconsciously or even unintentionally. However, other kinds of behavior can be both conscious and voluntary as well as unconscious and unintentional. For example, one can stumble intentionally or give assistance to someone unintentionally.

In addition, we are concerned here with a more or less. Action is a comparative notion not in terms of the event itself but, rather, with respect to the degree that it is voluntary and conscious. One's knowledge can be more or less clear and precise. It can just as well be intuitive as governed by strong and clear reflection. One can be concerned with only a subjective certainty of personal conviction or with an objective, methodically grounded knowledge—perhaps, even with an ever-improving knowledge of a science. Knowledge can be incomplete: Oedipus knows that he killed a traveler but not that he killed his father; Hamlet that he stabbed and killed an eavesdropper, not Polonius. We could see as a rule that, to the degree one doesn't know certain parameters, one has not intended one's action. Of course, what one takes to be the case can also prove to be false.

Even in the case of what is voluntary, we can be concerned with different degrees. There is a greater degree of voluntariness in an action in which one has invested conviction and enthusiasm than in one by which one must be convinced to act or is deceived into action. Nevertheless, as long as one is not a mere tool for someone else, there remains a degree of voluntarism. It belongs to the concept of intention that, when one undertakes an action knowingly, one does so because one wants to accomplish it or is consciously aiming at some further goal beyond the immediate action.

What are we trying to achieve with this concept of action? One attributes responsibility to someone who has done something consciously and voluntarily. He did something, and, in flagrantly negative cases, he did something outrageous. As a consequence, he can be praised or condemned, honored or humiliated. In any event, one can hold him accountable, and, in the case of misconduct, one can charge him with a crime. Behind the notion of conscious and voluntary events, of actions, lies our interest in holding one another responsible; responsible for our fellow beings as well as for oneself, perhaps even responsible before God.

5.2 Parenthetically: Ethical Realism?

To hold someone responsible for his actions means that one demands justificatory reasons in light of which the act or omission appears successful (good and right) or rather as a failure (bad, false, or evil). Human action is a world of justificatory reasons because it is conscious and voluntary. Precisely for this reason, moral action is concerned with more than merely subjective opinion; namely, it is concerned with objective knowledge. To be sure, moral action's justificatory reasons are radically different from those one evokes for one's knowledge about objects. The world of practical justifications is concerned with the appraisal of good and bad (or of evil), whereas the world of theoretical justifications is concerned with appraisal of what is true or false. As a consequence, action is capable of justification and of disputation but not in the usual, theoretical, sense of truth claims.

Ratio is the Latin expression that lies at the root of the word "rationality." Both the corresponding Greek word, *logos*, and *ratio* have a double meaning that can be found in European languages as "reason," *raison*, *ragione*, and *razón:* the expression means in the singular "reason," in the plural, however, "justification." This is the sense in which the world of justifications is in accordance with reason. Anyone who finds the term "reason" here too pretentious should consider that, since the beginnings of philosophy, human beings—along with other beings—have been understood to possess the capacity for reason (*logon echon*) because they are capable of providing a reason, an argument (*logon didonai*).

In contemporary meta-ethics, one finds the view that moral judgments are concerned with moral facts; hence, as in the case of claims about the natural and social world, they are taken to be true or false. This position is called moral realism, or more appropriately, as a theory concerning morality, ethical realism (see Brink 1989; Schaber 1997; for a critique of the same, see Scarano 2001, section 1). This is typical of a kind of thinking that takes theoretical philosophy as the standard of knowledge. This procedure, however, oversimplifies two options. *Either* it removes the moral dimension from the world of true or false claims: in this case, it pays the "ontological" price of an ethical relativism. This ethical relativism is comparable "epistemologically" to an ethical non-cognitivism that acknowledges in morality no knowledge or anything analogous to knowledge. *Or*, in order to avoid relativism and irrationalism, morality is included in the theoretical world of truths and falsehoods. Ethical realism follows the second option, and as a consequence it has two leading edges. In contrast to a strict ethical relativism, ethical realism maintains that there are objectively valid moral claims. Furthermore, in contrast to the assumption that its objectivity is distinguishable from theoretical claims, it presupposes that its moral claims are clearly obvious in the same objective sense of true and false.

The present study embraces the first leading edge of ethical realism: it seeks objective moral claims, acknowledges the critique of ethical relativism (see chapter 2.3), and maintains on the basis of a capacity for objectivity that moral claims are cognitive. However, in contrast to the second leading edge of ethical realism, it maintains the independence of the practical over against the theoretical. This is not a rejection of the crucial common elements between practical and theoretical reason. With respect to the critique of moralism, this study regards concrete actions descriptively: hence, there are true-false (i.e., constitutive) claims to be made in regard to such elements. The genuinely moral aspect, nonetheless, is distinct from such constitutive elements. It consists of judgment with respect to what is good or bad/evil and not true or false. At most, in a figurative sense one can call an action "false" and mean; thereby, it is morally unacceptable.

Moral facts are above all good or bad/evil, not true or false. Claims capable of true-false judgments play a considerable role, but for the primary task of moral judgment within the parameters of good-bad valuation, they are secondary. As a consequence, a position of valuation that transcends and relativizes all others has the character of reason or rationality. However, it is strictly distinguished from the "usual" theoretical reason because this latter is concerned with knowledge of facts and their explanation; hence, with a *know that*. Morality, in contrast, consists of a qualified form of *know how:* in the capacity and proficiency to judge from the highest level one's own life and its institutional context as it attempts to shape itself according to standards of value. (One can call this alternative to ethical realism "practical rationalism" because its acknowledgment of rational criteria makes it "rational" and because of its difference from theoretical rationality.)

There is a debate within the philosophy of action whether or not it is sufficient for the description of an action to trace out the effects of impersonal powers as non-intentional causes from the perspective of a neutral observer (pure causalism); or, in contrast, must one adopt the perspective of the actor himself and assume his intentions and justifications in order to give an appropriate description (intentionalism)? "Personalists" intensify intentionalism in that they take an action as such to be "caused" by a person and not by facts. According to a modified causalism, actions are events that, to be sure, can be traced back to justifications on the part of the actor, but these justifications in turn have the character of causes.

A closer examination of the different positions is necessary for ethics only to a limited extent. At least the following can be said: *First*, one can agree with intentionalists and personalists (and simultaneously contradict strict causalism) to the extent that not every human action but certainly those that constitute its uniqueness cannot be reduced to purely natural facts (explanations). The language of action is not only actually, but also, as soon as its uniqueness is to be grasped, necessarily interspersed with intentional expressions. *Second*, the fundamental aspect of human action is not, as many causalists maintain, a mysterious, unobservable mental state of action (see the thesis of the ghost in the machine in Ryle 1950, chapter 1, section 2). We are not talking about any "addition" to observable natural phenomena but, rather, about a structural complication within them, which requires that our descriptions include subjective elements. These include more than ever the necessary attention to an object that is already called in some circles "intentionality." However, with this intentionality one is speaking neither of a knowledge nor of a desiring that one could find in subhuman behavior. What is required is a conscious and voluntary directedness: a purpose (intention).

5.3 Practical Syllogism, Practical Reason

In order to understand this structural complication, one can represent intentional behavior by means of a practical syllogism. A theoretical syllogism based on knowledge draws from two antecedent propositions, for example: (1) All men are mortal and (2) Socrates is a man, the necessary conclusion: (3) Socrates is mortal. A practical syllogism asserts a deductively necessary connection as well: given an original premise (a goal) and a secondary premise (the means to the goal), an action (at least the decision for the action) follows with certain necessity. A person P_1 intending a goal G_1 pursues a sequence S_1 that he believes will lead to the goal G_1:

(1) P_1 intends G_1.

(2) P_1 believes that S_1 leads to G_1.

---

(3) P_1 follows S_1.

One can read the practical syllogism either from below ("bottom up") or from above ("top down"). In the former case, one formalizes (either in reflection or in reality) something that has already occurred. In the latter case, one anticipates an action. In both cases, one is advised not to claim that action *is* this way but rather: *action allows itself to be reconstructed in this manner.* This kind of reconstruction is acknowledged today as the standard model of action. One should call it, however, an elementary model since it involves significant simplifications.

An initial simplification is harmless: in the first premise the goal G_1 can, in fact, be an intermediate goal, whereby a kind of molecular action first occurs: a cabinetmaker searches out the appropriate wood in or-der—in the face of a higher goal G_2—to build a cabinet; a traveler goes somewhere in order to accomplish something. ("Atoms" in the molecu-lar action here are the still smaller elements, the smallest parts of an ac-tion: for example, that one moves one's hand in order as a cabinetmaker to grasp a tool or in order as a traveler to grasp one's suitcase.)

This first simplification can be accounted for by a chain of syllogisms in which the same individual, or also—a new complication—several in-dividuals are involved: P_1 produces a preliminary sketch of the cabinet, P_2 searches out the wood, P_3 glues or screws together the wood. A fur-ther complication of the syllogism here occurs when the intermediate goals are not clearly linear as in the case of the building of furniture or the climbing of a mountain. In such cases, the earlier goals create, rather, a new situation in which the new goal is established.

A second simplification is insignificant as well: the same goal can be reached by different paths between or among which one chooses. An additional complication, however, is that the choice can occur from dif-ferent perspectives. How quickly, certain, or efficient is this path; how much does it cost, and what are the hidden expenditures involved, and so on? One could invoke here a cost-benefit calculation that we will ad-dress later (see chapter 11).

No less significant is the circumstance in which the ends-means model applies only to an action in which it is not the process but the finished goal that matters (i.e., with the production of a product or in other respects when something has been brought about: the cabinet is finished, the mountain has been climbed). To be sure, one can under-stand a moral action as the combination of a goal with the contempla-tion of the appropriate means to that goal. In such a case, one combines an action meant to give concrete assistance to someone with reflection about how to be most effective with one's efforts. However, such a situ-ation does not apply to actions of procedure, which are called "praxis" in the narrow sense by philosophers. In such circumstances the fundamental model of action doesn't apply because, for example, in sight, musical performance, or walking there is no goal external to the action (on the concepts of production and process, see chapter 6.1).

Whether or not one is concerned with establishing the goal of a practical syllogism, wherever one's actions can be defended with good grounds, they are rational. They conform to a practical reason according to the three levels of the good of technical, pragmatic, or moral-practical reason (see chapter 2.2). For quite some time, there were two models for such rationality. In both cases the driving force of the action was external to reason. A first, "rationalistic" model takes reason to be involved in guiding pre-rational energies. Reason is their master (one finds this model clearly in Plato's myth of the chariot soul in *Phaedrus* 246a–249d). A second, "empirical" model declares by means of a non-dialectical reversal that reason is the slave. Peculiarly, David Hume notes in the form of a preface that reason has claim to no other function than to serve and to obey the passions (*A Treatise of Human Nature*, book 3, part 1, section 1). With respect to the practical syllogism, the empirical model of reason allows the application of reason only as a secondary premise, whereas, in the case of the rationalistic model, reason is involved foremost in the primary premise; in the case of a chain of syllogisms, reason is found in the highest premise.

Without too quickly undertaking a defense of the rationalistic model, one can, nevertheless, maintain that it is a defensible option. It can remain open whether or not we are considering pragmatic reason concerned with one's well-being or with moral reason in a more narrow sense. In any event, we are concerned here with three successive, constitutive possibilities, that is, three successive levels: a *limitedly* rational action is rational either (1) with respect to its means (hence, with respect to the minor premise), and thus instrumentally rational in a broad sense; or (2) with respect to its end (hence, with respect to its major premise), and thus rational as goal-oriented; and finally, (3) when concerned with both ends and means, an action is a *thoroughly* rational teleological striving. Likewise, there are three possibilities for irrational teleological striving: a merely instrumental, a merely final, and a thoroughly irrational striving.

It must be emphasized in opposition to a frequent misunderstanding that, even if it resonates with some philosophers, practical reason should not be viewed as a dualistic psychology—that is, viewed as independent from matter or the body—characterized by some philosophers as the proverbial "ghost in the machine." Rather, what is meant here is a relationship of the person to himself and his natural and social world that simultaneously is self-referential and because of its connection to action is called practical reason.

Furthermore, practical reason does not mean that pre-rational (i.e., sensuous) drives are not included in it. However, such drives cannot be the sole determining power, to which human beings subordinate themselves like slaves. To follow reason means neither succumbing to nor avoiding one's appetites. Rather, one controls them in an attempt to establish one's well-being: in the first place, one maintains one's distance and takes neither the ends nor the means as something prescribed, which one simply must accept without commentary or correction. Secondly, in light of this critical distance, one engages in personal reflection or seeks out the advice of others in a process of appraising and evaluating before one determines something to be a positive "good" as a final (teleological) reason and before one determines the "good" means toward that end and employs instrumental reason to establish a pathway to be followed toward that end. Even a restricted reason that is concerned only with means is primarily no theoretical (cognitive) reason but a practical reason, since it is directing an activity.

5.4 Reasons and Motives

In accordance with the distinction between "is" and "ought," reason can direct action in two respects. Understood normatively as the embodiment of grounds, reason can *legitimate* an action. Understood descriptively or explanatorily as the embodiment of an internal cause, the motives, reason can *explain* the action. In the two cases one expects an entirely different answer to the same "Why" question: "Why did someone do that?" When one is seeking a normative answer, one wants to know the objective authority on which one acted; in seeking a descriptive and causal answer, one wants to know just how the event occurred, more precisely: what were the decisive causes for the subject, what were the motives (i.e., the subjective incentives)?

As with the questions, so too are the answers related, but they should not be confused: one must distinguish between reasons in the sense of a possible justification and motives as possible causes. Even the best of justifications for an action do not necessarily bring about the action, and the actual motives driving the action can derisively dismiss every objective authority meant to govern the action. One calls this problem in everyday life the "weakness of the will," which is a conundrum that has engaged philosophers since antiquity. The response found among theory of action positions is this: a justification is a mere judgment with respect to the good, a *diiudicatio boni*, which is distinct from the execution of an action, the *executio boni*. The missing connecting link consists in the recognition of the good that is visible in the motives of the actor or is missing there.

The connection between reasons and motives can be accounted for by two fundamentally different perspectives. One maintains that there is an inner ("internal") connection between the reason and the appropriate motives. According to this internalism, it is not the reasons in themselves but, rather, conviction with respect to *justifying* reasons that constitutes the strong motive to act in a particular way. Of course, there can be competing motives, so that one doesn't *necessarily* follow what one takes to be justified reasons for the action. According to a second perspective, externalism, one needs an external motive in addition to the grounding justification for the completion of an act. For example, one may act morally out of fear of external or internal negative sanctions (punishment in the former case, or conscience—shame or guilt—in the latter), or out of hope for positive sanctions such as recognition on the part of others or self-esteem. Externalism, in other words, takes the connection between reasons and motives to be contingent.

The question whether the connection between reasons and motives is internal or external depends upon a more careful determination. Internalism comes to the fore where, with Anscombe 1963, one strongly emphasizes the intention to the extent that even the description and explanation of an action depend upon the intention of the actor. Were the actor to be asked about, and be able to answer with, reasons for the action, he would possess knowledge of the connection between justified intentions and intentional action. In contrast to an empirical tradition, this knowledge is independent, not contemplative (perhaps one should say: not theoretical) but practical. It conforms with this study's concept of practical reason. Whereas theoretical knowledge is dependent upon observations, practical knowledge occurs without observations. Instead, it is linked to a wish that constitutes the primary premise of a practical syllogism (for example, P_1 wishes to give a lecture in Berlin), which, when combined with the appropriate secondary premise (P_1 is convinced that the necessary precondition is a flight to Berlin), results in the future action.

The question whether the conclusion of the syllogism is an actual action, only a decision to act, or even merely a demand to act ("P_1 should fly to Berlin") results in subtle debates that lose their significance when it comes to causalism, the opponent of intentionalism. The primary proponent of causalism, Davidson 1980, rejects the distinction between theoretical and practical knowledge in that he explains the relationship between the reasons for an action and its execution according to the model of cause and effect. In agreement with a basic empirical assumption, he integrates the world of action into a *unified* world and situates the explanation of action within a unified science committed to theoretical knowledge as its standard.

Davidson knows that there are difficulties here. For example, a decision often results in an action only as a consequence of an evaluation between alternatives: should I travel to Berlin by plane, train, or car? In addition, there are intentions that don't result in actions: in spite of the decision to fly, one doesn't because other motivations dominate—for example, the fear of flying or anxiety about giving the lecture. However, Davidson places the transition from evaluating reasons to intending an action under a principle of "continence": in order to make actions explicable, one sets aside "ricochets" and presumes a rational connection between reasons and intentions. Davidson doesn't grasp the consequences of this assumption. Because one needs it only for the world of action and not for the natural world, the assumption illuminates a fissure between the world of action and the natural world that shatters the supposed unity between them. To the degree this shattering occurs, the difference between intentionalism and causalism fades to the advantage of intentionalism.

Davidson believes that he can eliminate the difference between explanatory motives and justifying reasons with the thesis that "reasons are causes." Davidson's underlying interest in unifying action theory with a naturalistic worldview can even be strengthened. Rüdiger Bittner 2001 attempts to detach action theory from everything subjective and mental (i.e., so-called mental states). Reasons are neither wishes nor motives, intentions, convictions, nor some combination of them, according to Bittner. Neither are they rules, fundamental subjective principles (maxims), normative competencies, or dispositions (virtues); they are not even causes, although these latter can *explain* an action. Following the paradigm of a move in chess, the reasons for an action reside in the antecedent state of affairs. Therefore, they don't lie in subjective convictions but in objective conditions: P_1 moves his pawn because his opponent's bishop is threatening his rook.

Bittner takes himself to be critically progressive [*ein Aufklärer*] in the sense that he wants to reject the mentalist and accompanying normative ballast, inclusive of the notion of humanity's privileged position, found in action theory up to this point. Has he not thrown overboard more than mere ballast? Bittner's strategy depends upon the suppression of many subjective and simultaneously normative aspects. One finds in his example the first two subjective and normative moments in the fact that the chess player must (1) understand the antecedent state of affairs (2) as a challenge that he wants to overcome. Here we do have a theoretical aspect: P_1 has to perceive the bishop as a threat. However, the perception cannot remain theoretical and be satisfied with the mere indifferent observation: "Here is a threat." Rather, it must be practical (i.e., evaluative and prescriptive for the person concerned). He must himself determine that the threat is "bad for him" (the evaluative moment) and hold the evaluation for justification (the prescriptive moment) for undertaking a defensive move: "I want to eliminate the threat." Purely theoretical perception perceives something to be something (in this case: the opponent's bishop as a threat to one's rook); practical perception sees in this "something" the necessity for an action: protect one's rook from the threat. It makes no difference, if occasionally it is so simple, that practical perception occurs without great reflection; the experienced chess player acts automatically (i.e., without anything specifically consciously occurring).

One can perceive a third, subjective moment in the background of the second moment with its interest in victory: short of winning, one wants to play well and, in the event of loss, to maintain one's honor. In this case, there are considerable differences: great chess players are notoriously often masters of ambition and of psychological warfare.

Furthermore, there are other subjective moments in play here: should the game of chess not be against a weak opponent, it requires no small portion of attention and insight. Where these are absent, one can be misled: perhaps the bishop is really no threat because it is protecting the queen. Such decisions require a nuanced competency for the game of chess. Knowledgeable players are capable of perceiving the threat many moves in advance and can implement step-by-step a defensive strategy, which in the case of a competent opponent results in an early detection and countermeasures.

Obviously, in real life it is often ridiculous to respond to the question, "Why did you act in that way?" with a subjective conviction about means and ends and with a desired goal that governs one's actions. Instead, one points to an objective factor: I jump into the water because someone is drowning; I eat because I am hungry; I am carrying an umbrella because I think it might rain. These answers, however, are an abbreviated form, one calls them an enthymeme, that leaves out the full explanation as self-evident (left in the mind [*im Herzen*]: *en thymo*). In the game of chess, it is usually redundant to say that in order to win one wants to protect one's rook from the opponent's bishop. Likewise, it is seldom worth mentioning, although it clearly belongs to an exhaustive justification of one's actions, that one wants to help the drowning victim and supposes that one can get him safely to shore, or that one takes the umbrella as an appropriate means to keep from getting wet.

We have arrived at the interim conclusion: whoever throws out all that is subjective and mental not only gets rid of ballast but also loses something crucial.

5.5 Happiness (Eudaimonia) or Freedom (Autonomy)?

More important for ethics than the difference between production and action (or planned action) is the alternative between striving [*Strebens-*] and willed [*Willens-*] action. This alternative leads from one and the same moral concept, the unlimited good, to two entirely different moral principles: the principle of happiness and the principle of moral freedom.

The first, more obvious model ties in with the fundamental model that has concerned us till now: an agent establishes a goal or intention and applies the appropriate means and methods to attain the goal. Such goal-oriented action leads one on the basis of one's own ambition independent of external coercion toward an end. Aspiring to an end means that activity in which one acts spontaneously from within and is simultaneously shaped by a specific, final goal.

The kind of goal- or purpose-orientation that one finds in organisms is sufficient for a weaker concept of aspiration. The narrower and stricter concept, in contrast, requires that one represents to oneself an objective, affirms that it is what one wants to achieve, and with the appropriate means pursues it—or, in the case of a negative striving, seeks to avoid it. Aspiration in the narrow sense is not purely natural but is reflective—a conscious and voluntary activity. Therefore, the individual can be held accountable for the action; he is responsible for it. Aspiration in this sense is no natural philosophical but an anthropological and ethical concept because it involves a peculiarly human form of movement: that one intends something and works toward its realization. (For a discussion of aspiration according to the authoritative, classical example of Aristotle, see Höffe 2000a, chapter 11; and Höffe 2008, part 1, chapter 1.)

The goals that one intends can be organized into a formal hierarchy. The lowest goals serve as the means to achieving a higher goal. In this respect, the lower goals are transitional. The next-higher goals, already goals in their own right, are final goals. In the case where one can determine a ranking among final goals, one's aspiration finds its formal completion when it is oriented toward a goal beyond which no other goal can be thought and pursued—in this case, it is an absolutely highest goal. This singular goal constitutes the fulfillment of all of humanity's aspirations: it is the absolute superlative that one also calls happiness. What is meant here is not a chance happiness like winning the lottery. Rather, we are concerned here with a goal for which one can live and which can serve as the final goal of one's life. Such a life is good and successful, a happy existence. Included in this happiness which the Greeks called *eudaimonia* and which can be translated as "felicitousness" is the absolutely highest, hence moral, good with respect to all goal-oriented action: the moral principle of (eudaimonistic) happiness belongs to the concept of aspiration. This moral principle forms the horizon within which all aspiration finds its ultimate justification.

This first model of action as aspiration is so obvious that many, even philosophers, do not see any other alternative. This model, however, is possible only on the basis of a presupposition that is no longer questioned but can be questioned. This presupposition insists on the volitional side, on spontaneous goal-directedness and its complete fulfillment. If we understand human action as aspiration, one assumes that it always has a goal that can be assessed within the horizon of happiness. In part shaped by drives, needs, and passions, in part by one's sociopolitical context, and partially, also, through personal factions, the individual is always in fact motivated in light of specific goals. In the final sense, he seeks the epitome of all goal-realization: (eudaimonistic) happiness. Someone who acts morally is neither following convention nor natural impulses. Thanks to an appropriate upbringing and self-discipline, he chooses to act on the basis of morally proper goals. What is meant by "proper" here is yet to be clarified. However, an initial formal definition has already been established: it is the epitome of the fulfillment of all goal-directedness, and this definition is a guideline that is no longer disputable.

The precise justification for this formal definition will follow (chapter 6). As soon as one understands action as aspiration, it is oriented toward goals, which obtain their sense and meaning from the absolutely highest goal. Within the framework of action as aspiration, one cannot imagine an action that doesn't justify itself, in the end, on the basis of an interest in happiness. However, if one questions the spontaneity of one's goal-orientation, including the principle of happiness, one increases on the volitional side the uniquely human practical-reflective world-openness. One can say, as well: this openness is structurally radicalized. Rather than "intending something within the horizon of happiness," one distances oneself from the usual horizon of intention, happiness. On the basis of this distancing, an earlier unrecognized alternative becomes manifest: the alternative that happiness does not necessarily constitute the determining goal and horizon of all intentions. In this fashion, what was otherwise unquestioned in the model of action as aspiration becomes questionable; to be sure, not by means of an epistemological but by a practical strategy (i.e., practically effective). The philosopher identifies this structurally new activity with the concept of the will in the strictest sense (i.e., free will).

Whereas action as aspiration is governed by the *fulfillment* of one's goals, action as willing is primarily governed by the *framework* of goals themselves and, thereby, by the issue of ultimate origin. In the most preliminary of senses, we can say that the will in the vaguest sense of normal "intending to" is no longer so self-evident because one had no alternative within the context of (eudaimonistic) happiness. A free will emerges in the context of a simple intention. The moral principle that governs this free will consists in an absolute first willing, in the freedom of the will in the demanding sense of autonomy, in the freedom of self-legislation.

A moral theory grounded in the concept of aspiration has no difficulty contemplating modifications within the framework of intended goals. However, the modified factors remain within the horizon of a teleological ethic of aspiration: the principle of happiness. In this context, one is concerned with a change in desire and interest, with the means to their satisfaction, or with the kind of means (change in taste or fashion), which in turn can be invoked on the basis of economic, cultural, and also cognitive changes. However, these nonmoral conditions cannot explain all change. Someone who criticizes a dominant morality on the basis of moral principles or who protests in the name of justice against an established point of view of a community does not pursue the intended goals within the context of happiness. Rather, he calls into question the dominant fundamental framework of goals. A similar thing happens when one subjects oneself to prescriptions or proscriptions that diminish one's happiness. Such action can no longer be thought of as a mere spontaneous acceptance and pursuit of goals within the context of happiness or as an action of aspiration. This is because it distances itself from aspiration in the name of a willing in a narrower and stricter sense. What is meant here is that moment in human action which is chosen not because its goal is established within the framework of a eudaimonistic horizon but because it is—and this is the alternative— emphatically [self-]"willed." In this way, one takes to an extreme the nonnecessity of human action; what one calls in the philosophical tradition "a condition arising from the self."

In philosophical anthropology, the thought of an (absolutely) highest good, to which constructive semantics leads, is broadened by the thought of responsibility in light of an intelligently grounded world-openness. Both the notions of pursuit of the good and of free will are subordinated by action theory either, according to the model of aspiration, to the criterion of an absolutely highest goal, the good in the sense of eudaimonia, or, according to the model of willing, to the criterion of an absolutely first origin, freedom of the will in the sense of autonomy. Both models (aspiration and willing) are focused on human responsibility. Because the concept of aspiration addresses only the weakest conditions (that it is voluntary and conscious), it does not involve the idea of responsibility in its complete clarity and radicality. The latter occurs only with the concept of the will and with freedom in the sense of autonomy. Nevertheless, these two things (happiness and freedom), with which one is concerned when one wants to live in earnest, stand, to be sure, in a kind of tension with one another. This tension, however, need not turn into a duel. It is not necessarily the case that eudaimonistic happiness is achievable only by ignoring freedom or that freedom as autonomy is achievable only by subordinating happiness. It is possible that a categorical moment is to be found even in eudaimonia and that a good life is to be found in the autonomous moment. In such a case, without one collapsing into the other, the two moral theories (aspirational ethics in the sense of eudaimonistic happiness and the ethic of willing in the sense of autonomous freedom) would complement one another as a twofold task of humanity: that of the art of living and of morality.

Part 2
The Principle
of Happiness:
Eudaimonia

All human beings have a longing for happiness. Nevertheless, many fail to achieve it, and those who are successful are confronted with the criticism that their longing, when elevated to a principle, contradicts morality. Even a superficial examination of the principle of happiness reveals three peculiarities. The first makes the commencement of ethics easier. Whereas prosaic common sense says that "all humans want to be happy," an enthusiastic author once wrote: "The first of all our wishes that speaks loudly and clearly from every artery and nerve is the wish to be happy, and it accompanies us throughout our entire lives." The author, Heinrich von Kleist, was not speaking only of his contemporaries, or of European modernity, or even of Western culture, but of "our essence"—the very nature of humanity. The nature of humanity gives us a goal that unifies all cultures and epochs. Nonetheless, the claim of intercultural validity forces the question: with what right does one claim that happiness is the natural goal of humanity?

According to a second difficulty, there are such massive hurdles on the way to the attainment of happiness that ethics must solve more than its usual tasks. The mere conceptual clarification of the desire for happiness and its justification are not sufficient. One must also clarify the hurdles and the means for overcoming them. In this respect, ethics is pursued as the art of living; admittedly, philosophically. A third difficulty says that even the one who has mastered the art of living cannot be certain with respect to the primary concern of ethics, morality. The pursuit of happiness and morality appear to contradict one another.

Taken together, these three challenges delineate the topics of a philosophy of happiness. First, we must clarify the concept with respect to the first problem: what does one mean by happiness to the extent that it is a goal sought by all? The kind of happiness in question here is one that is accomplished by action. As a consequence, it is not a matter of serendipity, even when one likes what has occurred by mere chance. Rather, happiness involves a practical and a feasible happiness. This concept, then, raises a set of difficulties that quickly intensify into aporias.

The first difficulty: how is it that people in different cultures and epochs can pursue the same goal; why do they all long for happiness? According to part 1 of this present study, the answer depends not only on a general moral anthropology but also on a not entirely so general concept of action (i.e., on goal-oriented action or aspiration). This concept names a presupposition that rejects a moral critique of what turns out to be only an apparent general longing for happiness. It also raises the second difficulty that the content of happiness involves such dramatic differences—astonishingly less between cultures than among members of a specific culture—that the universality proves to be only apparent. Happiness could even scoff at any attempt to establish its content. This aporia can be resolved by means of a formal, hence interculturally convincing, concept of happiness (chapter 6). In the process, a third difficulty emerges: how can a merely formal concept of happiness make an art of living possible (chapter 7)? Broad and expansive life goals such as enjoyment, wealth, and power could point to a single path (chapter 8).

A still larger difficulty follows from the view that, because the pursuit of happiness is concerned with self-interest, it has little if anything whatsoever to do with morality. According to the acerbic formulation of one great philosopher, Kant: "If *eudaimonia* (the principle of happiness) . . . is set up as the basic principle, the result is the *euthanasia* (easy death) of all morals." Confronted with what is possibly a devastating critique, we examine more closely our threatened ethics. Kant suggests that the concept of virtue constitutes an essential linchpin (chapter 9) and that the heart of virtue consists of such morally friendly attitudes as self-control, equanimity, and benevolence (chapter 10).

In addition to this moral virtue, eudaimonistic ethics appeal to an intellectual virtue. Because of a further difficulty, this virtue has less to do with the empirical-rational character of utilitarianism's happiness calculation. Rather, one needs above all a moral-practical power of judgment, wisdom (chapter 11). Because not only moral but also intellectual virtues are so important, one confronts a counterquestion that constitutes our sixth difficulty: can the eudaimonia ethic deliver on its promise; does it bring happiness (chapter 12)? Finally, one can draw a conclusion in two forms: What potential does a eudaimonistic ethic of aspiration hold for morality (chapter 13)? Where are the boundaries that are imposed by the transition to an ethic of the will with its principle of freedom as autonomy (chapter 14)?

6 The Happiness of Aspiration

6.1 Aspiration: Production and Action

"Aspiration" is hardly recognized as a fundamental concept in philosophy; the student is reminded only of the contemptible eager beaver. However, the notion serves as a fundamental concept for characterizing human action if one means by it a motivation from one's inner self oriented toward a goal. Because one silently pursues a desired goal that one has classified (provisionally) as good for its own sake, the question arises: what is the goal good for? The ensuing inquiry finds its answer only in the thought of a highest, positively valued goal. Precisely for this reason, aspiration becomes a fundamental concept in ethics: as the anticipation of a highest good that we sketched at the end of part 1, which one can call happiness or felicitousness.

There are three identifiable moments to aspiration: activity, finality, and spontaneity. The first moment includes more than merely a potential energy or capacity; one must consciously undertake an activity. One is concerned with more than a mere preference. Rather, one wants to accomplish a task. Aspiration doesn't require that one actually achieve that for which one strives. The chosen goal can be erroneous, or the level of effort devoted to its accomplishment can be too weak. However, it is only someone who strives after something and undertakes (presumably) the path toward the fulfillment of the aspiration or, in the negative case, seeks to avoid the task (i.e., doesn't undertake the activity) who actually aspires.

The behavioral patterns of animals—the species-specific differences in drinking, courtship, brooding, and care for the young, even vegetative processes such as anabolic metabolism and self-reproduction—can be classified as a kind of aspiration because these involve activities that serve a strategic goal, the maintenance of the individual and/or a species, and because they are established by means of internal strengths, unlike processes of physical deterioration which are external. Nonetheless, what one takes to be human aspiration is distinguished from this broader concept by means of a fourth moment: that the one involved approaches a goal. In other words, aspiration in this sense requires an individual intention: one must know and give one's assent to what one does (or does not do). In the typically human sense of aspiration, then, spontaneous finality is escalated to a self-chosen practical process. Something subjective, a reference to an acting subject, occurs instead of a purely objective process that is, on the one hand, externally goal-oriented and, on the other hand, a sequence with no internal distancing.

In any specific instance, practical reflection can be very rudimentary. However, it is not so much empirically impossible as it is semantically and logically impossible to maintain that the aspiration, for example, to be healthy or to be successful in a career can somehow occur without one having either a sense of what these goals mean or knowing how one is to go about accomplishing them. The subjective connection is not something additional or accidental. Rather, a subjective moment is essential: the conscious establishment of a goal whose selection or avoidance requires a specific activity for its accomplishment. At the latest when one is asked, "Why?" one employs relevant reflection. Human activity transpires in the world of propositional language, which is in this case not a theoretical but a practice-oriented language. Whereas in the case of animals it is sufficient that they see something, in the case of human beings a propositional "something as something" must be involved in addition: first, the activity values something *as* desirable; second, this something is taken *as* goal-orienting; and third, both must be affirmed. Of course, in the case of a weakness of will or lack of restraint, one chooses the worst although one knows better. The notion of aspiration is not concerned with an abstract reflection but with a self-reference in light of a drive, a conscious and deliberate activity.

It is obvious that these four moments to aspiration are not concerned with four distinct time periods of an event but, rather, they are moments of a unified concept. Regardless of how the activity turns out, when it occurs under the concept of aspiration, it involves a spontaneous and goal-oriented activity. "Aspiration" belongs to the sphere of those concepts that serve to identify the latent or manifest self-understanding of humanity as a species because with this concept of aspiration one attributes to the activity an individual as the responsible origin of the action.

However, this sense of responsibility is not something distinct but is one moment in the transpiring of an activity.

One likes to view modern philosophy as having begun with the question of self-consciousness. However, as soon as one observes that a standard-bearer with respect to self-consciousness is the ancient philosopher Aristotle, one must correct this (self-) understanding of modernity. Furthermore, it is clear that a comprehensive theory does not thematize self-consciousness (either not at all or not alone) separately by itself. At the same time, it becomes apparent that this "rational" characterization of humanity avoids both extremes of "pure exception" and "complete identification": humanity is placed in the continuum with nature at the moment of action; spontaneous goal-orientation emerges as an immanent hierarchy in nature; and reflexivity with respect to goal- and means-orientation indicates a unique position, if not the pinnacle, for humanity in this hierarchy.

It is important to see that, with respect to aspiration as a fundamental ethical concept, action in relationship to a goal can involve two different kinds of behavior (see Aristotle, *Nicomachean Ethics* 1.1.1094a3ff.; *Metaphysics* 9.5.1048b23–27): production and praxis. In the case of linear aspiration, one has *production:* the making or generating of something in specific but by no means all circumstances: a work is concerned with a goal that is the object of aspiration, the product of aspiration's activity that ultimately results in an independent object, a work, product, or result. Whether the action is by a craftsperson or is industrial, or artistic, or even social and intellectual—production in the Greek sense of *poiesis* occurs wherever what matters is not the success or value of an accomplishment but merely that something is accomplished.

Production points beyond itself in a structural sense because one undertakes it not for oneself but for the sake of something other, namely, the result. Completion is indispensable, but only as a means for the eventual product. Production is a linear activity in which one loses oneself. It is an instrumental action in the widest sense of instrumental in that it produces works and in that the created work contains the meaning and value of the action. The clear indicator: success is measured not by the quality of the production process but by the quality of what is produced. In the case of the construction of a house, what is important in the end is not the process of construction but the usefulness and livability of the finished house, not to mention its affordability. In the case of a chair, the questions are: is it properly designed anatomically, is it comfortable, as well as durable; additionally: does it fit into the décor of the room and, again, can one afford it? In the case of a scholarly publication: does it reflect the latest development in a discussion, does it bring the discussion further, and is it readable?

The situation is different when it comes to immanent aspiration, action in the narrower sense of praxis. Whether seeing, thinking, or walking; whether engaged in a conversation or a musical performance; whether sober-minded and proper action or honest research—in all of these cases, aspiration accomplishes its goal in the process itself. For example, someone who sees, has seen; someone who talks, has talked; someone who thinks, has already thought. Success in these cases is decided in terms of the quality of what is accomplished. Does one converse amusingly or boringly; does one perform a piece of music rhythmically, melodiously, and with energy; has one done one's research without plagiarism and without fudging the empirical data?

In all such cases, the standard does not lie in some product distinct from the activity itself but in an internal discernment of the success of the activity, in the accomplishment of an internal perfection. The standard consists in seeing *well*, performing a piece of music *beautifully*, acting *justly*. Praxis is not judged in terms of whether or not something in addition has been accomplished or not, has succeeded or not, or is meaningful or not. Rather, praxis is judged exclusively in and for itself. This condition influences the kind of existence associated with what makes praxis good. It advances an "ontological" meaning. The object of ethics, what is morally good, is not something substantial at hand; it doesn't exist for itself. Rather, it exists exclusively as good praxis. Whether just, sober-minded, or honest; whether courageous, calm, or helpful: all such "objects" exist solely in the activity of (just, sober-minded, . . .) doing or avoiding something.

6.2 A Second-Order Goal

A desired goal is generally not an end in itself. Whoever seeks out a (geographical) location wants to work there, to purchase furniture, to meet someone, or attend a concert, in short, to accomplish something. Even what is to be accomplished isn't an end in itself but more likely a means to something else. In the case of a job, one seeks to cover one's living expenses and to pursue career goals; the goal of purchasing furniture is to furnish one's apartment; and so on. Even these additional goals allow one to still ask, "What for?" which in principle can continue as long as each goal exists more or less for itself. As long as the activity has the structure of production, there is no ultimate highest goal. On the contrary, an endless progression opens up so that structurally considered human action appears meaningless. Formally considered, one strives for an always higher goal without any final answer to the question "For what purpose?"

In everyday life, we provide a pragmatic answer to this open question: one stops the questioning when the goal speaks for itself. Furnishing an apartment is a goal that for most is so obvious that one doesn't ever question it: one needs a bed in order to sleep, a kitchen for cooking, and a desk for writing, a set of bookshelves, an easel, or a grand piano.

There are occasions, however, when the pragmatic answer is not adequate. The question of a structurally higher goal, a final goal, is unavoidable when one finds oneself in a life crisis or contemplates what should be one's profession. One seeks to bring the never-ending aspiration to a halt, to stop the progression of goals. For example, one can attend a piano concert as a music critic, in order to write a review for the newspaper, or as a pianist, to draw inspiration for one's own performances. The concert serves an external goal in both cases. In another sense, the concert has—not necessarily exclusively, but also—an instrumental character. One can attend a concert out of pure pleasure in the experience of a musical performance. In this case, perhaps one encounters a possible final goal: pleasure, by which more is meant here than sensuous enjoyment or a feast for the ears. Whether it appeals only to the senses or to the mind—as a feeling that accompanies and affirms an unhindered free activity, pleasure is no longer the mere yield of a production process, but is in a certain sense (though *only* in a certain sense) sufficient in itself (see chapter 8.1).

The highest point of the hierarchy of "What-for?" questioning, however, has not been reached, even here. There are further final goals (for example, knowledge in itself or self-development) and, therefore, a host of conditions that demand an answer to the question: why does one want ("motive") or should one ("ground") seek pleasure rather than knowledge in itself, self-development, or some other final goal?

If we are to bring our questioning process to a satisfactory conclusion, there must be an absolutely highest goal beyond which there can be no higher goal. To the extent that such a highest goal itself allows for the "What-for?" questioning of all other goals, it is an extraordinary final goal, a final goal of a second order. This veritable conclusion to the hierarchy of goals, this conclusion arrived at methodically by means of a constructive semantic with its absolutely final "for this reason," carries the name "happiness" or "felicitousness." When one, nonetheless, asks further ("Why does one strive for happiness?"), one surreptitiously transforms the notion of happiness under discussion. For when purely conceptually considered, there can be no higher goal over against an absolutely highest, purely superlative goal. Though certainly one can still ask which concept of happiness satisfies such an absolutely highest goal.

Just as the aspiration associated with action is found for all intents and purposes in all cultures and in every epoch, so, too, there is also an interculturally shared answer to the "What-for?" question. At least one finds the name for the answer in a shared sense in many languages, and this speaks for an intercultural commonality. One is allowed, as a common denominator for humanity, to give the longing for happiness even an anthropological status. In the sense of a final "What for?" happiness is called in Greek *eudaimonia*, in Latin *beatitudo* or *felicitas*, in English *happiness* and in French *bonheur*, Russian *stscháse*, Arabic *al sa'ada*, Chinese *xìngfú*, and in Japanese *kōfuku*.

When life reaches this goal, one calls it "fulfilled" or "meaningful." The Greeks speak of *eu zen*, the Romans of *bene vivere* and mean not just any kind of happiness—especially not the happiness that merely occurs, the happy chance or capricious fortune; and also not simply the subjective sensation of feeling comfortable. Neither a fortunate fate nor a comfortable satisfaction are indeed excluded; they can play a "supporting role." What is critical, however, is something else: one must personally take one's life in hand and do well with it. The expression "life" is understood here primarily not as a concern of biology but from the perspective of a model of aspiration. Life here is meant not as a vegetative process that occurs (to a great degree) entirely independent of the agent or like the course of history that occurs (to a great degree) behind one's back. "Life" here means what one accomplishes oneself, consciously and freely, in light of one's own responsibility.

The principle of a teleological ethic of aspiration, therefore, does not cover everything that resonates with the term "happiness" or with its equivalents in other languages. Happiness here means that which gives meaning to one's personally responsible life and success to existence as a whole. The fact that at the same time things go well or that one fares well is an addendum. Just as an individual in the case of the theoretical is distinguished by a desire for knowledge, by curiosity, so in the case of the practical he is distinguished by a desire for a goal that he aspires to at all times and from which he never wavers. This practical sense consists in that self-responsible happiness that is to be distinguished conceptually both from having luck (the luck of fate or in winning the lottery) and from a mere subjective satisfaction.

6.3 Happiness as Longing or as Aspiration?

Difficulties with the concept of happiness commence with the speechlessness expressed by Wittgenstein, who claims of "men to whom after long doubting the sense of life becomes clear" that they "could not then say wherein this sense consisted" (*Tractatus*, 6.521). Philosophy's task of overcoming speechlessness commences with the observation that one finds in all places and at all times an aspiration for happiness, and that aspiration accompanies the individual his entire life. However, philosophy is not satisfied with mere observation, and, therefore, it seeks for explanations and suspects that the desire for happiness is universal and a general condition of humanity.

Humanity's driving forces are, of course, highly differentiated in their structure. One finds appetites, desires, and passions, and also interests, wishes, and longings. What these all have in common is that they all urge toward their satisfaction or fulfillment. To the extent that the individual is responsible for them, the epitome of satisfaction and fulfillment is called happiness, as we have suggested.

A second difficulty: a more precise determination, of course, turns out to be so varied that one must beware of a mere similarity of names. Some seek happiness in prosperity or power; others in friendship or love; others in scientific and philosophical research, art, or meditation. (The understanding of happiness in different cultures and epochs can be found in Bellebaum 1994 and in the *Lesebuch* [Höffe 2007b]; on the philosophy of happiness, see Pieper 2003.) This variety in the understanding of happiness has legitimate grounds. In one respect, all of them are dependent upon life circumstances: someone who is lonely wishes to have friends; one in poverty wishes prosperity; should one be sick, one desires health. And a castaway floating on the open seas without food and water receives again, as a bright day dawns, "the strength to wait" and is for the first time in the twenty years of his life "completely happy" (Gabriel García Márquez, *The Story of a Shipwrecked Sailor*, chapter 4).

For others, happiness is a question of personality. What brings happiness to a mathematician but in a different fashion to a philosopher and even otherwise to a chess player, the pleasure of solving a tricky problem, is of no consequence for the gourmet, the dancer, the soccer player, or the physically or socially talented person. In short: as long as individuals are different with respect to needs, interests, and experience as well as in terms of hopes and desires, the concrete fulfillment of their aspiration, real happiness, can by no means be the same for all and at all times.

Certain perspectives, however, do evoke agreement across cultures. These with few exceptions are found in Aristotle's list of common Greek convictions. The list is not by accident in the *Rhetoric* (1.5.1360b19–24) rather than in the *Nicomachean Ethics* because it includes elements that are irrelevant to the aspiration principle of happiness: "good birth, plenty of friends, good friends, wealth, good children, plenty of children, a happy old age, also such bodily excellences as health, beauty, strength, large stature, athletic prowess, together with fame, honor, good luck, and virtue including its components of wisdom, courage, justice, and self-control."

Above all, there remains the formal commonality of an uttermost and final element: happiness means that which is unsurpassably worthwhile. The mere segments of a biography are in this respect inadequate. When one means happiness in the sense of perfection, one refers to a complete life. Of course, life has the character of praxis—the one who lives has simultaneously already lived—so that the highest goal cannot be placed outside but only within the completion of a life itself. Happiness is not concerned with specific accomplishments in the course of one's life that stand independently for themselves and are more valuable than one's life itself could be. Rather, happiness is concerned far more with one's quality of success, and even more accurately: the quality of excellence that in the end constitutes the successful, happy life.

Differences in the understanding of happiness do not begin first with differences in content but occur already with the formal concept of happiness. What is common to all of these differences, however, is that they are concerned with something uttermost and final. More precisely, they depend upon the relationship that one has to what is uttermost. One can set one's mere hope, exaggerated to a desire, on the coming to pass of that for which one wishes but do nothing actively to bring about its realization. The alternative consists, however, in active engagement (i.e., in aspiration).

According to Judaism, Christianity, and Islam, humanity's beginnings were in an absolutely sensuous and pleasure-filled location: in paradise. Plato speaks of an "island of the blessed" which one, admittedly, reaches only after death. Nevertheless, he describes for life in this world an experience that approximates the "island of the blessed" in the afterlife. The genesis of his multistaged polis begins with the (arguably, consciously utopian) stage of a "healthy polis." Here the citizens, free from envy, jealousy, and other "asocial passions," live in freedom and harmony with one another; they lead their lives in the best of health and die only at an old age; they enjoy the joys of love; thanks to an adequate productivity, they can nourish themselves with bread and wine; and they wear garlands and praise the gods (*Republic* 372a-c).

Although such a happiness is hardly achievable, humanity craves it with a certain necessity. For wishes are not concerned only with that which is close at hand and easily achieved, but also with what is extremely remote and extremely difficult to achieve. Why do human beings wish for what is unachievable? A prerequisite: because their power of imagination knows no bounds. The main reason: because they experience an everyday world of hardship and suffer privations. Therefore, they wish for a condition in which not only the present affliction but also all future afflictions, including all possible troubles and plagues, all difficulties and suffering, are eliminated. This is why many fairy tales end with the statement: "Since all their problems were solved, they lived happily ever after."

Everyday life knows this wish for happiness, this fairy-tale or Sunday happiness, at least in passing moments. For example, two total strangers accidentally meet, they smile to one another, are aware for a moment that they share the same world and that what is shared is beautiful, then they pass on their various ways. The author Christa Wolf describes the experience of sharedness under the title *Divided Heaven* (1965, 91–92): "Shortly afterwards, the summer holidays began. Together . . . they combed through the countryside around [their] village, bathed in the lake and filled their lungs with clear, pure summer air. . . . They were in love and were full of new expectations." What happens to them? Unfortunately, they enter a time of year which contradicts the "ease of summer"; which brings dread for the loss of the "shared heaven": "their second winter."

One wants to hope for this desired happiness—the ease of the dreamer exceeds the limitations of actual experience with all of its contradictions.

Because fantasy knows no limits, it can focus on a utopia in the literal sense of the term, on an *ou-topos,* a no-where. At least in the world inhabited by *Homo sapiens,* there is no place for a world, first, where there are no limited resources, where there is a society of excess in the strict sense of the word; second, for a world in which there is an abundance of hanging goodies (as in "The Tale of the Land of Milk and Honey") that are constantly present before one's mouth; third, in which all services should be unlimitedly available without, fourth, being accompanied by any effort, burdens, and "sweat of the brow"; in which, fifth, given the absence of conflict and competition, everyone lives in love and friendship with such high respect and self-esteem that one never experiences either envy, jealousy, or shame; sixth, in which one remains free from illness and accidents; and seventh, in which no one dies prematurely, either according to one's own expectations or those of loved ones and friends or others, and in which many wish never to die.

Obviously, this wish list is ambitious and long. Nevertheless, even this list is not exhaustive. For many, the desire for happiness includes the desire that animals be included, at least those closest to one (i.e., household and domestic animals), and even those in the wild with the qualification that they experience no animal anxiety and with a second qualification that they live among one another in peace. Included, as well, can be plants, especially those domesticated plants, but even those encountered in the woods on one's walks. Some people wish for omnipotence: for an unlimited dominance over nature and other persons. Others wish for a wholeness that extends to a unity of what is true, good, and beautiful.

The list can be closed at this point because the decisive point has been established: the notion of well-being that includes a manifold of needs and interests and also reaches the highest imaginable maximum of strength and duration of its fulfillment—this wish for happiness is so pretentious that it is not achievable or is anything that could be temporarily attained with the greatest efforts either by an individual or by humanity as a whole. Even the Kantian concept that is a bit more humble and wants everything to go according to plan ("Doctrine of Virtue" [part 2 of *The Metaphysics of Morals*], "Fragment of a Moral Catechism," 6:480) is an unachievable desire for happiness because it presupposes an omnipotence over natural and social relationships.

The desire for happiness is a quixotic happiness that runs up hard against the reality of the natural, social, and psychological world. For example, the stressed-out city dweller as a rule seeks out the quiet of nature only for a limited time and even then only with the aid of highly developed clothing and instruments, not to mention a well-thought-out first aid kit that includes necessary prescription medicines. A fundamental caveat is imposed by one element of human nature that we know from moral anthropology: humanity has no species-specific limits even when it comes to essential matters of life and death. Humanity is driven by a propensity to excess. Included here is the appetite for finer things and luxury, which indicates in the broadest sense how "according to nature" humanity's desires can never be ultimately fulfilled. This multifaceted insatiableness confirms the individual's conflict with himself, as well as with others and with nature.

The consequences are obvious: whoever experiences this wish for happiness despite the dangers of such conflict will never be immune from ever-new disappointments. He will sink into resignation and think what was already expressed by the Greeks and has been repeated down to Freud: "The intention that humanity be 'happy' is not contained in the plan of 'creation'" (*Civilization and Its Discontents*, 1961, 25). Perhaps, though, this is the reason why many "escape" into addiction: because of an incapacity to follow a more realistic and simultaneously more humane concept than the concept of desire.

The alternative that one could seek a happiness that is not a mere wishing but has its own chance of realization is by no means quixotic. This is expressed in the proverb: "Each forges his own happiness" ["Jeder ist seines Glückes Schmied"]. Even in fairy tales, the hero's happiness is achieved only after great personal effort either in the sense of dangers survived or of deprivations. In any event, aspiring to happiness consists in the wish neither for a happiness that is too small, having good fortune, for which one may hope but can do little to achieve, nor for a happiness that is too great because it is unrealizable, a happiness for which one can only long or a blessedness that is reserved for the gods. What one now means by happiness in the sense of a moral principle is a model of aspiration "only" in the sense of achievable goals on the basis of the highest and most strenuous action and restraint. As long as one stresses achievability, one can appropriately speak of a human in contrast to a supra-human happiness.

This concept of the moral principle of happiness involves two moments. First, the desired happiness with respect to the hierarchy of goals is not an intermediate but a final goal that among other final goals is the highest that one can conceive. Second, such a highest goal cannot be "technical" (in terms of the consequence of an action) but only "practical" in the narrow sense. Happiness consists in successful living; it is realized, therefore, in every moment, perhaps with the addendum: "Only a man who lives not in time but in the present is happy" (Wittgenstein, *Notebooks 1914–1916* (*Tagebücher 1914–1916*), 8.7.1916). Given the first moment of aspiration, one excludes any exaggerated happiness, the prideful happiness of mere wishful thinking, and, given the second moment, one excludes a structurally false happiness, a perversion of happiness which believes that a perfect happiness is something that one can personally create.

A final goal of the second order has a new kind of goal-character. As a final goal by which one strives to accomplish the usual final goals, it is itself not a direct goal. It is the name, rather, for the reason why one strives and the specific and wider horizon of meaning in which one strives toward one's usual final goals. This horizon of meaning is characterized by three absolute superlatives that Aristotle, the standard-bearer for the philosophy of aspiration- and happiness-ethics, already identified (*Nicomachean Ethics* 1.5). As the utmost instantiation as a highest-, therefore as the *via eminentiae*, it is, first, the absolute highest (*akrotaton*); hence, second, it is the "most thoroughly goal-oriented" (*telos teleiotaton*), which at the same time, third, involves a self-sufficiency (*autarkeia*) not to be confused with every form of frugality that needs little.

The advice of self-humility: "Be satisfied in life with little" may be based in life experience (see chapters 8.1 and 10.2). It is often preached— prominently by Gautama Buddha: "Happiness is the solitude of satisfaction that has heard (and grasped). / Happiness is to do no harm in the world; / to exercise (self-)control over against other life forms. / Happiness is to be passionless in the world, / to conquer cravings. / Elimination of 'I' consciousness / is truly the highest happiness" (*Mahavagga* 1.3; reprinted in *Lesebuch* [Höffe 2007b], no. 25). However, the determination of a concept does not depend on life experience but on the formal concept of happiness. This formal concept does not consist in mere humility because it involves a unique self-sufficiency of a superlative nature. It is not to be understood in a restrictive sense: limiting and confining, but, rather, comprehensively: encompassing and inclusive. Aspiration for happiness is sufficient unto itself in the sense that, purely conceptually, there is nothing beyond it that one could yet strive for: a happy life lacks nothing; in this respect it is self-sufficient (*autark*).

Precisely because it "makes" the corresponding life worthy of choice for its own sake, aspiration for happiness is not an everyday superlative comparable to the geographically highest mountain or longest river. These kinds of "highest things" permit an escalation to a "superlative plus": the highest peak *could* be higher than the 8,848 meters above sea level of Tschomolungma (Mount Everest), and the longest river *could* be longer than the 6,671 kilometers of the Nile (including the Kagera River in Tanzania). Furthermore, a single continent could claim both superlatives, the highest peak and the longest river, or still other superlatives such as the coldest and/or the warmest location; the location of the densest flora and fauna. However, there is no "plus" to the peak that is happiness. If such were the case, then one would experience only an illusion of happiness, similar to the experience in mountain climbing when a peak turns out to be only a preliminary peak when the primary peak emerges in the background.

Aspiration for happiness allows for two further kinds of interpretation, although one often assumes that they exclude one another. Because the concept "highest" can mean supreme (Latin: *supremum*) or complete (*consummatum*), happiness could mean something monolithic, as a dominant goal that extends beyond all other goals; or one can take it to be something multifaceted in the sense of an inclusive and integrative goal that includes all other goals. The truth of the matter is that the concept of happiness is suitable for both meanings—with restrictions.

A logically highest-level final goal has a dominant character over against other final goals and reminds one of the ontological concept of God. What this concept says with respect to being (*ens*)—God is that being beyond which nothing greater can be thought: *ens quo maius cogitari nequit*—applies here with respect to the goal: *finis quo maius nihil cogitari potest*. Aspirational happiness is a goal (*telos*) in which the goal-character is escalated to the unsurpassable superlative of a "greatest goal" (*teleiotaton*). This superlative dominance of an absolute highest is not what one means by the usual concept of dominance, in the sense of the peak of a pyramid or the highest peak of a mountain chain. Self-development *could* be dominant over against an appetite within the same level. In the case of happiness, however, several final goals are combined so that the other sense of highest, the inclusive character, can be meant. When it comes to the moment of completion in contrast to supremacy, there are two things that must be added: that of the unhindered activity of an accompanying feeling of appetite/lust and that of the free development and unhindered "savoring" of one's own talents and interests (i.e., self-development).

Happiness has a (quasi-)transcendental character as the final horizon of meaning with respect to all aspiration. The question of whether or not it satisfies Kant's condition of transcendental, as a synthetic a priori, can be set aside. It obviously fulfills the other expectation of a "fundamental condition of possibility for . . ." something to be. As the final goal of the second order, it decides over the adequacy of all other goals: that they in the end are valuable only within the horizon of happiness. Thus, the aspiration for happiness acquires a characteristic that until now one knew only from modern, no longer eudaimonistic moral philosophy. As the condition that makes possible everyday goals without itself being dependent on any other higher condition, aspiration for happiness is unconditional. Hence, the concept of an unsurpassable, unconditioned condition has a legitimate place not first in an ethic of free will (autonomy) but already in a teleological ethic of aspiration (eudaimonia).

6.4 "Only the English Strive for Happiness"

As the modern critique of morality reached one of its summits, it jettisoned the principle of happiness. From Friedrich Nietzsche, who was such a sharp critic of Kant, who was such a sharp critic of eudaimonistic ethics, one might have expected a defense—even a praise—of eudaimonism because its primary defender, Aristotle, develops a this-worldly ethic entirely without religion, metaphysics, and otherworldly values just as Nietzsche demands. In fact, Nietzsche sharpens the criticism. Kant rejects happiness as a moral principle, but he held it to be a necessary goal of humanity. Nietzsche disagrees. In addition, Nietzsche maintains that happiness is in fact never pursued: "Humanity *doesn't* strive for Happiness, only the English do" (*Twilight of the Gods,* "Aphorisms and Arrows," no. 12). However, a closer investigation demonstrates that Nietzsche's claim is inadequate.

With the English, Nietzsche means two things. First, he is describing a kind of person who, with his demand for "comfort and fashion," is "incorrigibly mediocre" in contrast to the sovereign individual. Second, he is criticizing the respective theoreticians who defend such mediocrity, the "English utilitarians" (*Beyond Good and Evil,* no. 228). Admittedly, Nietzsche rejects the principle of happiness not only in its utilitarian form with respect to the general welfare. He dismisses even more the eudaimonistic form in general. His counterargument that the value of things is determined solely according to pleasure and suffering (ibid., no. 225) is appropriate only to one part, the hedonistic part, of eudaimonism or a life of indulgence, which itself rejects a reflective ethic of happiness (see chapter 8.1).

One perspective in the critique of hedonistic eudaimonism might also speak against a reflective happiness ethic: Nietzsche places humanity in the context of nature in his natural history of morality and maintains that beginning with plants, one finds only "propagation, absorption, growth" and "a struggle against resistance." The consequence: "Why do the trees in an old-growth forest fight with one another? For the sake of happiness?—For *power!*" (*Posthumous Fragments* [*Nachgelassene Fragmente*], 1887–89, 52–53). However, Nietzsche says with respect to humanity that this will to power needs something that hedonism and utilitarianism want to eliminate: suffering. To be sure, Nietzsche does not find in suffering an end in itself any more than he understands it in the Christian sense as sacrifice for the other or in the secular sense as suffering from the world. He is concerned not with sovereignty over physical illness or psychological afflictions but with the presupposition of a higher, enhanced humanity.

As long as one brackets the overtones of elitism, one can agree with Nietzsche's aphorism: "The gods placed sweat before the prize." As Nietzsche maintains, humanity possesses in comparison to its earlier forebears "a monstrous quantity of power," but no increase in "happiness" (ibid.). Furthermore, in order to achieve this power, humanity must undergo a strenuous educational process. The harshness of this process can hardly be understood as an increase of hedonistic happiness. Even more, the sovereign individual, for example the artist, seeks above all to increase his possibilities, not the balance sheet of pleasure. For this very reason, it is necessary—as is confirmed by psychology—to limit one's appetites.

Nietzsche's opinion is plausible that the individual must become "master over the powers of nature" and, thereby, "master over his own savageness and intemperateness" (ibid.)—indeed, he must become master more over inner than over outer nature. Nonetheless, for three reasons it represents no objection to the eudaimonistic principle of happiness. First, eudaimonistic ethics is not concerned with the natural history of morality. The biography of a concrete individual-focused ethic is—at least initially—unaffected by whether or not natural history is a struggle between an increase in life and power rather than happiness. Second, Nietzsche's preferred doctrine of a higher humanity has the rank of a concrete final goal, which is subject to the formal question: why should one pursue this higher humanity? The formal answer is: because a life is complete only when it appears to be successful. Whether as the enhancement of life or otherwise understood, a complete life necessarily includes, third, various exertions. The enhancement of life as the reason why one embraces such efforts can offer its own kind of pleasure. Nietzsche himself says: "Happiness . . . gives breathing room, light, and free movement" (*Daybreak*, no. 136). At the same time, it doesn't matter if one doesn't directly strive for this enjoyment. It is manifest more as a "corollary and a secondary appearance" (*Beyond Good and Evil*, no. 225).

In this respect, one can accept Nietzsche's critique of hedonism with the qualification that one changes the emphasis: "humanity does not *strive* for (hedonistic) happiness." However, when man achieves that for which he does strive, the accompanying aspect, hedonistic happiness, is, indeed, not certain but highly likely.

7 The Art of Living

7.1 *Savoir Vivre*

For a long time philosophy was understood to be an art of living, even the art of living happily. One didn't, of course, understand art as the cult of genius as it was understood in that modern sense of the later Enlightenment and the early Romantic period. Certainly, though, one meant what in Latin is called *ars* and in Greek *technê:* a kind of expert knowledge that was oriented to concrete everyday living, shaped by the facts, and in general graspable, teachable, and learnable. The art of living in the sense of *ars bene vivere* or *technê peri tou biou* does not seek knowledge in the sense of some state of affairs; it seeks no "knowledge of a that." Rather, its goal is a knowing, a familiar kind of "know-how" that begins with cooking, gardening, or oratory skills and extends from the art of playing the piano or chess to medical or judicial arts, that is, to the skill of healing the sick or judging disputes impartially.

The first three elements (orientation toward the concrete, rule-orientation, and teachability/learnability) apply only to a limited extent to the art of living. Whereas the usual crafts are limited to a subject area, the art of living is concerned precisely with the opposite: it is concerned with a nonsubject, namely, life as a whole. Only charlatans vaunt specific rules and recipes for a happy life. The philosopher is satisfied with rules of a second order, with certain precepts that correspond to an extraordinary know-how, namely, approaches to life that, because of their positive value, are called virtues.

This extraordinary know-how requires an equally extraordinary art of teaching and learning. From the art of cooking and piano playing to the medical and judicial arts, there are specific courses, even schools and postsecondary schools; whereas there is neither a school nor a postsecondary school for the art of living. Someone who possesses the true

art of living, not that flattened-out *savoir vivre* which is incapable of
enjoyment, this person deserves to be called a maestro, a master, in the
conduct of life. One doesn't expect, however, that he is capable of guaranteeing a happy life for himself, much less for others. One believes
even less that one can learn the art of living from books, which are
flourishing at the moment, like one can learn cooking from cookbooks
and chess playing from chess books.

In yet another respect, however, the art of living is distinguished from
other skills: knowledge in a certain discipline can go out of date (for
example, this is obvious in the art of healing). In the case of the art of
living, though, the recommendations of the ancients are still remarkably
contemporary, and with a proper interpretation they are almost as fresh
and convincing as they were hundreds of years ago. A feature of the
modern sciences, that they are always making new discoveries and producing new inventions, is foreign to the art of living. One of the reasons
for this is: the challenges of life and the adequate answers with respect
to happiness are in their core independent of cultures and epochs, given
their connectedness to the *conditio humana.*

In light of these substantial differences with respect to other disciplines, talk of an "art of living" could be misleading and the expression "wisdom of living" could be preferable. On the one hand, the new
expression accommodates linguistic usage in literature and above all in
other cultures. "Wisdom of living," often simply called wisdom, is considered in many places to be a capacity and deportment to live not within
life's partitionable subjects and disciplines, nor by restricting oneself to
what is at hand and before one's eyes, but rather to manage life "knowledgeably" as a whole; that is, wisely and judiciously. (On wisdom as
the object of psychological research, see Staudinger, Smith, and Baltes
1994.) On the other hand, the expression "wisdom of living" carries an
undertone of special knowledge that suggests an unusual capacity or
an extraordinary knowledge source ("esoteric") which contradicts the
actual medium of philosophy (i.e., general human reason). For this reason, we will retain the matter-of-fact and "democratic" expression "art
of living."

If one does not understand philosophy too narrowly as being limited
as much as possible to scholarly statements, the philosophy of the art
of living viewed ideally appears in three basic forms: the first provides
what is usually a loose collection of maxims and reflections. In a liter-
arily brilliant fashion, the European moralists, authors from the Seven

Sages of Greece to the stoa to La Rochefoucauld, Lichtenberg, Goethe, and Nietzsche, present reflections on the good life that include skeptical objections or, as in the case of Adorno, "reflections out of a damaged life." In almost every case, the style is essential: each of the great moralists cultivates his own form of presentation (certainly, one closely connected to the content in question). Montaigne's *Essays,* for example, love brisk provocation. Their decided "individualism of the moment" takes seriously the immediate present of the "I": every I is different, and the I of this moment is identical neither with the I just before nor with the I that comes right after it. In Nietzsche's case, one is struck by the acidic sarcasm and a school of suspicion that maintains itself in limbo between pathos and irony. The non-European counterpart can be found in the (life) wisdom of other cultures from ancient Egypt to the wisdom literature of Israel inspired by ancient Egypt to Hindu, Buddhist, Confucian, and Taoist texts.

A second form of the philosophy of the art of living consists of visions of the good life, above all of living well together. One finds in the representations of such ideal social orders, so-called utopias, not only religious but also nonreligious conceptions of paradise. On the philosophical side, one finds the already-mentioned healthy polis of Plato's *Republic.* The exemplary modern version is the very name-giving example of Thomas More's *On the Best State of a Republic and on the New Island of Utopia.* Authors of utopias encourage flights of fantasy as they attempt primarily to engage the wish for happiness.

Finally, there is the art of living that is oriented by principles and is also called practical philosophy. This present project is primarily devoted to it. The expression "practical" philosophy stands in contrast to "theoretical" philosophy and sounds, just like the latter, unusual and provocative. Since philosophy is already a form of theory, the addition of "theoretical" strikes one as unnecessary, whereas "practical" sounds contradictory. "Practical" means that which serves for coping with those concrete problems in life to which theoretical philosophy turns its back.

Theory, from which the notion of a practical philosophy is to be distinguished, is only knowledge for its own sake. Practical philosophy distinguishes itself from this "theoretical theory" not merely in a trivial way with respect to its object, human action. In contrast to knowledge for its own sake, practical philosophy also seeks its meaning and purpose in action—more precisely, in understanding that is concerned with concrete human beings. It seeks existential meaning. Nevertheless, practical philosophy remains true to its profession, philosophy, and serves praxis solely in a philosophical fashion, that is, in combination with concepts, arguments, and reflection. In contrast to an erroneous self-understanding and to unrealistic expectations, practical philosophy provides no recipes. Rather, it seeks understanding, and as fundamental ethics it seeks understanding of a basic kind. (On the difference between practical philosophy and an aphoristic art of living, see Höffe 2007a; for ancient philosophy, see Annas 1993 and Horn 1998; on selected theories of happiness, see Claussen 2005; for a foundation to "happiness and goodwill," see Spaemann 1993; see also Seel 1999.)

Already in the ancient world with Plato and Aristotle, the principle-oriented art of living reached a high point that has not been surpassed. Philosophy remained concerned with the principle of happiness through the Middle Ages and well into modernity in the work of Spinoza and Leibniz. Afterward, however, it disappears from the scene. There are at least four reasons for this.

First, it is maintained with respect to eudaimonia that it offers an insufficient, even an unserviceable foundation for morals. It was replaced by autonomy, the self-determination of the will. This development, which constitutes a veritable revolution, condemned the ethic of happiness to philosophical exile. It declared eudaimonia to be an antiquated *via antiqua* and accepted only the *via moderna,* the ethic of autonomy. Nonetheless, this revolution in moral philosophy did not make the question of the successful life irrelevant; it only lost its significance. It is no longer the question concerning happiness and human development that is at the center. In short: what humanity *can* do is replaced by what humanity *should* do. A philosophy of life *duties* replaced a philosophy of the *art* of living. Eudaimonia, which is an ethics of doing, was replaced by a deontology, an ethic of should. Admittedly, these all reach into the dimension of the art of living, as will be pointed out in part 3.

The notion of autonomy, however, can only disempower, not destroy, an ethics of eudaimonia. The Newton of the moral-philosophical and ethical-critical revolution, Immanuel Kant, affirmed that human beings as sensuous, rational beings necessarily long for happiness (felicitousness) (see, for example, *Critique of Practical Reason,* section 3, note 2). A scientific theoretical thesis speaks out in opposition to a philosophical theory of this kind for a *second* reason: philosophers should seek out objectively valid expressions, which do not exist for human happiness since this concept is too imprecise.

Third, so far as there is in fact objective knowledge of happiness, philosophy is confronted with a strong competitor. Whether in its own books, journals, or newspaper articles, whether from psychologists, sociologists, or theologians, or from journalists or compiled from women and men with life experience—guidebooks on questions of the art of living fill entire libraries. Weekly new titles are offered, and not only in grocery store checkout lanes for impulsive readers but also at "serious" locations. Philosophy can't and doesn't want to compete with them; it need not enviously turn up its nose because the circulation for such texts is so high.

There is no question that the scientific basis of such counsel, the empirical research on happiness, brings interesting insights (on the psychological research, see Diener and Suh 2000; from the side of economics with respect to the social and mental sciences, see Layard 2005). However, given the degree to which this research is indebted to philosophy, the latter has no reason to fear unemployment. This is because when it comes to the ethical concept of aspiring toward happiness (the properly philosophical question), the primary concern of empirical research into happiness, subjective well-being, plays only a secondary role. For the same reason, when it comes to the empirical research on happiness, a word of caution is justified: neither the conversion of the principle of happiness into an empirical concept nor the corresponding interpretations of the empirical evidence are uncontroversial. Precisely with respect to subjective satisfaction, one often depends too much on the self-assessment of the test subject. For example, for the popular case of country comparison, there are social indicators that to be sure provide no objective measure for happiness, but rather relativize merely personal self-assessments. To such observations belong the suicide rate, the number of drug, alcohol, and other addictions, and also the divorce rate, since both couples and their children are affected.

Surprisingly, research into happiness has stumbled onto a high degree of equal opportunity. Factors that in a (narrow) living context result in great differences (e.g., age, gender, appearance, intelligence, and education) are, fortunately, not decisive. Even one's standard of living proves to be not as significant as is often assumed when it comes to the question of happiness.

Fourth, at least philosophers in the West came to ignore the art of living and happiness because nineteenth-century Europe became ever more shaped by nihilism. In this respect, one does not think of the moral-philosophical and ethical-critical thesis that general obligations in life have no solid basis. Rather, what is meant is the historical experience in which those fundamental values that had endured so long came to lose their ability to shape life. When traditional norms and values are undermined because their sustaining principle (e.g., belief in God) has become questionable, the feeling of emptiness and meaninglessness becomes prevalent. Nihilism is not the consequence of rhetoric but of the pressures of existential experience.

A quick overview of the history of European nihilism discovers four phases. The first, *skeptical* phase emerges with Schopenhauer's question that Nietzsche also pursued: "Does life itself have any real meaning?" (*The Gay Science*, no. 357). The skeptic doubts that there is anything about life that is worthwhile, not to speak of absolutely worthwhile. The second, *constructive,* "terrible twos" phase of nihilism in which one encounters meaning in meaninglessness takes the fate of the Corinthian king, Sisyphus, as its paradigm: the punishment by the gods for Sisyphus's deception was his having to roll a huge rock up a steep hill. When he had almost reached the top, the rock always slipped and rolled back down to the bottom of the hill. Albert Camus' account made Sisyphus the master of the situation at that point where Sisyphus accepted this apparently absurd fate. The wisdom (a piece of the art of living) in this story can overcome much dejection: "The struggle itself towards the heights [of the mountain]"—the human struggle with illness, suffering, and death has this character—"is enough to fill a man's heart. We must imagine Sisyphus happy" (*The Myth of Sisyphus*, 1975, 123). The third phase of nihilism can be identified as Marquard (1986, 38) has as the phase of *lamentation*. One bewails the loss of meaning and in the face of it adds, as the fourth *longing* or *nostalgic* phase, the wish for a return to the pre-skeptical, no longer unsettled time before nihilism.

Someone who desires a return, but by no means a naive return, to the philosophical art of living is entirely familiar with this history of nihilism but sees nothing in it that is insurmountable. Rather, it presents a history of difficulties in search of solutions. Cognizant of the charge of meaninglessness, one seeks to overcome the speechlessness with respect to the question of meaning and happiness not merely, as suggested, purely semantically. Without rejecting autonomy as a new foundation for morals, one extends the ethic of *should* to include an ethic of eudaimonistic *can*. Here one is not dependent upon the certainty of the experts, those found in the empirical sciences; nor is one dependent upon the other form of certainty, that of the prophet who in the name of his God powerfully calls one to repentance and penance; nor, finally, is one dependent upon the powerful images of the poet. Confronted with the perennial danger for the philosopher to fail to live up to high expectations, he remains in the sober medium of concept and argument. In face of the profound differences among persons and cultures, he proceeds with care and circumspection with the claims of universal and objective eudaimonistic assertions. By no means does he fall into the resignation of "merely subjective" assertions.

7.2 Blueprint Knowledge

Following the example of the ancient archer who could better hit his target when it stood clearly before him, the principle-oriented art of living establishes as its veritable target the principle of happiness. However, as a final goal of the second order, the comparison with our ancient archer is limited, and it is precisely with respect to the limitations in the comparison that the analogy is different here from what it is with the other kinds of arts of living. Practical philosophy presents "only" a blueprint knowledge that consciously leaves open the differences among personal quests for happiness. This openness is welcome to the independent actor, but for the nonindependent agent it appears to be too little (on the concept of blueprint knowledge, see Höffe 1996, section 2, summarized in Höffe 2006d, chapter 2.2).

A principle-oriented art of living argues entirely multifacetedly and from life experience. It begins with the concept of happiness, develops out of it certain criteria, and determines by means of these criteria forms of living in which happiness can be expected in contrast to other forms that structurally block happiness. It works out the building blocks for the creation of lifestyles that successfully result in happiness, explains how these building blocks can be acquired, and identifies the fundamental obstacles that stand in the way of success. Taken as a totality, then, one can label it philosophical knowledge proper and if need be, also, philosophical knowledge saturated with experience. However, what this philosophical knowledge doesn't do is provide recipes that determine in advance how one alone or in cooperation with others at some specific point here and now should act in order to achieve happiness. The explanation for this is eudaimonistic: individual actions remain in their content entirely open with respect to the responsibility for the actions, the skills required for their accomplishment, the circumstances of their occurrence, and their cultural context, even though practical philosophy can provide insight into the structural grid and to a certain degree into the necessary eudaimonistic skeleton on which happiness depends.

Therefore, a principle-oriented art of living that comes onto the stage under the proud claim that it is a practical philosophy exercises unpretentious self-criticism. In the knowledge that concrete action (as well as refraining from action) must be left up to the agent, it recognizes that its judgment is no less, but also no more, than a structural framework in the sense of a floor plan. What is decisive, the actual performance, remains ceded to a nonphilosophical moment, the agent himself.

As an aside, practical philosophy suggests an explanation for how human life can be so varied and at the same time share a common quality: in this case, that of success with respect to happiness—without ethical relativism, on the one hand, or a dogmatism based on rigid rules, on the other. The structural grid identifies precisely this commonality that contradicts relativism. It also recognizes how necessary it is that the grid must be augmented by the mediation of individual uniqueness, to an extent with "flesh and blood," in opposition to rule-governed dogmatism.

Although philosophy is reserved when it comes to relatively concrete rules, it will be seen that it establishes more fundamental prescriptions that in part silently accompany any and all concrete rules. Otherwise, it leaves to the individual the decision with respect to concrete action with its cultural context. One reason: when it comes to moral actions there are three fundamentally distinguishable moments involved: the purely moral moment that consists in the thought of the morally good; the descriptive moment with respect to the general conditions of application under which the morally good is demanded; and, finally, the action in its individual concreteness.

Obviously, the moral moment belongs within the jurisdiction of moral philosophy. However, because in the second moment one is concerned with general human experience, philosophy is not exclusively responsible for morals, although it plays an important role. In contrast to these other two moments, when it comes to the third moment, the assessment of the concrete situation, it is confronted with a capacity, the power of judgment, for which philosophy possesses no special competence. In this case, every mature person is competent because each must lead his own life and must depend upon his own power of judgment—even when advice is sought from competent friends in cases in which he encounters serious and complex life questions.

A further argument speaks against holding expectations for practical philosophy that are too high. For example, in order for a physician to make an appropriate judgment with respect to his patient, he needs a moral orientation in addition to his medical expertise: the willingness to help the patient. In a similar manner, the power of judgment in the case of moral action seeks a moral solution under the presupposition of a moral orientation for the given situation. Philosophy can clarify this moral presupposition, but it cannot simply instruct it. Therefore, as Aristotle correctly said (*Nicomachean Ethics* 1.1.1095a4ff.), if one is to benefit from ethics, one must free oneself from one's passions and orient one's aspirations according to reason (*kata logon*).

What is the orientation that philosophy accomplishes? Philosophy can solve fundamental difficulties; for example, it can properly establish the moral perspective in opposition to the radical skepticism of relativism and nihilism. In the conflict over the final principle of action, philosophy begins with a conceptual analysis and derives from it a concept, then a standard. Finally, philosophy can make available general points of judgment. This rich arsenal for assisting one's orientation is no help, however, with respect to immediate action. However, as a consequence of philosophy's contribution, one can understand the goal, in the case of eudaimonism the goal of striving for happiness, far more precisely and can reach it more readily. An art of living governed by principles combines its fundamental orientation with a high degree of freedom and a right to differences. In terms of the crowd, it votes for an ethical liberalism that, when it comes to concrete living alternatives, holds itself independent from all materialistic and paternalistic perspectives that "know better."

7.3 A Dual Strategy

Although primarily concerned with the art of living in terms of the orientation based on principles, this study does appeal on occasion to life experience, wisdom literature, and empirical research. However, it focuses essentially on a discursive art of living.

Second-order reflection with respect to objective assertions concerning happiness commences with the experience that a happy life is threatened by an abundance of illusions. These start with small illusions; for example, someone "who is all thumbs" wants to be a goldsmith, or someone with "two left feet" wants to be a ballet dancer or a soccer player. The relevant principle that one can find happiness only in proportion to one's capacities perhaps sounds trivial. The individual who doesn't take it to heart, however, will hardly be happy. For this reason, there are two aptitudes that one needs to acquire: first, an intellectual aptitude that realistically assesses one's own skills (i.e., the power of judgment); and second, the aptitude of character that enables one to lead one's life appropriate to one's self-assessment—the aptitude to adjust one's dreams to the often painful process that accompanies the limits of one's skills and the difficulties of one's life situation. For example, someone who despite the oversupply wants to become a goldsmith must be especially talented, committed, and able to be satisfied with a low income.

The same two aptitudes are needed when confronting moderate illusions (for example, when, in seeking friendship, one stumbles upon an opportunist or a deadbeat). Once again, one must be capable of assessing properly the situation (in this case other persons) and be capable of adjusting one's way of living accordingly.

Philosophy, however, usually commences with the next level of illusion. It is the great illusion that expects happiness to come from a strategy that disregards one's current situation and personality structure because the structurally conditioned does not allow for a happy life, since situations and relationships violate the conceptual condition for the aspiration for happiness (i.e., the character of an end in itself).

Yet there is an even greater illusion with which philosophy meaningfully begins: whoever recognizes happiness only as a yearning for happiness or only as a vertiginous, effervescent joy will not be happy for any length of time either in the world or in his own skin, namely as a human being with conflicting needs; with a tendency to excess; with a jealous gaze at the fruit in his neighbor's garden; with the danger that he will be abandoned or betrayed by his friends; with the further danger that he will meet with an accident, grow old, and become fragile; and not least with the anxieties and cares that come not from the actuality of the former but from merely worrying about their coming to pass.

The frequent complaint about a lack of happiness consists in the gap between the expectation and the fulfillment of happiness. There are two strategies for overcoming this gap. Either one reduces one's expectations or one increases the range with respect to the fulfillment of the expectations. In light of the difference between wishful happiness and the aspiration for happiness, the philosophy of the art of living commences with the first task: prior to increasing one's activity, one restricts one's expectations. This kind of life strategy consists in the aptitude to lead a happy life without living on the "island of the blessed": in perfect deliverance with complete reconciliation and eternal peace. In short, it is the capacity for happiness despite the enduring deficit with respect to one's wishes.

Philosophy consists in more than mere subjective advice when one considers the semantic presupposition that the first moment in the concept of happiness, the "ultimate and last," cannot only be more ambitiously but also more modestly understood, and when one considers the empirical condition that the realization of a too ambitious concept can collapse under the *conditio humana*—that is, when one combines the semantic option (the "ultimate and last") with real anthropological conditions. The first cornerstone of an objective art of living rejects an excess of expectations that can only necessarily result in dashed hopes. In opposition to a hubris with respect to the search for happiness that in the end only punishes itself with disappointment, the first eudaimonistic advice is: "Nothing in excess," or more professionally, social scientifically formulated: "One should practice a tolerance of sensuous frustration!" Only someone who is capable of fulfilling this (by no means moralizing) advice can satisfy a critical aspect of happiness: that the aspired goals constitute together a totality that is complete.

Already with the Greeks, the well-known maxim "nothing in excess" (*mêden agan*) was an answer to the general danger of insatiability (*pleonexia*). Here the maxim is directed toward the insatiability that accompanies the wish for happiness. Absolute deliverance is a concern of the gods, finite deliverance is the concern of humanity. However, in order to protect against too quickly being satisfied with second best, philosophy knows that the divine is already to some extent within us, if usually only for a short period of time. Nonetheless, what Aristotle said with respect to the theory of philosophically scientific life practice can be applied elsewhere (i.e., to one's relationship with others, to nature, to one's own needs, and, according to the reports of some mystics, even in relationship to the divine itself): it is an escalation of life that takes one to the very edge of the unattainable perfect happiness for which we yearn.

A second-best happiness does not necessarily exclude the absolute best. The first advice of practical philosophy does not command any hasty satisfaction; it does not expect that one forget one's longing for happiness (for example, the dashing of all youthful dreams). Whoever is still "able" to yearn can, to the contrary, lead a full life. Satisfaction with second best is only merely a happiness "based on security." Hence, one doesn't give up one's hope for that great happiness: that, for example, unexpectedly one receives something or that one for a period of time finds oneself in harmony with a group of people or with nature. Therefore, we encounter a second point of advice: "In the midst of everyday happiness, one holds oneself open for Sunday happiness!"

In contrast to Marquard's (1986, 41–42) fundamental reining in of an unrestrained expectation of meaning, one is advised here not to go on a "meaning diet" by pursuing a reduction of one's sensuous expectations. In place of a reduction in expectations, a double strategy is recommended: one hopes for the greatest reconciliation, yet understands, nonetheless, that one must live with estrangements. Satisfaction with smaller happiness (by no means with the smallest happiness) maintains a reserve of expectation with respect to that greater happiness. This double strategy carries with it the consequence that there is always a potential for disappointment. Whoever is satisfied with the "smaller happiness," with what is usual and the routine, avoids the risk perhaps of never achieving the authentically worthwhile. The price for this "insurance mentality in leading one's life," this rigorous rejection of any escalation of expectations, is obviously high. Routine only aids survival through periods of thirst when it comes to the search for happiness, but it doesn't satisfy the thirst. One can reduce the thirst, but it remains and wants to be satisfied. Routine—as is confirmed by empirical research with respect to happiness—is incapable of satisfying the thirst.

8 Four Life Goals

It is quite seldom that a person experiences his life in all of its aspects as perfect. Certainly, perfection is not and cannot be an enduring experience. If and when it does happen, it is due to a set of circumstances over which the individual has little if any control. For this reason, there is no art of living for this kind of "Sunday happiness." For someone, however, who chooses to find happiness without excessive dependence upon his external circumstances but on the basis of his own powers, he contemplates how one goes about arranging one's life as a whole: what style or strategy of life more likely permits a successful existence?

According to some social philosophers, those communitarians known to focus on specific communities, lifestyles are culturally specific. In this case, there is only an ancient and a modern lifestyle, and within the modern there is a North American form. Many cultural differences, however, are irrelevant when it comes to the question of happiness. In fact, one can identify a threefold intercultural commonality that is identifiable in wisdom literature. First, in almost all cultures one finds the same four life goals. Second, these four goals have different weights for persons in the same culture. Without entirely neglecting the other goals, some seek above all sensuous pleasure; they live a life of indulgence. Others are concerned more with affluence (an "economic existence"), whereas others are concerned with power (an example of which is a "political life"), and still others seek prestige (one can provisionally call this a "life of ambitions"). There is a third intercultural commonality: these four life goals appear in the wisdom literature not as desirable but as goals critically dismissed.

Ancient Egyptian wisdom literature, for example, is opposed to wealth in that it rejects avarice and miserliness (see *Lesebuch* [Höffe 2007b], nos. 1 and 11). One of the Seven Sages of Greece, Periander of Corinth, is even more dismissive: "Profit is ignominious" (ibid., no. 45).

Another of the Seven Sages, Thales of Miletus, says more cautiously: "Avoid wealth in an ignominious fashion" (ibid.). With both Greek authors, the term "ignominious" affirms the fourth of the life goals sketched above: in order to acquire desired prestige, one should avoid "defamation and shame." In contrast, the Taoist, Yang Zhu, introduces a hint of skepticism: "In restless haste, one struggles for vain praise" (no. 35). Another of the Seven Sages, Cleobulus of Lindus, advises that one exercise control over one's lust (no. 45), whereas the Buddha rejects the "lust of passion" (no. 24). In the Old Testament book of Ecclesiastes, one finds: "'Now then, I want to try it with joy' . . . but, see, this too was vain!" Philosophers like Plato and Aristotle question the happiness of power.

Aristotle's succinct arguments against these specific life goals (*Nicomachean Ethics* 1.3; although power appears here only as an aside) were so convincing that they maintained an influence for centuries. As late as the threshold to modernity, one finds in the Renaissance philosopher Marsilio Ficino (*Lesebuch* [Höffe 2007b], no. 102) a free paraphrasing of Aristotle. With Søren Kierkegaard we reach a new high point in the philosophical investigation of the proposition and possibility of happiness. (On aesthetic existence that seeks nothing but sensuous happiness and on ethical and moral-social existence, see *Either/Or;* on the third level of religious existence, see *Concluding Unscientific Postscript.*) In what follows, we are not concerned with authorities but with content: Can one subject these four life goals to more than merely subjective moralizing judgments? Are there objective, eudaimonistic estimations of these ground plans for happiness? In any event, one should not expect here more than a modest sketching out of insights.

8.1 Pleasure

Our first life goal, the happiness of pleasure, seems to allow for an easy conclusion. Who doesn't crave pleasure and seek to avoid pain? Who doubts that someone who is joyous and completely free from suffering is happy? Nonetheless, the philosopher questions more deeply and begins with the clarification of the concept itself.

More often than not, one thinks only of sensuous pleasure and displeasure. In fact, on the negative side, displeasure, one has everything from hardship, pain, and suffering to material and above all psychological (emotional) affliction. On the positive side, pleasure includes the entire spectrum of physical, psychological, social, and mental (intellectual) pleasures: from craving a fleeting ecstasy all the way to an enduring pleasure; from a more physically modest pleasure ("The sun gives warmth, and I am free of troubles") to a Sunday spent with good friends over a glass of wine, to Jean Paul's "Idyll" of the amusements of the schoolteacher Maria Wutz from Auenthal, to the rapture of a "Rejoice! Exult!" from Bach's first Christmas cantata. Indeed, this positive side can also include a distancing from sensuous pleasure which can itself be a passion, the "contra-happiness of the mind" (Gottfried Benn, *Einsamer nie*). Some find pleasure in solving tricky (mathematical, chess, or philosophical) puzzles, some in the performance of music, painting, reading, or writing poetry. Don Juan enjoyed his talent of seduction. Another finds pleasure in strolling or in sitting on a park bench from which one can observe the activities of others and be alone with oneself in the midst of a crowd. One can find a general joy in life as well as a general joy in work; one, of course, is familiar with the smaller but more healthy pleasure found in eating whole wheat bread, just as one is familiar with the far greater and unhealthier joy in pralines. In short: the world of pleasures is varied and rich.

In contrast to a widely held opinion, pleasure in the more familiar sense is no product that jumps out at one. It belongs to a process—hence, it has no technical or artisanal character, but rather a practical one—and, precisely in this respect, it functions as a final end. Certainly, it refuses to be classified as common to other everyday ends or as superior to them. One can be happy about the recovery of something even though one wasn't seeking it. When it comes to such elemental needs as hunger and thirst, one doesn't *seek* pleasure but nourishment, even when the satisfaction of one's hunger and thirst can be accompanied by satisfaction.

It is this situation that explains why the philosophical conflict over the principle of pleasure often consists in the opponents talking past one another: the defender of pleasure is right to the extent that it is almost always an *accompanying* end or a *concomitant* state, at least when experienced in the sense of pleasure in an activity. The critic can in contrast maintain that pleasure is usually only a *secondary* end, rather than the primary end: to lose oneself in a task that one enjoys doing is to do it with pleasure. In this respect, formally considered, pleasure is not a feeling of its own kind but a subjective sensation that accompanies any and all actions (or avoidance of action) in which one isn't seeking it directly but to which one "completely surrenders oneself."

Already the mastermind of the philosophy of pleasure, Epicurus, made an important distinction. He spoke not merely of the "dynamic" emergence of an episodic pleasure (dynamic pleasure) that, for example, is experienced with the satisfaction of a need, with the modulation in the sensation of pleasure, or with the reduction or cessation of pain. Rather, he spoke of a second kind of sustained, permanent, "peaceful" pleasure (*katastêmatikê*) in the sense of a wakeful life; this mental pleasure is a "condition of pleasure." Diverse experience allows us to draw an initial conclusion: in the course of life, one finds more joy in free self-determination rather than in ever-changing particular indulgences, which latter, of course, can themselves be integrated into one's free self-determination.

In addition to the unmediated enjoyment to be found in the performance of living, one may also identify a pre- and post-joy. These both have the advantage that they can prolong an episodic pleasure. Incidentally, episodic pleasure is not limited to the five senses since one can experience, as well, a concert, a lecture, or the solution of a particular problem as a pleasure or with pleasure. This leads to a further distinction: pleasures of the senses are distinguishable from those of the mind, those someone experiences in the application of one's nonsensuous capacities. It is not unimportant, furthermore, that there are great differences here from one person to another.

The label for a life lived according to the principle of pleasure comes from the Greek word for pleasure, *hêdonê* (literally, sensualist). The associated philosophical school of hedonism makes pleasure the single and final motive for all psychological states of mind, and, in its ethical form, hedonism makes pleasure the ultimate justification for one's actions. In the first case, pleasure alone is the motivating factor; in a second case, it alone is the legitimating power. In egocentric hedonism everything hinges on the respective individual; in hedonistic utilitarianism, in contrast, one is concerned with all who could possibly be affected. (On pleasure, the principle of pleasure, and hedonism, see the still pertinent *Philebus* of Plato, Aristotle's *Nicomachean Ethics* 7.12–15 and 10.1–5, and Epicurus, *Philosophie der Freude;* more recent works, for example, are Freud's *Beyond the Pleasure Principle* and Marcuse's "Zur Kritik des Hedonismus" ["Towards a Critique of Hedonism"]; for the most recent discussion, see Sumner 1996 and Diener, Kahneman, and Schwarz 1999.)

According to a third, semantic (i.e., in the sense of a logical meaning) hedonism, in whatever one strives for one necessarily seeks a quality of feeling that one calls pleasure, namely, satisfaction or fulfillment. In fact, only the following qualifies as logically meaningful: whatever one strives for, one holds that to be good. Whether or not one in the process experiences pleasure is, in contrast, an empirical question that often is answered with "Yes!" though sometimes with "No!" Some remain happy even though they don't achieve what they set out to do, whereas others are unhappy despite success.

For a teleological ethic of aspiration, neither the psychological "is" nor the ethical "ought" is significant, but the methodologically mediating thesis that pleasure is *capable* of serving as a final end is significant. The corresponding eudaimonistic hedonism maintains neither that pleasure is something actual nor that it is a final end on the basis of conceptual grounds, nor that it should be. It simply maintains that pleasure is capable of serving as a final end; it has the potential for a successful life. Should, however, pleasure turn out to be the exclusive life goal capable of bringing happiness or, at the least, be an indispensable final end for happiness, then it would constitute a "Should," namely the fundamental eudaimonistic basis: "Aspire for pleasure!"

Our reflections concerning eudaimonistic hedonism commence with arguments in support of pleasure and leave the "encomium-inebriated" "Ode to Joy" to poets like Schiller. Elemental, but by no means therefore ignoble, sensual pleasures are fulfilled by the satisfaction of primary physiological needs such as hunger, thirst, the need for sleep, and sexual craving. To the degree that they serve the biological end of self- and species-preservation, they have a utilitarian meaning from which, however, they can be distinguished: one can take pleasure in landscapes, works of art, natural spectacles, or the movements of animals and humans; a thundering surf, the songs of birds, and music can please the ear; the scent of flowers or meals can please the nose. In such fashion, one can experience great enjoyment in feelings and tastes. Not the least is the cultivation of the finer cultural senses that long for even more enjoyable experiences.

Sensual pleasures turn pathological when transformed by greed or addiction. In order for the pathological character to be manifest, there is no need for anything external to the individual to be invoked, such as a socially dictated specification of an established standard for what is excessive. An internal, to a certain extent objective as well as subjective, criterion suffices: are other crucial needs and interests strongly influenced (objective) in the same individual (subjective)? Does, for example, the individual himself experience the consequences as destructive, or will he be limited in his activities and responsibilities by them?

Someone who knows only sensual pleasures, the indulgence of the five senses, pursues a concept of sensuous pleasure. The nondogmatic, definitely not subjectively moralizing but anthropological critique of such sensuous pleasure emphasizes the almost banal fact that humanity does not live by the senses alone. Humanity's other capacities have corresponding functions that involve in part social, in part intellectual, in part aesthetic, and perhaps also moral, even religious pleasures. In addition, there is a function that combines sensuous with emotional pleasure, and often with social pleasure. We are referring here to the game in its simple and also its highly developed form: such activities stretch from skillfulness with a ball, with cards, and with parlor games to theater and music games, and also dancing. Finally, one is familiar with organized pleasures, the festival and the celebration, and further with the escalation of joy: from jubilance to enthusiasm and to pleasure-filled delirium.

What argues against a life merely of pleasure, so long as it is open to the broad spectrum of pleasurable possibilities (i.e., is not merely the life of an unrestrained bon vivant) that includes social, artistic, and intellectual activities? Certainly the experience of sensuous pleasure alone is nothing that speaks against pleasure, since in the strictest sense no one can escape pleasure. As a reversal of a yet-to-be-discussed principle of discounting hedonism (chapter 11.1), whether in terms of a freely chosen or forced asceticism, phases of deprivation can be followed by an escalation of pleasure: even the ascetic who has not eaten, drunk, or slept for a long time finds pleasure when he commences again to eat, drink, and sleep even when the food isn't necessarily tasteful and the sleeping conditions are uncomfortable. The reason is obvious: quite simply because a human being has a body with sense organs, no one can lead a life without bodily and sense-perceptions to which, according to the principle under discussion, the necessity of pleasant sensations belongs.

Another social pleasure is also not entirely to be avoided. It may be true that there are misanthropes in the strict sense of the term who feel only uncomfortable when among others—especially if they are like Alceste in Molière's (tragi-)comedy *The Misanthrope,* who views his fellow human beings as entirely egoistic and calculatingly diabolical. However, as a rule one has a relative, a friend, or a colleague with whom one lives amicably. When one meets her/him to play music, a sport, or to share "a meal with animating conversation," one enjoys social and emotional joys. Pleasure is not so much unavoidable as positively valued where it is effortlessly integrated in a life that is meaningful, or even promotes humanity.

With what right, then, does the wisdom literature of so many cultures and philosophers reject a life of pleasure? Where are the difficulties? Since it accompanies every form of success, pleasure is present in and can arise in every moment. Now, whoever pursues his momentary impulses lives, as no one can say more concisely than Aristotle, "like a slave" (*Nicomachean Ethics* 1.3.1095b19–20). He subordinates himself to the needs and interests of the moment. Since in such a case one is merely passively a victim of one's appetites, one can say that they are passions that correspond to the foreign word *Affekte* (i.e., strong emotions). It is better, however, to distinguish between passions and strong emotions and to classify under the latter those quickly passing surges of feeling like anger, whereas with passions one is concerned with enduring fixations like hate, envy, and jealousy: "Affect works like water that breaks through a dam; passion, like a river that digs itself deeper and deeper into its bed" (Kant, *Anthropology,* 7:252).

Why shouldn't the individual succumb to his emotions and passions? The preferred answer that they contradict reason is, first, only a term that is followed with another question: What does reason mean here? Above all, why would a life of indulgence need reason? The non-moralizing answer consists in internal, often trivial difficulties. The first difficulty, a three-dimensional *pleonexia* (excess) that seeks the more-and-more of amount (quantity), strength (intensity), and kind (quality), is threatened by sensuous pleasure. In Shakespeare's words: "The ocean is limited, desire is unlimited" (*Venus and Adonis,* verse 89). One might perhaps counter: "Yes, and what's the problem? Why should one ever have enough, fundamentally?" An initial suggestion that pleasure ever and again runs dry and often only with great effort can be reanimated is really no counterargument. Two kinds of "never-enough" need clarification in advance. The one, temporally linear in its sequence, is the kind like that related to eating, drinking, and sleeping. Whoever has had enough, takes a break, and as soon as he is hungry, thirsty, or tired, he eats, drinks, or sleeps again. The same temporal experience is found in other areas of an unproblematic, often even unavoidable, "natural" ebb and flow of need, satisfaction, and renewed need.

However, what is problematic is the other, neither nonlinear nor horizontal, namely vertical "never-enough": the need for refinement and luxury that knows no measure of satisfaction ("satiety") or, above all, is never satisfied at all. As in the fairy tale "The Fisher and His Wife," one is never happy because a necessary ingredient of happiness, satisfaction, is missing.

A *second*, equally internal, difficulty is: different needs and interests are only concerned with themselves individually; they are not coordinated with one another. In combination with the first difficulty, the danger of unlimitedness, individual needs tend to compete with one another in a ruthless quest for dominance that consequently leads to a tyranny that threatens the whole: where one succumbs to one need, others can be forgotten, repressed, or eradicated, which threatens the fulfillment of the diverse needs as well as the resulting cumulative pleasure; consequently, it threatens happiness itself.

A *third* difficulty, the potentially negative ancillary consequences of our actions, is hinted at in the Polish proverb: "God created wine, the Devil the hangover." With (far) too much food or alcohol as well as too little sleep over an extended period of time, one risks consequences that often are harmless but occasionally are serious. As Schiller said in his poem "Lied von der Glocke," "Rapture is short, regret is long."

A *fourth* difficulty is expressed by the saying "Before victory, the Gods require sweat." The accompanying argument doesn't need to make two questionable assumptions. It is neither necessary to argue for asceticism nor for the so-called Protestant work ethic or to maintain a fundamental superiority of mental over sensual pleasures. Life experience independent of both assumptions demonstrates that many things which require little effort have a limited quotient of pleasure, whereas an enduring and deep satisfaction is often only achieved where one shoulders real effort. Readiness to abstain temporarily from pleasure, even to endure displeasure, is a hedonistic investment that pays a premium in the long run. Someone who meets an increasingly demanding challenge with ever-greater effort does more than increase performance. What is eudaimonistically important is that he often experiences a deeper and more enduring satisfaction that is later supplemented with the joys of memory. A satisfaction of its own kind can then be added to our appreciation of effort: the awareness that one did not capitulate to the challenging difficulties but, far more, managed to conquer them. In this light, a pedagogic of excess (one must have everything immediately) is damaging to adolescents, just as the "culture of amusement" is damaging to itself. In contrast, whoever pursues high goals raises the potential of gratification and does something good for himself.

Fortunately, the importance of experience has been rediscovered with respect to certain "social experiments"—for example, one encounters it in the film *Rhythm Is It* (2004; Enrique Sánchey Lansch and Thomas Grube, directors): the conductor Simon Rattle rehearses a classic dance project along with two choreographers. Rather than the usual performers, he chooses as his artists fifty young people from twenty-five nations who have neither the physical training nor the required discipline (and, for the most part, have never had anything to do with classical music). After the success of the performance, the students improved their performance in other areas, particularly in school. Above all, they were proud of their accomplishment far beyond the confines of the original performance. There is no question, though, that in such a situation sensitivity and a feeling of proportionality are necessary. What generates for one person a eudaimonistic creative performance can drain the self-confidence of another and simultaneously reduce his sense of satisfaction.

A *fifth* difficulty with a life of mere indulgence involves its effect on others: whoever is concerned with the exclusive satisfaction of his own desires takes for granted interference with, even impairment of, others' satisfaction, which aggravates the *sixth* difficulty: from relatively harmless Schadenfreude to the pleasure of outperforming someone else in a sport, politics, or academic discipline to the knavish pleasure of deception or violence that can turn into sadism, some find pleasure in the suffering of others. One doesn't need to recall the great deceivers of world literature, not even de Sade, who in today's sense was hardly a sadist. One can quote the "protagonist" of a little-known "loveless comedy," Stefan Zweig's *Ben Jonsons "Volpone"*: "You surely know, chum, that things taste better to me properly spiced: I acquire an appetite best after a peppery maliciousness or a juicy deception" (act 1, scene 1). A variation with respect to suffering is enviousness. As Jean Racine writes in his *Phedra:* "I can't stand a happiness that doesn't happen to me" (act 4, scene 4).

In addition to the social, *inter*personal conflict that is manifest with these two difficulties, one can experience an individual, *intra*personal conflict as well. It amounts to a *seventh* difficulty: should one cultivate a ruthless satisfaction of one's own pleasure even though it contradicts another kind of pleasure, the desire for a good reputation? One is not so much concerned here with the frequently evoked conflict between egocentrism and altruism as with an internal conflict with respect to one's own personal satisfaction: because one's own joy usually involves a genuine shared joy in terms of one's status in the opinion of others, a happiness based exclusively on one's own pleasure damages the entire balance of personal happiness. This imbalance is already experienced when one's ruthlessness leads to "an uncomfortable feeling," perhaps even shame and the bite of conscience.

Even here, however, one has not exhausted the complications. By no means tethered to the present, humanity experiences pleasures out of the past and in anticipation of the future. It is difficult to classify these pleasures, but to them belongs the joyful resonance of a remembered pleasure or one's memory of an accomplishment over which one is proud, as well as the joyful anticipation of a future delight. The situation is similar with respect to displeasure in the face of "anticipated travails" accompanied by anxiety and worries, as well as with "remembered troubles" like memories of anger, feelings of shame or of bitterness. Although not actually capable of being addressed directly, one can influence them through "internal technical controls." Everyone knows the simple advice that one balance out everyday worries by doing gymnastics, sport, and dance or by the enjoyment of music, a film, meditation, reading, or family life, undertaking an activity with friends, or participation in a social organization. The number of options is endless—with the danger that one loses oneself in the options and does not address the fundamental problems of one's lifestyle.

A further, now *ninth* difficulty: one with few joys, with too low a threshold for frustration, or with too high and too quick expectations can seek a "shortcut" by turning to chemical manipulation of one's body, "intoxication." Freud's down-to-earth appraisal continues to apply: an intoxicant provides one not only with the optimizing of pleasure "in the struggle for happiness and in keeping misery at a distance . . . [but also is] highly prized as a benefit . . . [for achieving] independence from the external world." However: "as is well known, it is precisely this property of intoxicants which also determines their danger and their injuriousness. They are responsible, in certain circumstances, for the useless waste of a large quota of energy which might have been employed for the improvement of the human lot" (*Civilization and Its Discontents*, 1961, 28). In addition to the loss of this energy and the increased "hangover phenomenon"—in which one feels physically and psychologically worse than one did before consuming the intoxicant—one can become addicted, which in turn can lead to the destruction of the body and the personality.

This cascade of difficulties is sufficient in the absence of a completed argument to establish a solid foundation with respect to pleasure: on the one side, none of the difficulties constitutes an absolute veto. The experience that some pleasures pass with ease into a meaningful life is just as beyond dispute as the fact that pleasure usually accompanies success with a self-selected activity so that there is no such thing as a successful happiness without pleasure. What the difficulties do establish is that there is more to life than pleasure; in order to overcome the difficulties, something else is necessary.

The principle of pleasure already fails internally because desire is directed exclusively toward the concrete and momentary and is dependent upon the givenness of motivations that are themselves contradictory and can atrophy just as well as proliferate out of control. Pleasure cannot provide a harmonious realization of the different kinds of pleasure that confront the individual. Just what the alternative to pleasure is must yet be determined. We can call it "reason" because it must be capable of establishing a distance, and because it is in the service of an optimal balance of pleasures, it can be labeled "hedonistic reason." Without this hedonistic reason, it is not possible for there to be a hedonistic creativity and art of living that can oppose displeasure from the perspective of pleasure—for example, one which sees in difficulties a chance for future pleasure, and thus ameliorates the difficulties by anticipating joy or, in the case of suffering, introduces the memory of past joy as a source of present consolation. What is missing in a life of mere pleasure is the internal relationship to the totality of life that is necessary for the happiness of teleological aspiration. It is missing hedonistic and, even more, eudaimonistic reason.

8.2 Affluence

The ethical evaluation of the next two goals for living, affluence and power, is easier. The same basic pattern, which consists of a critique that avoids any moralistic taking of sides, applies to both and calls to mind right at the beginning the different levels of human goals and values. Precisely because there is a hierarchy of goals and values, there is always the danger that one will value lower steps of the ladder over higher ones. From the perspective of the happy life, this possibility of the confusion of values runs the risk of perversion. According to the slogan of a bourgeois insurance director, the father-in-law of Otto Dix (according to Schick 2005, 19): "Happiness is order, discipline, and punctuality"; only such goals are emphasized that have a functional value. Were they truly to be turned into final ends, they would suppress the only true ends that can bring happiness and would jeopardize a successful life. In English one calls it "medium maximization": one maximizes a means without considering what one wants to accomplish with this means.

A life that strives only for affluence suffers from perversion. The reason that this is so does not come from a lofty idea of what it means to be authentically human, for affluence is not suited even to the "smallest of life's meanings." Persons who are interested in nothing but money and material things like furniture and securities or art that is collected only in speculation over its potential increase in value are obsessed in the literal sense of the word. A confirmation from experience: one gladly lives "in affluence," but not "in order to be affluent."

The non-moralizing critique does not follow Kleist's perhaps comforting but unrealistic opinion (here abbreviated): "The great ones of this world live in grandeur and opulence, which is why one calls them the favorites of happiness. However, displeasure clouds their sight, pain discolors their cheeks, and affliction pours over their tongues. In contrast, when we observe a day laborer, we see contentment in his eyes, joy shines in his face, and cheerfulness and ecstatic oblivion hover around him" ("Weg des Glück," 867).

First of all, we must readily recognize the important value here: money is a universal means of exchange; as capital it is even an object of trade, a commodity, and affluence opens a plenitude of possibilities of exchange. Whoever strives for money abandons a key moment of the principle of pleasure, its focus solely on the present, and engages in a "reflective" life (to be sure, within narrow limits). Eudaimonistically, a modest standard of living is the totality of material means presently available in a sufficient amount which also allows one to fulfill one's needs and interests in the future. In such a circumstance, one has additionally the emotional gain of a sense of security. As an elementary example: because we can look into the future, we can already be worried today about the hunger of tomorrow. In this case, affluence functions to overcome the anxiety of the present. Affluence, therefore, performs a dual eudaimonistic service. Directly, it serves the enjoyment of tomorrow; indirectly, the enjoyment of today, namely, by overcoming one's anxiety in the present. There can also be another advantage derived from the continual pursuit of affluence (or in a difficult situation, the preservation and enhancement of one's affluence): it stimulates creativity and performance and aids, consequently, the cultivation of one's talents (admittedly, often in a one-sided fashion).

Despite these advantages, there remains a structural problem: because of its exchange- and commodity-character (i.e., from its very concept), money and capital and their exaggerated possession, wealth, are only intermediate, not final, ends. As a rule, they are, in fact, actually only a means of a second order: namely, a means for the acquisition of first-order means like merchandise or services by means of which more normal needs and interests can be fulfilled. What is meant by a second-order means here is not those second-order interests like: no longer to be poor or to be able to purchase all that one's heart desires. Someone who organizes his life only in terms of money transforms a second-order means, a thoroughly significant intermediate end, into a final end, which structurally hinders a meaningful life. Once more from Zweig's "lifeless comedy": "Money, money stupefies the world, / . . . Then, even the one who has it, is never satisfied" (act 1, scene 1). In addition, there is a second path to affluence: someone without any greed can be rich and without a shopping addiction can be affluent. (An enjoyable adviser, Schönburg's *Kunst des stilvollen Verarmens* [*The Art of Stylish Poverty*] was a bestseller; see as well the "Leitfaden für Menschen mit geringem Einkommen" ["Guide for Persons with Little Income"] from the Hungarian author Sándor Márai's *Schule der Armen* [*School for the Poor*].)

However, before one intones a sentimental praise of poverty, one must not forget that there is (almost) "nothing so degrading as the constant anxiety about one's means of livelihood." William Somerset Maugham's literary character in *Of Human Bondage* (1965, 274) avows from bitter experience: "I have nothing but contempt for the people who despise money. They are hypocrites or fools." Voltaire wrote: "L'argent ne fait pas le bonheur, mais sans l'argent le bonheur n'est qu'une farce" ("Money doesn't create happiness, but without money happiness is a mockery").

The structural critique does not maintain that all aspiration for affluence suffers from perversion. As the biographies of such wealthy personages as the Fuggers, Rockefellers, or Rothschilds demonstrate, something else, at least unconsciously if not often enough consciously, is involved. Many of them sought success and, in addition, power, but only tangentially a comfortable life. Sometimes the angry diagnosis one finds in Toni Morrison's novel *Love* is accurate (2003, 45): "Rich people could act like sharks, but what drove them was a kid's sweet tooth . . . adoration, obedience, and full-time fun."

Other ends extend beyond the scope of these limits: with generosity, one wins friends; with increased generosity, patronage, one even acquires public esteem that can lead to fame. Large social, cultural, and scientific foundations like the Bosch, Gates, Rockefeller, and Thyssen foundations, but also smaller foundations, preserve for many generations the memories of their original benefactors. The assumptions here are generally held, praised attitudes, which possess their own eudaimonistic justification: largesse and generosity. A plea from another culture—from the *ghazal* of the Islamic poet Hafiz (2004, 255): "O rich one, take in your hand the heart of your beggar [i.e., don't ignore the needs of others]; (your) gold and money vault will not endure." Indeed, the stingy one gambles away this opportunity for happiness, just as the avaricious one does, who in his "always wanting more" never has enough.

The often banal little sister of the aspiration for affluence is the desire for material goods. However, their acquisition depends upon whether the conditions are favorable or not. Anxious single-minded pursuit of material goods can create necessities that often enough prevent the enjoyment of deeper and enduring joys. Furthermore, contrary to what one takes as the promise of a happy life that is to come with material acquisitions, they can be damaging in that they can produce envy, can attract thievery, and, possibly, make one attractive to a kidnapper. Above all, material possessions and their presupposition, affluence, taken in themselves represent at best a chance for happiness that must be recognized but also relativized.

A provisional conclusion combines four eudaimonistic insights that have four corresponding eudaimonistic imperatives. The *first* insight consists of the eudaimonistic ambivalence with respect to affluence: in light of its fundamentally instrumental nature, one can deploy one's affluence for good or bad ends, which leads to the advice: "View affluence as not so important and the incessant pursuit of ever-greater wealth, avarice, as the wrong track to happiness!" The *second* insight: the question of which direction the pendulum will swing, whether to the eudaimonistic good or bad, depends upon the capacity to follow unambivalent ends. Hence, the second piece of advice: "Orient your life primarily according to unambiguous ends!" The *third* insight, that a successful life is enjoyed by one who recognizes his opportunities and understands how to take advantage of those opportunities to achieve happiness, leads to a variation of the general advice: "Make the best of it!": "If you are born or become wealthy, take your affluence as the general framework within which you can pursue non-ambivalent goals in concrete form!"

Together these three insights suggest: affluence may be helpful, but it is not decisive for determining happiness in life. As a consequence—the *fourth* insight—it is imprudent to envy the rich. One does not need to follow Kleist's surely sentimental assessment that poverty has a eudaimonistic advantage. Rather, one should cultivate one's eudaimonistic creativity and rationality, which takes as its orientation Jean Paul's "cheerful teacher." Included in his art of living was the capacity for anticipation even under the most agonizing of situations: "Before you get out of bed," he says, "be glad for breakfast, the entire morning anticipate lunch with pleasure, at snack time and at the evening meal, be happy for what is placed before you"; and he reports that "in order to always wake each day with joy," he always "saved from the day before something pleasant for the next day." Without a doubt, one can mock the idyll expressed here: more intelligent, however, is the one who follows the advice: "Seek in your circumstances to be eudaimonistically creative!" The fourth insight, then, warns one to be humble toward those less well off than one: a comparatively higher standard of living does not improve the chances of one's being happy all that much. Research into happiness gives us two impressive conclusions. The one is that "although those in the West are increasingly richer, they are by no means happier" (Layard 2005, 13). The other conclusion: in those countries where one finds more poverty (e.g., Indonesia, Colombia, and Mexico), the percentage of happy persons is on average similar to that in richer industrialized countries (ibid., 46).

8.3 Power

The insatiable aspiration for power (and ever more power) fares just as poorly as an end in itself and the condition of a happy life. One variant of this aspiration for power is an insatiable careerism. When it comes to happiness as a principle of ethics, we are not concerned with power as a basic concept of society and politics but, rather, of power as a guiding life goal.

The powerful in our world arouse our skepticism over their happiness because they give us so many counterexamples. An example is the painting of *Emperor Charles V* in the Alte Pinakothek in Munich, Germany. The artist, presumably the court painter Titian, portrays the ruler in 1548 at the height of his power. Nevertheless, the ruler over half the globe looks neither proud of his accomplishment nor formidable. Even though the emperor is only forty-eight years old, he looks much older, with his face shaped more by the burdens of his office than by his honor and power.

The founder of modern political philosophy, Thomas Hobbes, defended an incessant aspiration for power. In chapter 13 of his *Leviathan,* he declares power to be not a form of meaningful life but its necessary condition. Rather than concern ourselves here with Hobbes's primary interests (the justification of an all-powerful state government, as well as its historical context, the civil wars of the early modern period), we turn to the question of the relationship between power and personal happiness. In this latter respect, an individual's power consists in the totality of means presently available to fulfill (even in the face of resistance) both present and future needs and interests.

Just like affluence, when eudaimonistically considered, power is a means of the second order because with it one cannot fulfill any of the usual first-order interests but one can overcome obstacles to their fulfillment. These obstacles can be of various kinds. Therefore, one needs different kinds of power depending upon the obstacle. Against the external obstacles of nature, one employs technical power (see Höffe 2000c, especially chapter 8), and against obstacles internal to the agent, one needs among others a specific kind of attitude (see below, chapters 9–10). Here the power to be discussed consists of the capacity to overcome obstacles that occur in social relationships. Because such obstacles are inescapable, it appears that the desire for power in the eudaimonistic sense is rational.

Although we don't need a detailed phenomenological description of power, a formal and functional distinction with respect to power would be helpful even if the frontier between them cannot be clearly marked. A defensive power helps protect against failure, humiliation, and (latent) exploitation. An offensive power, in contrast, aids in the acquisition of what one desires. An extreme case: someone strong enough and disposed to use his power to beat up others is feared, is quick to find followers, and obtains access to merchandise and services without having to pay the market prices. Only one thing functions as a defense against the capacity of externally aggressive power to dominate over others, to extort, and to humiliate. This one thing is a defensive power that, admittedly, sometimes is too weak in the absence of one's own external power.

The argument in favor of power is similar to the justification of a modest affluence: because when one looks into the future, one can anticipate barriers blocking the fulfillment of one's needs and interests, and because one is anxious that one will not be able to overcome those barriers, one develops strategies for overcoming those barriers today. The desire for power, viewed from a eudaimonistic perspective, performs a threefold service on behalf of one's happiness. Directly, it is conducive to enjoyment in the future; indirectly, to enjoyment today, namely, the overcoming of present anxiety; and, because of the difficulty of acquiring and maintaining power, it unleashes creativity.

In opposition to the mere instrumental character of power, one can point to the politician as a model because political power is not limited to merely this aspect of power. In economics and the sciences, even in the arts, one can identify three types of political activities: the designing of general frameworks for the accomplishment of a task, decisions concerning personnel, and the self-administering of specific departments and/or programs. In the economic sphere one thinks of trade associations, labor unions, industry boards, chambers of commerce, and guilds; in the sciences one thinks of university rectors or presidents, conferences of rectors, and scientific advisory boards. Whoever in these contexts strives for power may appear to pursue the power of such offices for its own sake. If one looks more closely, however, appearances are exposed as deceptive. To fill an office involves in most cases not merely the performance of certain tasks but also the generating of creative solutions. As a consequence, the pursued power is in the service of the completion of tasks and of organizing events and, hence, it retains its instrumental character. Even in those cases where power appears to be otherwise, mere power without a desire for organization (instrumentality) is an empty concept.

There is no question that there are those who enjoy power in and for itself. They enjoy the pride of the "hunter" who runs down an opponent, or the elation of the victor who leaves all competitors in the dust, or the feeling of superiority that believes itself for all intents and purposes capable of handling all situations. There is also sadistic power that doesn't shy away from any cruelty but even enjoys inflicting it. Fortunately, there are far more of those who use their power to accomplish something good.

However, when it comes to its eudaimonistic meaning, power is not taken so narrowly. Usually, one considers four kinds of power: the economic, the social, the political, and the power of the public media. One can add to these four the power of the mind, of which the natural sciences constitute only a small portion. Which of the so-called "powerful" possesses even remotely so much power as the founder of a religion or the power of a great philosopher, whose influence is continually being renewed?

The common instrument of the usual forms of power is called a power "network." For most of us, a modest if not unassuming measure of power is sufficient. Personal well-being for the private individual is satisfied by a good livelihood with adequate savings; when it comes to social power, one needs no more than the respect of colleagues and friends; for political power, citizens' rights and the franchise. In place of the power of the media, one needs a certain capacity to convince others of one's abilities and legitimate interests. Each of these kinds of power contains a certain opportunity for happiness that, as was the case with affluence, requires one's personal recognition of, and personal effort in seizing upon, the opportunities. These necessary capacities, likewise, have the characteristics of power in a eudaimonistic context.

Power serves happiness in the form of three personal capacities by means of which one masters new situations: with cleverness one adjusts intellectually, with psychic mobility one adjusts emotionally, and with social sensitivity one adjusts to new social constellations. Not least, power consists of the fourth capacity of renunciation. Here, depending upon the situation, one is capable of being satisfied with less than what one normally expects, whether with respect to consumption and comforts, or with respect to fewer goods and services, or with diminished recognition. These four capacities, which constitute power over the self, are in fact more important for one's happiness than the other, more usual forms of power that constitute power over others.

In light of this broadly sketched understanding of power appropriate to a eudaimonistic justification of power, it follows that the quest for power is rational, but not as an incessant activity. Philosophers like Hobbes overlook the fact that anxiety about the future is not the only "passion" driving humanity and the fact that the absolutizing of such anxiety results in a threat to the present satisfaction of other needs and interests. As with the quest for pleasure and the longing for affluence, there occurs an inner conflict within the quest for power that is based on its dual function: the first function consists in the placation of present anxieties, and it can collide with the other function, the satisfaction of the tendency that serves the pursuit of security. In addition, experience teaches that embracing certain risks enhances the chance of happiness. As a consequence, the question arises: just how much anxiety over the future is "rational" without the actual happiness of today sacrificing the potential happiness of tomorrow?

Precisely because it is wise to think about the future just as it is wise not to absolutize one's conclusions about the future, no unlimited quest for power recommends itself. Rather than maximizing one side or the other, everything depends upon an optimizing. The eudaimonistic reason involved in such an optimization combines two imperatives: the first focuses on the danger that one day one might be negatively surprised because one no longer has control over the means for the satisfaction of new needs. It can be summarized: "Rein in your limitless aspiration for present consumption in favor of a rational limiting of your appetites!" The second imperative: "In the name of present consumption, stop your exclusive concentration on the acquisition of future power!" The reason: except for the conquering of an anxiety, one should not always employ ever more means in the pursuit of a possible pleasure to the exclusion of an actual pleasure. In addition, there is the threat of power (especially the great power of envy) that in turn impairs one's own happiness and in addition threatens others.

8.4 Prestige

The prestige that one enjoys in the company of others, reputation, has more the character of an end in itself than do affluence or power. Its minimum consists in a good reputation. It escalates to honor, which emerges from distinguishing oneself; and reaches its superlative in fame, which at its best endures forever. With the quest for prestige, the quest for happiness in its inherent social dimension is manifest more clearly than with power. One can choose to pursue prestige and still not be able to achieve it alone by one's own efforts, because the accomplishments that bring with them prestige have to be recognized and appreciated *as* accomplishments by others. Consequently, others are in fact responsible for the acknowledgment, whereby one unwillingly makes oneself dependent on others. Whether sought from parents, teachers, peers, colleagues, or the public, many people court prestige, and not a few fail. Since humanity has a fundamental interest in acquiring and maintaining a good name, its presupposition, recognition, belongs to the fundamental conditions for happiness. Surprisingly, prestige became a foundational philosophical concept only in modernity and even then relatively late, with Fichte and Hegel. Its actuality, of course, is found much, much earlier and presumably in all cultures.

In an unadorned sense, "recognition" means praise. In a more ambitious sense, it means an acknowledgment with esteem for an unusual accomplishment. As a fundamental concept of philosophical ethics and normative social philosophy, recognition, in contrast, involves a relationality of reciprocal respect that cannot occur on its own either between individuals or between groups, legal communities, or even cultures.

Hobbes's thought experiment of the natural condition demonstrated a difficulty in reciprocal recognition that in a fundamental respect can be solved only on the basis of a legal relationship dependent upon public power (i.e., the state). Hegel picks up the theme and takes it further. In a properly famous chapter of his *Phenomenology of Spirit,* he sketches under the title "Master and Slave" the struggle for recognition that is necessary for the development of humanity. At the beginning there is no relation of respect but a reciprocal, even life-threatening, danger. In the course of this conflictual relationship with its truly existential weight, there arises in the end a recognition of the other as a person, although only after passing through various stages of interaction. Hegel's description of this dynamic process is not to be taken primarily as a historical sequence but as a mental construct that seeks to grasp the relationship between being a person, the socialization of the individual, and the law. The core thesis consists in a "self-recognition in the other": at the outset, one encounters the other in limited confinement that results in an initial struggle for exclusive dominance and leads to a life-and-death struggle. It is only after very painful experience that one reaches the point of reciprocal recognition, which necessarily, though not exclusively, has a legal character to it.

This struggle is meaningful because the recognition involved has a tremendous significance, since it involves acknowledgment of the person and the establishment of social parameters. Nonetheless, such recognition doesn't result in happiness as such, but is the presupposition for happiness. It does have the priceless advantage, in contrast to money and power, that it doesn't suffer from scarcity: as is demonstrated by a democratic state system, the relational recognition of the individual as a legal entity and as a citizen of the state is not a scarce good only possessed by the few; rather, it benefits everyone.

When it comes to concrete recognition, the personal reputation of an individual, we have a different situation. Acknowledgment of one another is a scarce resource over which, within a constitutional state, there is a struggle that is in part open and in part concealed. This struggle is especially obvious in the public sphere, especially in the national press, radio, and television. When it comes to recognition from colleagues in one's own discipline (and in other ways with customers or clients), the struggle for recognition cannot be counted on to be equal. One can hardly establish equality as a starting point, much less equality in the conclusion. Special skills and giftedness, an extraordinary effort, outstanding achievement (of whatever kind), differences in expectation, and (not least) fortunate circumstances aid and abet the chances of acquiring high prestige.

Some of these factors are under the control of the individual, so that one can after a fashion work toward prestige. However, since other factors are out of one's control, one has little personal responsibility for the total process. This accounts for why the happiness from teleological aspiration can hardly consist in mere prestige. What also speaks against prestige satisfying this definition of happiness is the danger that, since one is dependent upon others, one knows one does not build only on the basis of one's own efforts, but in terms of how others view those efforts. It is not unusual that in order to influence their social status, people play up their own accomplishments while downplaying the accomplishments of others; they don't even hesitate to use deception. Some allow themselves to be celebrated for an achievement that they did not accomplish; they choose to live with a veritable life-lie.

There is an obvious alternative, and it consists in the following imperative: "Seek accomplishment as such, create out of one's own self-respect, and seek the recognition of others only by the measure of two criteria: one's actual accomplishment and its valuation only by persons who are capable of judging it impartially." In this case, the concrete recognition by others—one's personal acknowledgment by the stranger—is in part supplemented, in part even replaced, by one's own self-respect.

A eudaimonistic result of our four proposed life goals turns out to be varied: pleasure is to a certain extent a final end, but it is more an accompaniment, a complementary factor, that alone as a principle cannot "guarantee happiness." Furthermore, pleasure is no exclusive, "only true" final goal. Affluence and power, in contrast, are not unimportant but also only as intermediate ends—to be sure, they possess the status of relative universal means of a second order. Prestige, finally, is indeed a possible final end. However, similar to pleasure, it is only an accompaniment to a final end that is achieved with certain accomplishments; in addition, it is threatened by distortion, deception, and manipulation.

In addition to these differences, there is a dual similarity. On the one hand, the four goals have an established place within the happiness of teleological aspiration; they are indispensable for a comprehensive and integrated concept of happiness. On the other hand, when taken individually and made absolute, they are not adequate to the two moments either of happiness or of teleological aspiration. Even when taken to be pre- or supplemental conditions or taken as opposition to hindrances to happiness, which allows them to be integrated in a larger concept of happiness, they are in themselves alone not suitable for happiness. Instead of one carrying responsibility for the success of one's life as far as possible, one is made, stated pathetically, a slave of one's momentary needs and interests: a slave of the principle of pleasure; or of one's concerns for the future: a slave of the principle of affluence and the principle of power; or of one's estimation in the eyes of others: a slave of prestige.

The common counterforce to these goals is called eudaimonistic reason. According to the approved method in philosophy, that of determinate negation, the bottom line that emerges from our evaluation of these goals gives us direction: in contrast to power and affluence, eudaimonistic reason keeps a true final end in sight; in contrast to pleasure and prestige, it pursues these final ends neither exclusively nor actually directly; they are if anything side effects that occur when one is successfully on the track to the authentic final end.

9 Virtue

9.1 Moral Virtue and Life Wisdom

One may call eudaimonistic reason that which establishes one's relationship to the incentives that serve the principle of happiness. Eudaimonistic reason is necessary for happiness because neither sensuous incentives nor the desire for affluence, power, or prestige is capable on its own of adequately determining a plain and simple life or even a happy life. As a defense against the threat of personal chaos, eudaimonistic reason is needed to provide at least coordination and control over one's motivations. Its function can be an intentional pruning, an empowering, or even a new acquisition of aspects of one's character.

With respect to this personal relationship to one's motivations, reason may be in part a matter of knowledge. However, knowledge is not primary when it comes to this cognitive or intellectual moment. What is more important is that one's motivations spontaneously follow ends conducive to happiness. One's motivations need to be trained so that they follow a pathway on their own that is suitable to bring happiness. One can speak here of a power over power, namely, of a power over the power of pleasure, over avarice, and over dominance, and, not least, over the power of ambition or the craving for recognition. However, this is no power that suppresses these other powers. Rather, it is concerned that these other powers take as their goal those ends that are conducive to happiness.

Furthermore, since what is crucial is an entire life, a temporary orientation toward happiness is not adequate. This orientation needs to be an established aspect of one's personality, of one's orientation and skills (know-how). As a successful lifestyle, it consists of a spontaneity of its own kind that is a second nature in contrast to one's inborn capacities.

When this spontaneity is appraised positively, it is called "virtue" in contrast to negatively appraised attitudes that one calls "vices."

It is not enough in this context "to be able"; for in addition to being able, one must apply one's capacity. Of course, virtue is a predisposition that one also attributes to someone who is not presently exercising it. This occurs, however, only under the assumption that the appropriate conditions for its application are at the moment not given. Someone is called helpful even when he is not presently helping because, for example, either no help is needed or his specific help is not needed. In contrast, someone who witnesses a stranger's suffering but does nothing out of a desire not to be disturbed cannot be called helpful. "Virtue" is not a label for success because the help in our example can be too late, too weak, or simply the wrong kind. Virtue is, however, related to execution or performance: where one's own help is requested, one must do something.

In order to be happy, though, the mere determination of ends conducive to happiness is not sufficient; one must, in addition, actually follow the route toward the accomplishment of those ends. In order to accomplish this, one needs another kind of virtue in addition to that concerned with one's motivations or moral virtue. One needs intellectual virtue, as well. Intellectual virtue is a eudaimonistic power of judgment—cleverness in the sense of life wisdom—that is responsible for determination of the ways and means; admittedly, not just any ways and means. In contrast to a neutral power of judgment in opposition to moral virtues (i.e., cunning) or a power of judgment in service to what is non-virtuous that can lead to vices associated with shiftiness, intellectual virtue contemplates solely those ways and means that lead to those final ends conducive to happiness compatible with moral virtues.

Both moral and intellectual virtues depend upon interaction between them: without life wisdom, the means conducive to the happiness of moral virtue are missing; without the fundamental orientation accomplished by moral virtue, life wisdom cannot accomplish what its name says; it cannot aid the achievement of an entirely successful, happy life. Eudaimonistic reason, then, consists of two entirely different but reciprocally dependent aspects. Because it is only their interplay and the internal connectedness between moral virtue with life wisdom that makes a person suitable for happiness, we can identify a further, non-moralizing imperative of an objective art of living: "Learn both moral and intellectual virtues, and practice them!"

These days the notion of "virtue" strikes one as a merely dusty arti-
fact; it sounds like moralizing. However, once one remembers its core
meaning, one no longer need experience virtue in this way. In fact, the
core meaning can constitute a moralizing-free virtue. In its conceptual
origin, virtue identifies all of a specific kind that cannot be surpassed in
that kind: a general "best" or excellence that one also finds with respect
to organs (e.g., a "most sharp-sighted eye") or in animals (e.g., an exceptional racehorse or an excellent guard dog). Persons, too, can perform
certain activities in an astonishing manner to become an extraordinary
cabinetmaker, physics instructor, musician, or soccer player.

Ethics frees itself from all particular perspectives and asks: what is
an extraordinary individual? In this abstraction, the concept of virtue is
not restricted by any specific task-oriented limits; it distinguishes a person as a human being so that one can speak of his humanity. Whereas
the Latin word *virtus* literally means the extraordinariness only of the
man (*vir*, "man"), the German (*Tusend*) separates itself from gender-
specific limitations and understands under "virtue" the Greek word *arête*
or, more closely, (outstanding) capableness, competency, and power. In
ethics the word refers to the adoption of the capacities and readiness to
live as a superlative human being.

Just as the individual is a unity, so also is his excellence. As a consequence, the concept for this excellence, virtue, can function in the
singular and label one's moral virtue as rectitude. Surprisingly, however, it also occurs in the plural. Since antiquity one has spoken of the
four cardinal virtues, even though one knows that there are far more
inclusive lists of virtues. One could fear, though, that such pluralization
would signal a fallback into a pre-philosophical, task-specific concept.
Actually, virtues like helpfulness or honesty do not belong to a specific
profession: musician, physician, or soccer player. They are nothing but
virtue in the singular schematized according to general human types,
rather than according to roles or task-specific situation types.

Just as there are three levels of appraisal (chapter 2.2), there are three
levels of virtue. At the lowest level one finds technical virtues in the
broadest sense, the instrumental, functional, and strategic virtues. These
virtues are not good in themselves any more than are the "bourgeois"
virtues of punctuality, love of order, frugality, and industriousness, or
even the will to follow through and a perseverance that does not allow
itself to be too easily discouraged. Everything depends upon the reason

for the invocation of such bourgeois virtues. In terms of a system of virtues, however, they are merely secondary. Many people are satisfied in life with mere substitute virtues like, for example, the "work-addicted" attorney general in the "ballad" by Max Frisch: "Work as virtue. Virtue as a substitution for joy" (*Graf Öderland*, scene 1).

For philosophical ethics, the virtuous alternative does not consist in the idea of an escalated living. Authentic life may by all means earn admiration (i.e., in accordance with the original meaning of a virtuous character). However, it is not the only path to a meaningful life. On the contrary, in a humanistic respect, authentic life has an aristocratic character, since only a few can live up to the idea of authenticity, but the lives of others need not be considered failures on that account. Philosophical ethics for this reason embraces dispositions that are open to all. Philosophical ethics grants the rank of truly primary virtue to dispositions such as honesty, helpfulness, or justice, which belong to humanity as humanity. Only these are not concerned with some character advantage but with an excellent character.

A comment on a new but by no means the newest moral philosophical debate: according to a legend prevalent in so-called virtue ethics, the concept of virtue is supposed to be unknown in modern moral philosophy. This claim comes primarily from English-speaking neo-Aristotelians and—one must, unfortunately, say—attests to their ignorance. With the standard-bearing representative of modern ethics, Kant, virtue plays an essential role. This is demonstrated already in the thought of universalizable maxims. It is portrayed even more clearly in Kant's systematic moral philosophy, *The Metaphysics of Morals*. The second part of that text devoted specifically to virtue has the title: "The Doctrine of Virtue."

In addition, there is an indirect argument against the thesis that virtue is unknown in modern philosophy: the great German neo-Aristotelian philosopher of modernity, Hegel, is skeptical about the concept of virtue, for example, in the section "Virtue and the Way of the World" in the *Phenomenology of Spirit*. Further, one should recall the more recent rehabilitation of virtue since Max Scheler 1913/1972 to be found in the philosophy of value and in phenomenology (e.g., Hartmann 1926, part 2, sections 5–8, and Hildebrand 1933; see also Bollnow 1958, Guardini 1963, and Jankélévitch 1968). As a consequence of the recent widespread forgetfulness of the tradition, this rehabilitation is found neither in the English-language *virtue ethics* that goes back to Anscombe 1958 nor in the German reception of that tradition. (On the most recent debate, see French, Uehling, and Wettstein 1988, Crisp and Slote 1997, and Rippe and Schaber 1998; on the history of the concept of modernity, see Höffe and Rapp 1997.)

9.2 Learning Virtue

Experience teaches us that virtue is not something that we possess by nature. When it comes to a natural aptitude, there is a capacity that exists prior to its application: human beings already possess completely formed capacities (e.g., of seeing, hearing, and feeling) at birth and, for example, need only open their eyes to be able to use them. The dual, not only moral but also intellectual, rational deportment toward natural incentives, in contrast, has to be learned. This is what distinguishes an education in virtue from a natural development like physical growth. Whereas there are developmental phases from shyness, through the terrible twos, and on to preadolescence that have to be passed through by everyone, rational deportment has to be learned. Furthermore, since this rational deportment isn't satisfied with words but requires manifestation in actions, even "verbal acts" such as consoling another are not something that one learns like "words" acquired through class instruction and reading, but rather through deeds, namely, through one's own doing and neglecting: through practice and habituation.

One just doesn't learn virtues the way one learns music history. Rather, one learns virtues the way one learns a musical instrument (i.e., practically, through copying the good example of another and practice). This introductory practicing is combined with a strong social component as the good replication is praised and the bad criticized. Moral philosophy follows this practical kind of learning in contrast to theoretical learning, since it maintains from the beginning that whoever always acts sobermindedly will become levelheaded; whoever predominantly acts with courage will become a courageous person, and by means of repeated just actions, one will become upright or, rather, just (e.g., Aristotle, *Nicomachean Ethics* 2.1.1103a31ff.): first, one learns to act virtuously, and only after one has learned virtuous behavior successfully can "doing right" become one's second nature.

Whether or not one possesses a virtue is not established by declarations of intent or with "pious words." Not even individual actions are sufficient. What is required is dependability, and accordingly, a relationship to natural impulses that endures by virtue of a disposition, a character or personality trait, what can be called a second nature that is not merely given, but for which we are responsible.

Although virtue as a whole is a secondary nature for which we are responsible, we do possess a natural inclination to it, or at least to two natural interests: children and adolescents prefer to be praised rather than criticized, which demonstrates that behind this interest is a concern for recognition. (Admittedly, the responsible "authorities"—parents, teachers, and peers—do not all praise the same things.) Furthermore, all possess a natural desire for happiness, which in the absence of an education in virtue hardly has a chance at success. Interest in praise and recognition binds one to a concern for the regard of others. Nevertheless, one makes oneself dependent on others in one's education in virtue only when one acknowledges social conventions ("one doesn't do that") or the personal preferences of a person of authority ("that is something that he likes/dislikes"). In the former case, one acts in the end on the basis of convention; in the latter case, on the basis of authority. The alternative consists in a kind of praise and criticism that seeks to empower the person concerned to develop his independence and personal responsibility.

In individual cases, it is not easy to establish the true justification for one's action. What one actually maintains as the reason for one's action all too often turns out to be blocked by illusions and self-deception. For example, the distinction between an orientation toward the other ("authority figure") and one's own orientation ("autonomy") with regard to praise and criticism is concerned with a justification that is often clarified only with difficulty and in truth is never entirely unequivocal (see chapter 16.3).

Within the framework of an ethic of aspiration, autonomous praise and criticism have a eudaimonistic character. They are experienced not as something foreign but as the very happiness that one in the end seeks for oneself, so that in autonomous praise and criticism one encounters oneself and can affirm it. One experiences oneself as properly praised and is able to be (at least a little) proud of oneself; or one experiences oneself as properly criticized and is disappointed or angry with oneself.

9.3 Morality in Virtue Ethics

Someone who acts on the basis of deportment acts not by accident or a happy mood. He is also not the plaything of externally imposed emotional and social influences. He lives out of his own personality and, hence, with inner conviction and with great dependability. The process of learning that leads to virtue is, therefore, only successfully complete when one, first, does what is right with consistency and, second, does it without any internal resistance.

Duty ethics distinguishes between two relationships toward what is morally correct: between what is legal and what is moral (see chapter 22.3). The first is understood to be an agreement with what is right regardless of the reasons for the agreement; the second consists in an escalation: a free agreement with what is right for its own sake. This escalation is found most frequently in a eudaimonistic virtue ethic. It is not someone who simply acts properly on the basis of inner effort who earns praise, but, rather, someone who has passed through a strenuous learning process and in the end spontaneously does the right thing with pleasure and without reluctance. Well-rounded happiness includes that one is pleased with the manner in which one acted: one does the right thing gladly and experiences it with pleasure. What is decisive, however, is not the pleasure itself but the free compliance with the right thing that is the basis for the experience of pleasure.

Where this kind of free compliance occurs, one is not satisfied with mere conformity with that which virtue demands (i.e., with legality). One performs the "more" of morality. This "more" does not play a role only in a duty ethic, but already and far more in a eudaimonistic virtue ethic. This escalation is relevant not merely to duty ethics but also to virtue ethics; it has its place not only in an ethics of will but also in a teleological ethics of aspiration.

Already in the writings of Aristotle, who to this day provides the standard of a virtue ethic, one finds the thought that what conforms to virtue should be done not for the sake of other ends but for its own sake. For example, by means of a felicitous escalation, Aristotle explains at the beginning of his discussion of justice that by being just one becomes *competent* for justice, will act justly, and, moreover, will *want to* act justly (*Nicomachean Ethics* 5.1.1129a8–9). However, even according to Aristotle, it is not enough that one does the right thing. One must be pleased with what one has done (ibid., 2.2.1104b3ff.). In this respect, we encounter a further agreement between a eudaimonistic (Aristotelian) and an autonomous (Kantian) ethic: without pleasure in a free and unconstrained assent, there is neither a complete happiness according to the former nor a full morality according to the latter. At the same time, it is confirmed that pleasure is an integral part of happiness, which leads to a further eudaimonistic imperative: "Seek those activities which you can affirm in freedom and 'with your entire being.'"

It remains to be seen whether or not one can equate this nonphysical, mental pleasure with unrestrained and freely chosen activity itself or whether this pleasure is to be taken as something added to the activity once it is completed—the latter option is comparable to the recognition of beauty in plants and animals as well as persons that only emerges in the course of one's development. Nonetheless, in both options pleasure enhances mere life itself as well as the good life. Someone who engages in an activity with delight magnifies its quality and intensity. Such pleasure can be achieved only collaterally through complete concentration on an activity. Above all, secondly, one must choose those activities to which one can commit oneself completely. Even before one can make that choice, thirdly, one must orient one's life according to one's talents and life circumstances, first, with the aid of one's upbringing; later, with a certain kind of self-discipline, so that one can be completely committed to one's chosen action. Once more, happiness shows itself as a goal that one neither quickly nor shortsightedly strives for but, rather, pursues with great deliberation and planning. One must reach that point where one is consistently aware of the eudaimonistically correct and the eudaimonistically false pleasure.

To reach this goal it is not sufficient to develop virtues. The mere cultivation of virtues can occur on the basis of less elevated motives. There are instrumental reasons even for primary virtues (i.e., as in the case of honesty—that one creates trust which brings with it social, political, and economic recognition). In order to achieve the complete self-respect of an all-around praiseworthy individual in both social and personal respects, one must embrace moral virtues not merely as the means to some other end but also to practice and perform them for their own sake. Only in this manner can one recognize the purity and strength of virtue's demands and live out of an all-around, free commitment to them in a way that takes one beyond mere proper action to an ethos of rightness, and even to morality.

How far does resolve extend the concept of deportment? If one is optimistic, one believes that the truly virtuous person is above all danger; he aspires to the proper goal without wavering. Although this expectation belongs to the concept of disposition, it is rarely achieved in reality. Rather, it is an ideal that one can only approximate. Life experience warns one to be soberly realistic, as Friedrich Dürrenmatt presents in his "tragi-comedy" *The Visit:* there are such overwhelmingly strong temptations to which even the otherwise virtuous person succumbs that lead to reckless, uncourageous, and dishonest actions. One can formulate it "ontologically" or anthropologically: humanity can never turn its second nature, virtue, exclusively into its nature.

9.4 Subjective Objectivity

The actual content of moral virtues is open for extremely different cultures and individuals. However, this openness is no relativistic capriciousness. Hence, one can assert the objectivity of moral virtues in a way that is legitimately qualified as subjective with respect to the uniqueness of different cultures and especially with respect to the individual. Let's take as our example a virtue that has not yet been discussed. Universally, one can recognize the kind of circumstance in which a danger arises because of the menace of an antagonist or a circumstance in which a disaster threatens. This universality calls forth a eudaimonistic response and suggests that there exists a common virtue of courage, which can also be called bravery, spunk, constancy, or dauntlessness, across cultures and individual circumstances.

Even though one may have survived one or another variety of danger, there are always others, and in addition new ones arise, so one can acknowledge that their challenge can be seen to have an anthropological meaning. One can, however, identify two natural and in themselves contradictory ways of addressing danger. Either one reacts in fear (i.e., with nothing but anxiety and shock that cause one to freeze or to seek flight in the face of the danger) and the individual is judged in retrospect as a coward; or one shuts one's eyes in the face of the pending danger (i.e., one trivializes or mistakes the danger and approaches it in reckless foolhardiness, blindly). In one case, one risks too much: one acts audaciously, foolishly; in the other case, one does too little: one is paralyzed. A more appropriate response, of course, consists in the mean between the two extremes.

This concept of the mean that comes from antiquity and above all from Aristotle suffers, unfortunately, from misunderstanding. Because of this misunderstanding, this crucial element in the classical definition of virtue has become opaque and empty, although for many centuries it exercised an extraordinary influence. One thinks too readily today of a segment on which there is a middle point. The consequence is that one thinks of virtue as a compromise between two emotions or passions that we then call vices. The virtuous mean would be condensed into an undamaging mean, and its innocuousness makes it a virtue. In truth, though, virtue and vice are not merely different by degree.

In antiquity, the notion of "middle" did not merely have the mathematical meaning of a point equidistant from two other points or from two straight lines. Just as well, and primarily when it came to the concept of virtue, it meant something consummate, the mean in the sense of the best form of life, which included the best manner of dealing with one's emotions or passions. The image best suited for representing this mean is a circle for which, of course, the middle is not on the circumference but assumes a prominent and exceptional position. To the extent that classical ethics determined virtue by the concept of the mean, it had nothing to do with compromise that one ennobled by the name "golden mean," but if anything with a new and at the same time excellent quality, sovereignty.

The mean also doesn't suggest that one could do too much or too little good"; for example, with bravery, that one could somehow show too much or too little courage. Rather, the mean concerns simply the capacity to think and to do the good. For this reason, it maintains a practical and reflective relationship to naturally occurring motivations. The fact that courage and civic courage are the mean between foolhardiness and cowardice does suggest that someone foolhardy has too much and the coward has too little courage. More important, though, is that both indulge in a natural tendency whereby the one knows no danger and the other cringes in the face of every danger. In contrast to both, "courage" means someone who in the face of danger acts with unwavering composure while understanding precisely what it means to be sovereign over the danger.

Exactly what the demeanor of courage is, however, is not independent of the subject. Aristotle's extension of the notion "mean" to "mean for us" evokes this awareness, although in many Aristotelian interpretations it is misapplied: in the first place, it is concerned with the kind and degree of danger. In another sense, something else is expected from someone who cringes before danger than from one who "blindly presses on." This difference in subjective temperament is not denied by eudaimonistic virtue. Furthermore, in certain professions, such as the fire department, the mountain rescue service, or the military, which are devoted to overcoming dangers, one expects an entirely different measurement of intrepidness than one would expect from a novelist or a financial adviser. (Switching from courage to generosity: generous is not only someone who because of great wealth establishes a foundation, but is also someone like the poor widow praised in the Bible who sacrificed her last mite.) The courageous person does follow a mean insofar as he neither shoulders any and all dangers nor seeks to avoid them. The appropriate attitude is achieved only in that one establishes a proper balance between one's emotions which one takes to be "reasonable" and which one assumes with sovereignty.

One is not courageous (also in the sense of civic courage) because one experiences no trace of or only a little fear and, therefore, ignores or underestimates the danger. What is decisive is rather to acknowledge fear in the face of danger but not to let that fear have the last word, thus not to be fainthearted and despondent. This capacity maintains a distance from mere fear and out of this distance first contemplates and then seizes upon the appropriate response. Both the recklessly foolhardy and the coward succumb to a quasi-instinctive, merely emotional reaction. The one believes himself capable of conquering even an overwhelming power; he succumbs to an emotional fantasy of omnipotence. The coward is terrified of even the smallest danger; he considers himself powerless. Both are missing the reflective relation to natural inclinations. The courageous person (for example, one who is courageous in the military or civic senses) confronts danger intrepidly.

The objective side of courage consists in dauntlessness and in the superior, analytic relationship to danger. The subjective side consists in an openness to differences with respect to temperament, lifestyle, and life goals established by a strategy of determining the "mean." The same applies to other moral virtues. Someone who wants to be great in terms of an athletic or political career, wishes to create an artistic or academic work, or wants to follow a life of meditation makes a huge commitment. A highly talented individual in a specific area leads quite a different life from a less talented person. Individual fate also plays a role, of course. The subjective objectivity of moral virtue consists in its recognition not only of one's ownmost possibilities on the subjective side, but also of the differences in one's situation and the skills necessary for success in that situation on the objective side.

Rather than speak of objectivity, ethicists would prefer to speak of universality. However, even defenders of virtue ethics doubt the universality of their fundamental concepts. They actually see an advantage in the nonuniversality of those concepts. In truth, though, eudaimonistic virtue ethics does have a universal core. The decisive universality in virtue ethics is content with a concentrated universalism not only of a specific kind but also with respect to principles ("duties") and motivations ("virtues"). Further, a more extensive, trans-human, and absolutely universal universalism is entirely reasonable. Just as is the case with the theory of objects, ontology, where certain fundamental claims are "true in all possible worlds," so also morality maintains that there are fundamental claims applicable to all physically conditioned, linguistic, and rational beings. If this is the case, why shouldn't there be other virtues and duties that are valid for nonhuman but morally capable beings to the degree that they experience challenges similar to humanity (e.g., with respect to the experience of pleasure and pain, the possibility of danger, and the possibility of not only oneself encountering danger but also of aiding others in an emergency)? One is justified in accepting the claim of a species-specific universalism because only human beings are known to be moral. Convinced that the concept and the principles of morality are valid for the entire human species and not solely for specific groups, societies, or epochs, this species-specific universalism neither binds itself to any particular culture, tradition, or community nor does it stop at any political, religious, or linguistic frontier.

Eudaimonistic virtues satisfy both conditions. In terms of what is crucial, they are universally valid and fulfill the second criterion that they remain open for cultural and personal differences. The very governing principle of eudaimonia (happiness), including its formal determination as the highest end toward which one can aspire, is also universally valid: persons act in all cultures and epochs toward ends, and they establish their meaning and purpose only with final ends that, viewed from the second-order final end of the aspiration for happiness, appear to be entirely meaningful.

Our four candidates that have come to the fore as final goals (pleasure, affluence, power, and prestige) continue to be universally valid. However, they are nothing more than candidates, as is confirmed by critical evaluation. They can contribute to happiness only at that point when one grants to them a certain right (but rejects their possession of an exclusive right) and when one, in addition, subjects them to a eudaimonistic reason that consists of the interaction between moral virtue and (intellectual) life wisdom.

Those who maintain that there are no universal virtues point to the fact that one does not learn virtues in a world society (already discredited as an abstract concept) but only within one's own society. This argument is correct to the extent that moral education begins within the family and similarly small groups. To draw the conclusion, however, that one lives solely according to the norms of one's own society substitutes the manner by which one acquires a particular virtue in one's social world for its status as a universal concept and its justification as a universal virtue.

Even if one's acquisition of a virtue is tied to some socially dependent particularities, one relatively quickly learns their formal and simultaneously universal core. For example, in the case of helpfulness, one learns quite quickly that one should not only help when someone has lost something but also in other emergencies; and, further, not only when one's playmates are involved. Someone who has not learned a general sensitivity for the plights of the stranger as well as the readiness to help compatible with this sensitivity (recognizing that there is a hierarchy of responsibility), for such a person this universal core of helpfulness is unknown, and he cannot claim to possess the true virtue of helpfulness.

The same is the case with courage. In one's recognition of the manner in which it is colored by one's own social context, one cannot ignore the universally valid core that in the face of danger one should neither act cowardly nor recklessly but, rather, intrepidly. The same applies to other virtues: there is a situation-specific type of behavior, a particular kind of challenge, and the principle of happiness of a particular kind depends not upon the conditions of Greek antiquity or on European contemporaries but, arguably, upon universal anthropological conditions. At the least the fundamental virtues are not signs of the habits of a particular culture, but, rather, schematizations of a praxis conducive to happiness and undertaken with respect to general human norms of passion and realms of action.

When one strips the concept of virtue from specific tasks and roles, one frees it from cultural particularities, and it achieves a universal status. Both moments of the concept of virtue maintain this anti-particularistic character and at the same time contradict the persistent prejudice that a universal ethic is incompatible with a culturally specific coloring of morality: the situation-specific type of behavior that establishes a characteristic task for each virtue depends not upon culturally distinct conditions but upon general ones. This is true for courage because there is no culture in which dangers that threaten body and life do not occur; it is true for generosity because almost everywhere one finds exchange and wealth as well as the danger of lavishness and avariciousness with respect to them; and it is true for helpfulness because, although hardship is found everywhere, there are, fortunately, persons who can respond to it. These universal conditions can manifest themselves in thoroughly different cultural and individually distinct forms. The same can be said of the concrete responses to them. The exact form of courage, generosity, and other values may full well be partially conditioned by the given society and its habits of behavior. The fundamental form, however, is independent of these particularities: the consequence is that one does in fact overcome one's natural instincts—the one to cowardice and the other to recklessness; or the one to profligacy and the other to greed—learned by normal development. Instead, one acts on the basis of reflection and with sovereignty on the basis of practical reflection or practical reason.

10 Prudence, Composure, Selflessness

Introductions to ethics are in great demand. Astonishingly, although they discuss virtue ethics, they do not engage in an analysis of particular virtues. Even representatives of more contemporary virtue ethics practice restraint. A nice exception is MacIntyre's 1981 discussion of a non-classical eudaimonistic virtue, patriotism. Another philosopher whom virtue ethicists do not yet recognize as one of their own demonstrated three years later in an exemplary way how one might go about renewing the philosophical tradition of the art of living. Under the title *L'usage des plaisirs,* which appeared in German with an echo of frivolity as *Der Gebrauch der Lüste,* Michel Foucault developed the notion of what philosophy customarily calls "prudence": this means the work of an individual on himself that is opposed to mere pleasure in life, but without succumbing to a hostile snuffing out of all sensuousness.

The specific analysis of a particular virtue is not easy, since it must avoid two opposite dangers: the temptation to be either too abstract or too concrete. Rather than succumbing to vagueness and assuming the position of a paternalistic "know-it-all" who attacks the peculiar sense of propriety of cultures and individuals, the art of blueprint knowledge is required (see chapter 7.2). One is not concerned here with traditional lists of virtues, whether they be Plato's fourfold of cardinal virtues: prudence, courage, justice, and insight (or wisdom) or Aristotle's larger catalog, although both lists can survive a skeptical examination. Our purposes are satisfied by a set of exemplary reflections based on the four life goals discussed in chapter 8. Because the two goals of affluence and power are concerned with the same virtue, equanimity, we will concern ourselves with the three other moral virtues, to which we will later add life wisdom. The consequence is a somewhat anomalous quartet of virtues, which combine the three moral virtues of prudence, composure, and self-effacement with the intellectual virtue of life wisdom. These deserve to be called cardinal virtues appropriate to *cardo* in the sense of a "door hinge" on which much depends; for example, generosity and serenity are aspects that depend upon these cardinal virtues. However, our four virtues are not exhaustive; for example, not included are virtues that we've already discussed (e.g., courage or civic courage; see chapter 9.4).

In terms of their logic of justification, our three moral virtues emerge out of the weakness of all four candidates with respect to final ends (i.e., on the path of determinate negation). What they share is a deficiency with respect to eudaimonistic reason in terms of their goal-orientation. Our moral virtues have to overcome this deficiency by cultivating a consistency of deportment.

10.1 Prudence

As with the different types of pleasure, the virtue appropriate to pleasure appears under different types. With respect to physical pleasure, there is the danger that one merely follows one's appetites (i.e., enjoyment of the joys of eating, drinking, and sexuality without considering either the context or the consequences). With respect to sensuous pleasures, the following is obvious: *omnis determination est negation* (in this context: everything that we can desire is possible only because it is accompanied by a cornucopia of exclusions and rejections). Whoever eats, doesn't sleep; and whoever does eat, prohibits someone else (at least in the moment) from eating what one is eating.

In extreme circumstances, self-indulgence can lead to licentiousness (i.e., to vice). As Thomas More's predecessor as lord chancellor, Thomas Wolsey, said of Henry VIII, he would rather risk losing half his kingdom than curtail his appetites in the least degree. In contrast, there are those who are opposed to sensuousness or who, out of anxiety, or perhaps from being overcareful, repress their sensuousness to the point of diminishing certain sense-capacities and in the extreme case losing them entirely. The alternative to both is prudence: the simultaneous coordinating and controlling adjustment of one's relationship to pleasure; hence, an adjustment in the practical sense of reflection over pleasure.

Eudaimonistic counsel in the sense of a double strategy includes the partial recommendation, first, that one reduce one's expectations for happiness. The counsel called for here points in the opposite, second, direction because it recommends an increase not of expectations but of capacities: in order to increase the capacity for happiness with respect to pleasure and pain, one develops both a hedonistic rationality and within its parameters the virtue of prudence.

What one normally understands as prudence does not expect the repression of all sensuousness, which can be accomplished only at the price of diminished strength and a shortage of agility. By no means should one become like the sensuously handicapped who live in *pace dei senso* (in freedom from the senses and longings) by refusing to develop their feelings and sentience merely to avoid the "challenges of the world." Prudence does not demand a boring lifestyle. Whoever fears from philosophers the rejection of pleasure and sensuousness learns a valuable lesson from Spinoza: "It is . . . the part of a wise man to refresh and invigorate himself in moderation with good food and drink, as also with perfumes, and with the beauty of blossoming plants, with dress, music, sporting activities, theatres and the like, in which every man can indulge without harm to another" (*Ethics,* book 4, proposition 45, note).

Prudence perpetuates an openness that is characteristic of this virtue. No philosophy presumes to decide for someone else what is good or bad for him. Prudence is a highly formal concept to the extent that it is defined as the individual's relationship to pleasure and pain. It forces no particular lifestyle. Rather, it leaves up to each person the question of lifestyle in acknowledgment that there are differences in temperament, circumstances, and interests.

It is similar with emotions. Prudence does not require that one never experience anger. Someone who never gets heated up, never gets angered by inconveniences, never is disturbed by a small affront or an experience of personal injustice, or in the face of a humiliation does not react with indignation, is emotionless. Such a person has no self-respect, which is the reason why his reaction appears to be contemptible. In contrast, someone who possesses prudence is neither disturbed by every little thing nor angered by justifiable criticism, but he does fulfill two conditions: his "revenge impulse" is invoked only in the case of justifiable provocation, but in that circumstance he reacts in an appropriate fashion (i.e., not with exorbitant anger or uncharitable vengeance).

One often equates prudence with self-control and self-restraint. In fact, prudence is not content with this merely negative power (i.e., the rejection of the false). It consists far more in an attitude toward what is proper. The acquisition of a positive fundamental attitude of the self toward its own emotionality opposes not only uncontrolled emotionality and self-indulgent desires but also their elimination. One who is prudent pursues, with respect to pleasure and pain, provisional and final ends that together constitute a coherence which makes possible a successful and meaningful life.

Corresponding to the levels of the good, one can distinguish three levels of prudence—even when one often does not name the first level "prudence": this is the unassuming, *technical* prudence that enables one actually to accomplish some kind of pleasure to the extent that one pursues it. It is to be distinguished from the more challenging *pragmatic* prudence, which answers the question of which pleasure allows its integration into an overall successful life. In order to successfully achieve an enduring well-being that is compatible with different kinds of pleasure, one must refrain from the despotism of momentary desires, as well as frequently delay the satisfaction of some, restrain some, and even entirely repress other desires. Finally, the highest, *moral* prudence resists the reckless pursuit of pleasure. It avoids any pleasure that harms the self-esteem and the legitimate interests of others.

Life experience contributes some other pieces of advice. Two of them have already been identified. The one says: "Don't seek mere instantaneous gratification, but where needed practice restraint as well as exertion!" These latter practices are capable of increasing cumulative pleasure. The other piece of advice: "In good times and bad, remember joys of the past that can mitigate the unpleasantness of the present!" A third piece of advice appeals to the higher pleasure of anticipation: "Think about anticipated pleasures in advance and delay their realization in order to lengthen their pleasure!" A fourth piece of advice: "Learn the capacity of pleasant anticipation and hold to it even when one knows that not all dreams are realized!" Socrates offers a further piece of advice: "Be prudent in that, with respect to the many options one has, there is much that one doesn't need!" A further piece of advice: "Don't be captive to anger or hate!" The capacity to distance oneself even from something that one desires greatly also belongs to the art of living.

Prudence is neither something one has by birth nor something that automatically occurs as a course of physical growth. Furthermore, obtaining control over particular and obstinate, naturally occurring motivating drives is not something that one accomplishes in one heroic decision. What is in general true for all the other virtues is true for prudence, as well: even broad outlines of the power to nullify egocentricity are acquired only through a lengthy educational process that is, above all, practical and not theoretical: it comes through practice, not mere memorization. Biographically, this educational process begins before any formal learning, namely in the earliest childhood phases of devoted parental care and concern for the child's welfare, which provide the emotional basis for a self- and world-confidence that decidedly aids later development. Only through the course of parenting do ever more elements of self-development emerge.

Although the threat to prudence (above all the incessant drive to consumption) is a general danger, it is manifest in terms of epoch-specific challenges: today's world with its huge population and worldwide, ever-rising individual expectations requires more than mere personal prudence. In order to slow down if not reverse the multifaceted and uninhibited depletion of the environment, we also need a global and collective prudence.

However, there is an analogous kind of depletion of one's personal resources. No matter how healthy, vigorous, talented, skilled, and robust one is, one's reserve of physical, psychological, social, and cultural power is capable of development and can benefit from undiscovered reserves, but it is not limitless. Just as each generation has a responsibility to preserve the natural order for the next, so also the individual is not permitted to exhaust his personal resources. In fact, one needs to hold oneself open with respect to one's physical, psychological, and intellectual strengths in full recognition that there are limits involved. Which contemporary proportion of self-challenge and overload is going to prove beneficial can be determined only by experience: Will the excess of stimulation like the growing power of the visual media be beneficial? Will it depend upon a flood of information? Will it depend upon a concentration of regulations and, simultaneously, a greater amount of social networking? By no means last or least, will it depend upon cell phones, faxes, and e-mail?

Even the most superficial examination of cultural history warns against a moralizing critique of contemporary society, because the problem here is by no means new. Already the Stoic Seneca complained in *On the Shortness of Life* (section 9) that people devote their lifetime to meaningless activities rather than to engage their limited time rationally. Seneca was concerned that one establish a proper balance between one's private and public life. One should not forget one's "own" time for philosophical and literary study by investing all of one's energies in "public" time.

This critique can be directed at least in part at our contemporary culture, whose spectrum of engagement is so broad. However, a core, which is the limitedness of human life, belongs to the human condition. Independent of any specific diagnosis, one cause is obvious: whereas many are "condemned" to inaction because of unemployment or sickness, others suffer from the loss of leisure time without which one cannot begin to find time for reflection, for nonvocational activities, or for an enduring personal relationship. A small word from the mouth of a great thinker, Blaise Pascal: "When I have set myself to consider the various agitations of human life, . . . I have discovered that the unhappiness of men arises from one single fact: that they cannot stay quietly in their own chamber" (*Pensées,* no. 139).

There are many kinds of prudence known to the philosophical tradition. In light of them, we need a (relatively) "new prudence," given the danger over the pretensions associated with the concept. This new notion of prudence consists in the cultivation of reserves of resistance: in the capacity to be able to say "No!" to one's own desires and to a certain extent to abstain from certain temptations; further, in the capacity to limit the tasks one undertakes, as well as the talent to be able to say "No!" to others without alienating them. Often, the "Yes!" one says comes less from magnanimity than it does from cowardice, which tries to take on everything out of anxiety that one not be accepted.

10.2 Composure

When it comes to the second life goal, the striving for affluence, there are two "temptations" that often emerge: an avarice that only wants more and more and a miserliness that does not want to share with anyone ("hard-heartedness") and that often doesn't want to spend anything even on oneself. The alternative to miserliness consists in profligacy. Both avarice and miserliness are combated by the attitude with respect to material goods that they are to be neither "thrown out the window" nor clung to in anxiety. Someone who is generous and guards against profligacy as well as miserliness practices the eudaimonistically proper valuation of material goods. Rather than "being married to" his possessions, he is their sovereign and disposes of them in ways that are appropriate—above all, with respect to others—without giving away so much that one puts oneself in the poorhouse.

There is a virtue that is deeper than generosity. This virtue restrains that motivation which succumbs to a life driven by affluence. Because this same motivating power is found in combination with the third life goal, the aspiration for power, there is a common alternative to an addiction to both money and power. This alternative is concerned among other things with combating one's anxiety over the future: in one case with one's concern that one will not have enough material resources in the future; in another case with one's concern that one will not have enough power. The sphere of application for this alternative, however, extends much farther. This circumstance increases the importance of an attitude of anxiety that is absent from the classical Aristotelian list of eudaimonistic virtues. The reason for this absence might be its breadth of applicability. It establishes limits to the core interest itself, one's own happiness, in a way that relativizes eudaimonism as a whole.

The network of forces within which life occurs is dependent upon natural and social parameters that are only partly capable of being influenced by the individual, and often enough one is not even aware of them. If there is to be success in life despite these limits, one requires a paradoxical skill: one must be capable of taking control of something over which one has no control. Therefore, one needs—according to a further piece of advice—the capacity and readiness to perceive and to acknowledge the parameters. One must add to this an acknowledgment of a second order: one must be able to accept the limits that constitute the parameters of one's own capacity to grasp the parameters. Someone who accepts his own limits and develops this open acceptance as a fundamental orientation is skilled in a second virtue, composure. Once again, we're not talking about some paternalistic concept of life but about a practical self-relationship that remains open to the differences of temperament, life situation, and life interest.

Composure opposes an impatience that is incapable of adjusting to a situation but, rather, already in its perception of the situation wants to modify the situation to make it conform to its own preconceptions. Composure is also to be contrasted with mere compliance and weakness, by means of which one surrenders spinelessly to a situation. The extreme example of what in the end is an ominous indecisiveness is presented by Karl-Heinz Ott in his novel *Endlich Stille* [*Finally Still*]: the first-person narrator is so pressured by a perfect stranger into a self-serving pseudo-friendship that, initially, the narrator over weeks drinks himself to near-unconsciousness and only afterward flees his own apartment because he was not "master of his own house." Upon his return, he convinces the intruder to go on a hike in the mountains where, apparently as planned by the narrator, the intruder plunges to his death from a cliff.

Situated between using force and passive tractability, between activity and passivity, composure consists in the readiness to accept nature, others, and not least one's own self with all of its personal history while, simultaneously, not denying that one is a free and creative agent. Neither too accepting nor too petty-minded with respect to one's self, one seeks, where required, to develop one's capacities without agonizing over one's failures. Furthermore, one accepts that life is accompanied by unpleasant surprises as well as by unsurprising unpleasantnesses like aging. Nevertheless, one lives in equanimity. Composure also escapes the dictatorship of the rat race and is satisfied with "wasting" time in leisure.

This virtue, which is an expression of self-confidence, basic trust in one's world, as well as a strong ego, includes the readiness neither to remain undecided nor to act hastily. Someone is composed who knows how to wait for the right moment and understands not only how to estimate but also how to implement a proper measure in his actions. On occasion, composure demands that one overcome that restlessness that Goethe counters with experience in his poem "Remembering" ["Erinnerung"]: "Do you always want to ramble?/See, the Good is so close by." Properly, the poem emphasizes a creativity of a particular kind ("Learn to seize happiness"), which allows the conclusion: "For happiness is always there."

Because the German word *Glück* (happiness) has so many meanings, one sometimes wants to speak rather of meaning (*Sinn*), although often with a negative overtone. One readily speaks today of a "*Sinnkrise*" (a crisis of meaning) but doesn't mean by it a life crisis that everyone can at some point experience, but a crisis in society. One makes a "*Sinnverlust*" (a loss of meaning) responsible for the crisis. In opposition to this pessimistic-moralizing undertone—"everything was better in the good old days"—one attempts another diagnosis: in contrast to the defeatism of the loss of meaning, one calls attention to a gain in meaning that lies in the heretofore unrecognized and unknown wealth of possibilities for a meaning-filled life. If one cuts away the structurally illusionary expectations for meaning (i.e., pure indulgence and mere striving for affluence and power), there is always left over an excess of meaningful life possibilities. In their fullness is mirrored again the *conditio humana*, an openness to the world and multiplicity of skills.

An excess of possibilities also has its costs. A first example: a form of life that to this point appears to be the only valid one is relativized, which jolts one's security. Whoever, nevertheless, continues to talk about a "loss of meaning" constructs a perspectival illusion. It is not meaning itself that is lost but, rather, the certainty with respect to the form in which one can expect such meaning. A second cost lies in the complexity and consequent crisis of decision that one in turn craves in its former familiar simplicity. This craving is social-psychologically always understandable as a "nostalgia for meaning." However, it pursues the "pleasure principle" and not a "reality principle," and, therefore, is an inadequate strategy for dealing with the challenge of this new complexity of possibilities.

Because human beings have different talents and interests, the curtailing of the wealth of possibilities would result in the elimination of important opportunities. The alternative, however, means that those concealed possibilities confront the individual who is tied only to the sensuous with great challenges. As a consequence, expansion of the horizon of meaning brings with it new opportunities and new dangers. We encounter here as well as elsewhere the cost-benefit analysis formulated by Friedrich Nietzsche with a pinch of provocation: "Man is more sick, uncertain, changeable, indeterminate than any other animal. . . . Certainly he has also dared more, done more new things, braved more and challenged fate more than all the other animals put together. . . . How should such a courageous and richly endowed animal not also be the most imperiled, the most chronically and profoundly sick of all sick animals?" (*On the Genealogy of Morals*, section 3, segment 13).

Dangers to the wealth of meaning require a new capacity for the discernment of meaning. This new capacity is an orientation toward the future that holds itself open to life's possibilities. It begins as "a small openness": whoever is disappointed by a friendship does not close off the possibility for a new one. The second, "median openness," is concerned with changes associated with life stages: falling in love, career success, the raising of children—all are possibilities that contribute to a meaningful and happy life, but they aren't possibilities available at every stage of life. Finally, we can speak of a "large openness" which knows that certain projections of meaning are used up and emptied: for the individual, a society, or a generation. With the unavailability of such projections, humanity is forced to seek new meaning.

No person, either the philosopher or the nonphilosopher, either the religious believer or the nonbeliever, is immune to the danger of both the small and the great loss of meaning. As a consequence, it belongs to the human condition that the stumble into a crisis of meaning is no "disgrace." More likely, such crises are an indicator of a free and venturesome style of life. Here one is not talking only about a readiness to embrace certain risks of meaning but also about the capacity to live with a (temporary) despondency without falling into self-doubt. In addition to a small composure, one also requires a "large" one that knows how to live with crises of meaning. A small part of such a large composure: "Allow no mournfulness! The most difficult work in the world" (Uwe Timm, *Rot,* 2003, 206). A further piece of advice proposes, therefore: "Develop opportunely the capacity even when still in despondency to find one's way back to the 'hope' that is the vital force of life, whether it be to a hope beyond all hope for which there are religious models, for instance in Christianity, or also nonreligious examples like Sisyphus!" Because: "Have courage! Hope is something that can be very dangerous, but without it, life would be horrible, empty of joy, and well-nigh immoral" (Anthony Doerr, *Winklers Traum vom Wasser,* 2005, 42 [*About Grace,* 278]).

Life acquires an internal splendor should the two virtues of prudence and composure occur together. Life escalates to the serenity of an enduring joyous heart when sustained by a calm cheerfulness free from all melancholy. As Epicurus said, one who possesses these virtues in their fullest sense walks "like a god among men" ("Epicurus to Menoeceus," 33). Nature gives a paradigm of a perfectly blue sky without clouds. Serenity is not confined to cultural boundaries. In the Chinese philosophy of the legendary Lao Tzu, the founder of Taoism, serenity brings one close to the ideal of a truly authentic person: *zhenren* (*chen-jen*). What is meant by this term is a state of mind arrived at through self-cultivation in which one is free from desires and the calculation of self-interest and leads a simple, calm life free from torments (see Shen 2003).

How does one acquire this virtue of serenity? Epicurus attempted to achieve it through rational means: he explained that humanity's anxieties are baseless, its appetites are capable of being controlled, and its pains are conquerable. The poet, Schiller, claimed that one can experience it through "beautiful art"; the speculative philosopher, Hegel, in contrast believed in his profession. The gap between the knowledge of a rational explanation and actually being able to live according to that knowledge (the gap between a "knowing that" and a "knowing how") speaks against Epicurus. The fact that the stage is not life itself speaks against Schiller. Philosophy can grasp principles, but it cannot bring about a life in complete conformity with principles. What is true in general for virtues remains valid in this case: the poetic arts, philosophy, or other things (e.g., music, belief in God, etc.) may be helpful, but serenity is something that one can acquire only through practice in life circumstances that one cannot wish either for oneself or for someone else: through practice in serenity itself in the face of the dark clouds of life.

10.3 Selflessness Out of Self-Interest

Composure contributes to our discussion of the fourth form of life. Composure's *modest* rank, discussed here, resists the danger that one becomes too much a slave to one's ambitions—in other words, resists the danger that one neglects one's other interests to embrace the aphorism "more appearance than reality" or that one succumbs to recklessness. It may be that not everyone finds such composure easy, but it is recognized because its eudaimonistic value is obvious. In contrast, though, it is a different story when it comes to a greater composure within the framework of human interaction.

The conditions for the application of this greater composure are found, as with other virtues, in many cultures: friendship, partnership, and love have a special place when it comes to a successful life. Philosophy is familiar with these forms, from Plato and Aristotle to Scheler (1913/1973); and to Spaemann (1993, 141ff.) and Frankfurt (2004) via Epicurus, Augustine, and Kant: someone for whom material goods are too superficial and profane finds wealth in human relationships and doesn't exclude the exceptional case of falling in love, which the poets correctly praise as an eternal elation. With Goethe one praises this love as an extension and a savoring of the heights and depths of life: "Cheerful/And tearful/Then pensive again./Yearning/And burning/In quivering pain;/Soaring to heaven,/Cast down from above/Happy alone/Is the person in love" (*Egmont*, act 3).

Stable relationships contribute twofold to happiness: they are the presupposition for and simultaneously a form in which happiness occurs. Above all, close personal relationships draw upon two peculiarities. *First*, partnerships and parenting are especially dependent upon an expanse of time, if not an entire life. They do require a restricting of freedom; however, this restriction occurs "in freedom" and simultaneously increases it: on the one hand, as long as the ties endure, they offer a protective zone in which one can pursue one's interests unconcerned about any hostilities and in which one can acknowledge one's weak-nesses. To that extent, one can live in freedom and seek new contexts and activities for the expression of freedom. However, in order for the ties to endure, one must accept others as they are and acknowledge their differences. At least by this point there occurs what one can most appropriately call a paradox: one gains through loss; personal expansion comes through personal restraint. Wisdom literature names it: "Liberation from the confinements of one's own heart" (Psalms 18:20).

Within the principle of happiness, personal restraint is not the consequence of a noble, in any case a frequently self-deceiving altruism. The reason lies in an unusual form of enlightened self-interest: out of self-interest one denies self-interest as the final basis of one's actions. In Nathaniel Hawthorne's short story "Egoism," there is a snake in a man's chest that consumes him. Only when he follows the advice to "forget yourself in the idea of another" is he able to conquer his illness. Authentic but not self-addicting, happiness reveals itself in a paradoxical tendency: in order to find oneself, one must outgrow oneself, and in a certain sense lose oneself. A highly unusual side to humanity emerges with its social character, which results in another piece of advice: "If you want more than usual happiness, you should follow your self-interests in the extraordinary form of selflessness."

This piece of advice contains far more than the somewhat trivial, negative form of the Golden Rule with its challenge not to harm one another: "What you don't want others to do to you, don't do to others!" Even the escalation to the positive formulation is not adequate: "Do unto others as you would have them do unto you!" What is at stake is more than an anticipated reciprocity because, with the maxim: "Give to others so that you will be given!" one is merely making a strategic investment in the future. Instead, here we have in mind an investment by means of which one hopes for and perhaps even expects a successful return, but which is nevertheless not a merely strategic move.

Whoever engages in an escalated concern for others in an attitude of selflessness develops behavior that bursts apart the usual alternative between egoism and altruism. These patterns begin with the already acknowledged largesse that doesn't cling to one's own material resources. True largesse does not act on the basis of strategic grounds; for example, to make friends or to acquire prestige. Rather, the magnanimous person gives simply because he has what others lack. Although the truly magnanimous individual does not invest in the economic sense, he is making an investment with respect to social capital that can pay out positively with respect to connections and prestige.

Magnanimity is not limited to material objects. Whoever employs his resources for the benefit of the public and, for example, voluntarily engages in some form of public service without thought of strategic interest practices a social, cultural, or scientific magnanimity, depending upon the sphere of engagement.

Some philosophers in their discussion of the principle of happiness recommend avoiding any form of social happiness. The following maxim is attributed to Epicurus: "Live in concealment" (Usener 1887/1966, fragment 551). One should seek neither public office nor recognition, neither honor nor fame, because one has no defense against the malevolence and intrigues of others. Epicurus's advice is not unreasonable, but it entirely ignores eudaimonistic openness. Depending on personal idiosyncrasy, one enjoys avoiding dangers or perceives them as challenges in which one seeks to prove oneself, whether it be in sports, society, art, science, or politics. The status that one obtains by such efforts, even when not sought directly, can be understood as a happy bonus. For example, writers like Franz Kafka and Samuel Beckett conspicuously avoided the public media and were averse to any and all kinds of praise. Nevertheless, they achieved the highest fame.

Included in selflessness is the capacity to wish, on occasion, that one could harm others either out of "revenge" for some injustice or out of jealousy, resentment, or envy by preventing someone from achieving greater success than oneself. Appropriately, in the Middle Ages one called the last two emotions *vitia poenalia:* vices that punish the self. In agreement, popular wisdom warns against being "eaten away by resentment or jealousy." It is self-evident that one should avoid any and all forms of sadism and also that one avoid any feeling of deep gratification (perhaps a touch is okay) over the suffering of others, and, above all, no strong Schadenfreude.

A special kind of selflessness consists in that form of friendship in which one is concerned neither with mutual pleasure nor profit but with friendship for its own sake. In such a relationship one combines closeness with distance, so that in reciprocal respect each remains himself while, nevertheless, connected in close togetherness.

Another kind of enhanced selflessness consists in the negative and positive aspects of sympathy. In circumstances of an accident, disappointment, or suffering by others, one experiences the negative sympathy of com-miseration [*Mitleid*] and not merely an aesthetic-passive feeling. Rather, one tries to assist either with an appropriate consolation or a proper action. True sympathy is not a concealed kind of scorn, but arises out of respect for the other. In contrast to any aspect of negative sympathy, though, one recalls the positive that consists in a desire for the well-being of the other, even in a shared *joy* [*Mitfreude*] that celebrates the joy of the other in a way that strengthens it for him. Sympathy is summarized by the proverb: "Shared suffering is half-suffering," whereas shared joy is expressed by the proverb: "Shared joy is double joy." Where jealousy and envy reduce the joy of success, shared joy brings with it a positive duplication: shared joy reciprocally increases the joy of all concerned. For this reason, it is understandable that one shares joyful events with others, so that one can without hesitation say that the escalated form of shared joy, common celebration, belongs to the art of living.

Many cultures have a formal sense of ecstasy, a release of the self from everything normal, an experience in which sensuous pleasure and materiality, even the respect of others, lose all meaning. In classical philosophy, namely in Aristotle, ecstasy means a *bios theôrêtikos,* or a life dedicated to philosophy and theoretical knowledge. The Christian and Islamic Middle Ages turned this life ideal into a *vita contemplativa* or contemplative life that dedicated itself to religious meditation beyond theoretical knowledge and found its highest expression in a direct experience of God. Buddhism seeks ecstatic selflessness in a form of meditation that takes several forms but, in the end, seeks an enlightenment free from all religious content. According to the Buddhist masters, enlightenment can be described only in paradoxes. For example, a student complained to his Zen master: "I have nothing," whereupon the master demands: "Then throw it away!" The anecdote ends with: "And then he experienced enlightenment."

The neutrality demanded by a philosophical art of living, an ethical liberalism, does not view such suggestions as silly. It remains open to them all without privileging any. It doesn't even take sides with that which is extraordinary. It leaves the decision up to the individual whether or not he expects a successful life in the exceptional or within the framework of the ordinary; in other words, the individual must determine for himself what is satisfying by means of prudence, composure, and a modest form of selflessness.

11 Wisdom Rather Than Calculation

11.1 An Empirical-Rational Calculation

Obviously a successful life requires more than the right goals. It needs the appropriate means, as well. The competency required involves far more than a simple technical reason in the service of well-defined goals, since this competency is pledged to the service of the difficult goal of a happy life.

Affluence, for example, can be easily measured—at least with respect to the financial part, although it is more difficult to measure when it comes to an investment portfolio, real estate, and art collections. However, when it comes to establishing their value in terms of the goal of personal happiness (i.e., their "existential" value), these tell us very little. Many value only their personal accomplishments, what they have achieved on their own, whereas others seek affluence to get the recognition of others. Regardless, eudaimonistic worth does not increase proportionally to the size of one's affluence. Even if one denies proportionality, the following axiom is not valid: more affluence brings more happiness. Whoever out of avarice aspires to affluence lives with the worry that his absolute value will decline. Whenever envy is added, the sense of well-being declines—even when it comes to a Croesus—as soon as one's affluence is surpassed by another's. In contrast, one who lives modestly without avarice or envy is already entirely satisfied with very little.

Power, too, is difficult to measure. At a time when a country possesses hegemonic control, one may declare its president the most powerful person in the world. However, one is then speaking only in terms of the currency of political power, although there is also intellectual, moral, and religious, not to mention media, power as well. A further difficulty: there is no "conversion table" for these other power currencies that would allow one to convert one into the other: is the president of a country with 270 million citizens more powerful than the leader of a church with a billion members? The most difficult form of power to measure is the eudaimonistic one, and without question it would be incorrect to believe that the more power one possesses the happier one is.

With the third option of honor or prestige there are even more evaluative options. One can speak of social, media, and political prestige, artistic, literary, intellectual, and scientific reputation, as well as recognition in sports, humanitarian service, and much more. In addition, one must speak of limitless "small change," for example, easy listening and electronic music, poetry, and dime-store novels, as well as the multiple disciplines in the academic and sports worlds. Not least, we encounter here again non-proportionality: there is no guarantee that with growing prestige one's happiness will also grow; it can just as well stagnate or decline.

Given that the eudaimonistic value of the three life goals of affluence, power, and prestige remains unclear, the pressure mounts to seize on the final goal, pleasure, and to concentrate exclusively on a pleasure-displeasure sum. This fundamental thought is by no means new, and it is well known to critiques of a mere ethic of pleasure. Already Plato sketched in his *Protagoras* a pleasure-calculation according to which one adds up the pleasurable on the one hand and the unpleasurable on the other and evaluates what is closest and most distant, and, finally, chooses the course with the best pleasurable-displeasurable sum total.

Even according to a modern critic of such a pleasure ethic, Kant, what counts for a life of mere indulgence is simply "how strong, how long, how easily attained, and how frequently repeatable" the pleasure is (*Critique of Practical Reason,* section 3, note 1). The positive program driven by the notion that one can calculate pleasure and even happiness on the basis of empirical knowledge emerges in the work of the first classical representative of utilitarianism, the legal theorist and social reformer Jeremy Bentham. Because he defines happiness according to pleasure and displeasure (i.e., hedonistically), one calls his happiness calculus "hedonistic" or a "hedonistic calculus." His example allows for an empirical testing of the possibility of a happiness calculus.

According to the definitive formulation of Bentham's *Principles of Morals and Legislation* (chapter 4), one calculates the pleasure or happiness value of an action or rule of action by appraising its consequences according to six criteria: with respect to (1) its intensity, (2) its duration, (3) the degree of certainty with which one can expect pleasure or displeasure, and (4) the closeness or remoteness of its occurrence, as well as (5) its fecundity and (6) its purity (by which one means the likelihood that the pleasure will bring collateral pleasure and that displeasure will bring collateral displeasure rather than their opposites). One treats each of these criteria as if happiness were a sum total of money. Positive values of pleasure are added, from which negative values of displeasure are subtracted, so that one calculates the total hedonistic utility in a mathematical and certain manner. In the last step (7), one adds up the happiness values for everyone concerned. The choice of an action is rational in the sense of the utilitarian principle to the extent that the collective utility is larger (or at least not smaller) than any other possible course of action.

In order to be applicable, the calculus makes three assumptions. First, we can accept for the moment the hedonistic assumption that everything important in life can be grasped by means of the concepts of pleasure and displeasure. As we saw in chapter 8.1, pleasure has the character of a final end, and the questionable exclusive claim of this final end we can leave aside. According to the second, empirical assumption, two elements are given as data of objective experience: the possible actions among which one must choose and the pleasure-displeasure values of each possibility.

The third assumption consists in the demand for calculability combined with the thought of maximization. Happiness is taken to be capable of being increased, and included in humanity's pursuit of pleasure is the interest in achieving the highest level, the maximum. This gradation is not foreign to the principle of happiness because one can certainly evaluate the course of life of an individual as more or less happy. The utilitarian calculus, however, demands more. It presupposes the quantification of pleasure and displeasure in the exacting form of cardinal numbers. An ordinal knowledge is not sufficient (i.e., that one option is first, another second, a further one third, etc.). In order to arrive at a pleasure-displeasure sum total, one must be able to say that one option, for example, is 2.65 times more pleasurable than another.

In an empirical and rational age, a calculus that combines both elements, an empirical-rational happiness calculus, is warmly welcomed. For one cannot achieve what is eudaimonistically correct purely rationally, say by derivation from a highest principle or by mere calculation; one is concerned rather with empirical knowledge and its appropriate research. Nor can one achieve what is eudaimonistically correct purely empirically, because the information must be "rationally" processed.

Nevertheless, it is legitimate to ask whether such a calculus is not simply welcome but also true to its subject in a functionally valuable way. With respect to the more modest demands of a cost-benefit calculus (rather than a happiness or pleasure calculus), its proposal is unquestionably valuable. Not only for economic questions but also with respect to life-style, cost-benefit reflections are helpful, sometimes even requisite. For example, one deploys one's financial as well as time resources within a tolerable limit because over the long haul one cannot live beyond one's means.

How does it fare, however, with such a highly formidable goal as happiness? Bentham's calculus has been subject to many adjustments (e.g., Mill 1861/1949 and Broome 1995). These do not eliminate the fundamental difficulties of the calculus, however; several doubts are obvious (see Höffe 1985, part 1, especially chapter 4). The first difficulty, actually a bundle of difficulties, is concerned with the foundation. Bentham's calculus is not directly concerned with pleasure and displeasure but with actions whose hedonistic meaning not only must be sought but also worked out.

One can commence the challenge so: although this calculus does not start naively with pleasure and displeasure themselves but with the "expected" pleasure/displeasure, it sounds, nonetheless, like it is concerned with an objective value (to be sure at the moment still unknown) that is comparable to weather conditions or stock market prices which transpire independent of one's behavior. When it comes to the weather or the stock market, one responds to uncertainties by combining two strategies. The first strategy simply accepts the more moderate prognosis, which one can accept with the weather or stock averages, but, in the case of pleasure/displeasure, it is questionable whether one can establish cardinal values for them. The second strategy develops more complex prognostication instruments. When it comes to the weather, one employs mathematical chaos theory; with the stock markets, the theory of wholes whose parts correspond to the basic model of the whole, fractal geometry. However, when it comes to balancing pleasure and displeasure, these two strategies come up against the limit that in the end the manifest hedonistic relationships are not only subjective, namely, different for each individual, but also in a strong sense they are subject-dependent. They are co-determined by a person's behavior, including his manner of perception. What is important is not first the mathematically calculable sum of utility or "utility expectation" but the sobriety and probity with which one goes about establishing the foundation for the valuation.

Take as a simple illustration of the second strategy a party that offers each participant an equal hedonistic potential. Should the festival actually take place, it can be the case, despite the presumed equality, that some experience more, others less, pleasure, and others actually experience displeasure. This is because hedonistic potential presents possibilities only in a global sense that each individual must see, seize upon, and transform into personal well-being. A festival that starts well but turns out sour makes very obvious how individual happiness, despite a long time of exhausting but in the end even successful work on the part of others, occurs as a consequence of the active and creative interaction with elements in part presented to it and in part influenced by the individual's own particular life circumstances.

The phenomenon of anticipation confirms the fact that neither the size of the hedonistic potential nor even its positive or negative promise are subjectively independent determinations. Anticipation of a festival or of a reunion contributes an important element to the sum total of joy involved. In addition, the actual enjoyment can turn out to be greater than the expected pleasure, which only magnifies the total pleasure. However, the actual enjoyment can turn out to be smaller than one expected and when it turns to disappointment can erode the bottom line. Finally, there is a pleasure of remembrance in which a "happy temperament" holds the past pleasure in an enhanced (a less happy temperament in a reduced) pleasurable memory.

Obviously there are counterstrategies. In the expectation of a disappointment, one can engage in a kind of hedonistic discounting; in other words, a dampening of anticipations in which they are adjusted to more realistic expectations or even more sparingly indulged as a precaution. Anticipation, however, is already a form of pleasure, a hedonistically important factor that discounting reduces in advance. As a consequence, hedonism shoots itself in the foot, namely, by degrading the sum total of happiness. Should one's anticipation be too strongly disappointed, one experiences displeasure even when in the eyes of others the event under consideration appears to have been a success.

Furthermore, the primary pleasure one has been anticipating depends upon one's own efforts and the efforts of strangers. Neither a reunion nor a festival are "determined" events with respect to their hedonistic value. Their pleasure-displeasure balance sheet depends upon those involved and the participants' hedonistic creativity that is capable of mastering a given situation with respect to a possible highest sum total of pleasure when in conformity with the life rule: "Make the best of it!" Similar to anticipation, the preliminary apprehensiveness can be unrealistically high or, in the form of insouciance, carelessly low. It is extremely difficult to determine by which set of expectations one best discerns the balance between apprehensiveness and the primary pleasure. Not even for one and the same person are there halfway-certain expectations.

One could name this *first* bundle of difficulties "hedonistic uncertainty." In fact, though, we are not concerned with a lack of knowledge (there is no cognitive deficit) but with a practical life task. In order to fulfill that task, one does not need the knowledge of a state of affairs but two hedonistic skills. In the preparatory phase, it is important to establish the proper attitude toward pleasant anticipation and apprehensiveness; in the primary phase, what counts is creativity with respect to already experienced and yet-to-be-experienced pleasure as well as in the avoidance of already experienced and possibly yet-to-be-experienced displeasure. In any event, before one can calculate at least some of the sub- and special tasks, one needs general experience in common sense.

A *second* bundle of difficulties is buried in the task of determining from among the alternative courses of action the one(s) relevant to one's goals. Once again, here we are not concerned with an objective standard [*Vorgabe*] but with a subjectively dependent task [*Aufgabe*] because the options are not like how one discovers a strange but already existing continent. Someone who wants to maximize his pleasure balance requires in addition to hedonistic-practical creativity a hedonistic-intellectual creativity, more precisely: commonsense practical-intellectual creativity. Its concern is the determination (if necessary, the discovery) of the best options for the accomplishment of one's goals.

The *third* difficulty arises from the object of one's calculations. In the classical utilitarianism of Bentham and Mill, one is concerned with an action or with a rule that governs action. For example, should I honestly answer only the question of the moment (a hedonism of action), or when it comes to questions of honesty should I decide fundamentally *against* lying and *in favor of* the truth (a hedonism of rules)? According to the theory of life goals, these questions stand together and require in advance a decision with respect to their theoretical legitimacy: do I want to live a life of pleasure, affluence, power, or prestige, or do I want to lead a life based on moral virtues? Depending upon which option one chooses, there is a different currency when it comes to pleasure, and there are different values of pleasure, and, finally, there is a difference with respect to the balance sheet: whoever wants to be upright experiences shame when it comes to a lie (i.e., displeasure); whoever, in contrast, wants power, affluence, or indulgence can decide on occasion that a lie is instrumentally good and thereby experience pleasure. There are some who even experience satisfaction in having tricked someone when it comes to a successful deception.

A *fourth* difficulty is caused by the necessary comparison of pleasure-displeasure totals for the same person, the inner-personal comparison: Should one dine alone, with one's family, with business colleagues, or rather with a friend? If the situation arises, should one cook with them, alternatively cook in turns, or go to a restaurant? Should one prefer a theater performance or a concert over a visit to a restaurant? Should one aspire to what promises to be a pleasurable career that will require an education over several years, in which at least some part of those years will require great sacrifice? The answers to such questions depend obviously not only on social constraints but also on personal preferences. These latter preferences, however, are not so determinately given that the person deciding about what will maximize his happiness could simply know them like independent facts.

Fifth, concrete situations make a quantitative comparison (almost) impossible. For example, one does not merely have to compare the joy of dining with that of a visit to a concert. One must also weigh the pleasantness of satisfactions that come with varying wants (i.e., the pleasure of change) against the pleasantness of successfully pursuing a career or of a successful partnership (i.e., the pleasure of an enduring state of affairs). Given the absence of a currency exchange rate (a "pleasure" currency rate), the very comparison by one and the same individual is an illusion; at best there are values determined by rules of thumb.

A *sixth* difficulty threatens an inferior optimization: given the complexity of the situation, there is a danger that one will privilege those aspects for which there appear to be easier formal determinations and that one will push the more difficult aspects into the background. Because sensuous pleasures and material success are easier to determine, one is inclined to orient oneself more toward these and to give lesser weight to those eudaimonistically essential but hardly quantifiable goals like a social relationship or self-respect. Thereby, there is the danger of maximizing certain aspects that impair the whole; namely, suboptimization.

Bentham is well aware of the diversity of pleasure. In the *Principles of Morals and Legislation* he distinguishes, purely formally, between simple and complex, self- and other-oriented (chapter 5), as well as between primary and secondary pleasures (chapter 6). Furthermore, with respect to concrete content, he proposes a rich palette of fourteen kinds of simple pleasures that include subsets. The palette begins with sensuous pleasures, joys with respect to affluence and craftsmanship, and extends over the pleasures of friendship, good reputation, and power to joys of memory, the imagination, expectation, and, finally, to socially anchored pleasures as well as the pleasures of relaxation. This colorful bouquet of pleasures is a potpourri of popular conceptions that lacks any phenomenological examination that would clarify the "essence" of each. It is only on the basis of their presupposition that one would be able to commence that crucial calculus, but Bentham does not adequately determine them, much less adequately compare them.

11.2 The Alternative

Were the attempt to determine happiness empirically and rationally only aiming too high, one could take advantage of our double strategy and not only develop more complex instruments but also lower one's ambitious expectations. In fact, however, one would fall short of the goal structurally in three interrelated respects: first, from the perspective of the theory of action; second, in terms of a crude empiricism; and finally, with respect to a correlatively crude cognitivism.

In terms of the theory of action, every calculus of a sum total of pleasure, not only with respect to the life phases of the individual but also in terms of life as a whole, is a producible (*poiesis*) goal. The paradigm is *homo faber*, the one who produces something. To this paradigm one can add a crude *homo oeconomicus*, the one who wants to maximize profits in the most simple fashion by treating the possibilities for engagement and their expected pleasure-displeasure values as objective data on the basis of which he can determine the hedonistically favorable balance and choose the maximum bottom line. In fact, though, life is a kind of praxis that exists only in a creative process, and only here can one find a "favorable balance of pleasure": whoever seeks happiness in friendship must cultivate relationships conducive to friendship; whoever expects something out of science or music must personally engage in research or in music in order to enjoy the process involved. In contrast to crude empiricism, there are no objective data that one can convert by calculation into a maximization, as is the case in a crude cognitivism.

According to the method of determinate negation, the proper alternative emerges from the preceding critique: First, one must creatively determine, and in part even invent, whatever leeway there is in the action. Second, everything depends upon the subject's hedonistic-creative engagement of the pleasure-displeasure chances involved. Therefore, one can indeed conduct a qualitative but at best only an ordinal appraisal (A promises more chance at happiness than B, which in turn promises more than C). However, one cannot conduct a cardinal appraisal that is the presupposition for a determination of a maximum pleasure. For that one requires an intellectual capacity of a particular kind which presupposes the eudaimonistic moral virtues and at the same time supplements and completes them. This capacity constitutes the other side of eudaimonistic reason. Methodologically, part of this capacity can be subjected to a critical hermeneutic. This critical hermeneutic does not limit itself to understanding what is merely cultural; it must establish itself, above all, in terms of the particular individual's life practice.

Whether texts, images, or music, great art can definitely simulate life and evoke an intelligent interpretation. Experience informed by literature, theater, and film has the advantage that it can be powerfully moving without hurting physically or psychically. In sympathy with Oedipus, Antigone, or Othello, with the young Werther, Thomas Buddenbrook, or Effi Briest, one suffers or celebrates with fictive characters. One's own existence, in contrast, must be lived here and now, really and concretely. Here there emerges a different kind of hermeneutic. This hermeneutic is concerned with a practical understanding with respect to one's own personal life. Nonetheless, just as in the usual hermeneutic of the human sciences, this hermeneutic includes the capacity of personal critique as well as a critique of the other.

Before a calculus can even occasionally perform a certain service— and then only in a secondary sense—this calculus requires the capacity of self-awareness and self-explanation, including the capacity to learn from good as well as bad experience. What is necessary is the capacity for sober (neither too positive nor too negative) self-appraisal, and, further, the capacity to give advice to oneself and to accept it from others. Not least, it helps to be able to attract good advisers, by which one means persons who not only have life experience but also are sensible, above all are of good judgment, and are open to the interests of the person seeking advice. Yet even this long list of ambitious competencies indicates only the necessary components of a decisive capacity, namely, the capacity to focus all of these components on the primary end, a life of happiness. The capacity of reference is called, generally, the power of judgment; when the reference is to one's own experience, and with reference to the entirety of existence, it is called life wisdom, or eudaimonistic reason. The intellectual complement of moral virtue, the cognitive side of the art of living, lies in the subject's own capacity and not in an objective calculation.

The ambiguity that wisdom shares with other basic philosophical concepts can be bracketed here (see the collection of essays in Kersting 2005). Any misunderstanding that arises from this ambiguity should be avoidable through the designation "*life* wisdom." One calls the art of living the capacity to lead a successful life given the vicissitudes of life. It consists in the interaction of two fundamentally different capacities, a moral and an intellectual capacity. Whereas moral virtues are responsible for ends that are suitable for happiness, life wisdom is concerned with determining the ways and means for the accomplishment of those ends. Only someone who possesses both capacities, who can discern correct life goals and possesses the capacity to realize properly those goals in ever-new particular and concrete situations, can establish himself well in life as a whole.

Scientists and philosophers think primarily of their own kind of capability in terms of a theoretical competency when they hear the phrase "intellectual capacity." Such a theoretical competency belongs in the world of knowledge, not in the world of character, although in the world of knowledge it refers to a life-practical intelligence. Life wisdom is a honed power of judgment acquired out of appropriate life experience. The one who possesses such life wisdom knows how to help himself in difficult situations. He pursues personal interests but always with a second-order interest in long-range well-being, an interest in happiness in life. Whoever has life wisdom is able to engage every situation but is able to treat both factors, the constraints and above all the leeway for action, not as some kind of determined guidelines but as factors that he must discover for himself.

With life wisdom, one combines the necessary cognitive skills with an awareness of what is at stake. Therein lies an invaluable gain incapable of being offset by any wealth: an orientation- and life-security by means of which one can establish oneself properly in life as a whole. As soon as this security by continuous practice has become an enduring element of one's way of life, life wisdom reaches a condition of reliability; it reaches the form of an (intellectual) virtue.

How far does this intellectual virtue reach in life? Virtue ethicists eagerly emphasize its sensitivity to contexts and situations; in fact, life wisdom is responsible for far more. Above all in pluralistic societies in which the framework of life and lifestyle are not as extensively established as they are in traditional societies, one requires not only more life wisdom but also a higher-ranking kind of life wisdom. Whether explicit or more likely implied, it is concerned, for example, with the presuppositions of a valuable life and with the leeway within which emotional experience, social conditions, and gratifying activities are possible. This higher-ranking life wisdom is evoked when it comes to such significant decisions as the choice of what one will study and one's selection of a career, like the search for a life partner or for friends. Life wisdom deliberates only in a eudaimonistically secondary sense, when one remains within the parameters of a pleasure-displeasure thought process that asks how one leads a hedonistically creative life within these limits and conditions. Precisely because there are neither certain ways and means nor trustworthy recipes for happiness, life wisdom engages ever and again in a reasonable as well as creative reflection. Rather than trust blindly in preestablished guidelines, it seeks realizable possibilities for action and evaluates their advantages and disadvantages in light of a successful life. (On evaluative and deliberative reason, see Bormann and Schröer 2004.)

Life wisdom already begins in a systematic sense more fundamentally with the choice of lifestyle. The normal person's engagement of life wisdom seldom begins with the radicality of Plato in the *Republic* (374a-e), Pascal with his famous wager (*Pensées,* no. 233), Kant "through a [moral] revolution in the disposition of the human being" (*Religion,* 6.47), and Kierkegaard in his total philosophical oeuvre. The arguments of these philosophers are not so weak that one could simply set aside the theme of a fundamental choice as foreign to life.

We can formulate an interim conclusion: a generally high expectation of "commitment to duty" belongs to the art of living; its elementary task is to seek an appropriate lifestyle. Within its framework and according to the requirements of moral virtues, the art of living seeks the optimal option for the situation. It knows, however, that often it will find only a suboptimal option.

11.3 Back to Aristotle?

Aristotle's reflections on practical living remain definitive (see, above all, *Nicomachean Ethics* 6.5 and 8–13). The central concept of *phronêsis* is best translated by "wisdom" because it is concerned with "life wisdom" in relation to life as a whole but not with insight into "morality" or the "moral." In contrast to a morally neutral, merely instrumental power of judgment, perspicacity (*deinotês*) and the tendency toward an immoral power of judgment (i.e., "Machiavellian" cunning or shiftiness [*panourgia*]), *phronêsis* is concerned entirely with the eudaimonistic meaning of a moral good. This orientation, however, is not accomplished by one's own power alone but on the basis of moral virtue to which *phronêsis* is bound. Situated in the middle between cunning and simplemindedness, life wisdom is responsible solely for the ways and means toward the fulfillment of goals, although not with respect to every capricious end. Rather, it is concerned with a fore-orientation toward a specific goal in the singular that constitutes a successful life. Whereas moral virtue is responsible for this orientation toward happiness, practical intelligence, wisdom, sees to it that the orientation is an appropriate concretization for the given situation.

Aristotle's life wisdom is, therefore, practical and not theoretical because, in contrast to understanding (*synesis*) and thoughtful understanding (*eusynesia*), it does not merely formulate a judgment but applies it to a concrete situation. It has a power to determine action to the degree that it establishes what one should and should not do. Nonetheless, this practical wisdom is not capable of ignoring those powers that blur the proper goal, the passions. Since it is incumbent upon moral virtue to pay attention to passions, life wisdom necessarily works in tandem with them. For example, when it comes to someone with courage, virtue is concerned that one reacts neither cowardly nor recklessly but, rather, calmly; whereas with the aid of wisdom, one evaluates the kind and intensity of the danger as well as the appropriate response. There is no such thing as either a specifically moral power of judgment that is concerned only with moral goals or a morally indifferent power of judgment. *Phronêsis* is nothing more and nothing less than a morally practical capacity for judgment. The first individual to address the power of judgment responsible for moral commitment itself was Kant (see Höffe 1990).

In contrast, there is another limit in Aristotle's doctrine of virtue that is shared with Kant: the structurally difficult moral problems of our age confront us with the task of the evaluation of multiple moral obligations that neither Aristotle nor Kant adequately addressed. Neither discusses the situation in which virtues collide with one another and require a moral virtue of a second order, a kind of meta-virtue, as well as a power of judgment devoted to the conflict of virtues. One does indeed find in Kant certain theoretical strategies, for example, the privileging of owed duties over duties owed to oneself, or the thought that something "that is in itself not permitted [is permitted] (indulgently, as it were) in order to prevent a still greater violation" (*Metaphysics of Morals*, 6:426). Further, Kant speaks of an "exceptional right" that leads to the violation of the rights of others but is not punishable although not upright (ibid., 6:235–36). Not the least, Kant acknowledges in a conflict situation the priority of the stronger ground of obligation over the stronger commitment (ibid., 6:224). Because such strategies, though in need of further development, are at least in an initial fashion addressed by Kant but nowhere by Aristotle, in this area one cannot expect to gain much by an appeal to Aristotle.

Although a theory of life wisdom can surely learn from Aristotle, an exclusive reinstatement of Aristotelianism is not recommended.

12 Can Virtue Make Us Happy?

Classical, eudaimonistic ethics is appraised as simultaneously attractive and inadequate. It is seen to be attractive because it doesn't overwhelm the individual with altruism but "obligates" one to a good life and designates the good in life as true happiness. Just this vocation, however, is what is inappropriate; it truncates morals, even contradicts it, by subordinating morals to incentives that would undermine it. Kant's pointed critique declares succinctly: "All eudaimonists are for this reason practical egoists" (*Anthropology*, 7:130). However, both assessments prove false upon closer examination. If one begins with the claimed attractiveness, it appears to be smaller than expected (chapter 12.1). Added to this is a second limit to the eudaimonistic value of virtues, the phenomenon of evil in experience (chapter 12.2), which requires a new kind of virtue: the creative engagement with the occurrences that can befall us (chapter 12.3).

12.1 Usually

Before one praises eudaimonistic virtue ethics for its orientation with respect to one's personal well-being, one must ask the preliminary question of whether or not the virtue in virtue ethics brings happiness at all. Although since antiquity one has heard the complaint that more often than not it is not the just but the unjust who are happy, neither today's defenders nor detractors of classical ethics pose the preliminary question. This question is not meant to undermine the eudaimonistic potential of virtues. However, what needs clarification is whether or not that potential is sufficient with respect to happiness.

According to the aphorism of an anonymous Spanish garden architect, we have not been given a happy world, we must create one. Appropriate to his profession, he thought in terms of plants and flowers as well as their beautiful arrangement, which no doubt bring happiness but, in the absence of the efforts of the gardener, would not exist in the form of gardens and parks. Is this the kind of happiness one means when it comes to eudaimonistic virtue? Does virtue bring happiness?

If we place the word "bring" on the jeweler's scales, the answer is "No!" However, to make something in the sense of creativity means to bring forth an object that in the end will stand on its own. The kind of happiness that occurs in virtue ethics arises in its execution. A constructed landscape continues to exist long after the process of its development, like a scientific, artistic, or political life's work. However, this is not the case with happiness in the present. Purely conceptually, it is by no means a product that can be constructed; hence, it is incapable of being produced. This is also the case with the two cornerstones of virtue ethics, moral virtue and life wisdom: neither is an accomplishment in the sense of a product one can produce. The question, then, whether or not virtue brings happiness cannot be meant literally. Virtue is not the cause of happiness, and happiness is not the necessary effect of virtue. What is really being asked is how closely virtue and happiness are related to one another: does living according to virtues bring happiness?

The moral advantage of an eventually affirmative answer is obvious. It consists in a "natural internalism." When it comes to the question of why one should be virtuous, the term "why" has two well-known meanings (see chapter 5.4 and chapter 25). Because both the justifying ground and the motivating force are either irreconcilable or complement one another, there are two paradigmatic answers. According to the inward (the "internal") answer, the justification of virtue is sufficient; according to the objective (the "external") answer, it is not. A virtue in the sense of eudaimonism is satisfied by the first answer. An enlightened self-interest speaks in its favor, so that the grounds that justify the virtues simultaneously have the status of motives for their acquisition and for living one's life according to them. Assuming practical rationality, for example, the bracketing of weakness in the will, the justifying ground and motivating power complement one another.

Before concluding that this complementarity is an advantage for virtue ethics, one certainly should clarify whether it claims to, and/or does, fulfill this advantage. Does virtue ethics claim that happiness, if not the direct effect, is arguably the certain expected reward of virtue? When one adds the expectation that one will be happy according to the measure of his virtue so that virtue alone determines happiness, is the following proportion correct: the more virtuous, the more happiness? Does double virtue result in twice as much happiness? Above all: according to the standard of virtue, is the best person in the sense of the completely virtuous person also the happiest? Does the reverse also apply: is the one who enjoys the maximum of happiness also the most virtuous; or is the one most unhappy the most evil person?

No less than Plato offers an affirmative answer to all of these questions. Whereas the just individual serves not only the other but also himself, and the unjust, in contrast, harms himself the most, the just person enjoys not only self-respect but also the respect of the other on whom he depends. As a consequence, the most just individual is the happiest (see *Gorgias* 468e–470e). Indeed, Plato assumes and we would reject what we would today call a metaphysical psychology: that the unjust person lives with internal chaos. In the case of ruthless individuals who nevertheless possess a moral conscience, this is rightly the case; if they do something wrong, they experience shame. However, someone who has never acquired this moral consciousness or who has entirely eliminated it is undisturbed by any such internal conflict.

A philosopher like Spinoza goes even further than Plato; he actually maintains an identity: "Happiness is not the reward for virtue but is virtue itself" (*Ethics*, book 4, proposition 42). In Beaumarchais' comedy *The Marriage of Figaro*, we are told: "We should incessantly follow the path of virtue without guile. Sooner or later, intrigue will ruin those who scheme with it" (act 5, scene 17). Heinrich von Kleist writes in the essay "Weg des Glücks" ["The Way to Happiness"] that "only virtue is the mother of happiness, and the best person *is the happiest*" because "a huge unrelenting law" governs "all of humanity whether prince or pauper. Reward follows virtue, punishment vice" (869ff.). Whether or not "follows" is meant in the sense of "causes" in this passage remains open; nonetheless, a necessary relationship is expressed with "unrelenting law."

The authority of such demanding theses depends on both concepts: virtue and happiness. However, we don't need to engage in the clarification of these concepts because we remain within the paradigm of the teleological ethic of aspiration and its virtue- and happiness-concepts. Aristotle as the authoritative representative maintains realistically and soberly in the introductory chapter of the *Nicomachean Ethics* that one is harmed by virtue; in the case of courage, one can come to one's death (1.1.1094b17–19). He therefore concludes: the claim that it is possible for courage or some other virtue to lead to happiness does not always mean that this will be the case. Unexpressed here is the acknowledgment that happiness is impaired by the occasional harm that comes from virtue.

One could undertake a eudaimonistic balancing of interests and on the basis of it declare: when we compare someone who loses courage and saves his life in the face of a deadly danger with someone who stops at nothing and calmly clings to his convictions in the face of a threatening harm, the one loses esteem in the eyes of others whereas the one demonstrating courage, specifically civil courage, acquires esteem. The consequence is that it would be better to die with the honor of courage than to continue to live with the disgrace of cowardice. One could even prefer "premature" death out of mere self-respect according to this rationale: should it be the case that no one is ever aware of the cowardice, for example, because it remains concealed by deception, one still experiences shame that impairs whatever happiness one might experience. Just as the aphorism says and Aristotle acknowledges (*Nicomachean Ethics* 1.13.1102b10–11): a quiet conscience sleeps through thunder. There is an objection to this aphorism, but it is not found in Aristotle. As a self-sufficient, inclusive end, the concept of happiness includes the survival of the individual, so that an estimable but premature death cannot be a "complete happiness."

Courage may indeed play a special role. For as the sovereign attitude with respect to dangers, it cannot prevent one from nevertheless being harmed. This danger seems ruled out for other virtues by definition. For example, in one's reflective relation to pleasure and pain (i.e., temperance), dangers in this area of the emotions appear by definition to be overcome. One who seeks too much pleasure or bears too much pain cannot be called prudent. Likewise with composure as well as generosity and well-being: the endangerment of happiness on the part of virtue is difficult to imagine here.

We can set aside the question of whether or not only courage represents an exception. At least in the case of one kind of virtue, "one is concerned with a 'usually' the case" so that the exercise of its guiding principle, happiness, can be contradicted. Whereas Aristotle was concerned only with the theoretical consequence that virtues usually, though not always, bring happiness, there remains an ethical- and principled-theoretical consequence: happiness loses its status as the absolutely highest and all-encompassing principle of human action.

That Aristotle doesn't misapply the corresponding phenomena on the basis of his "system" confirms him to be undogmatic and open to experience. That he also doesn't entirely embrace the consequences also shows his limits. The philosopher relativizes the principle of happiness, but only incidentally without noticing the complete consequences, which would have led to rejection of the notion of eudaimonism, or to a certain degree to an acknowledgment of its collapse.

A possible basis for Aristotle's failure to draw the theoretical conclusion with respect to eudaimonism might be: in order to dismiss a eudaimonistic ethic, one needs more than an occasional contradiction between virtue and happiness. It requires perhaps not a common but, nevertheless, an extreme contradiction (for example, the provocative sufferings thematized in the book of Job in the Old Testament or, in another manner, Europe's experience of the Lisbon earthquake of 1755): in order to become skeptical with respect to the principle of happiness to such a degree, one must have had the experience that even the thoroughly righteous (Job) or tens of thousands of innocent victims (Lisbon) were devastated by calamity. Aristotle rightly knew that such a righteous person as Socrates had to drink the hemlock. From Plato's dialogue *Crito* we learn that Socrates according to his own self-appraisal is not the victim of a calamity comparable to that of Job. Socrates saw his death as a relatively small evil; far smaller than the injustice that would have occurred were he to have escaped death.

The eudaimonistic "usually" possesses in any case an ethical- and principled-theoretical meaning that is ignored by contemporary defenders of Aristotle's virtue ethic. Their rehabilitation of Aristotle's ethic is too hasty. Virtue in the classical sense is incapable of fulfilling the task of making humans happy because of the crumbling of the internal relationship between virtue and happiness. Happiness in the sense of eudaimonia is a task that virtue alone is incapable of achieving. Even when humanity is capable of cultivating and applying virtues, from at least the perspective of virtue it is only partially responsible for complete success in life. Eudaimonistic fulfillment of life is not something that depends exclusively on human beings.

12.2 Evil and Good Occurrences

Eudaimonistic happiness is active and focused on the present. Hence, it is far less dependent upon the course of events than a passive happiness. Nonetheless, it is not entirely independent of the course of events. Someone who experiences the death of a life partner or a child, whose friend deceives him, who innocently suffers a permanent physical disability, or who like Job loses all his possessions, including his family and friends (see Joseph Roth's novel *Job*), such a person cannot seriously be called happy: "a fissure tears creation apart. There are no crutches of meaning, nothing, despair, rage" (Uwe Timm, *Rot*, 2003, 85).

Everyone, the righteous person just as much as the scoundrel, is subject to the danger of devastating bad luck. Evil experiences neither are capable of discriminating between the fair person and the cheater nor have they the power to descend only on the bad or to spare the good. Virtue is neither an amulet that can protect one from burdens and sufferings nor a vaccination that can make one immune from them.

A virtue ethic of Aristotelian stature is not blind in this respect. It declares explicitly that happiness must endure "over an entire life" (*Nicomachean Ethics* 1.6.1098a18). However, here neither Aristotle nor his newer rehabilitators pursue the ethical-theoretical consequences of this insight. It is clear that in his *Poetics* Aristotle gives great attention to the important theme of tragedy in Greek culture. Nonetheless, he discusses the tragic constellation of events neither in his action- nor in his virtue-theory. One could rightly say that, because according to Aristotle tragedy includes a moment of personal fault (*hamartia*), the truly virtuous person experiences no tragedy in the strictest sense. Nonetheless, with respect to the everyday meaning of tragedy in terms of the danger of an overwhelming disaster, virtue is no protection. Therefore, in this respect it is correct to say that neither Aristotle nor today's virtue ethicists pose the unavoidable question of how ethics is to respond to unfortunate occurrences.

Incidentally, the question of one's experience of evil is independent of the eudaimonistic concept of virtue. Whether defined with regard to happiness or already defined from the beginning with regard to moral ends in themselves, virtue has no power over the absurdities of life. Nonetheless, the virtuous person is not completely helpless in the face of evil. He is aided by life wisdom's ability to place events in a greater context that can reduce the threat of evil in experience. Furthermore, life wisdom is able to transform disappointments and evil surprises into something positive. However, unfortunate occurrences in the strict sense of the term are incapable of transformation into something positive when it comes to the avoidance of unpleasantnesses and to the extent that they do not have midget but giant dimensions, as in the case of Job.

Things stand better when it comes to an unusual virtue; more precisely, a kind of virtue that, in contrast to the usual virtues, performs essentially only a negative service. The quasi-virtue in question neither can protect one against misfortune (it doesn't consist of a form of prevention) nor can it reverse the consequences of a misfortune (it doesn't understand itself as negation). There is no doubt, however, that it can confront a misfortune in such a way that one can one day come to terms with it in terms of the "sequence of moments of disjunctions" that is life (Anthony Doerr, *Winklers Traum vom Wasser*, 2005, 52). This appropriate virtue can help one deal with misfortune without enduring deep and incurable, festering wounds.

The quasi-virtue with which we are concerned here has two levels. The minimal level consists in *tolerantia*, in Greek *karteria* (see Aristotle's *Nicomachean Ethics* 7.8.1150a13–15 and a32–36), which is not originally an attitude toward others but toward oneself: it means tolerance not of some-*one* but of some-*thing*. Even today, one calls someone courageous who not only actively masters a dangerous situation but also endures deep suffering without breaking down under its weight. Such a circumstance presents tolerance as a kind of passive courage, namely a fixity of purpose, that in the case of difficult conditions can shade over into forbearance. Related to prudence, it refers to the capacity to endure pain and other unpleasantnesses. One is tolerant in this sense who knows how to patiently endure pain, the vicissitudes of fate, and if necessary even torture.

Even when endurance escalates to heroic (mental) strength, which when confronted with the most extreme suffering neither complains nor crumbles, it remains in essence a *negative* achievement precisely as a *not* collapsing. In order to be a *positive* achievement, this passive enduring must be transformed into a new kind of virtue unknown in the classical catalog of virtues: it must be transformed into an active and creative engagement that inventively processes the evil occurrence.

Creativity begins with the capacity to perceive a difficulty as an opportunity to prove oneself. In Joseph Conrad's short story *Youth* (1903/ 1922, 13–14), the protagonist, Marlowe, gets himself hired as second officer on an old and decrepit ship. After a daylong storm, the ship springs a leak, and everyone "pumped watch and watch, for dear life . . . as though we had been dead and gone to a hell for sailors." However, "there was somewhere in me the thought: By Jove! This is the deuce of an adventure . . . I was pleased. I would not have given up the experience for worlds. I had moments of exultation. . . . [The ship] to me was not an old rattle-trap carting about the world a lot of coal for a freight—to me she was the endeavor, the test, the trial of life."

How do things look, however, when the adventure ends not in deliverance but destruction? What is valuable here are advantageous coping mechanisms. Whoever has such mechanisms at his disposal, whoever is not merely familiar with such but understands how they apply to life, is capable of overcoming even the most extraordinary difficulties like unemployment, the death of a loved one, or a serious illness. Such skills allow one after a while to regain one's vitality, and later one can even return to a fulfilling and satisfactory life.

In the case of a misfortune with respect to which one feels oneself personally responsible, one experiences not only despondency but also shame. However, as soon as one notices that one is beginning to master the situation, self-respect returns, and one's self-worth increases. Admittedly, mastering a misfortune can involve such a demanding effort that one speaks here of trans-formation [*Ver-arbeiten*], for example in the case of mourning [*Trauerarbeit*] the death of a partner or of a child. Even when one cannot expect to recover entirely from all injuries, for example, childhood sexual abuse or other traumas of childhood or youth, resignation is neither the only nor a creative alternative.

Many seek a renewed sense of meaning in the arts. Perhaps they believe that only music, painting, dance, or literature is still important. Given the breadth of human talents, however, any sense of exclusivity here is inappropriate. Some conceal their suffering in research, while others seek to conquer it through meditation or, to the contrary, even in social engagement. There is no doubt that one can discover a functional life in this fashion, even happiness. Whoever has learned to live in the appropriate manner, in other words, has acquired the skills for such activities, possesses a virtue that up to this point has no label. The reason may be that the task in fact is recognized in psychotherapy and psychology but not yet in the discipline responsible for virtues, ethics.

Classical ethics—in this case one means such different thinkers as Epicurus, the Stoics, and the Skeptics—is familiar with an attitude that approaches the determination in question here, a "competency to overcome misfortune" ["*Widerfahrnisbewältigungs-kompetenz*"]. It is called equanimity, peace of mind, and imperturbability (Greek: *galênêapatheia, atarxia;* Latin: *aequanimitas, tranquilitas animi*). With equanimity in the face of the blows of fate, they named a result that one achieves with the tolerance of misfortune. It is expressed in the popular form of the conclusion to an opera: "Happily I praise, the one who grasps / Everything from the right perspective, from which storms can never shake, / Chooses reason as one's guide. / . . . Should dangers threaten in this world, / He looks on the bright side" (Mozart, *Così fan tutte,* conclusion).

Included in the "techniques" of endurance is, for example, the overcoming of a fourfold fear by means of insight. According to Epicurus, one need not fear God because He doesn't interfere in the affairs of the world, and one does not need to fear unfulfilled wishes because little is needed for humanity to be happy. (Correctly, Nietzsche said in *Human, All Too Human,* vol. 2, no. 192: "A garden, figs, a little cheese, and three or four friends—that was the luxury of Epicurus.") Further, inordinate pain is also not to be feared because it doesn't last long and can be offset. Even death need not be feared because evil consists in a sensation, but death consists in the loss of every sensation. With such techniques one can master a great deal, certainly. However, to the extent that they emphasize the cognitive, they have clear limits; above all, that emotional work is left out without which evil occurrences are difficult to overcome. Someone who possesses the positive virtues, the creative competence to overcome misfortune, is not immune to adversity. However, he is capable, once again, of leading an almost happy life even in the face of great troubles and suffering.

The examination of the ways of the world would be inadequate, in a certain sense even unfair, if it did not acknowledge the other side: there is more to life than misfortune. A good that can come to one without one's own efforts can also befall one beginning with the smile of a child, the loving glance of a partner in an unanticipated happy encounter, the aphoristic "gift from heaven" that one neither sought, nor which stood in any fashion within one's power—all this has a right to ethical appreciation. The one who properly acknowledges that not everything good is the consequence of one's own efforts but who, nonetheless, recognizes the reality of unearned happy experiences, senses a relationship between an insight that much is beyond one's control and an appreciation for an anonymous addressee who has control over that which is not at one's disposal and "who" has one's best interest in mind. This relationship does not have a proper name; only crudely can one use the word "humility." However, it demonstrates a further limit to the teleological aspiration for happiness.

12.3 Eudaimonistic Composure

No virtue ethic can be so distant from life that it denies the possibility of evil occurrences and their eudaimonistic consequence: whoever experiences adversity and suffering finds it difficult to be completely virtuous. As a consequence, there is no unlimited capacity for happiness accomplished by the combination of moral virtue with life-practical intelligence. The corresponding risk factor in life cannot be avoided by the righteous.

Virtue remains a necessary condition for a successful life, but it is incapable of guaranteeing it for two reasons. On the one hand, as one saw with the example of courage, virtuous actions can have devastating consequences for happiness; on the other hand, no one can escape the possibility of fate's devastating blows. Smaller strokes of fate can, indeed, be offset, and in the face of great adversity they aid against being smothered by it. The fact that happiness can be blurred and for many even squelched is not something that virtue can prevent.

Anyone who maintains to the contrary that virtue can protect one from all dangers and uncertainties, and who believes that happiness is the consequence of one's own efforts alone, suffers from an omniscience fantasy. He believes that no matter how great the difficulty, it can be conquered by an equally sovereign facility that one may call "triumphant." One is triumphant over the world: over fate and all of its adversities; one is triumphant over oneself: over one's burdens, anxieties, and weaknesses; and not the least one is triumphant over one's fellow human beings to the extent that they make life difficult by their resentment and jealousy. Aristotle, the philosopher of eudaimonia, does not share this delusion of grandeur.

The recognition that the teleological aspiration for happiness consists in a fragile good can be discerned in the Greek word *eu-daimonia*. It means to be guided by a good (*eu*) deity (*daimon*). The German expression *glücklich leben* [to live happily] forces one to recognize what life experience confirms: whether one is successful with such important things as an education, a friendship, or a partnership depends, no matter how much upon one's own efforts, also upon a pinch of fortune. There is no difference when it comes to life as a whole. Complete happiness is not something over which the individual alone has control. Even the highest form of asceticism and the skill of self-absorption are something only momentary like the moment of ecstasy, not absolute: complete happiness is not simply one's own accomplishment. Even when the primary source of happiness lies within, in virtue, happiness requires in addition a lucky fate that includes an external gift.

One can liberate oneself more or less from those external goods given by the capricious god Fortuna, which can be taken away by others and which she steals back in the course of most people's lives only to give them back again. Even here one must acknowledge: in contrast to the ideal of Stoic disinterestedness, one finds general practical success in grappling with the vicissitudes of life. Hardly anyone remains unaffected by frailness and fragility or intense physical pain. Even when one maintains that one can realize such an ideal, there remain the other non-external goods such as the reverberation that can come from another person or another thing: from love, compassion, great art. Indifference is in such cases hardly possible. One cannot, for example, find a partner for life, experience a fulfilling relationship with her/him over the years, and in the end remain indifferent to her/his death. If so, then either one is indifferent to death (and one's partner was dispensable for one's happiness) or the partner was essential for one's happiness, and one cannot be unaffected by the loss.

The eudaimonistic consequences are obvious—with respect to the art of living they are: virtue is the best that one has available for a successful life, but it is not sufficient for a completely successful life. The life-practical consequence is: composure contains a new fundamental task. Without restricting the requirements of virtue, it does not expect that all happiness comes from virtue. Virtue remains indispensable for happiness without happiness being identical to or being combined causally with virtue. Virtue neither *is* happiness nor *produces* happiness.

Moral virtue is not even a necessary condition for happiness. The claim that no evildoer was ever happy is a bold claim that only an ivory tower moralist such as Kleist would dare to make. There is no way a priori to maintain that it is impossible for a rogue to experience well-being so long as he lives untroubled by punishment and a bad conscience. Perhaps he even enjoys his misdeeds and gloats over them as a consequence of his exceptional amoral status, of the ills inflicted on others, and of his intellectual skill, his cleverness, at escaping punishment for those misdeeds.

This second intellectual factor, not cleverness but life wisdom, is as good as indispensable for a successful life. A sleepwalker without any reflection with respect to the means and ways of his situation cannot be a happy person. Someone who possesses life wisdom does not realistically expect any guaranteed product of happiness from reflection. Rather, he embraces life wisdom for its insight into the perilous nature of existence.

As a consequence, a virtuous life contains an internal sovereignty that is capable in the literal sense of "mastering" life as a whole. Rather than being a knave or a slave to the fateful nature of one's life, one demonstrates for the most part one's lordship. Even when one is far from even knowing, much less being in control, of all the factors, one understands how to ascertain, and the way to lead, a happy life based upon just actions.

This result that virtue cannot guarantee the meaning of a virtuous life, happiness, rejects the too optimistic hopes of the Stoics as well as the standard and example of the righteous. The wise person can be happy even when he suffers under poverty and illness, even torture. Despite all one's personal efforts that are required in order to achieve a successful life, success itself, happiness, remains a fragile good. Over against the Stoics, the diluted expectation can be supported by life experience. Whereas the non-virtuous path easily leads to the abyss of failure, virtue does not protect one from every adversity, but with its help a happy life is highly probable.

13 Euthanasia of Morals?

The combination of the teleological aspiration model of action with the most formal concept of morals, the absolute good, results in the concept of an absolute highest and simultaneously comprehensive goal: happiness in the sense of eudaimonia. What potential does this goal have for morals? The immediate impression is that we are concerned with two contradictory expectations: a thesis and an antithesis. According to the *thesis:* teleological aspiration constitutes a fundamental model of human action, so that one must be able to conceive of morals according to a model of action. The action principle of eudaimonia occurs within this model, which means that one should expect a high, aspiration-theoretical, even comprehensive, potential for morals to be associated with eudaimonia. However, one usually thinks here only of one's personal happiness, one's own well-being, and hence of precisely the opposite of morals, which is concerned primarily, if not exclusively, with the interest of the other. The *antithesis* emerges here: eudaimonia is an unsuitable theory for morals; in fact, it amounts to the euthanasia, the gentle death of morals (Kant, "Doctrine of Virtue" [part 2 of *The Metaphysics of Morals*], 6:378).

Both theses have enormous consequences. On the one hand, should the concept of eudaimonia possess a comprehensive moral potential, then the respective ethics from antiquity constitutes the proper paradigm, and its neo-Aristotelian rehabilitation is correct. Today's ethics claims that the good has a priority over the right. On the other hand, the contrary thesis that eudaimonia has no role to play in ethics would mean not merely that one rejects antiquity and affirms the high point of modern ethics, Kant, as correct. Because eudaimonism has dominated from antiquity through the Middle Ages and up to modernity, our antithesis would mean that Western philosophy with its culturally dominant, positive morals (the good in terms of eudaimonia) either is an incorrect theory, or the theory is correct but its object, positive morals, contradicts the demand of critical morals. It would mean that Western philosophy would be an immoral morals. Both options to a certain degree appeal to the self-consciousness of modernity, that is, the demand to do everything in a fundamentally new and right way for the first time. Anyone with critical distance from this demand, though, is skeptical.

We begin with the antithesis, which raises three objections to eudaimonism. When it comes to Aristotle, the standard-bearer of eudaimonism, there is a fourth objection. The defensive move on the part of the antithesis for the neutralization of the objections maintains, in the form of an anti-antithesis (i.e., a thesis), that it is incorrect, first, to conclude that eudaimonism amounts to the opposite of morals as an egotism rather than an altruism (chapter 13.1); it is incorrect, second, to conclude that virtuous, including moral, behavior is demanded not by an absolute but only by a prudential standard of one's own well-being (chapter 13.2); it is incorrect, third, to conclude that Aristotle's eudaimonism leads to a lifestyle of *theoria* (contemplation) that contradicts the high standards of a long-standing moral understanding (chapter 13.3); it is incorrect, fourth, to conclude that eudaimonism privileges the good above the right in an improper fashion (chapter 13.4).

13.1 Beyond the Alternative Between One's Own and Others' Well-Being

The fact that those virtues represented by eudaimonism are overwhelmingly of a social nature speaks against the first objection, that of egoism. Analogous to Kant's distinction between duties to oneself and duties owed to others, there are two classes of virtues: those virtues directed toward oneself and those toward the other.

When it comes to the primary virtue in the truly appropriate sense, the relationship to others or its social character is obvious: justice regulates the relationships of persons to one another in terms of their cooperation (for example, in the different kinds of exchange), in terms of distribution, and not least in terms of conflicts. Other virtues are directly related to the self but are indirectly concerned with others: one is generous who is magnanimous with money and, when it comes to lots of money, is cautious in balancing profligacy and avarice. One with a sense of honor exaggerates his reputation neither "too highly" nor "too lowly." Nevertheless, these virtues have an essentially social character. Generosity or magnanimity does not refer to someone who demonstrates an ability to satisfy whatever personal desire one has but to someone who administers his affluence to the advantage of others. Prestige, furthermore, is nothing other than the value one has in the eyes of others.

A clearly social phenomenon, friendship, is a quasi-virtue with formidable weight in classical eudaimonism: because one seeks a friend and partner in part out of necessity as well as in part freely, the well-being of the other is important to one's own well-being. To an enlightened pursuit of happiness belongs a concern for the welfare of the other for no other purpose than his welfare alone, without any calculation of one's own gain. Appropriately, the concern for the welfare of others is not limited to one's friends and relatives but extends to all with whom one comes into close contact. Even one who seeks his happiness in a limited social context is dependent at least on the preservation of an external peace. Because his well-being depends in fact upon society in a broader sense, one extends this quasi-virtue, now better called solidarity, to the larger life-world. In an age of globalization, solidarity obtains even a global dimension: it is extended to a cosmopolitan solidarity.

Two further virtues, prudence and courage, appear only at first glance to be exclusively concerned with the self. A reflective relationship to highly personal feelings of pleasure and displeasure safeguards not only against personally destructive licentious conduct as well as apathy but also against, for example, (intemperate) anger. Furthermore, someone who in a cooperative exercise "blindly surges ahead" in the face of all danger risks harming not only himself but also the others in the group.

These examples are sufficient to make clear the decisive response to the charge of egoism: eudaimonistic virtues are either—as in the case of justice and friendship—directly concerned with others or—as in the case of generosity and prestige—only indirectly, admittedly, but nevertheless essentially concerned with others. Finally, a third set of virtues, prudence and courage, is not necessarily, yet is to a large extent, socially relevant.

In response to the question of why one should be virtuous when it comes to the principle of happiness, the answer is: out of one's own self-interest as well as out of one's deference to others. Whoever seeks an enduring and satisfying happiness goes beyond what is merely legally required and beyond the renunciation of ill will toward others. He extends his generosity to non-pecuniary aspects of life and cultivates a general largesse. In the face of the charge that one clings here to a cultural relativism, one need only look at other cultures. The Chinese term for virtue, *de* (*te*), means, above all, a largesse combined with thankfulness (Nivison 2003, 234).

The virtuous person in a eudaimonic sense is driven by compassion and a sense of shared joy to seek the well-being of others. This is accomplished appropriate to a spectrum of responsibility whereby the ranking can have a culturally dependent component (i.e., it can and will be different in Western and Asian cultures). A possible ranking: above all, one is responsible for one's life partner, then for one's friends and others whom one knows (e.g., instructors for their students). One also takes into consideration one's social world; not least one takes into consideration, especially in a global world, all peoples and their social and natural environments.

Because many moral philosophers take it to be difficult to overcome the conflict between personal interests and the interests of others, they take the easy way out by excluding personal interest and limiting morals to responsibility for others. Upon careful examination, however, this altruistic strategy turns out to be superficial because an important part of moral obligation arises out of an enlightened self-interest. As much as a meaningful life helps one's fellow travelers and as pleasant as it is to cultivate relationships with others who lead a successful life, to lead a meaningful life means, first of all, to support oneself, which in a communal species like humanity necessarily occurs socially.

Enlightened self-interest is known as a legitimizing criterion from economics. The question with respect to a meaningful life indicates that the criterion extends further and can serve for the appraisal of life as a whole. In the process, however, any too narrow, exclusively economic, definition of self-interest will be rejected. Incidentally, religion is aware of the connection between morals and self-interest. The command "Honor thy father and mother" includes an addition that many often overlook: "that your days may be long, and that it may go well with thee, upon the land which the Lord thy God giveth thee" (Deuteronomy 5:16; see also Exodus 20:12). At least the fourth of the Ten Commandments in the Old Testament is not based on mere altruism.

Enlightened personal well-being, in any event, "demands" successively and with increasing expectation: first, adherence to the civic law; followed by considerateness; further, readiness for cooperation with others; goodwill; and as a form of perfection, even love.

There is not only a happiness that exists *along with* the suffering of others (for example, the happiness of affluence simultaneously with the distress of the poor). There is a happiness that occurs *at the expense of the suffering of others.* Anyone who only wants to be better than before possesses a socially neutral ambition; as long as he only competes with himself, he evokes neither envy nor jealousy. Should one, however, want to be better than others, he is necessarily their competitor. No matter how civilized the competition works itself out, with respect to happiness there looms only the well-known natural condition of a war of all against all. It might turn out that the collective sum from the competition turns out to be positive, since the contest can increase engagement and creativity and as a consequence boost accomplishments in economics, the sciences, arts, and sports. In addition, it could be that the higher performance alone will come to the especial benefit of those most disadvantaged. Nonetheless, competition results in a winner and a loser, and the winner's happiness occurs inescapably *at the expense of* the loser's unhappiness.

Some social utopians want radically and entirely to avoid this state of affairs. Not satisfied with the mere civilizing of competition, they seek a happiness that is concomitant not with the suffering but with the happiness of others, that even arises *from* the happiness of others. In order to accomplish this goal, they seek alternative social structures; above all there should be no economic oppression or exploitation, perhaps even no dominance of anyone over anyone else. These expansive, though from experience unrealistic, utopias constitute an alternative to eudaimonic virtue ethics. Without disputing the need for a change in social relations, virtue ethics commences with the individual and not with others (e.g., one's fellow human beings) or with other factors (e.g., social structures): a virtue ethic emphasizes the responsibility of each individual himself.

Nevertheless, a virtue ethic is not satisfied with mere personal responsibility for oneself. To the extent that eudaimonic virtues are for the most part concerned with others, they account for the opposite of social competition. Rather, they contribute to a social utopia, to a happiness, that lives from the happiness of others without having to turn society upside down. This in part indirect and in part direct service to others, however, is not a contradiction of one's personal well-being. Having overcome the opposition between self and other, eudaimonic virtues contribute to both sides, one's personal as well as others' well-being. In the case of friendship, they directly encourage one's own well-being by contributing to the well-being of others. In this circumstance, one who serves the other serves himself.

13.2 More than Only Prudent

Arguments that are based upon self-interest are called prudent. The term is supposed to help avoid a conceptual, historical difficulty: whereas the virtue-ethical concept of cunning serves to a great extent that which one calls morals, in modernity cunning has been disconnected from morals. It has descended to the cleverness of the snake or the shrewdness of a fox, which are employed for nothing other than self-interested ends. "Prudential," to the contrary, means those arguments that understand self-interest neither too narrowly nor shortsightedly but broadly and enduringly, without making self-interest an independent moral element. Prudence acts out, to be sure, an enlightened but morally indifferent self-interest; Kant speaks in this case of the appropriate maxims as pragmatic imperatives.

Whoever appeals to self-interest in support of virtues usually argues legitimizingly: self-interest declares itself for these virtues. A closer examination shows, however, that the argument has not only legitimizing but also simultaneously limiting power. To this extent eudaimonic virtues can be proposed as prudential in a double sense: with respect to justification and with respect to limits.

Insofar as virtue promises that for which humanity ultimately lives, happiness, it is "wise" to acquire and to employ virtues. The opposite side, however, is: as long as virtue is calculated only with respect to happiness, happiness is the measure of virtue as long as happiness coincides with virtue, as Spinoza said. This second prudential argument limits the scope of, and can propose, virtue only to the extent that it actually serves happiness. The consequence, then, is that the prudentially legitimizing virtue is placed under a prudential caveat. Even in the event that a eudaimonic legitimation is successful, it constitutes a limitation. Does this caveat apply, as well, to the teleological aspiration-ethic's concept of virtue?

Whoever from time to time complains about the limited happiness of the virtuous understands happiness for the most part to be concerned with external well-being, which is visible in objective conditions that can actually be absent like health, affluence, power, and prestige in the life of the virtuous. According to an alternative understanding, happiness is internalized and simultaneously privatized; instead of "objective, but external" it is now "internal, however subjective." Accordingly, happiness consists of an internal condition like an exaggerated feeling of well-being or elation. Here everyone is his own judge who agrees with the comic poet quoted by the Stoic Seneca: "No one is happy who maintains he isn't" ("Letter to Lucilius" in 2004a).

The standard of eudaimonic ethics, Aristotle, rejects this alternative. To the extent that he connects happiness not exclusively but predominantly with virtue, he relativizes not only external but also internal well-being. Admittedly, he emphasizes something internal but not an experience; rather, an attitude that is manifest in appropriate objective action. These objective-subjective virtues (see chapter 9.4), to be sure, do not necessarily, though they usually do, have a remarkable eudaimonic value.

Within this framework, virtues are no pure final end, but merely a means. However, they are no capricious means but one that serves the happy life. Furthermore, they are a final end, but they don't assume this rank exclusively. They stand, first of all, on the same level, that is, "next to," three other ends: prestige, pleasure, and mind in the sense of reason that is responsible for principles (*Nicomachean Ethics* 1.5.1097b2). Because these three other ends remain obligated to happiness as nothing other than alternative final goals, one must maintain a distance from them wherever there is no chance for happiness, above all where something like courage threatens happiness.

However, Aristotle rejects this prudential restriction. As in chapter 9.3 where morals was discussed in terms of virtue ethics, virtues are also pursued for their own sake. Although they are "only" a final end of the first level, a *teleion*, that must justify itself in the face of the superlative, the *teleiotaton*, eudaimonia, they have their own value. In contrast to a commonly held opinion, obligations that are not based on self-interest but are (intrinsically) valid in themselves are not first manifest in so-called deontological ethics, but are already present in eudaimonic ethics.

Since Kant, one has called obligations categorical that are absolutely valid without reference to one's own self-interest. To the extent that Aristotle in the prudential sense renounces the limitation to one's personal interest, it sounds—stated carefully—as if already with him we encounter a categorical character. Therefore, it is neither originally in Christianity nor in Kant's secularized ethics that one finds an aristocratic morals in the form of virtue's value in itself, but already in the "ancient pagan," Aristotle.

One finds three arguments in support of the "end in itself" character and a rudimentary categorical claim for virtues in Aristotle and, generally, in classical eudaimonic ethics. *First:* the authority of virtues is not restricted by a "most-case" logic. "Mostly" is a theoretical (an epistemological), not a moral, qualification. One is concerned here not with the breadth of virtue's obligatoriness but with its contribution to happiness, its eudaimonic value. The claim is not that one should be courageous "for the most part"; for example, the claim is not that if life is threatened, one may and even should steal off. Although virtues ultimately are eudaimonically justified, one finds no mitigation of the obligation to act courageously either in Aristotle or in classical virtue ethics.

This observation, once again, has a huge significance for theoretical principles: within the framework of the principle of happiness, one expects only prudent obligations; but Aristotle does not embrace any such restricted validity. For example, when he calls courage "in the usual sense" (*kyriôs*) one's "fearlessness in the face of death" (*Nicomachean Ethics* 2.9.1115a32–33), then he is speaking of courage as an "end in itself" and of its demands as of greater worth than one's personal interest in life. The question how these two functions (eudaimonic service and self-interest) are related, however, is ignored. That they might be in tension with, even in contradiction with, one another is not addressed by Aristotle.

One finds a *second* moment in opposition to a prudential caveat in that both conceptual elements of virtue speak against it. The generic concept (e.g., preservation of life) speaks of a personal attribute that might be acquired for the sake of happiness. However, in the case of one's holding fast to one's position in a difficult situation as a second nature, self-preservation conduct consists in a reliability and autonomy by means of which any manipulation in the sense of a prudent eudaimonic provision is rejected. The species concept (e.g., the means) profiles the attitude of self-preservation, but it is to occur without any eudaimonic control that claims some right to express any caveat. Whoever encounters the situation of fearlessness is required to reject, *eo ipso* from the concept of fearlessness itself, any relativizing of the concept in the name of happiness (in the sense of a possible avoidance of death). As a matter of deportment, the virtue of courage has its own value just as with all other virtues, that is, a value that does not permit its compromise in the service of happiness.

Of course, one can ask whether or not real people are in fact so fearless that they conduct themselves this way in absolutely every situation:

is there such a thing as not merely a "to a great extent" but an absolutely unshakeable consistency? Even in the event that the answer would be "No!" because one cannot depend on any single person to be truly perfectly virtuous, the deviation would be a sign of moral weakness even when understandable and perhaps even excusable. The individual would be judged not to possess a perfectly dependable deportment. The moral deportment itself, however, excludes the following alternative by its very concept: in a situation which promotes happiness, one would retain a deportment which one would intentionally renounce in a situation in which happiness was diminished.

The *third* argument for an "end in itself" character to virtues is found in the concept of humanity's unique work (*ergon*). Aristotle employs this concept to give the concept of happiness more content (*Nicomachean Ethics* 1.6). He declares the unique work to be the activity of reason that is manifest in two forms: a commanding and an obedient form. He ascribes to each a special kind of virtue: life wisdom along with other intellectual capacities apply to the first, the "commanding" form; whereas moral virtues apply to the second, the "obedient" form. The concept of the unique work of humanity includes an "end in itself" character: reason does not serve something other and higher; it stands for the essence of humanity and, simultaneously, in this respect it stands for itself. Once its right has been established, it follows its own laws: reason leads its own life in such a fashion that, once again, eudaimonic "manipulation" is eliminated.

13.3 Provocative *Theoria*

The pinnacle of the teleological aspiration for happiness according to Aristotle is surprising, even provocative, to contemporary moral sensibilities: the perfect form of a satisfactory life that really matters is scientific-philosophical existence, that is, theoretical life. Aristotle's allegiance to only a very small group of people, in fact his own guild, philosophy, is surprising. *Theoria* bursts the accord between one's own and others' well-being because, although it distances itself from all utility, it doesn't even indirectly concern itself with the well-being of others.

One side in the plea for a disinterested knowledge is thoroughly welcome: in contrast to a utilitarian view of human life, it shows in an exemplary manner that, in the end, one is not in the service of others but of oneself. Still a *second* side may be welcome: because *theoria* is independent not only from external goods but also from one's fellow human beings, it provides a paradigm for happiness that actually is within our power and, in its independence from everything external, has something divine about it.

However, in opposition to a widely held conviction that *theoria* is not merely an example of an end in itself but is also its ideal form, there is a polyphonic protest: first, scientists and philosophers are no pure intelligentsia. They, too, have needs and interests, and they cultivate relationships not only with colleagues but also with "normal persons," so that even they need the "usual" form of happy life. Furthermore, one can ask why a thinker or researcher who operates in an ivory tower should possess more human value than, for example, the kindhearted Samaritan. Not only Christianity but also other religions and not least the greater part of nonreligious world literature raise their objections. A brilliant attack against the personal overestimation on the part of science and the arts was undertaken at the time of the Enlightenment by its heretical thinker, Jean-Jacques Rousseau.

What counts for an evaluation of eudaimonism, however, is not the provocative estimation of the theoretical life itself but ultimately the question of whether or not the theoretical life is essential for a happy life. There is no easy answer to this question. If one follows the argumentation in the definitive text, the *Nicomachean Ethics,* there is a privileged status for *theoria* neither in terms of the aspiration-theoretical concept of action nor in the concept of an absolutely highest end. Neither the spontaneous pursuit of a positively evaluated end nor the thought of an end that cannot be surpassed appears to establish the privilege for *theoria.* The privileging of *theoria* does not arise even in the adjunct thesis that reason is the characteristically human capacity. This occurs for the first time with the investigation of the concept of reason—more precisely: with the distinction between two levels of reason and the equation of the higher, "authentic" level with that reason essential for knowledge (*Nicomachean Ethics* 1.13.1103a2–3). This equation of reason with knowledge ignores the prior question of whether there might not be an authentic reason that is concerned with action. The priority given to knowledge follows, of course, inescapably only because this latter possibility is not examined. Precisely this possibility confronts a teleological aspiration-ethic with fundamental difficulties (see chapter 14) whereby the privileging of *theoria,* then, appears to be inessential.

At least as an option, the following alternative is obvious at any rate: one develops a pure reason also for the domain of action and distinguishes between two domains, a purely theoretical and a purely practical

reason, whereby one obtains two basic forms for the successful completion of life. If so, then pure practical reason appears as a competitor to
theoria. In a further step of the argument, one could maintain its superiority to pure theoretical reason, which decisively abolishes the privileging of *theoria:* the privilege no longer lies in utility-free knowledge but
in a morals that rejects any end higher than itself. Something that no
longer shows itself in the prudential character of eudaimonic virtue then
becomes a principle: that which is the unique characteristic of humanity and which by all means can be called "reason" culminates neither in
scientific-philosophical research nor in mere happiness but doubtless in
the practice of morals that has no other (wider) utility.

13.4 Priority of the Good Over What Is Right?

One part of the contemporary debate in ethics comes to a head in the
question: to whom does the conceptual priority apply; the one whom one
takes as good or the one whom one takes to be morally right? According
to utilitarianism, which has long dominated the English-speaking world,
the priority is found in the subjective good. One asks what one holds to
be good for oneself in light of one's needs and interests, attitudes and
tendencies; then, what proves to be good for all those involved; and
finally, one declares the conclusion, the maximum collective well-being,
to be the standard for what is morally right. However, since the anti-
utilitarian Rawls, a large segment of Anglo-American ethics has been
inspired by the Kantian point of view that the morally right has priority
over the subjectively good: "A just social system determines the domain
in which the goals of the individual"—that is, his needs and interests,
attitudes and tendencies—"must be held" (Rawls 1972, section 6).

Eudaimonism appears to contradict Kant and Rawls because it takes
the final goal to be an absolutely highest good, the teleological aspiration for happiness, and thereby privileges the good over the right—in
Greek: the privileging of *agathon* over *deon.* However, the weight given
to justice in eudaimonic ethics generates doubt about the validity of
this popular reading. According to Aristotle, the criterion of justice is
not like the other virtues, which are dependent upon the subject (as a
"subjective-objective mean for us"), but is the solely objective "factual
mean" (*meson pragmatos: Nicomachean Ethics* 5.5.1131a14ff.). Justice is
independent of that which the individual determines to be good for
himself; one may pursue one's personal interest only within the frame-

work of justice. It may be that ultimately the virtue of justice assists the individual (better: assists the personal good of an entire life). However, the objective demand of justice is independent of the individual and demands its fulfillment entirely without any concern for eudaimonia. In addition, none of the other virtues has any license to ameliorate the demand for justice. Even the one corrective to justice, equity, permits no deviation. On the contrary, it functions as a "higher justice" that in extraordinary situations aids in the realization of justice.

The same is true for the other virtues, as well. They, too, involve a privileging of the right over the good. A reflective relationship to the emotions consists in a service to happiness; hence, to the good of an individual. However, when we take into consideration the range and depth of legitimacy, the virtues have the status of an end in themselves that is a long way from serving only as a measurement of one's personal well-being. A prudent appeal to life wisdom in order to refrain from a virtuous act is excluded. When it comes to virtue, the morally right enjoys the absolute priority.

There is a further consideration in favor of this priority that is simultaneously opposed to the assessment of eudaimonism as a superior, even nonmoral theory. Because a morally right act occurs for its own sake, it does not merely correspond to the modern concept of legality. With the renunciation of the constraints of a merely prudential cleverness, even a eudaimonistic virtue is elevated to morals.

14 From an Ethic of Teleological Aspiration to an Ethic of the Will

Neither an alleged dominance of egocentrism nor an ostensibly objective prudential virtue stands in opposition to an ethic of teleological aspiration and its principle of happiness. Furthermore, the feared euthanasia of morals is avoided because there would be no privileging of the good over the right. Critique commences, however, with the illegitimate prioritizing of theoretical over practical reason and encounters a further, more fundamental, limit: when one thinks of reason as practical, it is as a driving force that in the case of *pure* practical reason is free from anything nonrational, especially from sensuousness. This is not to say that action as a whole has this freedom, but only a single moment, the final motivating force, and only in the case of a pure practical reason.

However, this claim is based on an entirely different model of action from that of teleological aspiration. It is a model based on willing. Popular discourse doesn't distinguish between aspiring and willing. When someone says, "I want x," he means: "I have a desire for x and I engage a course of action that leads to it." Willing in a more narrow sense, however, is different from desire. Willing is confronted with the question: "Should I or should I not do x?" Whereas teleological aspiration is oriented toward a goal, and consequently is concerned with "where to," the strict concept of willing looks at "wherefrom," at the origin of the movement in what moves (i.e., at the will). This new model of action doesn't ignore normative principles, however. When it comes to teleological aspiration, the highest, normative point of orientation, the superlative of unlimited happiness, consists in an absolutely highest "where to" in the sense of happiness as eudaimonia. In the case of willing, on the contrary, the point of orientation is an originating "wherefrom." A superlative beginning replaces a superlative end, and this origin is established where the commencement of an action is not driven by something external but receives its impetus from the individual himself.

How we are to think about this principle, as well as the engagement of a host of objections to it and misunderstandings associated with these objections, will be the concern of part 3. Here one can say this much: the will that is self-determining does so on the basis of a fundamental ground, its "law" (*nomos*), by itself (*auto-*); hence, auto-nomy. Liberated in this sense, although only in relationship to elements that themselves have no will, one is a pure and, *to this extent,* a free will. Appropriate to the rational nature of the impetus, it is synonymous with pure practical reason. As a consequence, we are concerned here with an investigation of a fundamentally different ethic in contrast to a theoretical ethic: after having examined an ethic of teleological aspiration, here we are concerned with an ethic of the will with its principle of autonomy.

Already we can see that, although it wants to be a counterpoint to modernity, contemporary virtue ethics is not concerned with the distinction between antiquity and modernity. One who takes Aristotle as the protagonist of eudaimonistic- and virtue-ethics and Kant, in contrast, as the primary representative of a willing- and autonomy-ethics, accomplishes by means of the contrasts between them more than a mere contribution to the history of moral philosophy. He engages at least four debates: that with respect to the difference between antiquity and modernity as historical epochs; that with respect to the fundamental nature of ethics; that with respect to ethics' exoneration from eudaimonic success; and, not least, that with respect to the contemporary meaning of moral consciousness.

For a long time Aristotle and Kant were viewed not only as important but also as alternative moral philosophers. One was either an Aristotelian or a Kantian, but not simultaneously both. There was hardly even a conversation between the two schools. However, if one is not led astray by the differences in conceptual frameworks, one discovers weighty commonalities between them. These begin with an extremely formal concept, to be sure, that is fundamental to all moral praxis. Ultimately, the normative principle of action consists for Kant neither in autonomy nor in the good will and for Aristotle neither in eudaimonia nor in happiness. Both—as one can see by a quick glance at the appropriate passages—are more concerned with the superlative, with the idea of the absolute good.

The famous introductory sentence from Kant's *Groundwork of the Metaphysics of Morals*—"a good will is alone without qualification good"—

provides ethics with a semantic criterion: "morally good" means "absolutely" or "unconditionally good." In addition, Kant makes the claim of exclusivity: only a good will satisfies this criterion. Aristotle maintains something similar with respect to happiness at the beginning of the *Nicomachean Ethics*. Happiness, by means of the characteristic of a superlative good, shows itself to be that goal we seek for its own sake and for the sake of which we seek all other things; as the highest of all practical and practicable goods; as something that is self-sufficient and desirable for itself alone to which nothing could be added; and above all as the goal that possesses the greatest-goal character as the absolutely perfect goal.

It is only against the background of this commonality, the idea of an absolute good, that their differences emerge. With Aristotle, the superlative is teleological; with Kant, it has in a literal sense an "archaeological" character: one who evaluates praxis raises a question that in the case of teleological aspiration finds its answer first with the idea of an absolute or an unsurpassable goal (*telos*); in the case of willing, in contrast, the question finds its answer in an unsurpassable and ultimate wherefrom (*archê:* "beginning," "origin"). The difference between the eudaimonic-oriented antiquity and the autonomy-oriented modernity is based not in the idea of an unsurpassable good, but in the concept of action to which the idea of the good is applied. The decisive difference, then, doesn't occur on the genuinely normative side but from the side of the theory of action. In this respect, Kant changes the focus radically in contrast to Aristotle. What now matters is no longer the goal but the beginning. The appropriate superlative rests in laws or principles whose origins are not external to the will but are located within the will itself.

The fact that the normative moment, the superlative moment, is shared by both, but the conception of action is different, is the point at which questions arise for both authors. It is not the recognition or the rejection of the concept of virtue that distinguishes antiquity and modernity; it is the theoretical framework of teleological aspiration and willing that distinguishes them. The usual distinction between an "ethic of the good life" (Aristotle) and an "ethic of duty or deontology" (Kant) is, therefore, of secondary significance; it is appropriate only in a limited sense. The end-in-itself character of virtue contains the eudaimonic deontological element; and according to duty ethics, the one who follows the principle of autonomy leads a good life.

On the one hand, the ultimate "where to" of happiness lies, as we have seen, not exclusively in the hands of humanity. It could look different when it comes to the first "wherefrom," the free will. Interest in the intensification of responsibility speaks in favor of a shift from teleological aspiration to willing. In the case of happiness, the individual is only *for the most part responsible,* whereas in the case of autonomy and right action the individual is potentially *totally responsible.*

On the other hand, the individual remains interested in a successful life. That the ethic of teleological aspiration, because entirely replaced by an ethic of willing, loses all claim to being right appears, therefore, to be implausible. Humanity wants both: to be right or moral and happy, so that the question is raised whether or not they can be combined and, even, whether or not they might be equivalent. With respect to an ethic of teleological aspiration, the question of how it is possible for a (morally) correct life to be a (eudaimonic) good life is answered in two steps: First, one determines the virtuous or moral life to be mostly, but not always, happy. Second, the principle of happiness is not allowed to become the feared euthanasia of morals. With respect to an ethic of willing, the question becomes how a good life is possible as a morally correct life: is it conceptually thinkable, and, in addition, with respect to life practice, is it possible that a moral life can also bring one happiness?

None of the following four elements is restricted to a particular epoch or culture: neither the thought of an unlimited good, nor the two fundamental models, teleological aspiration– and a will-based theory of action—the orientation of an ethic of teleological aspiration toward (eudaimonic) happiness and an ethic of the will toward an autonomous will—nor, finally, the further questioning of these two basic forms of moral philosophy. There is only a single attestation that these elements are universal: because they are formally open to different conceptions of life, not only happiness as an unsurpassable highest goal but also autonomy as the absolute original beginning are such that it is appropriate to view them as binding for a single culture and, therefore, only culturally relative. They deny not merely every attachment to a specific culture; they are not even limited to humanity as a biological species. Every species that strives for goals desires to achieve its goals. Ultimately, the desire is also for happiness as a consequence of the fulfillment of those goals. The same is true for autonomy. It is such a formal principle of morals that it applies not only to all human beings in all cultures but also to nonhuman species—*insofar as* they are both sensuous and rational beings.

Part 3
The Principle
of Freedom:
Autonomy

Freedom is a key concept of European modernity. Likewise, it is a concept that even helps one to understand the distinctiveness of humanity. In philosophical ethics, it is a principal concept that distinguishes an ethic of the will from an ethic of aspiration. An ambiguity is jointly responsible for this ability of freedom to undertake such diverse roles, namely, to serve as the concept for an epoch, as an anthropological concept, and as a moral principle. Within the framework of this ambiguity, the form that is determinative for an ethic of the will, moral freedom, will first be located (chapter 15), then developed step-by-step until, finally, the highest level, the freedom of the will, is reached.

Moral freedom is concerned neither with political freedom nor with any other form of social freedom but with the freedom of the individual (but not the isolated individual), with personal freedom. This personal freedom shows itself at two levels: in the freedom to act with which we are already familiar in the ethic of aspiration, and in the freedom of the will that is proper to the ethic of the will. Even the more elementary level (that of the freedom to act) does not consist in capriciousness but in the capacity to act on the basis of one's own reasons, which is also called practical reason. It will be necessary to examine more thoroughly the concept of practical reasons and practical reason that was introduced in part 1 (chapter 16). According to the three levels of assessment in constructive semantics, one can distinguish among three levels of reason, which correspond to three levels of freedom: technical, pragmatic, and moral freedom. The notion of a practical reason reaches its highest formulation in a certain respect at the third and highest level of freedom. Three additional and just as difficult and controversial concepts will come into play at this point: freedom of the will in the strictest sense, autonomy of the will, and pure practical reason (chapter 17).

Political freedom involves something disturbing which a citizen of Geneva, French intellectual, and European philosopher expressed as provocatively as he did paradoxically: "Man is born free, but everywhere he is in chains." This thesis from Jean-Jacques Rousseau applies just as well to moral freedom. There are internal chains in addition to political and social chains. Determinism maintains that because of these internal chains the freedom to act, or at the very least the freedom of the will, is an illusion (chapter 18). Recently, neurobiology has embraced this conclusion with missionary enthusiasm (chapter 19).

Only when counterarguments have been at least in part neutralized will it be possible to develop the criteria for moral freedom, that is, universal principles for life (maxims), and confront these with two popular alternatives, consequentialism and discourse ethics (chapter 20). On the basis of a discussion of two examples of universalizable principles of life (chapter 21), the question arises of whether or not there is any such thing as the highest level of moral freedom (i.e., freedom of the will). In addition to the preliminary question of which conditions are to be fulfilled for the possibility of the freedom of the will, there is the more fundamental question of whether these conditions can be fulfilled (chapter 22). In addition, one must at least provisionally discuss a concept that raises such difficult problems that many moral philosophers would prefer to ignore it: the problem of moral evil (chapter 23).

One usually attributes questions about the art of living exclusively to theories of the good and happy life (i.e., to eudaimonic ethics). A philosophy of the freedom of the will (that is, an ethic of autonomy) calls this attribution into question. Just as the eudaimonic art of living reaches into the area of strict morals, so conversely could moral autonomy be significant for the art of living. Even the highest form of autonomous morals, authentic morals, can be integrated into the human desire for happiness (chapter 24). In conclusion, the question of the consummation of morals is raised for autonomous morals: does it bring happiness? (chapter 25).

15 Locating Moral Freedom

As with almost all of the fundamental concepts of human thought and life, the notion of freedom has multiple meanings. This is not primarily because of the ambiguities of language but because of the development of the natural and social world. Freedom at its core has a bipolar meaning. Negatively, it means independence. As "freedom from" in the sense of free from determination by others, it has an emancipatory character as a freedom from specific conditions. Positively, however, freedom means self-determination or "free for": one establishes for oneself what one will do and provides oneself the impetus to do it.

According to the negative and emancipatory concept, the fewer the precepts and requirements placed on one, the more free one is. We are concerned here with a more or less; this notion of freedom is a comparative concept, and one can speak of different grades of freedom. In addition to the gradations of freedom in this sense, one finds an enormous spectrum of its application: a folk song says that thoughts are free and means by this that they are not censored. Research is free (art, as well) that is unrestricted by political restraints; another freedom is unrestricted by economic restraints; and a third form of freedom is unbound by any sense of usefulness.

When it comes to free rhythm, the free market, and free trade, and also in the case of "Free Churches" [*Freikirchen*], free jazz, or freedom from debts, "free" means that one has detached oneself from something or from prior rules and burdens; in other words, that one has experienced limitations and overcome them. In this sense, someone can be free who has not capitulated either to inner desires or to the external "vanities of the world" like power, affluence, or prestige. According to a vagabond, someone is only truly free who is unattached to everything but the essential human needs like food and drink, sleeping and rambling. Finally, someone who has been released from restricted conditions, especially prison or a compound, has a feeling of freedom.

If the jester is considered free because he can say anything he wants, he is so at the price that no one takes him seriously. Here there is the announcement of an ambivalence with respect to negative freedom that is also manifest where one is not bound by responsibilities or obligations. In Silvio Blatter's *Zwölf Sekunden Stille* [*Twelve Seconds of Silence*] (2004, 273), the protagonist, a retired cultural editor of a Swiss newspaper, finds while visiting an exhibition: "He no longer needed to manipulate art to please a readership. That was a liberation, a never-known freedom. But it also showed him that he was here without a task. Without a task. Without responsibility." At the very least when freedom is intensified to the point of liberation from all obligations, "emancipatory freedom" loses its positive sound: whoever has already lost everything unquestionably possesses no enviable freedom because he has nothing more to lose.

Given the ambivalence that surfaces with negative freedom, the question arises whether one is free who, like another character in Blatter's novel, admittedly renounces all possessions but doesn't view the renunciation as ascetic but celebrates it as an artistic performance. Mind you, he is captive to the necessity to do something that attracts notice. Furthermore, is one free in any real sense who, like the "hero" in Pascal Mercier's novel *Night Train to Lisbon,* to be sure, breaks free from a secure career but holds on to his considerable wealth? Is not, rather, that person really free who in addition to all social bridges has also burned all financial bridges behind him? Or to the contrary, is a person really free who opportunely chooses a lifestyle that is entirely free from the dictatorship of every power be it convention, applause, money, or others only because he has broken away from the life led up to that point? Is not that person really more free who, thanks to careful planning, doesn't need any spectacular emancipation?

These questions are not the responsibility only of philosophers: a reflective understanding from everyday life, self-evidently on the part of many specific sciences, and not the least by great authors—novelists and dramatists—can be called upon. Contrary to the opinion of many philosophers who are lovers of provocation, neither a single external nonphilosophical competency nor any combination of such competencies alone is in charge here. Indeed, a theory of moral freedom depends heavily on philosophy for conceptual clarification, for raising provocative challenges, and, finally, for a constructive thought process.

When it comes to a discussion of freedom in this respect, anyone who is not content merely to reject long-standing (social, scientific, or artistic) governing rules needs new content and standards and, to satisfy them, requires creativity and originality. For this reason, there is a constructive freedom of emancipation devoted to the reversal of established rules; it is, once again, a comparative concept: on the one hand, someone enjoys more freedom the more he establishes and accomplishes goals for himself; on the other hand, he enjoys more freedom the more unconventional and challenging his selected goals. Obviously, the "on the one hand" depends upon one's physical, mental, and affective capacities but also upon one's economic, political, and cultural circumstances; the "on the other hand" in contrast depends upon self-confidence and a confidence in the world, as well as courage.

Conceptual history (see Conze et al. 1975; on antiquity, see Raaflaub 1985) evokes an additional meaning for freedom as a legal concept. Here freedom means, first of all, a higher right, a privilege, that distinguishes "the free" from submissive dependence, hereditary serfs, bondsmen, and slaves. "The free" live for their own sake as full-valued members of a legal community. Free individuals are "in the same boat" because the protection guaranteed by their shared legal community depends upon reciprocity—with the consequence that freedom is related to solidarity. In addition, because free individuals know and also work with one another, they can be united with one another in friendship.

The ambiguity of meaning announced by these examples permits neither classification according to a single scale nor assignment to a single family of concepts. Rather, there are many different perspectives under which the meanings may be grouped. Six perspectives will be addressed here, although in most cases we are concerned with a binary division.

The first binary division is concerned with the prognostic symptoms or perspective with which one engages freedom. In this case the emancipatory concept, the independence or "freedom from," stands over and against the primarily constructive concept of self-determination, "freedom for."

With the second thematic ambiguity, freedom qualifies such different objects as musical forms and the market, relationships of civil and public rights, and natural persons. Especially important, however, is the binary distinction with respect to social freedom (with legal and political freedom constituting a significant subspecies) and the personal freedom of a natural subject.

Thirdly, freedom occurs in two modalities: either as an experienced actuality or as a demand. When it comes to its empirical meaning as in, for example, a group of free individuals in a social unit, freedom means "is" in contrast to the prescriptive and normative meaning of "should" expressed, for example, by the demand for legal protection.

With natural persons, freedom consists in an elementary sense of the capacity to act out of one's own free will. This concept of action theory is obviously not bound to the status of rights possessed by "the free," and, precisely as a consequence, it harbors revolutionary power. It contains the potential for a universalization that destroys the privilege of certain groups and allows freedom to be an attribute of every individual. As the peculiar right of each person, freedom loses its discriminatory power: with the elimination of slavery each individual obtains the status of a free legal subject. (With the elimination of colonialism and satellite states, all societies have acquired freedom, to be sure often only as regards foreign policy.)

With this process of liberation there emerges a fourth ambiguity, the extent of freedom. Here two levels become obvious: either a few representatives possess freedom or everyone does. In the first case, freedom is a particular, in the second, a universal concept. The corresponding development—that at first one, later a few, even later many, and in the end all are free—could develop linearly. Actual historical experience, however, demonstrates that the development is more likely to involve gaps, regressions, and then again erratic progress.

There are different levels within the parameters of personal and positive freedom, in which—this is the fifth ambiguity—once again, a binary division occupies the foreground: the self-determination of action, or freedom of action; and the self-determination of the will, or freedom of the will.

In addition to these five ambiguities with respect to freedom, there is, sixth, a gradation related to freedom. A child has narrower limits than an adult; the ill, poor, or weak in certain respects have narrower limits than the healthy, rich, or powerful. Furthermore, one possesses more freedom insofar as more intelligence and experience allow one to see possibilities for action, and one possesses more freedom the more one likes the available possibilities because they fit one's temperament and character. Even further, the fewer restrictions that are established by society and the state, the freer one is. Not least, one can say that that individual possesses complete freedom who does not have to say in advance what he plans to do; in contrast, he has partial freedom who has to announce a good bit in advance what his plans are (Sten Nadolny, *The Discovery of Slowness* [*Die Entdeckung der Langsamkeit*], 1987, 36).

As an addendum, one can point to a further meaning of freedom as generosity that is important for ethics as the art of living: free is one who with his financial and other resources is neither parsimonious nor lavish but, rather, sovereign and generous.

What is the location of freedom as an ethical concept (that is, moral freedom and its consummation in freedom of the will) in light of this broad, confusing conceptual field? In everyday experience, in the social sciences, even in philosophy, one likes to view morals as an exclusively, or at least primarily, social phenomenon. Within the parameters of our second, thematic ambiguity, one could therefore view social freedom as overriding. However, fundamental ethics is concerned with subjects who are responsible for their actions and who not only derive their sense of responsibility from their fellows but also from themselves. Freedom on the part of the responsible subject, in other words, personal freedom, constitutes the primary concern of ethics. It leaves open whether or not morals are exclusively or above all a social matter. Two prognostic symptoms play a role for personal freedom: not only independence from determinism by others, but also self-determination.

With the third, modal ambiguity, it appears at first glance that only a "should" is at stake because, on methodological grounds when it comes to empirical ethics, it is less philosophy that is affected than the wide spectrum of the social sciences. However, philosophy is also concerned when it comes to the question of the actuality of freedom. Philosophy aids in clarifying whether or not there is any such thing as personal freedom, even if only with respect to the first level, freedom of action, or also with respect to the second level, freedom of the will.

When it comes to the question of the extent of freedom, philosophy tends toward the more pretentious option common to all humans. Philosophy works with a universal human capacity, reason; views personal freedom—at first only somehow—as united with reason; and expects for both freedom and reason a universal meaning common to all. The assumption from the very beginning of this universal meaning by philosophy is, of course, prohibited; it is no premise but a thesis that must be defended against alternatives.

The last perspective, the gradation of freedom, is not as important as the two levels for fundamental ethics. For morals, the highest level is to be expected, the elevation of free action to freedom of the will. However, as long as the question remains open whether or not there is anything valid to the second level, one speaks of moral freedom as neutral with respect to the distinction between freedom of action and freedom of the will. Moral freedom constitutes the primary concern of ethics within the parameters of personal freedom, whereas freedom of the will reflects a controversial thesis.

16 Practical Reason: Freedom of Action

An ethic of the will is aware that its primary concept, freedom of the will in the sense of pure practical reason, is unusual; hence, not only is it in need of clarification but also of justification. In order to *clarify* the concept, it starts with the uncontroversial concept of the simple agency of an action. From this starting point, it develops step-by-step first the concept of free agency; then, by means of the concept of practical reasons it develops its clarification further by means of two additional concepts that remain a bit controversial to aspirational ethics: freedom of action and not pure, but at first simply practical, reason.

16.1 Free Agency

Imagine that someone as he falls over a cliff reflexively attempts to catch himself by grabbing the person next to him and, thereby, causes serious injury to this other person. In a second incident, someone stumbles toward a vase and breaks it; and in a third, one falls on a switch and sets off an alarm. All three events can be described by an "on the one hand" and an "on the other hand."

On the one hand, the persons involved are agents. Although the consequences are nothing that was intended, nonetheless, they are directly attributable to the individuals. The first is the direct cause of the affected person's injury, the second of the damage to the vase, and the third of the alarm sounding. On the other hand, it is at least assumed that the falls are neither affected nor "orchestrated." What the individuals caused is not under their power; they "couldn't help it." They are agents but not authors in the exacting sense of having intended the consequences; they merely accept them. Because the persons concerned neither wanted to happen what happened *to* them, the fall, nor wanted what occurred *because of* their action, an injury to someone, damage to something, or the setting off of the alarm—to the contrary, they were surprised—one cannot hold them accountable for the specific actions. One can attribute the cause to them but not any intention.

The same is the case with more successful consequences. The individual who by falling blocks a dangerous passage and protects others from danger no doubt caused the consequences. One cannot, however, attribute to him the benefit. He is merely the agent whom one neither praises nor condemns. He cannot assume any responsibility for the consequences.

Clearly, simple agency is not limited to humanity. A mosquito bite causes an itch. A virus or bacterium initiates a disease or genetic damage. A clinging ivy can damage the surface of a house. One does not need any "someone," a person, for simple agency. Other agents include animals and plants to the extent that they can actuate an effect by their own power and within their own possibilities. Plants grow freely that are neither trimmed nor cut. Animals live freely when they conduct themselves within the parameters of their traditional environment and develop according to the laws of their species and self-preservation. Even the accompanying space is appropriately called free; the animals in question live "free in the wild." One even speaks of a free fall and means thereby that an object moves exclusively according to the law of gravity without any (other) external influence. However, because gravity is already a form of external influence, there is no real freedom here, not even a free agency.

One is more than a simple agent, however, who unintentionally falls off a cliff and in falling takes into consideration alternatives. When he contemplates, even if only for a split second, whether there is a bush or a person on the edge available to hinder his fall and then ends up causing an injury because he decided to grab the person, it may be that the consequence was unintentional. Nevertheless, the agent assumes responsibility because he acted with knowledge and intent, since he met the characteristic conditions for freedom of action: he was aware of a range of options among alternative possibilities, seized upon one option, and simultaneously blocked the realization of other possibilities.

An initial taking-stock here draws two conclusions. On the one hand, the fundamental level of personal freedom, the freedom to act, is joined to agency even though not every agency involves the freedom of action. Everything that occurs because of someone may count the "someone," the agent, in a loose sense of the term as the author of what happens. The more demanding concept is realized where the simple agency escalates to intentionality, the actor becomes a free agent, and one can attribute to him free action, including personal responsibility for the action. On the other hand, four meanings of freedom are manifest, which build on one another and demonstrate an increased freedom with each stage. We are concerned here with a unique, increasingly complex kind of activity. Since the first three stages are not characteristic for persons, they can be called preliminary stages. Nonetheless, because they are also found in humans, the frequently discussed anthropological question of whether humanity is "natural or an exception to nature" can be answered with a "both/and": humanity is inseparable from nature but simultaneously rises above it; humanity clearly distinguishes itself from nature in which it nonetheless remains imprisoned.

A movement is free in the most modest sense when, like a free fall, there is no external impediment. At this first stage, freedom is entirely negative; it is an independence from external restraints. The activity associated with freedom at this stage that one can see in lifeless objects is not even a behavior but a mere movement. The ground for any such effect is simply a cause and by no means even a simple agent.

Freedom is enhanced when, by means of a moment of self-determination, it first becomes positive. According to this second preliminary stage, a sequence of movement is free, in the literal sense spontaneous, when it arises out of the agent itself. In this case, the appurtenant activity is reflexive but still has no conscious character. It is a self-movement (along with the corresponding freedom that it represents) that is already found in simple organisms but not in minerals. Nevertheless, it is "light-years" from anything like what one experiences as peculiarly human freedom. One does find this stage of freedom, organic self-determination, in animals and humans when it comes to purely vegetative processes like digestion.

With the third preliminary stage, we encounter practical consciousness. At this point, for example with hunger and thirst, the reflexive moment is ramped up to a practical (admittedly at first only sensuous) self-consciousness, to feelings of pleasure and displeasure. This sensuous-conscious spontaneity opens up a whole new range of behavior. One can understand hunger and thirst as a warning signal to the brain in the form of a feeling of deficiency in food and drink that is combined with the drive to satisfy it. The feelings are originally only a drive and not yet an obedience to the drive that allays the hunger or appeases the thirst. This elementary practical consciousness is by no means found only with such highly developed species as primates but also in other animals, although only at a rudimentary level. Nonetheless, the fact that it extends into the personal realm means that it constitutes a transition stage to the primary level, which consists of action and freedom of action.

The primary stage presents itself with three levels so that, more precisely, one can speak of three primary stages. What they share in common is the capacity, thanks to thought- and language-aptitude, to develop one's own activities with their appropriate reflections; in other words, to act according to one's own and not someone else's reasons. For example, in the case of hunger and thirst, these reflections include when and how to satisfy one's need; further, how one is to avoid other feelings of pleasure and displeasure, and not least the question, how one could avoid them: shortsightedly and insularly, or, rather, sustainably and with interconnectedness, or even, when it comes to more ambitious goals, with long-term renunciation. This structurally complex behavior that is self-conscious with respect to thought and simultaneously a self-controlling and self-directed spontaneity is what is called "action" in the narrower sense of the word, which is characteristic of humanity. It encompasses not only making or producing, *poiesis*, but also action in the sense of praxis (see chapter 6.1).

With respect to the additional question of the "ontology" of action, there are two points of view: event individuation (attribute or accidents) theory [*Eigenschaftstheorie*] and event identity theory [*Ereignistheorie*]. In addition to their clear advantages, both have obvious disadvantages. The associated, quickly sophisticated debates (see Pfeifer 1989) are not essential for the discussion of moral freedom and, therefore, are not considered here.

As a capacity to act (self-)consciously ("with representation") and freely ("spontaneously"), freedom of action permits the attribution of actions and taking the agent to be of sound mind and a person capable of taking responsibility. Soundness of mind and personhood therefore belong together, but certainly not so narrowly that one could in any way deny personhood to persons without soundness of mind; for example, babies, the mentally challenged, and those with severe dementia. In contrast, someone who acts only recklessly and carelessly is a person whom one can accuse of and to whom one can attribute precisely these characteristics of riskiness and carelessness.

There is only one important point with respect to the other no longer personal but social meaning, one's room for maneuver, which is made possible by one's social and political environment: even in the circumstance of a high measure of social freedom, one's own actions are in many ways conditioned by physical, mental, and affective limitations, even as a consequence of one's unique experience. Whether or not this multifarious determinism contradicts the very freedom for action is something yet to be examined (chapter 18). However, now we can already say that the concept of freedom of action does not consist in a pure freedom. Freedom of action is not something opposite to determinism but to necessity and external conditioning.

According to an existential heroic freedom, real freedom is manifest only in the dramatic transformation of one's previous life, in the abrupt escape from familiar and occupational responsibilities, and also in religious or political conversion. According to the existentialism of a Jean-Paul Sartre (1963, 34), humanity is condemned to be free because it is nothing other than what it makes of itself, with the consequence that it must assume the entire responsibility for its existence. What a person makes of himself does not arise, admittedly, from a conscious will but from an originating projection. Nonetheless, the individual is responsible for this projection; and in addition, one also bears responsibility for all other persons.

It is not necessary here to test this highly ambitious claim. The concept of freedom of action is far more restrained and less emotional and doesn't have to address every element of its condition to begin radically anew out of nothingness. Just as little must one make a break with all convention and lead a preferably eccentric life. "Freedom of action" means simply the ability to act out of knowledge and approval. Conditions definitely remain given, but they do not have the weight of immutable factors. A person is capable of engaging them consciously and deliberately. This engagement of practical self-relationality as an activity is called "volition," as a capacity or ability "will."

"Volition" here means a selection or intention, even a wish, assuming that it results in some effect of action. A mere wish is not sufficient. One can indeed wish that one is immortal, that one's train will run on time, or that tomorrow the sun will shine, but one is incapable of willing such wishes. Immortality is unattainable, the punctuality of trains is not under one's control, and one has no influence over how the weather will be tomorrow. Likewise, a mere wish to see a drowning person saved doesn't alone undertake anything to accomplish his rescue. Already known to and compatible with the aspirational model's notion of volition is the requirement that one has an effect upon the world as a consequence of the application of one's own powers—or at least one's attempts to do so. Furthermore, the "will" means the fundamental capacity that is assumed by volition, without turning this capacity into some kind of real substance as some kind of quasi-empirical but nevertheless objective mental substance removed from experience, which is alleged by over-hasty critics.

Where does freedom begin and end? Is someone acting freely who with a gun aimed at his head turns over his wallet to a robber? Is the captain free who in the midst of a violent storm seeks to save his ship and sailors by throwing part of the ship's cargo overboard? Is the patient free after a serious accident to whom a medical doctor discloses: "We have to amputate your leg; we have no other choice," or the person who in honest self-defense shoots someone else? In each case the spontaneous answer is "No!" but upon closer examination this answer demands correction.

Without question, none of these persons is a simple agent because each is free to refuse to hand over the wallet, to throw the cargo overboard, or to refuse the operation.

When the perpetrator of violence asks not for the wallet but for a life, a refusal even seems obligatory (see chapter 22.1)—one has no choice. Whoever chooses, then, not to turn over the wallet calls into play things that one usually values more than money. In light of this unexpressed assumption, he can maintain (as in the case of the captain or the medical doctor) that he has no choice. Nonetheless, he acts knowledgeably: he sees an alternative reaction; and he acts willfully: even when, driven by the terror of the loss of his life, he reacts "automatically," the action occurs on the basis of consent. An alternative kind of reaction occurs when someone suddenly confronted with danger is so powerfully affected that he is overwhelmed by a panic attack and acts only reflexively or, as if paralyzed, just stands there. (From the captain, of course, one certainly expects a "cool head.")

It doesn't take any special knowledge either from the sciences or from philosophy to recognize in these examples that one neither entirely possesses nor entirely lacks room for maneuver. Common understanding acknowledges a gradation: depending on the situation but also on the person, one has at one's disposal more or less room for maneuver.

Let's first consider the extremes, the pure "No!" and the pure "Yes!" Those events in which there is no freedom of action are, for example, the digestion process, movements while one is sleeping, the involuntary twitching of an eyelid, and an epileptic seizure. In contrast, one cannot solve a mathematical or a chess problem without knowledge and intention. In such events one explicitly encounters all of the moments that otherwise are only silently present: one sees alternative possibilities of action; frequently, one must even discover or create those possibilities; one weighs the possibilities against one another; one chooses among them the one taken to be the (relative) best; and one seizes upon the chosen possibility.

Between these two extremes are limitless intermediate degrees. The moment of volition can occur in a strong but also in a weak sense, which for its part can depend upon the degree of knowledge: beginning with the half-conscious condition at the moment of waking, through automatic answers and thoughtless routine actions, up to thoroughly conscious decisions. There is also the possibility that, as a consequence of alcohol or drugs, one is no longer sufficiently in control of one's senses to pursue a clear goal. In such cases one is on the edge, at least, of unaccountability. Someone who is judged to be unaccountable commits an *actio libera in causa,* which is a free action (*libera*) with a cause (*causa*) that leads to a non-free status so that one is not responsible for the action *but is* responsible for having made oneself not responsible. (On the case in criminal law, see Lackner and Kühl 2004, section 20, and Gläser 2005; on the concept of responsibility, see Höffe 2000c, chapter 2.)

Elsewhere, a structural complication can occur, as well. One can forgo something but, also, bring oneself to do something. One can surrender the initiative to someone else or snatch it for oneself ("taking the notebook back into one's own hands"), which raises the question to what degree something lies in one's power—even when the power is very little. In this case two levels are distinguishable: volition at the first level is concerned with normal actions, whereas at the second level volition is concerned with the responsibility for the standard employed for measuring the level of volition at the first level.

That one trips up or forgets something can happen to anyone. However, such things occur less frequently to the degree that one is attentive and vigilant. Another is only in part free, for example, because he grasps only a certain aspect of the event: one intentionally eats a mushroom, but unintentionally a poisonous one; Oedipus intentionally slew a man, but unknowingly his own father. In general, human action depends upon factors that, beginning with natural laws, are not in the control of the agent, are not even conscious to him (see chapters 18–19). Furthermore, in hindsight one can give different, even contradictory justifications for one's action.

Philosophy is not concerned with deciding the extent of freedom of action in particular cases. That decision is the concern of the agent and

those affected by him; in serious circumstances it is the concern, in the
first case, of conscience and, in the second, of the law. Both, however,
can be aided by applied ethics. Fundamental ethics is concerned with
the structural indications to which we have referred: based upon knowledge, opinion, and intention, one's freedom of action extends beyond
mere agency. This extension can possess a strength of different degrees:
from a minimum of knowledge and volition to an appropriate measure
of one or the other, and finally up to a maximum of both. The extreme
claim, however, that everyone acts intentionally in every situation and
with complete knowledge (not only with respect to a given situation but
with respect to the consequences of the chosen action) and with complete volition (without any aspect of an internal or external necessity) is
entirely alien to a deliberate philosophical theory of freedom.

16.2 Acting According to Reasons

According to a widely shared opinion, freedom is taken to be a "wild"
freedom that acts just as impetuously as it does unreflectively and wan-
tonly, and even delights in unbounded capriciousness. Because in fact a
practical knowledge is constitutive for freedom of action, it at least rules
out a pure unruliness, that anarchy which makes action unpredictable
and surprises others, perhaps even the agent himself.

When it comes to practical knowledge, one must distinguish the concept of its indispensable minimum from optional additions. Optional
are genuinely normative parts, those insights into norms, values, and principles that establish what is normative, practical knowledge. Its degree of
knowledge (cognitive level) extends from normal moral consciousness to
its carefully reflective form, and finally up to philosophical knowledge of
principles. Likewise optional are those parts relevant to action but theoretical that are concerned with the description of a situation and with
means-ends relationships. In contrast to a nonacting but pure, epistemologically relevant knowledge, we are concerned here with a normative-
practical knowledge. Both normative-practical and theoretical-practical
knowledge increase free agency; they belong not merely to the basic
level of agency. Only a third kind of knowledge is no longer optional
with respect to norms, a practical knowledge that is concerned with
what one does or does not do; this is "reflective-practical knowledge."
Where this kind of reflective-practical knowledge is absent, there is also
no freedom of action because one doesn't know what one is doing, as in

sleeping, contemplation, or in a certain respect as with Oedipus and the aforementioned mushroom eater.

Knowledge does not need to be objectively valid and undoubtedly correct in these three cases. Sufficient is a presumed, even only an alleged knowledge, an agent's opinion, a practical belief. Decisive is that the knowledge affects the action of the respective agent and that it consciously influences him. Neither of these may just somehow and somewhere happen, but must come into play in his actual action. As an (eventually, only alleged) knowledge out of which the action arises, this knowledge has a practical and simultaneously subjective character.

Knowledge can be limited to the mere "what" of an action. For example, someone wants to overcome his lethargy and finally do something without determining the kind of action. Since knowledge influences only the motivation but not its nearer goal and the means to it, the corresponding freedom of action is limited. It is content with a freedom of exertion (*libertas exerciti*), which consists of the freedom to act or not to act, and does not include the freedom of discretion (*libertas specificationis*), which consists of the freedom to act one way or another.

If one asks about the cause in the case of simple agency, it is impersonal not in reference to a subhuman being ("Why did the bee sting?") but in reference to a person, even oneself: "Why when I fell did I reflexively grab the ledge?" The "self" is turned here into the third person *about* whom one speaks and not *with* or *to* whom one speaks. Consequently, the answer consists in a practical knowledge independent of the agent and is an a-personal cause. In the case of the bee, the answer might be: "It was frightened." One says the same of a person, whether another or oneself: "He/I began to fall, panicked, and tried to cling to the closest object."

As we have said, the situation is different when the falling individual thinks about whether he should grab on to another person, who could be then injured, or grab the ledge, or grab the certainly seizable root rather than attempt to cling to the apparently slippery rock. Only at such a point is one confronted with multiple possibilities, weighs them against one another, and makes a decision. Even if to the most rudimentary degree, this free agency allows the question that appears to be improper when asked of the bee that stings out of nervousness, and altogether improper when asked of plants and animals (at least most animals). This is the question of accountability: "With what right did the cause occur?"

The question of accountability can be applied to all three grammatically possible persons and ultimately applies to one and the same person, the agent of the action. Whether singular or plural: in the first person, the agent asks himself: "Why did I grab the person and not the root?" In the second person, the agent is questioned by a victim and often with an undertone of upbraiding: "Why did you grab me and place me in danger?" Finally, a nonvictimized third person, for example a judge, can ask the agent why he acted as he did.

The answer in all three cases consists in a reflexive practical knowledge (it consists in providing practical reasons) and, indeed, in the reasons themselves, not in theoretical knowledge about practical reasons and not at all with respect to indifferent causes opposed to practical knowledge. One can attribute to the reasons the character of causes, as we've said, because they are mental events that bring forth actions that are visible events in a shared world (Davidson 1980, e.g., chapter 3). However, the "ontological" question of the kind of being possessed by the reasons is not asked initially. Even someone who holds reasons to be causes hardly doubts that the essential reasons here, the arguments for and against an action, have the character of practical knowledge, which distinguishes them from the usual, knowledge-independent causes. Normal causes are external to the accountability of a person: they are external causes of accountability; practical reasons are, in contrast, internal causes of accountability. In contrast to external causes of accountability, causes based on reasons are subject to the choice between approval and disapproval. External causes actually change the world; reasoned causes have merely the potential to do so. Whether or not they actually change the world depends upon the subject who has accepted or rejected the reasons—silently or explicitly.

Practical reasons contain a demand character, and therefore one also speaks of imperatives. What is meant here is not the capricious command of an overwhelming power. The demands to close a window or to stop smoking have the status in a moral sense of imperatives only when in the background there is an argument, in this case: either one's own or the other's health, which justifies the demand. Whoever wishes to lead his life well in the technical, pragmatic, or moral sense must capitulate to the appropriate imperatives. Whether or not he does so in fact is another question.

16.3 Reasons and Pretense

Reasons can occur in combination with other reasons and constitute a network, in the end even a world, of reasons. This world can be valid only for a single individual, or for smaller or larger groups, and finally for all of humanity. Furthermore, this world can establish order in different fashions. Not least, one can run up against compatibilities and also against incompatibilities, even contradictions.

With respect to the question of effectiveness, there are three known modalities. Practical reasons apply either possibly or actually or even necessarily. In the first case, they *can be* effectual (problematic-practical); in the second, they are actually so (assertorically-practical); and, in the third sense, something unavoidably occurs (apodictically-practical). These three levels of effectiveness or validity [*Geltung*] are certainly to be distinguished from the three levels of applicability [*Gültigkeit*] even if one employs for both the same technical Latin language (chapter 2.2): modal technical reasons are problematic, pragmatic reasons are assertoric, and truly moral reasons are apodictically valid.

Each of these three modalities occurs in at least three functions within the framework of accountability. (In addition, one can throw in an independent explanation of accountability.) Either reasons should justify the action as good and right, at least as "definitely defensible"; or reasons should excuse an action although it is not good. And finally, they can expose an action as bad. In terms of function, then, there are justifying, excusing, and exposing, compromising reasons.

When it comes to more important decisions, it is often the case that a partly hasty and partly thorough evaluation of reasons with their respective negligent or attentive weighing of alternatives transpires in advance of a decision. One can compare this creative task with the construction of a geometrical figure. For a given goal one constructs in thought an action that one believes will lead to the goal and is in fact realizable. Because in many cases the goal cannot be achieved directly but only as a consequence of a long chain of events, the calculations for such a chain of events flow backward from the goal until they—this, too, corresponds to a geometrical construction—reach the starting point, the agent. In contrast to a geometrical construction, however, practical calculation often has the character of an internal pushing and pulling. It is often the case that an ambivalence, equivocality, and ambiguity prevails that is compounded by indecision and combined with an uncertainty that can endure even after the decision has been made. It is not necessary that the subject's action-effective knowledge consist in a pettily ordered world of reasons.

Both aspects of practical knowledge (the knowledgeable and intentional moment, as well as all three modalities) and not least the three functions are susceptible to a double deception. In an attempt to avoid reproach or even punishment or in an attempt to accept an unearned praise, one can deceive others. Furthermore, one deceives even oneself when it comes to saving one's self-assessment and self-worth, one's carefully cultivated self-image of "moral integrity."

There is a second hemisphere to the world of deception. It consists, as well, of two parts: deception of the other and of the self. With respect to unintentional self-deception, an agent usually can have only a partial clarity about events; other aspects emerge after the fact, while some become clear only after many years, and some things remain forever concealed. Not least, one can succumb to a deep disappointment, a fundamental illusion, or an ideology.

It may seem that this huge world of deception is aggravating. Surprisingly, however, it is not. Subjective, practical reasons are far too important, too consequential, and of too serious consequence, even often existentially decisive, for one to take them constantly only at face value. Like the still-underaged Briony in the novel by Ian McEwan, many a person is sheltered by means of "a ruthless, youthful light-heartedness, a self-serving forgetfulness well into puberty" (*Atonement*, chapter 1).

The capacity to intentionally mislead others even when one knows better, thus, the capacity to lie (additionally, the capacity to lie to oneself or to deceive oneself), appears to be specific to humanity. The only species that is capable of more than a rudimentary morals is just as capable, as well, of more than a rudimentary immorality. Whoever in fact never lies is a highly moral individual; whoever, in contrast, is incapable of lying is not in some respect even more moral; rather, he is not a human being.

Both hemispheres, of deception and of nondeception, constitute together a "world of reasons and pretenses."

16.4 Levels of Practical Reason

Subjective-practical reasons have a fourfold individualizing index. A person P_1 performs the action A_1 in the situation S_1 on the basis of the reason R_1: in order to hinder the event, P_1 grabs toward the cliff within reach. According to the individualizing index, there is a specific reason for every concrete action; individual actions have individual reasons. Already contained in their linguistic character, reasons have more than individual validity; they are a possible rule: whoever (P_i) finds himself in a similar situation (situation segment $S_{a,i}$) and with the help of a cliff

within reach (situation segment $S_{b,i}$) seeks to stop his fall (situation segment $S_{c,i}$) has a good reason (R_i) to grab toward the cliff (A_i).

However, what is the meaning of "good" here? The expression "good"
says that the reason for the action, the justification, actually fulfills its
task. Whoever in the given situation seeks to stop his fall does well to
grab toward the cliff (it is a good thing to do). In the process, though,
one aspect is consciously, the other potentially unconsciously open.
Consciously open is the question of whether the grabbing toward the
cliff was the only possible action and whether, in the case of multiple
possibilities, it was the best possible action. This openness amounts to a
prudence when it comes to the demand for justification; it is not unusual
that justification is combined with a silent addendum; a higher demand
would realistically not be meaningful. (When it comes to competitions
or life-and-death struggles, "merely good" is not adequate.) The other,
often unconscious, openness is concerned with the kind of justification:
according to which kind of being good is the reason good? The answer
involves the decisive role of the three levels of technically, pragmatically,
and morally or categorically good.

If the agency is determined by practical reasons, it achieves the rank
of being rational. Once again, decisive here is not knowledge but the
kind of reason that governs the action. To be sure, there is only one reason, the capacity to act according to reasons. This one reason, however,
is concerned either with knowledge or with action. In the first case, it is
called theoretical reason; in the second, practical reason. Their respective
reasons are not necessarily moral. There are, in addition, technical and
pragmatic reasons, so that at first we are concerned here with the more
modest practical reason and not with the more exacting, pure practical
or moral-practical reason.

Someone does not already possess practical reason (whether pure or
in a broader sense) who merely knows how to evaluate his actions from
the standpoint of the (technical, pragmatic, moral) good; only someone
does who knows how to live according to the good. This "knowing how
to live" arises in three levels: as a negative partial power, as a positive
partial power, and as a completely sovereign power.

One has command over practical reason at the weaker level who regards the perspective of the good not as a neutral observer. A neutral observer possesses only a theoretical reason even when it is directed toward
"praxis" as an object. Reason is first practical where one perceives the demands as affecting oneself, as applying to oneself, and feels subjected to

them even when one doesn't always adhere to them (code word: weakness of the will). In the case of practical reason, the good is a *should* that is recognized by the individual involved; simultaneously, though, because of the actual acknowledgment of a *should*, it is a "being." This paradoxical manner of existence, the being of a *should*, becomes clear when someone doesn't conform to what should be according to the internal judgment of the subject—as one feels in cases of regret, remorse, or moral shame. Already at this first level, the level of a negative partial power, the good is no pure *should*, but it is at the same time a being; it contains a descriptive-prescriptive double character (see chapter 22.2): it has an experienced as well as a lived presence in the form of negative practical feelings.

Practical reason obtains a positive but also only a partial power when it finds recognition in actual action, but this is the case only occasionally, not dependably. Already at this second level, practical reason contains a complete presence and power, but only transiently. With this positive partial power, the recognition of a should is combined with an obedience that corresponds to a positive practical feeling that is manifest as the satisfaction that one has lived up to the demand of the good without any weakness (of the will). Admittedly, such a feeling occurs only occasionally.

Reason reaches the third level—complete, sovereign power—when one practices ever and again its recognition, when it is constantly renewed, and, finally, when it is made a solid component of the individual; then, it becomes a mark of one's character.

Whether negative or positive, in the case of partial power, practical reason is recognized first "in principle." Like a tree that has not yet set its roots, this level of recognition of practical reason cannot hold its own against the storm of anger, desire, or passion. Practical reason as a partial power is an (occasional or frequent) weakness of the will that is overcome when it possesses complete power. Obviously, partial or complete power is not a simple either/or. The presence of practical reason occurs far more in the form of innumerable gradations comparable to the continuous spectrum experienced with the force of wind. We focus here on four points on the scale of gradation: that of extreme weakness of the will whose practical reason is already lost with the slightest breeze, the usual weakness of the will, then the tolerably strong will, and finally the extremely strong will capable of withstanding a hurricane of temptation and seduction.

If practical reason maintains command, then one's justifying reasons simultaneously have motivational power. So-called internalists attribute this motivational power to justificatory reasons; externalists reject them. This conflict—it can now be seen—can be solved only practically, not theoretically. According to the theory of action and its reasons, both options occur. Which of the two actually occurs in a particular situation is determined by an idiosyncrasy of the acting individual; it is dependent upon the power or weakness of his practical reason.

Philosophers of action and moral philosophers have engaged this theme since antiquity. It appears under the theme of "weakness of the will" (Greek *akrasia*, Latin *incontinentia;* authoritatively, Aristotle's *Nicomachean Ethics* 7.1–11; in addition, see Höffe 2006a, chapter 13.3). Such a weak will generally consists in one's practical reason possessing too little power. In the case of moral weaknesses, the power of practical reason acknowledges morals (in contrast to evil) as its guiding light and offers competitive resistance to the storm that is too weak in the face of this competition. Otherwise than with vices, reason in the face of weakness of the will is only occasionally and not usually powerless. (One must here contradict Dante, who in his *Divine Comedy* attributes to weakness of the will sins like gluttony, avarice, and anger as habitual misconduct; for example, *Hell,* canto 5, verses 55–56: "Lechery will so dominate you, / that its law allows desires.") Within the framework of a nuanced phenomenology of moral weaknesses, the weak-willed is not the one who pursues morally corrupt habits but the one who permits his good habits to be dissuaded not constantly but time and again by anger, desire, or passion.

As has been suggested, weakness of the will is sensibly understood as a deficiency of practical reason without assuming that the weakness has too little knowledge. It knows full well what would be the good thing to do; only, this knowledge is—temporarily—a useless possession; more precisely: it is comparable to a competency that doesn't adequately assert itself. Whoever acts contrary to the good out of habit and without remorse suffers from a chronic wickedness, intemperateness, something like what Dante calls lechery, and which is difficult to cure. However, someone who, in contrast, is still capable of remorse and honestly regrets what has been done recognizes the good but only "in principle," not through actual actions. He suffers "only" from a transient and frequently curable wickedness, precisely that of the weakness of the will.

17 Autonomous Reason: Freedom of the Will

17.1 Three Levels of Freedom and Remorse

Viewed negatively, practical reason is the ability to allow one's desires to be governed ultimately neither by sensuous feelings of pleasure or displeasure, nor by the desires and dispositions of others, nor by authorities (including one's tradition). Viewed positively, practical reason is the ability to comply with reasons and, also, to hold firm to those reasons as an imagined good against sensuous temptations and social distractions. Practical reason is set off from pure sensuousness and simple authority.

Let's focus on the domain of sensuous impulses. Here practical reason rejects as its governing motive the current dominant popular needs and desires as well as the seductions from advertising and other persons. Nonetheless, practical reason calls one to action. Precisely because it consists of an instance of motivation that does not submit to the yoke of momentary pleasure and displeasure, practical reason demonstrates that it consists a double freedom, negative as well as positive. It does not consist merely negatively in freeing oneself from pleasure and displeasure as the final authority for one's decision-making. Positively it is an incentive that subordinates itself to the demands of reasons.

Motives of pleasure and displeasure such as hunger, thirst, sleeplessness, and sexuality (in short, sensuous motivations) may by all means have a certain power. It would be preposterous were humans to lose this drama that is often enough driven by strong passions, with its dramatic and at the same time productive tensions. "Practical reason" simply means not to grant superiority to sensuous motives and passions. It must, however, integrate the requirements of reasons; in other words, it must overcome pure immediacy to benefit from a motivating power shaped by the good. Whoever has done so has left behind the preliminary levels of freedom and finds himself at the three-part primary level with its equally three-tiered practical reason.

There are three levels to freedom corresponding to the three levels of the good, depending upon the scope of the reasons contained in reason's demands and not on the degree with which they are fulfilled, that is, not according to the power or powerlessness of practical reason. At the first level, the technical or functional good, reasons conform to a means-ends relationship. Whoever conforms to such laws appropriate to a practical activity has in this, but also only in this, respect a will; he has at his command a technical or functional freedom. Recall the example from the previous discussion of affluence in which one is able and must be willing to bring in more income than is expended. In this case, one does not exercise a technical freedom who already knows the relevant laws governing earnings (economic, stock market, etc.), or who has the wish to conform to such laws but does not possess the power to realize this wish. Only he is free who neither succumbs to a consumption addiction nor recoils from the effort required to increase his income. Such a person is able, in fact, to subjugate his lifestyle to the imperative: "Earn more than you spend!"

At the second level, that of pragmatic-practical reasons, "good" essentially means "good for the well(-being) of someone." The corresponding freedom extends not only to the ability *to pursue* the goal of the natural end of a species with a body and sense organs, admittedly a pre-moral end, but also to the ability *to oppose* internal as well as external resistance to the goal. In the case of affluence, when the goal contributes to one's well-being, there belongs to practical freedom the ability to pursue a relativized understanding which recognizes that affluence alone does not make one happy. As a consequence, whoever is free in the pragmatic sense does not simply aspire to ever more affluence.

It is similar with a second example, career development. With respect to a career, one is technically free who has acquired and effectively applied the necessary knowledge and skills. To one's pragmatic freedom in this case belongs the ability to pursue a career, including its success, to continue it in anticipation of an enduring well-being, or to know when to abandon it if there are slim chances of success either because of a lack of talent or because of superior competition. Pragmatic freedom also includes the capacity not only to know but also to live according to the knowledge that a successful career alone does not make one happy.

Obviously, there is still another level beyond pragmatic freedom. At the third, moral level, practical reasons push aside all consideration of one's personal welfare. At this level the more fundamental, immediately functioning motivating powers (sensuousness) are repressed. The will becomes the sole ruling motivation; it is free as such, and not only in a particular respect. Freedom of the will comes into play only at this third, moral level. This freedom is defined by a special kind of practical reason, its highest normative level.

Whether or not the radical rejection of sensuous and social "temptations" constitutes a world-denying conception or is, to the contrary, an essential aspect of the world, and perhaps constitutes the core of everyday moral consciousness, is a question still to be considered. Furthermore, the question arises of whether or not within moral justifications and the freedom of the will that accompanies them a binary division presses to the fore: an initial partial level, civic morals [*Rechtsmoral*], might constitute the common basis that all should acknowledge; in our example, this would mean that it would be improper to acquire wealth or to establish a career by deception. A second partial level, meritorious morals, would demand benevolence and charity beyond the mere avoidance of debt.

The three levels of freedom can be illustrated by the case of a person who wants to end his life by jumping from a bridge. We will assume that the person actually jumps and does not fall by mistake or is not pushed by another. We start with the preliminary level: the individual is in this first sense free when he in free fall is not thrown back over the railing by an extremely massive blast of wind. He is free in the second preliminary sense when the fall is a self-initiated movement and not the consequence of any push. Finally, the individual is free in the third preliminary sense when he is not so thoroughly under the influence of drugs that he has jumped only out of a dazed knowledge and desire, in a certain sense even unconsciously.

Insofar as the suicide is carried out with clear knowledge and desire, it can demonstrate volition with respect to the three primary levels of freedom: the *technical* level with respect to the effectiveness of the chosen means; the *pragmatic* level with respect to the appraisal of one's life situation; and *morally* with respect to the assumption of responsibility not only for oneself but also for others. While falling, the suicidal person can experience uncertainty in any or all three respects and feel regret or remorse in three levels of increasing scope.

The broadest sense of *technical* remorse overwhelms the individual when he is suddenly uncertain whether or not on impact he can expect the desired sudden death. Perhaps—the person reflects—the bridge is not high enough, or the ground is not hard enough, so that he must fear becoming a paraplegic or a slow, agonizing death when he is discovered too late. Technical remorse involves the reflection: "I should have chosen a more certain means."

The suicidal person experiences a second, *pragmatic* remorse when during the fall he suddenly realizes an alternative way out of the mess that led to the jump. In the face of the new chances for life, even happiness, that occur to him, he thinks: "I should have thought through the options more carefully, or I should have sought advice."

Finally, he can feel a *moral* remorse when he acknowledges the actual meaning of a heretofore undervalued, perhaps even repressed, point of view. For example, he admits that, with the choice of suicide, he violates such high-ranking responsibilities as the care for his life partner, child, or parents. Moral remorse amounts to the thought: "How could I place my own well-being above all other responsibilities?"

17.2 Autonomy as Pure Practical Reason

The suicide example with its levels of freedom and any possible remorse demonstrates once again how sober the concept of morals is that constitutes a philosophy of free will. Without any undertone of moralization, morals are equated with the highest level of practical reasons that corresponds to the highest form of value-estimation, an unconditional good. Only at this level is the potential for freedom fully exhausted as the capacity to act according to practical reasons. According to its philosophical concept, freedom of the will in the strict sense does not consist in a will that is undetermined and unconnected from practical reasons, even groundless as an irrational will. It means the ability to pursue practical reasons and to actualize this "willed" ability with respect to its third and highest level.

One can defend, of course, a broader concept of free will and speak of a modest first, a more demanding second, and a maximal third level of free will. Modest free will consists of the ability to sway one's willing in light of some kind of benefit or detriment (technical freedom). The more demanding freedom of the will consists in the ability to sway one's willing with respect to one's own well-being (pragmatic freedom);

however, the maximal or radical freedom of the will consists in the ability, in addition, to sway one's willing by means of restricting one's own personal well-being (moral freedom).

The three levels of freedom and practical reason are not necessarily connected. With respect to the ascending direction, this disconnect is obvious and is indicated by the examples of aspiration for affluence and career success: technical reasons (the first level), even when strenuously adhered to, are not "automatically" oriented toward a successful, happy life (the second level), much less toward morals (the third level). Such a connection is even conceptually, on the basis of a mere functional goodness, impossible. Nor do pragmatic reasons as such contain any connection to morals.

With respect to the descending line, there is a connection but no close interlinking: aspiration for affluence or a successful career according to the most strenuous avoidance of deception safeguards against a guilty conscience (that is, it eliminates some of the barriers to one's own well-being, but it cannot guarantee a successful life). There is almost no positive connection between moral and technical reasons for action. Whoever refrains from all deception and every other moral misstep indeed avoids certain threats to affluence and career success but makes no constructive contribution to them, either.

Between pragmatic and technical reasons for action, however, there is a close connection. Whoever wants to live happily must pursue and integrate happiness-conducive aspects like health, friendship, and professional success into his lifestyle; in other words, one must pursue technical-pragmatic grounds for one's actions.

Above all, moral freedom does not include technical and pragmatic freedom. As is confirmed by the simplest experiences of life, the highest level of free will is not synonymous with full, personal freedom: a moral, thoroughly scrupulous person can lead a thoroughly chaotic but only barely successful life from the perspective of moral integration. At that point where practical reasons for action do not bear on a narrowly defined character model but, rather, on a larger range of life, one speaks of practical principles, as well as of maxims (see chapter 20.3). Principles, for example the moral principle to help those in need, resemble laws, but they are distinguished from their prototype, natural laws, by means of two features: their object is personal actions, not natural events; and, according to the features of their occurrence, they have predominantly, but not exclusively, a character of *should*.

Where do practical reasons or principles come from; where do they originate? This is not to be taken as an empirical question. We are not concerned with a historical origin; that is, we are not asking why certain reasons develop an action-guiding power either in a single person (a question for biographers) or in a group or culture (a question for intellectual historians). We are asking about the origin of legitimation: where do reasons get their justification?

When it comes to morals, there are two decisive possibilities that constitute a strict either/or. If one takes reasons to be laws with respect to their rule-character and invokes the second paradigm for laws, civic laws, then one encounters either autonomy or heteronomy. Here the opposite of autonomy is not authority but heteronomy. Within the conceptual framework of this project, the nonauthoritarian character of reasons for action belongs to all levels of practical principles. It is a (self-evident) precept and not a distinguishing feature; even laws that are heteronomous in the legitimating sense are not authoritarian. When it comes to the law, auto-nomy means self-legislation: a corporate body in the public sense, for example, a state, or a private subject, for instance, a natural person, does not allow laws (*nomoi*) to be determined externally by an extraneous (*hetero-*)authority; rather it legislates the law for itself (*auto-*).

Where does the binding character of practical principles come from? Technical and functional grounds are nothing other than the demands of a particular field of action. They are specific laws governing an area of action that can be quite complex, and in their "application" they can demand a dizzying degree of judgment. Whoever adheres to such situational laws acquiesces to their previously established goals or interests. For example, someone who lives according to rules that result in his having much more income than expenditures acquiesces to an interest in affluence. Whereas the specific laws governing the focus of action are rational (hence, internal), their preestablished interest is established externally. A technical principle does not establish its own legitimacy; it obtains its obligatoriness externally. In this sense, as an external law in contrast to practical reason, technical principles have a heteronomous character.

One can also approach pragmatic principles as specific laws governing an area of action. The proper concern, one's own well-being, does not have the typical limits of an area of action, since it is satisfied not with a more or less delineated area of activity but with one's entire life. Other than that, however, pragmatic principles share the origin of technical principles: since they make a demand on practical reason ("Focus on your own well-being!"), their obligatoriness ultimately arises externally. Once again, we encounter an extrinsic legality. Its ultimate authority does not lie in the will (in the sense of practical reason) but in the previously given goal, one's own well-being.

The alternative to heteronomy is autonomy, self-legislation, with the crucial addition: oriented toward practical reason, that is, the will. Autonomy is not meant here in the broader sense of some kind of self-commitment, say that one establishes an (internal or external) demand as one's own. In everyday discourse, of course, this self-obligatoriness can be called autonomy. However, it consists in a weakened, if also common, understanding. Autonomy in the sense of the ethics of the will is more demanding. Within the capacity to act according to reasons and principles in general, one encounters the decisive question: is one concerned with a demand external or internal *to the will*?

What is meant by the second option, a lawfulness that is internal to the will? The answer is so difficult that many philosophers prefer not even to attempt a response. Some even go so far as to make an advance-defense, that is, to hold the concept of autonomy to be irrelevant and to declare the attempt to ground morals in the autonomy of the will to be very murky, perhaps even abstruse. One properly gives up, however, only when one has good reasons to do so. Before we engage objections in the next two chapters, let's rebut here one objection to the freedom of the will. According to a popular counterargument, freedom of the will rests upon a presupposition that is too strong. It pushes aside, namely, all "usual" concerns with sensuous desires, social conventions, and legitimate laws. Schopenhauer assumed that the thought of a pure practical reason attempts to secularize the conception of a religiously established moral law (*Preisschrift über die Grundlage der Moral* [*On the Basis of Morals*], section 4), and Tugendhat agrees with him (2006, 15).

In truth, someone is not free in the exercise of his will who "wills what he wills irrespective of any precept." Freedom of the will also does not consist of some kind of wishing at a second level but in a specific kind of reflection. Rather, someone has at his command a modest conception of the freedom of the will who subordinates himself to principles of practical reason. However, only where the principles have an internal origin within the will are we concerned with the more demanding sense of autonomy. It is not someone who in the final instance allows himself to be shaped by the power of the appetites or passions, feelings of sympathy and antipathy, or a dominant custom, and also not one who chooses the best means to pre-given goals, but, rather, only someone who leads his life according to the laws of the rank of autonomy who is free in this sense.

The demand of morals is directed, indeed, toward a being who can discard neither his sensuous nature nor his historical-social origins. Precisely for this reason, because one remains a being with desires, a history, and a social setting, morals have a *should* character. It consists in the challenge to admit one's desires and one's social dependence, even to affirm them as long as they don't contradict morals, but not to allow them to be the final grounds of determination of one's actions. Autonomy in this sense means to be more than a being with mere desires and social concerns and in this "more" to discover oneself.

The "more" does not include a casting off of the "less." Besides, it is impossible for someone to simply lay aside the manifold conditions of his personal, social, economic, and political nature. One is prohibited from making a new start out of nothing. The freedom of the will consists neither in the rejection of vitality, sensibility, and social orientation, nor does it pursue a "sincere" morals principally in terms of an escape from life, a lack of tradition or history, or a critique of a developed form of living. Like the freedom of action, the freedom of the will does not consist in indeterminateness but in a qualified obligation; in our case, it consists in giving oneself laws out of which one's willing finally results. The autonomy of the will in this morally decisive sense is itself the origin of its willing so-and-not-otherwise.

In this respect, the level of the freedom of the will repeats what was said about the freedom of action: conditions may by all means be present, even unavoidable, but they may not claim the weight of unalterable facts. This "not allowed" is by no means so remote from everyday life as some critics maintain. Humanity is capable, namely, of putting itself in a relation to conditions. It can name, judge, and recognize them in the form of a creative "making them one's own" or it can refute them as it strives to change its obligations along the path of nurturing, self-developmental, and if necessary also therapeutic procedures.

18 Objection One: Determinism

Sound philosophy comes to grips with any appropriate skepticism that is relevant. Even a theory of moral freedom must pause in the construction of its argument to engage a point of view, determinism, that counts as its radical, skeptical challenger. However, determinism's fundamental thesis is incapable of offering a convincing argument that constitutes any real challenge to freedom.

Action counts as one of those things for which one identifies causes. Causes explain why something occurs in some specific manner and not another so that with sufficient causes the phenomenon under consideration appears to be necessary. Sufficient causes, of course, claim to provide a relative, not an absolute, necessity. The circumstance could have turned out differently, but that could be the case only under a different constellation of causes. Should someone walk out in the rain without an umbrella or some kind of rain gear, he will necessarily get wet. Had he used an umbrella or a poncho or had he found shelter from the rain, he would have remained dry. The effect is therefore not necessary; it can, however, only be avoided by changing the network of causes.

Even a sufficient network of causes is no challenge to freedom because freedom consists in independence not from causes but from necessity. The person sketched above would be unfree only if he were forced under the given conditions to walk around in the rain without an umbrella or any rain gear. He would be unfree in a social sense were the necessity to stem from his social environment; he would be unfree in the personally decisive respect for ethics, in contrast, were he to be internally forced to walk in the rain.

In order to challenge the notion of freedom, however, one requires at least an additional argument; an argument that permits one to infer "compelled" from "caused." Skeptical of freedom, determinism concludes that one is allowed to infer compulsion when one can extend the usual, external causes to involve the internal causes of action. Should one extend explanatory power to include internal causes, action appears to be the consequence of a sufficient network of causes that makes the action an inescapable, thus (relatively) necessary, effect: it is not only in part but completely determined. However, this is not the fatal consequence that it appears to be. The apparent extraordinariness of humanity's freedom is not, thereby, exposed as an illusion. It is, of course, frequently claimed that anyone who wants to "save" freedom must question the causality, the determination, that shapes action and must maintain the contrary: that human action is uncaused, undetermined, or at least in part uncaused, a consequence of partial indeterminateness. In truth, "internally caused" does not mean "compelled." Whoever assumes so succumbs to a logical fallacy.

A debate over freedom that succumbs to this logical fallacy transpires under the title "Determinism Contra Indeterminism." One also says that freedom and causality are contradictory to one another, that is, incompatible with one another. In contrast, someone who conceptually distinguishes between cause and necessity and sees the reason for the distinction in practical reflexivity, as escalated to practical reason, defends a unification of cause and necessity, a compatibility, that allows no mere indeterminism. He does not take freedom to be action without determination, but action without compulsion. Nevertheless, a closer examination of determinism is worthwhile.

18.1 Methodological or Dogmatic Determinism

Everyday understanding already knows about the multiple conditionality of human action. Some perspectives are long since trivial and have acquired more precision from the empirical sciences: as a body, the individual is subject to the laws of physics and chemistry; as a living body, the individual is subject to the laws of biology and physiology. His driving forces, motives and passions, depend upon needs and interests as well as upon temperament, and even further upon constellations of appetites and character features that are influenced for their part by genetic factors, (early) childhood impressions, and environmental elements, including the influence of parenting. Those whom one meets, what one hears or reads, and what happens to one can all fundamentally change one's life.

Everyday understanding, of course, knows something that the sciences can more precisely determine but can hardly dismiss, practical reflexivity. Above all because of it, the driving forces and the ways and means by which they are developed are subject to an evaluation in terms of their acceptability or inadequacy. No matter which, one's behavior is not forced in either case. In the event of rejection, one can even work toward a modification; to be sure, not everyone can in every single circumstance—anyhow, not in every respect and completely. It might even be that there are persons who experience their life stories as pure fate and then, admittedly, view themselves "as an animal": "I feel too strongly that each of our actions is an absolute, a thing complete, necessary and inevitable. . . . Involved in a series of decisions each final in itself, I had had no time to consider myself as a problem, no more than an animal does" (Marguerite Yourcenar, *Coup de grâce*, 1957, 30).

Some are incapable of doing anything but stealing, others, like Don Juan, nothing but seducing women, and undoubtedly there are even more serious fixations. "In principle," motives and means are combined with practical reflection, a self-knowledge that is accompanied by a self-evaluation open to self-modification. This occurs along a wide spectrum. One extreme is the complete acceptance not only of a particular action but also of one's entire character. In the case of such an all-around self-adulation, there is a danger of an all too hasty self-satisfaction. The other extreme consists in the absolute rejection of the entire person, including a complete self-abasement, perhaps even self-contempt. Between these two extremes, one finds the complete palette of more or less with respect to acceptance and rejection. Furthermore, the self-evaluation can occur according to many different aspects of the person.

No serious philosopher questions this conditional nature of experience. On the contrary, he is open to life experience and, in addition, acquaints himself with the insights of the particular sciences. All that is contested is the scope of the conditionality. Only at that point where one maintains an equally comprehensive as well as pervasive conditionality does one draw the conclusion of a questionable determinism from out of the neither questioned nor surprising conditional determination. This is manifest in many forms. An initial form is at the core of all scientific research. Whether in the natural or social sciences, empirical research alleges that all factual circumstances of the natural and social world are explainable by means of causes or out of understandable motives and that these are graspable in terms of laws or regularities. The responsible laws do not have to take the form of classical physics. There are also statistical law-like regularities; furthermore, there are quasi-laws or, as in the case of the subatomic realm, relations of indeterminacy.

Obviously, research doesn't assume that it can already explain and understand everything—although it does claim so in principle. If that were the assumption, there would be an end to any search for novelty and even an end to research itself. Naturally, the region of human action falls under the same conditions. Even in the event that its causes are for now only incompletely recognized and their interrelatedness still inadequately illuminated, curiosity on the part of the natural and social sciences will be satisfied only when there are no more gaps in our explanations.

Methodologically considered, the in principle explicability and comprehensibility of all facts and circumstances is a regulative idea of each research focus. The notion of a regulative idea in research means, first of all, nothing other than a never entirely satisfied thirst for knowledge. A regulative idea consists in interests, facts, and circumstances of all kinds not only in respect to their givenness but also with respect to their origin, and, not least, it consists in the linkage of all of these factors with other facts and circumstances. When it comes to the regulative idea of research, determinism can mean a methodical determinism or a research governed by determinism according to regulative ideas. Determinism implies: whatever is the case in the world, it is to be understood as an effect for which the causes (including motives and reasons) can be sought. To the extent that determinism consists in the challenge to keep on investigating, it has a prescriptive character. When one cannot identify a cause, one does not substitute a miracle in the scientific sense, that is, some fundamental indeterminacy (something denied by philosophy since Plato [*Timaeus* 28a]). Rather, one assumes that one just doesn't know yet: in place of a never-able-to-know, one assumes an ignorance that is in principle capable of being overcome. Whenever there is a knowledge deficiency with respect to causes and grounds, it is attributed to the researcher, the subject, and his current state of knowledge rather than to some fundamental condition of the object itself. Instead of being concerned with indeterminate facts and circumstances, one supposes two things: that there are causes and that they can be discerned by means of fundamental and creative research.

The insatiable thirst for knowledge that is methodological determinism, however, does not justify the tendency, especially in the younger sciences, to propose that one possesses absolute knowledge and to explain or understand everything according to only this standard. For example, if all that was acknowledged for the explanation of human behavior consisted of exclusively physical or exclusively biological, neurological, psychological, economic, or sociological causes, methodological determinism becomes a form of epistemic imperialism that declares itself either to be exclusively or exhaustively competent or to be a hegemony that is primarily competent for accounting for that behavior. Rather, as long as these appropriate orientations still perform modestly as an attempt to plumb the depths of each orientation's manner of explanation, they are hardly alarming. A modest, merely methodological physics, just like a methodological biology or neurobiology, applies to its own narrow area of specialization only a generally valid methodological determinism. Such an application by all means can inspire a strategy of creative research. Why shouldn't one, for example, at least attempt to explain biological phenomena as far as possible chemically, and chemical phenomena as far as possible according to physics? Equally, why should it be dubious to seek an explanation not only of mercantile, financial, and service markets according to economic rationalizations but also as a consequence of the conduct of parties, governments, and organizations, and, not least, as a consequence of the partly political or cultural rise and/or fall of states or regions?

As long as such questions are pursued with mere curiosity and not motivated by a desire for epistemic dominance, they permit others the same right, so that something can emerge that is difficult to find in politics: an imperialism capable of epistemic coexistence among disciplines. Although their spheres of application are different, a modest physics, for example, is compatible with biology and economics so long as they, too, remain modest in their claims. They along with other "isms" could live peacefully with and next to one another in epistemic competition and, simultaneously, in tolerance of one another. Things get dubious only when one maintains that one's own way of thinking is exclusively valid and infallibly correct. In such a case, an open, epistemic determinism is turned into a closed and likewise intolerant determinism. Having lost its capacity for coexistence, a research strategy originally inspired by curiosity is transformed into a dogmatic premise that limits curiosity.

However, in order to avoid any misunderstanding: the kind of closed determinism under discussion here is not equivalent to the thesis of a causal closure to physical nature that, in combination with a second thesis of mental causes, results in serious difficulties for the notion of personal freedom. Closed determinism is, namely, a scientific theoretical position that is to be tested scientifically and best rejected when it becomes a form of epistemic intolerance. The thesis of causal closure, in contrast, amounts to an action- and moral-theoretical determinism.

Methodological determinism is not without consequences for the notion of freedom. With its silent demand to seek unknown causes not in the object but in the knowing subject's inadequate knowledge, it declares all causal indeterminacy to be merely dependent upon the subject and his limits of understanding. It rejects any sense of an objective causal indeterminacy. All action is explainable once one has acquired sufficient knowledge so that to an omniscient being, such as God, all actions would appear to be determined. Even Wittgenstein defined freedom, admittedly freedom of the will, in terms of a deficiency in knowledge: "Freedom of the will consists in the fact that future actions are now not known" (*Tractatus*, 5.1362). However, as we have emphasized, freedom is not to be understood fundamentally as a strict anarchy in the sense of a capricious causal indeterminacy.

An influential position to this day, indeterminism (also called libertarianism) maintains precisely this option: free is someone who could have chosen otherwise; unfree is someone who has no other alternative. Freedom, according to indeterminism, involves a deficit of sufficient causation. According to the German dictionary *Duden-Rechtschreibung* (2006, 527), "freedom" means succinctly: "indeterminism . . . (*philos.* doctrine of freedom of the will)."

In the first place, a freedom-threatening oddity speaks against the notion of freedom as partial causal indeterminacy: because of methodological determinism, a person, including his actions and underlying will, would be free only "in light of our current state of knowledge"; strictly speaking, a person would be free only "with respect to the current state of knowledge on the part of the subject who alleges himself to be free." The consequence is hardly convincing: deficiency with respect to the pertinent expertise, in other words, ignorance, would be the measure of freedom. The more ignorant one is, the more likely he will declare himself and others to be free. Conversely, the more one can explain causally, the less one can maintain any presence of freedom. For an omniscient mind there is entirely no freedom either for the omniscient mind itself or for any other being because, for both, their actions are known in advance.

A fundamentally opposite position maintains that this curious argument involves a categorical, if not a perspectival, error: the confusion of an objective for a subjective predicate. Freedom, namely, is according to its content a predicate of objects who are beings capable of action. According to methodological determinism, causal indeterminacy is a predicate of the knowing subject. It is the consequence of a (temporary) lack of knowledge of the "real" cause of the action. Whoever explains his action or the exercise of his will on the basis of freedom (i.e., that actions and the will are causally and rationally groundless: in short, indeterminate) is actually only identifying a limit to human knowledge. In the extreme case of a principled causal indeterminacy or inexplicability, he assumes an insurmountable limit without, thereby, approving human freedom.

Furthermore, an argument known in moral philosophy as "Buridan's ass" speaks against indeterminism: in the absence of a cause for being active or remaining passive and, in the case of the activity, given the absence of a cause to act one way or another, one is like a donkey who starves to death because it possesses no cause to select between two equal amounts of hay equidistant from itself. Correspondingly, whoever is strictly an indeterminist remains incapable of action, and not even capable of choosing the alternative of doing or not doing something. He lacks a (sufficient) cause for acting one way or the other. Should he nevertheless act, then the action occurs entirely accidentally; it is, therefore, difficult to speak in such a case of the presence of a freedom that belongs in the ambit of (moral) responsibility.

Libertarianism is unacceptable for someone who plays according to the "language game" of responsibility. How could one be able to do what responsibility means: holding others or oneself accountable, and presenting justifying and excusing grounds for one's actions? In any event, libertarianism is unconvincing because it ignores the difference between cause and necessity and the practical reflexivity that speaks against necessity. Methodological determinism maintains, in contrast, that accidental actions only appear to be accidental: even when one doesn't yet know the cause or ground for the action, all events in the world are understood to be effects for which there are causes. Buridan's ass starved to death because it was incapable of choosing between the two piles of hay in spite of its threatening hunger, an incapacity that for its part has definite causes.

18.2 Only a Freedom to Act?

It is not a little surprising that determinism has been around since antiquity, but it has been taken to be compatible with morals, responsibility, and the corresponding freedom. In order not to chase a phantom, we will examine determinism in terms of two of its classical defenders. Whereas it is still possible today to make fine-tuning adjustments, the basic paradigm has long been known.

Augustine engaged in a thorough debate of the more exacting notion of the freedom of the will in his dialogue *On the Free Will* (see Brachtendorf 2006). Since his discussion is saturated with theological issues, we will turn to two authors who discuss the issue independent of theology. We have selected representatives from each of the two trajectories that have continued to be influential down to the present: on the side of rationalism, instead of Descartes, who is often referred to today, we have selected the first great Cartesian opponent, Baruch de Spinoza; and on the side of the more dominant empiricism, we will discuss its decisive classical representative, David Hume. According to today's labels, Hume is a compatibilist; however, he is a compatibilist only in terms of freedom of action and not freedom of the will. Spinoza is, in contrast, both: his approach is strict incompatibilism, whereas in execution he is a compatibilist; again, however, only partially because he claims to reject free will. In fact, however, he comes very close to accepting the notion of free will, so that, with respect to freedom of the will, one may call him a compatibilist against his will.

Baruch de Spinoza starts with a universal determinism, but he nevertheless maintains that humanity is capable of freedom. His almost encyclopedic magnum opus commences astonishingly, when one looks at the title *Ethics* with an ontology. According to this ontology, all elements of the world have an internal and, at the same time, necessary connection to the only real being, God. They are dependent upon God and, as far as this dependence goes, they are determined. In this essential respect, then, humanity is no different than plants and animals, even lifeless nature: humanity is "necessary or, rather, coerced." Only God is free because only He fulfills the two conditions that, according to Spinoza, belong to the exacting concept of freedom: exclusive self-causation and exclusive and pure self-determination: "*Free* means that something simply exists as a consequence of the necessity of its own nature and acts only through itself" (*Ethics*, part 1, definition 7). The two qualifications "simply" and "only" indicate that for philosophy freedom is to be thought of with respect to a rare radical thoroughness and comprehensiveness.

One might ask why Spinoza begins with such an ambitious concept of freedom in terms of a self-causative and self-determining spontaneity, since it applies only to God and is separated by an abyss from the concept that is his ultimate interest, human freedom. A possible answer lies in the thesis that is left unarticulated in the *Ethics:* any "rational" theory of freedom applicable to humanity would necessarily be far more modest.

Spinoza's ultimately practical interest culminates in the coincidence of freedom and a happy life, that is, in a harmonious unity of the two central principles of Occidental philosophy. In order to philosophically reconcile the two principles of happiness and freedom that often are taken to be competitive principles, Spinoza develops in the *Ethics* an intellectual drama in five acts. It begins with what is for humanity a deterministic ontology in order to finally arrive at a concept of happiness defined as freedom by means of a long detour: starting from what is initially human bondage, our ontological dependence upon God (part 1), through a theory of spirit (the "mind:" part 2) and a theory of emotions (part 3), Spinoza arrives at a second form of human bondage, our subordination to emotions (part 4), only finally to conclude (part 5) with the alternative, a theory of the power of the mind that is in conformity with the emotions.

Just how successful Spinoza is with this notion that the mind is in conformity with our affective lives can be left undecided here. (On the interpretation of Spinoza's *Ethics,* see Hampe and Schnepf 2006.) The fundamental thought is in any event plausible: that human freedom consists neither in emancipation from emotions nor in an absolute control over them but, rather, in their restriction and moderation. The presupposed theory of action here does not contradict in any way the incipient definition of freedom. It annuls "only" part 1, which applies to God and maintains that something "simply" exists as a consequence of the necessity of its own nature. Even humanity is able to exist, admittedly, out of the necessity of its own nature; it exists, however, not exclusively so. Rather, it settles for the second aspect of the incipient definition of freedom—"to act merely out of itself"—which approaches the usual understanding of freedom. Even this freedom of action is understood by Spinoza in such an exacting manner that it is not a human endowment. Although it is no supra-human ideal, it remains a perfection that only a few achieve.

Although Spinoza rejects free will, he in fact comes close in practice to affirming it. Namely, he speaks of action in the strictest sense only when a person through the aid of the mind liberates himself from external as well as internal necessity, that is, from dominance by the emotions. Thanks to this liberation, the individual is a self-determining being who is oriented not only with respect to his own well-being but also by moral reason. Spinoza, to be sure, doesn't use this expression himself. He even rejects the separation of the two kinds of reason—especially sharply in the final thesis, the famous proposition 42 of part 5: "Happiness is not the payment for virtue but virtue itself." According to Spinoza, a free person contemplates "pragmatically," on the one hand, not only his death but also his life (*Ethics*, part 4, proposition 67). He lives cheerfully (for example, part 4, proposition 44, note), refreshes himself by means of appetizing food and drink, and finds pleasure in beautiful plants, jewelry, music, and theater (part 4, proposition 45, note). Not least, he understands not only how to avoid dangers (prudence and foresight) but also how to overcome them (courage: part 4, proposition 69). On the other hand, he lives "morally" because he never acts deviously but always honestly (part 4, proposition 72). In addition, he distinguishes himself through self-confidence, respectively, strength of mind and generosity (proposition 72, note; already part 3, proposition 56, note). The individual strives for both pragmatic and good actions; simultaneously, he possesses both kinds, not only self-related (strength of mind) but also other-oriented virtues (generosity).

The mental foundation for self-determination is knowledge and self-knowledge. When one renounces the concept of the will rejected by Spinoza as an independent capacity and constructs instead a solidly grounded concept, the difference between freedom of action and freedom of the will evaporates in the case of a moral virtue such as generosity. In this case, Spinoza appears more like a subtle defender than an opponent of the freedom of the will. He even anticipates the criterion of free will, strenuous universalizability (chapter 20.4), because he says with respect to emotions that they divide whereas reason unites humanity (*Ethics*, part 4, propositions 32–35).

Admittedly, Spinoza sharply defines reason in terms of knowledge, which results in an overestimation of the theoretical and culminates in a false cognitive conclusion: the attempt to think about reason in the practical realm by means of the theoretical activity of the mind contradicts a genuinely practical reason. More cautiously, one can say that the theoretical program of the *Ethics* involves an internal tension. On the one hand, Spinoza opposes the emotions within a purely theoretical attitude: without any normative moment, everything counts as good that can be desired (part 3, proposition 9, note). On the other hand, emotions should also be appreciated with respect to their "true" significance, not merely as imaginary but as truly good. In this case, reason emerges as a command in contrast to desire (part 3, proposition 59, note). Reason is no longer descriptive but normative: "good" is what we are certain is to our benefit (part 4, definition 1; in this case, benefit is understood in both a pragmatic and a moral sense).

The result: a radical theory of determinism simultaneously makes room for moral freedom. According to Spinoza, someone is free who acts according to the standards of reason *in and with* one's circumstances. Because of the moment of reason, one is no longer under alien necessity, and especially is not subservient to the emotions. Ultimately, one is answerable only to oneself and to no other.

David Hume believes that he is capable of easily solving the problem. The belief—so one finds in section 8 of his *Enquiry Concerning Human Understanding*—that determinism and human freedom are mutually exclusive rests upon the confusion of two concepts of freedom: a freedom of indifference appropriate to indeterminism that rejects causal determinism, and a freedom of spontaneity which alone is important for moral judgment and action. The latter, "hypothetical freedom," means nothing other than a freedom from external determination that is subject to two conditions: the action is neither hindered by something external nor compelled by someone else. Whereas Spinoza approaches the freedom of the will in terms of independence from internal necessity, Hume is satisfied with a more elementary freedom of action: the agent is free in terms of action; the agent is determined, in contrast, in terms of the will.

Hume understands the opposing view, indeterminism, to be a "pseudo-experience," the illusion that the will is subordinate to no one. In fact, it is possible for an observer, as soon as he "is entirely familiar with every detail of his situation, temperament, and most hidden motives," to deduce all his deeds, and therein is found "the true essence of necessity" (section 8, part 1, footnote 1). Hume maintains, in opposition to the opinion that human action is as capricious as the weather, that even the weather is determined by unalterable principles, although they are not easily identified.

Hume anticipates the objection that, in addition to the freedom of spontaneity, the understanding of moral responsibility requires an indeterminism compatible with the freedom of indifference. This would in fact, Hume argues, nullify moral responsibility: where actions are not the consequence of some kind of cause found in the character and capacities of an acting person, they can lead neither to honor insofar as they are good nor to disgrace to the degree that they are bad. In such a circumstance where one is not responsible oneself for the condemnable action, the agent would be only a quasi-agent; namely, a mere initiator, with the absurd consequence that "a man is as pure and untainted, after having committed the most horrid crimes, as at the first moment of his birth" (*Enquiry Concerning Human Understanding*, section 8, part 2).

Obviously, more is needed for freedom than merely independence from external coercion. It is difficult to hold someone completely responsible who is not subject merely to internal motivations but to inner compulsions in the narrow sense of serious phobias or neuroses. Extended to motives and inclinations, freedom of spontaneity consists in the ability to orient one's willing according to pragmatic and moral obligations. One kind of such inner freedom can well be called freedom of the will. It is based, however, in something that Hume does not argue as distinctive to inner causes, practical reflection. Practical reflection contradicts in fact Hume's more emphatic claim that reason is the slave of passions and capable of nothing but service to the passions (*A Treatise of Human Nature*, book 2, part 3, section 3). For this reason, freedom of the will in the moral sense is not so easily integrated into his (here extremely empirical) thinking, as many friends of Hume want to maintain. A practical reason that is capable only of serving the passions is impossible as an appropriate basis for the justification of action according to moral freedom.

Hume's own lifestyle appears in fact to contradict his theory. He mentions in an autobiographical sketch that he developed a life plan as a young man to which he subsequently successfully adhered (Hume 1776/1988). A life plan demands more than a reason dominated by the passions. One might interpret the origin of a life plan purely instrumentally: Hume wanted to live within his means by living extremely frugally. The implementation of the plan demonstrates, however, that reason here was not driven by mere fleeting passions but by a long-range goal of personal well-being. The unconditional financial and mental independence that Hume wished to maintain is not independent of passions, but, on the contrary, this mental independence is sovereign over rather than subordinate to passions.

18.3 Intensified Determinism

Spinoza's and Hume's attempts to save freedom in the face of determinism have not been universally accepted. An important collaborator on the French *Encyclopedia,* the "aesthetic-materialist Enlightenment thinker" Paul-Henri Thiry d'Holbach, maintained in his *System of Nature* that humanity was so completely determined that any kind of freedom is an illusion. In an intensification of determinism, he maintained an uncompromising incompatibilism. Because d'Holbach is so little known today, it is appropriate to quote a few passages from his main work. Already in the first chapter, we read: "Man is the work of Nature: he exists in Nature: he is submitted to her laws: he cannot deliver himself from them: nor can he step beyond them even in thought" (1770/1970, 11). A little later he writes: "Man is a being purely physical: the moral man is nothing more than this physical being considered under a certain point of view" (ibid.). Chapter 11 (part 1) devoted to "The Doctrine of Human Freedom" declares equally uncompromisingly of the individual: "He is good or bad, happy or miserable, wise or foolish, reasonable or irrational, without his will being for any thing in these various states" (ibid., 88). Even Socrates, the model of virtue, was not free. His refusal to flee from prison was nothing that he had control over because "he could find no potential motive to bring him to depart, even for an instant, from those principles to which his mind was accustomed" (ibid., 96–97).

Surprisingly, the great philosopher of freedom, Immanuel Kant, accentuates this determinism that is as radical as it is universal. He combines it with a dig at what he views to be Hume's superficially prized compatibilism. Simultaneously, he relativizes what is taken to be the normal "situation" in today's debate over freedom. In the second preface to the *Critique of Pure Reason,* Kant declares that the human will acts in all "visible acts . . . subject to the law of nature, and [is] so far not *free*" (B xxviii). When he writes about materialism, fatalism, and atheism a few pages later (B xxxiv), it appears that he is writing directly in opposition to d'Holbach even when the name isn't specified. D'Holbach's primary work begins, namely, with a strictly materialist conception of the entire world, draws from it the grounds for the complete rejection of any notion of human freedom ("fatalism"), and declares, thirdly, that God is an illusion ("atheism").

Already for Kant and still today, Hume carries far more weight than d'Holbach. Hume's attempt to resolve the conflict between freedom and necessity applies to the project that Kant calls empiricism (*Critique of Practical Reason,* 5:96), namely: "One might call the actions of man 'free' because they are actions caused by ideas we have produced by our own powers." Kant declares this to be a "poor remedy" because one dares not believe that "with a little . . . [hairsplitting one has] found the solution to the difficult problem which centuries have sought in vain."

Kant rejects not only the materialistic "mechanical causality" defended by d'Holbach (he speaks of a "material automaton") but also Leibniz's "mental causality" ("spiritual automaton") based on mental experience. Wherever events occur according to a chain of cause and effect, they are necessary so that one may speak of the "mechanism of nature" without those things necessarily being "actually material machines." Mental machines remain automatons, namely, machines functioning on their own, whose freedom "would in essence be no better than the freedom of a turnspit, which when once wound up also carries out its motions of itself" (*Critique of Practical Reason*, 5:97).

Kant goes a step further. He speaks not only of psychological causality but also of "psychological freedom," by which he paradoxically declares causality and freedom to be equivalent, when they are usually taken to be contradictory. This declaration does not ignore the contradictory meanings. However, it criticizes as precipitous the opinion that sees freedom already present where one appeals merely to a representation of the soul and its internal interlinking.

The background: in his philosophy of freedom, Kant proceeds no differently than he does with any other theme; first, he accentuates the provocation. Defenders of materialism can even consider him an ally because he formulates their position clearly, stringently, and above all with justification like no other. Nevertheless, the recent debate over freedom from Ryle through Bieri and up to Roth does not take the Königsberg philosopher seriously enough. One could accuse Kant of exaggeration in his comparison of a freedom determined by mental representations to an automated kitchen appliance. In point of fact, both sides indicate the huge burden of proof that they impose: the opponent of freedom must demonstrate that psychological freedom, which is a consequence of consciousness and the ability to formulate judgments, is a variation of determinism. The defender of freedom, on the contrary, must know that this "freedom which lies at the foundation of all moral laws" (*Critique of Practical Reason*, 5:96) is not yet saved by the phenomenon of psychological freedom.

Kant's solution, in contrast to Hume's, is carefully constructed. First, he develops a new theory of causality that eventually accommodates the opponent of freedom. The second analogy found in the *Critique of Pure*

Reason rejects Hume's modest empirical concept of causality as habit and regularity in favor of a transcendental law of causality: an observable event does not permit of being known as something objective unless one presupposes four fundamentally nonobservable things: (1) the event that the street is wet when it rains is experienced as a sequence in time: "first it must rain, then the street is wet"; (2) the sequence is irreversible: the street cannot be wet before it rains; (3) the goal of the irreversibility is a "for this reason," for example: "the street is wet, *because* it rained or has rained"; and finally (4) a (not always already known) rule of connection maintains that the temporal sequence is necessary (admittedly hypothetically, not categorically, necessary): "*if* it rains on the street, *then* it will necessarily get wet" (on the Kant interpretation, see Höffe 2004, chapters 14.2, 18.4, and 21.2). This is a transcendental theory of causality because it is concerned with conditions of possibility. It places methodological determinism in a new epistemological light.

In a second step of the argument, Kant extends epistemological determinism beyond the usual natural events to include practical phenomena, acts of free will. Let's sketch an example of this new determinism that includes the theory of action: whoever takes the event of someone leaving a room to be a deliberately volitional event, maintains, first, a temporal sequence: First, there is an internal, spiritual, or mental event, the desire to leave the room; this is followed by an external, bodily event that consists of the eventual opening of and exiting out the door. Second, he affirms the irreversibility of the events: not even occasionally is it possible for there to be an opening of and exiting out the door prior to the desire to leave the room. As the goal of the irreversibility, one needs, thirdly, a "for this reason": "someone exits out the door *because* he wants to leave the room." The "because" doesn't occur out of what has already transpired; it presupposes rather a rule of connection that the (internal, mental) prior-event explains the temporal sequence between the necessary prior-event and the external following-event: whoever consciously and deliberately leaves a room must want to leave the room prior to actually leaving.

Only parenthetically: because the mental event, interpreted as a "for this reason," has the status of a reason, Davidson's frequently cited thesis, "reasons are causes," reads like a commentary on Kant's expanded determinism that holds for nature as well as human action. For this reason, the thesis is neither so fundamentally new nor provocative as one believes. Davidson's opinion that "causality is the cement of the universe" is not only defended by Kant, but he also gives it a philosophical basis.

Kant's third step in his argument, the third antinomy, distinguishes between two kinds of causality that are far more fundamentally different than external and internal causality. These are in fact two subsets of the usual notion of causality, the lawfulness of nature. Kant contrasts these two with the causality of freedom. This latter form of causality, which initially appears to be a strange expression, refers to a causality whose determination is established by reason (see *Critique of Practical Reason*, 5:89).

In a fourth step, Kant establishes—still within the third antinomy— the direct opposition between the two kinds of causality. Freedom is not an indeterminate causality as, surprisingly, the Kant scholar Schopenhauer maintained (*Preisschrift über die Freiheit des Willens* [*Prize Essay on the Freedom of the Will*]), but rather it consists in the capacity of practical reflexivity to acknowledge grounds of practical weight. Although Kant speaks of an unconditional free will, he nonetheless doesn't succumb to the "ridiculous thought" of a will that acts independent of our body and character or independent of thought, perception, memory, and wishes. He refers rather to an extraordinary kind of reasons for action: it is not the undetermined will that is unconditional but the free will in the autonomous sense discussed above that is unconditional.

In a fifth step, the direct confrontation is resolved to the advantage of freedom and to the advantage of a methodological determinism: the critic of freedom is correct insofar as all events, actions included, can be investigated in terms of external and internal causes, which can potentially be determining of what is taken to be freedom.

In the justification—sixth step—determinism is provoked in the sharpest fashion: not only the events of the external world occur in a temporal sequence and are, therefore, irreversible, but the same also applies to the relationship between internal and external events and, above all, to the representation of internal events: present thoughts are the effects of prior thoughts, which are not only *prior* but are also now *past*. The consequence for a theory of freedom: as prior thoughts, they find themselves "no longer under the control of the respective subject." Equally, the past thoughts for their part are caused by prior past thoughts, and they are also no longer under the control of the agent. Because this circumstance extends ever further into the past, it appears that the agent is entirely determined and, therefore, completely unfree.

234 THE PRINCIPLE OF FREEDOM: AUTONOMY

In Kant's example, a theft is to be explained "by the natural law of causality [and as] . . . a necessary result of the determining ground existing in the preceding time" so that it "was therefore impossible that it could have not been done" (*Critique of Practical Reason*, 5:95).

Only the next, seventh step exposes the appearance of total unfreedom to be merely an illusion. Dogmatic determinism does not follow from methodological determinism. Whoever declares freedom to be impossible because of the potential determinism of all human action misappropriates a limitation that at the latest in the sixth argument becomes obvious: actions are only determined to the degree that one is anchored in relationships of time and, as a consequence, in the dimension of the empirical and of nature. Time is absolutely indispensable for human knowledge only because knowledge is dependent upon an (external or internal) intuition. At that point where it requires no intuition, that is, in the area of pure thought, both the form of intuition as well as time are dispensable. As a consequence, actions are comprehensively but not entirely determined: within the confines of temporal imprisonment, including our experience of nature, actions are all in all determined, but not entirely, because the actions are relative to temporality, the empirical, and nature.

The two steps still missing in the argument will be completed later but can already be identified here. Kant's eighth step consists of the negation of temporally conditioned, merely empirical determinism: in order even to think moral freedom—the reality of this moral freedom results in the further, ninth step—it must be thought of as "independent from everything empirical and, therefore, from nature in general." One needs, then, nothing less than a freedom that relinquishes any attachment to the empirical. It is an absolute freedom in the strictest sense that is unknown other than in humanity. It is no substitute, however, for freedom of action or freedom of the will. It is also no further, third kind of freedom. As the condition of the possibility to think freedom (of the will), it is "transcendental" freedom.

19 Objection Two: Brain Research

Earlier it was physicists or psychologists, and more lately among scientists it is a few brain researchers and other neuroscientists who challenge the two cardinal concepts of modernity, "enlightenment" and "freedom of the will." Because the experience of liberation from internal compulsion is an illusion, they acknowledge primarily only what is in fact a remnant of freedom in the sense of "to make free"—the emancipation from the very illusion of a modest freedom of the will: "Neural circuits determine us: we should stop talking about freedom" (Singer 2004). At the most, it is still permitted for brain researchers and a few approving neuro-philosophers like Metzinger 2004 to speak of freedom. This is because there are two things to be explained: on the one hand, how is it possible for the illusion of freedom to occur in the brain as a by-product (an epiphenomenon) of neural processes; and on the other hand, why is it that the brain holds on to the illusion of freedom with such tenacity?

The exemplary supporting evidence for the illusion of freedom comes from the experiments of Benjamin Libet in 1985. Originally, this neurophysiologist wanted to experimentally prove freedom. To that end, he investigated the arbitrary, "free" triggering of a minimal movement, the raising of the right hand. Convinced of the "autonomous" power of the mind, he expected that the commencement of appropriate processes in the brain, the construction of an electronic readiness-potential, was preceded temporally by a self-directed act of the will. In fact, the unexpected occurred: the electronic readiness-potential occurred neither after nor simultaneously with the act of the will; rather, it temporally preceded the act of the will. Libet 2004 called it "mind time," which constituted something like 350 milliseconds.

Other researchers prefer to appeal to other discoveries. However, all of them constitute a seamless whole of further neurological knowledge that forces the conclusion that unconscious brain processes direct consciousness and not the other way around. Consciousness is not the "master of the house." Persons consider themselves to be independent and free. In truth, they perform only what the network of gray cells has previously determined: "We don't do what we want; but we want what we do" (Prinz 1996, 87).

In the event that humanity in fact possesses no freedom of the will because the brain steers its behavior, there are some serious consequences. For example, criminal law would lose the whole notion of criminal liability. It might be that a society would still impose sanctions for crimes. However, because the agent bears no guilt for the crime, the sanctions cannot be punishment but only a quasi-punishment, a forced therapy. (On the broad debate, see Geyer 2005 and Köchy and Stederoth 2006; the reflections of chapter 19 draw on Höffe 2006c.)

19.1 Extent of the Challenge

How does a philosophy open to experience react to the question of freedom? First of all, it appropriates the conclusions of the most recent research, beginning with the description of the brain as a complex organ that far surpasses any mainframe computer with its network of some 100 billion (10^{11}) nerve cells (neurons) and a thousand times as many connections (synapses: 10^{14}). With "ungrudging envy" it looks at the not merely technically but also optically fascinating processes of functional imaging. Then with the aid of neuro-tomography, electron- (EBT), magnetic resonant- (MRT), and above all proton emission tomography (PET) and functional magnetic resonance imagery (fMRI), one can above all *spatially* visualize the network of active brain structures. Not least, one can watch the brain in the act of "perceiving," "thinking," and "feeling" thanks to the enormous capacity for data processing.

Even so, one must make here a qualification, even a double qualification. It is not the brain that perceives, thinks, and feels but a human being. Above all, one can watch only in a certain sense. What is viewed is, namely, only the objective space-time architecture of the brain, not the subjective "concomitant phenomenon," perception, thinking, and feeling. One observes, of course, not merely brain processes in the narrow sense, the neurophysiological and neurochemical processes, but also their functional relationships with behavioral reactions and internal processes. (The named instruments are not adequate for this purpose; one needs other processes and resources.) Nonetheless, one cannot see the level of meaning that constitutes the functional combination that is perception, thinking, or, for example, an experience of anxiety. The researcher has to approach that which he sees in the brain—the functional combination of behavioral reactions and internal processes—"as" perception, thinking, and so on. Involved here is an additional contribution, an interpretation, that presupposes for its part a certain knowledge or interpretive model, a knowledge about the distinctiveness of perception, thinking, and feeling. The question with respect to the freedom of the will is not decided in the laboratory but in the classroom: not during the experiment but only when it is interpreted, which for its part is extremely controversial when it comes to its relevance to the freedom of the will.

This circumstance has momentous consequences: were it possible to decide the question in the laboratory, any peace between neuro-research and the day-to-day world with its consciousness of freedom would have devastating consequences for freedom. However, since the question is decided in the classroom, the situation looks more promising. Whereas the laboratory and the life-world are methodologically separated, the seminar is an authority with the power of mediation.

Still a further moment is imperceptible to the researcher but is something that must be brought to his research as a guideline, and this small gift [*Mitbringsel*] magnifies the suggestive power of the neuroscientific imaging: the differences in the activity are not displayed by means of the precise and, to that extent, more scientific numerical values. Brain researchers are far better adapted to the age of mass media and dramatize the differences in the brain. Highly active regions of the brain are marked in red, whereas the minimally and nonactive areas are portrayed in blue.

Philosophy is not merely influenced by the increasingly refined construction of our functional brain architecture. As a consequence of its own competency, namely its theory of living organisms, it shares with the neurosciences the basic view that the dynamic of the brain is best accounted for by a self-organizational process and hardly by a linear-process model. Even more than the research, philosophy is astonished at nature, which in the course of evolution produced the morphological and physiological miracle that is the human brain. Philosophy is not really surprised that the brain will be increasingly understood. Already one of its "church fathers," Aristotle, explained at the beginning of a fundamental text of Western thought, the *Metaphysics,* that humanity is by nature curious, and its curiosity is satisfied only by knowledge of causes and final causes (including reasons). The same author, who was the paradigmatic biologist and psychologist for centuries, determined that the concept of cause is not exclusively linear; when it comes to certain items, there are dynamic structures and self-organizing processes in addition to linear causality.

Appropriate to the adage "Philosophy, stay by your accomplishments!" philosophy refrains from taking a position with respect to experimental arrangements and research conclusions. It does, however, argue with the interpretation of the conclusions, especially with their "missionizing-enlightenment" construction. In this respect, it undertakes background reflections that clarify the presuppositions of the suggested enlightenment. In other words, it seeks that reflexive enlightenment with which philosophy has always been concerned: is freedom of the will an illusion, or is not the real illusion, to the contrary, the illusion of the freedom of the will?

Before philosophy takes up this question, however, it extends the provocation. In the event of a social world without freedom of the will, much more is lost than merely the notion of guilt in criminal law, although this loss alone is momentous. The alternative kind of criminal law that would be based on improvement of the "criminal" results in an extremely unjust criminal punishment that as a consequence is appropriately called "quasi-punishment": On the one hand, relatively harmless criminals could be severely quasi-punished when the punishment is judged to be necessary for their "healing." On the other hand, the quasi-punishment for even the most horrendous crime can be annulled, *insofar* as no recidivism can be expected, for example, by Nazi or Gulag archipelago henchmen.

Furthermore, the question can be asked, just what is the basis not only for political but also for personal morality? Self-determination! In addition, the presupposition for parenting, self-education, and self-respect must be established: in order for a society as well as for the individual to survive, individuals must program themselves ("wire" themselves) in a specific manner. They must, for example, distinguish highly eccentric but still allowable manners of behavior from criminally punishable crimes, and, appropriate to the distinction, they must be able to cultivate themselves, which is difficult to imagine in the absence of any freedom of the will. This discriminating task is pursued not only by the one wishing to pursue a virtuous life who avoids offense but also by the "ingenious criminal" who wants to commit crimes without detection.

Evolutionary biology adds: whether a construction or reality—for the evolution of hominids, the thought of responsibility, including at least a modest freedom of the will, is indispensable. As a consequence, the following preliminary conclusion imposes itself: loss of the freedom of the will endangers a huge portion of individual, social, and juridical culture that has been developed throughout human history and in the meantime constitutes its highest accomplishment.

Is there a danger that the philosopher overstates the provocation? According to Gerhard Roth, a human being is capable of a "responsibility without personal guilt" thanks to a self-evaluation of his actions and a consequent self-monitoring derived from his own experience (2003b, 544). This ability is even called "autonomy" by him. Since it contains nothing but what "most animals possess" (ibid., 531), it is too weakly conceived. For example, a foundation of private rights is endangered: the ability and, simultaneously, entitlement to make contracts, a private autonomy, hardly possessed by primates and certainly not by "most animals."

A distinctive feature observed parenthetically: some brain researchers tend to downplay the differences between humans and animals. When comparing their new knowledge with the insights of the human sciences and philosophers (in their opinion still backward), they prefer to exaggerate the persisting differences (between philosophers and scientists). In opposition to that, a question and a suggestion impose themselves.

The question: can one also detect in animals the sketched tendency or even only the suspicion of a tendency to under- or overestimate specific differences between animals and human beings, or is it dependent on a qualitative difference, and thus on a peculiarity of human beings? The (apparently) positive answer speaks for a considerable difference between animals and human beings.

The suggestion: one argues with an overly simplistic alternative. No one questions that humanity both physically and mentally-psychically is a part of nature any more than one questions the belief that it is ridiculous to make a sharp distinction between nature on the one side and mind, culture, and society on the other. What is asked about, however, is the structurally complicated ability to see both: the connection to the subhuman nature *and* the unique position of humanity. In any event, one should do both: one should value nature and culture not only in their connection but also with respect to their relative differences.

In addition to the extension of the provocation, there is an extension of the phenomenal basis: philosophy reminds us of the fullness of intermediate and transitional phenomena and, simultaneously, of the fact that humanity does not act consistently on the basis of its freedom of the will, not even in terms of simple freedom (see chapter 16). A person can make a blunder, miscalculate, or forget something. He can succumb to internal experiences in which his appetites, needs, and passions dominate; furthermore, he can succumb to external experiences in which he is the victim of evil (of course, also happy) blows of fate. Not least are the limitless physical, psychical, and social causal elements that absolve one of responsibility and freedom for some behavior, and others (for example, psychotic illnesses, dementia, and delusions) that absolve one of responsibility and freedom for almost all behavior: the notion that every individual at all times is perfectly free and thoroughly responsible is an illusion to which no one adheres.

Allegedly, the insight that the individual does not exercise absolute control over his life and life story is shocking; in fact, it's not shocking at all. The popular diagnosis of the great mortifications which humanity has suffered in the course of modernity can be taken confidently to be an overdramatization.

Even the common man in the street knows that the individual is not in control of his life. Since Greek tragedies and philosophy, Western culture has known that there are good reasons for this lack of control. Some religions and many wisdom texts from other cultures are even more skeptical although not always with scientific or philosophically sound arguments. Because one knows more precisely as a consequence of the works of Darwin, Freud, and the new brain research, philosophy is curious about the insights from evolutionary theory, psychology, and the neurosciences and takes seriously, for example, the arguments of the neurologist Antonio Damasio 1999 that limit the freedom of the will. However, thoroughly shattering surprises are expected only by those who ignore the well-known witnesses of culture and repress their own personal experience. Only such people can be fooled by the solemn staging of supposedly radically new discoveries that deny absolute control over life.

Unquestionably, one makes rash judgments. For example, one deludes oneself sometimes that one is still in thorough control; or one attributes to someone a morally reprehensible action only to discover later that he suffers from a tumor in those structures of the frontal lobe of the brain that are necessary for imputable behavior or, as brain researchers say, are necessary for the recall of acquired social rules. Or presumably, in the case of hard-core youth offenders, their cerebral metabolism is sensitively damaged. The film buff will remember Fritz Lang's film *M—A City Seeks a Murderer* (1931) in which at the end, a horrifying sexual offender and multiple child murderer cries out: "I don't want to, I must; I don't want to, I must; I don't want to, I must." In such circumstances, it is not the illusionary nature of the freedom of the will but two other things that are obvious: First, one must be careful with moral judgments. This is a warning that is by no means new, especially in court cases where the principle of the presumption of innocence is clearly nothing new. Second, it is only sensible to excuse someone suffering from a special tumor (or from a cerebral metabolism dysfunction) because other tumors don't offer such an excuse and many people—at least, one hopes—don't suffer from some other illness that limits their sense of guilt. These examples of absent or limited freedom of action are in any event controversial.

A second interim conclusion: both the principled limitation of the freedom of the will and false conclusions about its concrete presence are not contested. All that needs clarification is whether or not there is *any kind* of freedom of the will; is there "no freedom anywhere"? Is someone who allows himself to be bribed, who cheats on his taxes, or who kills a patient under his care necessarily not responsible for his actions? The alternative: whereas a brain illness, according to its kind and degree, makes one unfree, a healthy brain is not the only but is an important organic presupposition for freedom and responsibility.

19.2 An Exemplary Experiment

A third consideration addresses the consequences of the Libet experiments, which are often taken to be decisive. In tending to this consideration, the debate over causality and freedom of the will is taken further. Kant remains the authoritative figure here because he concerned himself with both themes: with the favorite opponent of brain researchers, René Descartes, and with David Hume, who is taken by most philosophers of the mind today to be paradigmatic. The first argument with respect to the question of causality which Kant held against the empiricist Hume remains valid (see chapter 18.3): an observable change is objectively recognizable only under the assumption of four nonobservable elements. Whoever declares in the case of the Libet experiment that someone who raises his hand is engaging not in mere reflex behavior but in a knowing and intentional behavior maintains, first, a temporal circumstance:

"first, the construction of the readiness-potential, then the application of the will." Second, he declares their irreversibility: the application of the will does not even occasionally occur prior to the development of the readiness-potential. As the goal of the irreversibility, he presupposes, third, a "for this reason" that includes causality: the application of the will occurs only *because* prior to its occurrence a readiness-potential has been developed. The "because" does not automatically follow, however, from the "prior to"; rather, it requires, fourth, a (not necessarily already recognized) rule of connection. This rule says that the construction of the potential over and against the application of the will is not accidental but is necessarily prior in the sequence of the progression.

An enlightened philosophy of freedom is, therefore—and this constitutes a third interim conclusion—not especially surprised at the Libet research: in order to recognize the application of the will as an objective event, one must assume the occurrence of a prior event and maintain that it is necessarily prior in the sequence of progression. (One finds in Kant a transcendental natural law for the nonlinear model as well, with the Third Analogy, the Principle of Reciprocity: *Critique of Pure Reason,* B 256ff.)

Further steps complete the clarification. They show that what appears to be an empirical refutation of the freedom of the will in fact depends upon an obsolete metaphysics that restricts all causality to natural causes. The contrary assumption of a causality of freedom does not presuppose, as we've seen, indeterminism, which maintains the will to be "ultimate and uncaused." It presupposes even less that freedom assumes with respect to the individual concerned that he could act differently under identical internal and external conditions.

Because freedom of the will does not consist in indeterminism, one does not need to fear that, in the presence of a true freedom of the will, individuals would conduct themselves unpredictably all the more often. To the contrary, one finds an additional argument why an elucidated philosophy of freedom should be able to be convincing even to brain researchers: responsible agency consists in the binding of the will to reasons, and moral agency consists in the binding of the will to reasons of a superior type. If such reasons were rejected with respect to character profiles, individuals otherwise with free will would not have been able to act otherwise than in the manner in which they did; they would as a consequence be predictable: an Achilles would always be brave; a Socrates would never deceive; the friend in Schiller's "The Pledge" would not be able to do anything other than act as Damon the True; and Mother Teresa would not have been able to do otherwise than help the destitute in Calcutta. However, lack of freedom is not the consequence of predictability.

Already as a consequence of its focus, the space-time architecture of the brain, brain research is not concerned with what is decisive for the freedom of the will in the sense of practical reasons for action. This brings us to a fourth interim conclusion: because someone who limits himself to the horizon of natural experience has already eliminated the freedom of the will, he shouldn't be astonished that he hasn't discovered it in the course of his research. It is commendable even for the brain researcher to stay within the limits of his accomplishments, that is, to interpret what he observes in a manner appropriate to the observations rather than to include interpretations that are very controversial for what otherwise, for the most part, are uncontroversial observations. Anyone who draws conclusions about the nonexistence of freedom on the basis of natural data succumbs to a naturalistic fallacy. The will is not free because it suspends natural causes. To the contrary, it is free because, or, more carefully, insofar as in spite of natural causality, first, it has at its disposal an ability to act according to recognized and adopted reasons, that is, through practical reflection instead of merely through external or internal necessity (i.e., it is in possession of a modest freedom of the will), and because or insofar as it is capable, second, of extending this capacity to include moral reasons (i.e., it is in possession of a complete freedom of the will).

It is downright obvious that one encounters freedom when one poses a question that brain researchers tend to cover up in their interpretations: to what extent are researchers and their subjects free? When one overcomes the usual "blind spot," one finds anew, surprisingly, a great deal about the levels of agency and practical reasons.

Let's begin with the research subjects! These, first of all, usually participate voluntarily and are, therefore, to that extent free agents. Second, they are able to act according to the expectations of the research plan. Possibly, the research promises, third, something that will contribute to the subjects' well-being; for example, they feel honored thereby, or as psychology students they need the research for their studies, or possibly they will be paid for their time. Not least, the research depends upon the honesty of the subjects involved even when one believes that one is able methodologically to eliminate an occasional dishonesty.

The researcher in turn is, first, free with respect to the initial levels even to a conspicuous degree: he is the conscious initiator of the action, who (a) considers alternative possibilities, (b) chooses among them, and (c) controls the sequencing for an orderly completion of the planned research. (d) A requirement of professional experiments of empirical research is that the research be repeatable, so that both the subject and the researcher in both the setup and the execution of the experiment be strictly replaceable.

Second, the colleagues who are responsible for evaluating the research at the very least hold the leader of the research team responsible for all three of the primary levels of freedom: (a) In the technical sense, they examine the alternatives that were under consideration in the research, as well as the choices taken on which the research was conducted, and not least the interpretation drawn from the research; they know that there could be professional blunders made in all of these respects. (b) In the pragmatic sense, they evaluate the research according to points of view of originality and power of explanation, and they bestow, according to their standards, scientific prestige on the project. (c) In the moral sense, they ask whether the data were faked or plagiarized, and, not least, they ask, as is expected in the advisory reports from foundations that promote the sciences, whether there are any conflicts with the legal principles of scientific ethics.

Should technical, pragmatic, or moral expectations be violated, some might wish, of course, that they be judged not responsible. Positive accomplishments, in contrast—that is, "my experiment" or "my publication"—one prefers to ascribe to oneself. One undertakes a challenge, perhaps even achieves a splendid success, for which one, then, expects the prestige and the scientific prize that one finally receives.

19.3 Further Objections

Since its early days, especially explicit in Kant's transcendental epistemology, philosophy has taught that optical, acoustic, tactile, and other everyday perceptions depend upon the interaction of two factors: assimilation of sensory inputs and their processing by the understanding. Only with this interaction can something emerge *as* something; for example, the noisy ball of fur in the garden can be taken to be a barking dog. Even the brain researcher does not "see" cells or synapse connections. Even less capable of such "sight" is that nerve system within the skull, the brain. It is incapable of doing what the book title of a brain researcher, *Aus Sicht des Gehirns* [*From the Perspective of the Brain*] (Roth 2003a), suggests: to have certain views with respect to perceptions, memories, thoughts, and feelings; and to constantly interpret with increasing distance from that which it observes. Beginning with the interpretation of certain sensory inputs or switching points, he passes through several intermediate steps to finally arrive at a physiological theory of the brain that seeks to understand neuronally the entirety of human activity, including thinking and experiences of freedom. Because of this multi-leveled interpretation, one needs the mentioned restriction that one can see the brain by thinking and feeling "only to a certain extent."

This restriction includes an objection already contained in Aristotle's advice: "To say that it is the soul which is angry is as inexact as it would be to say that it is the soul that weaves webs or builds houses. It is doubtless better . . . to say that it is the man who does this with his soul" (*De anima* 1.4.408b13ff.). The soul is treated here neither as a mysterious "something" nor in contrast to the body but as the embodiment of these powers of motivation. In fact, the person does what he does because of the powers of his brain. It does not follow from the circumstance that all movements of the body are seamlessly controlled by the brain and that all consciousness and mental activities are inseparable from neuronal activity in the brain, and hence that these activities *are nothing but* a bundling of neuronal conditions of stimulation so that the brain thinks, feels, decides, and acts. In truth, the person thinks, to be sure, "with" his central organ, he acts "with" the brain, but it is the person, not the brain, that thinks or acts.

Even more important is the fact that the object of these experiments can only with difficulty be considered relevantly pertinent. The Libet experiment is a classical stimulus-response experiment. On the basis of an internal stimulus, the urge to move a hand, the subject is given the option not to implement the "felt" urge. One is not concerned here with a truly free or an unfree decision but with a minimal reaction to a prior instruction, with an atomic action, that is insufficient when it comes to the question of the freedom of the will; and, in the strict sense, it is even irrelevant. A mere agency is attested to by atomic actions; however, in order to establish or to contradict the more ambitious authorship of free will, atomic actions are insufficient. The same applies to Singer's experiments with perception. The morally important brain processes that belong to the neuronal processes of lying, deception, or stealing; to levelheadedness, offering help, or forgiving; even those that belong to a threat or compromise, viewed temporally are no short haul, but medium hauls, and often even involve long hauls, more exactly long-term *periods of time*.

Thanks to the fact that their intelligence is almost never tied to the "peg of the moment," human beings live equally and often simultaneously out of the past, present, and future. Their actions consist of a complex linkage of short-, medium-, and sometimes also long-term goals that can be weighed against one another in light of guiding points of view like happiness and morality and to which they consider the appropriate means in light of opportunities and resources, but also in light of hindrances and resistances. And to be completely absorbed in the moment usually requires an extraordinary effort, an extreme concentration.

Those actions that are decisive for freedom and morality are not merely neuronally considered long periods of time. They must also be interpreted in a (morally) significant respect. If left uninterpreted, one has only a morally indifferent basic action, for example, one takes something. However, the morally significant action decides, first, to whom the thing belongs and whether or not the owner agrees to the object being taken. Should the owner not agree, one has stolen; when agreed, then something other than a theft has transpired.

Now to return to reflection: one must learn the required complex of capacities and skills in order to reflect. Such learning is less like the manner in which one learns music or art history than the way one would learn a musical instrument or the art of painting: that is, by means of demonstrating and imitating, by practicing, becoming acquainted with something, and refining one's technique until one is able, finally, to act with thorough deliberation and with circumspection. Atomic actions that are separated from all such things—not only independent of stretches of time and the framework of an action but also from reasons that organize and assist in structuring the context, and not least independent from appropriate skills—have nothing to do with the significant sense of free action.

These objections are in no way intended to diminish the significance of brain research, not to speak of denying the insight it has brought. In addition to knowledge, this research promises much of humanitarian value: for example, as a contribution to the diagnosis and indirectly to the treatment of illnesses. For example, it aids in the recognition of the causes for pathological, false perceptions or hallucinations; and, thanks to the assignment of carefully identified regions of the brain or nerve populations, such research makes possible (minimally) invasive procedures. However, the essential personality characteristics of moral freedom as well as non-pathological actions such as honesty or dishonesty, courage or cowardice, integrity and generosity, are items that develop over long periods of time and bring order into an entire life. The essential aspects of moral freedom do not emerge even on the horizon in the Libet or Singer experiments, or in other known investigations.

According to Roth, it is absolutely useful "to bring to bear understanding and reason when it comes to important things. Neither, however, is *decisive* for anything, they function as *advisers* for the emotional directing of the activity system" (2003b, 553). The author of the exemplary investigations, Libet (2004, 137ff.), in contrast, acknowledges a veto-potential to consciousness. The free will is not capable of initiating an action of the will, but it can control it; for example, to delay the completion of, and even block, the sequence of the willful process. Although not capable of initiating them, likely as not, freedom can influence the possibility of options, of linkage, and of the veto of actions. The fact that both Libet and Roth know the relevant experiments, but nonetheless estimate differently their significance, strengthens the fundamental reservation: brain researchers can only demonstrate very little; they are indebted far more to interpretation, and these interpretations turn out to be seriously varied.

How does one handle a situation of competing interpretations? One strategy is obvious. Either one subjects the interpretation to examination directly or subjects it to an interpretation of a second order. When it comes to the first strategy, the non–brain researcher, the plain philosopher, is advised to be careful and to exercise discretion. However, one of the philosopher's competencies, the clarification of concepts, allows the placement of a question mark after Roth's interpretation because it involves two contradictory partial theses: either the will is, as claimed, an adviser, and then it is no neutral third observer but an engaged authority that, to be sure, doesn't make the decision but can influence to an essential extent the reflections leading up to the decision; or the will doesn't have any power of influence, and then it is no adviser, only a neutral observer capable of offering only commentary irrelevant to the decision.

The second, meta-interpretation strategy affects Libet's thesis. He is, indeed, no philosophical authority—his attachment to a specific theory of knowledge, Karl Popper's falsification theory, is even questionable. Nevertheless, his warning to be careful and to exercise discretion makes sense (Libet 2004, 155–56): "Given that the issue is so fundamentally important to our view of who we are, a claim that our free will is illusory should be based on fairly direct evidence. . . . It is foolish to give up our view of ourselves as having some freedom of action and of not being predetermined robots on the basis of an unproven theory of determinism." Equally wise is a modest dualism that is only epistemological but not ontological. Libet strictly distinguishes between subjective and objective experience, that is, between the mental and physical world, and he modestly observes (ibid., 183): "The emergence of conscious subjective experience from nerve cell activity is still a mystery."

The fundamental assumption of the new brain research—that one needs the brain when it comes to the generation of the will and determination of a decision—is neither new nor spectacular; even free action has a neurophysiological background. Equally unspectacular is the insight that the brain has no dominating cognitive center and, because of its polycentric network, works without a director or captain, but is self-organizing. Philosophy is equally not astonished that mind and consciousness have not fallen from heaven but have developed by means of the evolution of the nervous system. In opposition to the not infrequent tendency to succumb to a neurological reductionism and in opposition to the insight that in the end everything amounts to a self-organizing activity of the synapses behind the back of the subject, philosophy recalls the significance of cultural evolution and social education (that afterward shows up in the synapses). Stated in terms of the social sciences: the natural development of the human individual is from the very beginning an interaction with others; it remains a history of interaction with a thoroughly cultural, coevolutionary environment; and, at a certain point of development, includes the encounter of the individual with himself whereby that encounter takes on increasing significance.

It is also not surprising that the individual is a "combination" that consists of a bundle of genetic factors, of prenatal and early childhood experiences, as well as of experiences that one has in youth, and, finally, as an adult. The neurophysiological knowledge that unconscious neural processes precede conscious ones, that only the result of certain weighing processes inside the brain enters consciousness so that one is only reputedly aware of all the significant variables in a decision which one could then freely evaluate, all this demands only that one conceive freedom differently, namely, not as indeterminism. This alternative way of thinking about freedom, however, was clear long before such physiological knowledge, namely, in that moment in which one grasped freedom to be in opposition not to determinism but to necessity. It does not follow from the circumstance that one is not master in one's own house that one is simply an unfree marionette or slave.

The actual insights of brain research offer in any event no dogmatic neuro-biologism according to which mind and consciousness *merely* emerge as natural events and according to which the social nature of humanity occurs exclusively on the basis of biological nature. Doubt is already raised in the critique by such a methodologically prudent natural scientist as Max Planck (1934/1949, 309–10) against the analogous tendency of physicalism. Physicalism succumbs to the attempt to explain our consciousness of the freedom of the will by means of Heisenberg's uncertainty relations. In that event, how should one—Planck asks— "reconcile the assumption of a blind accident with the feeling of moral responsibility?" In point of fact, the temporally imprecisely predictable quantum jump of electrons, which is by far a prior preconscious event, is no proper foundation for the freedom connected to consciousness.

The alternative to physicalism that is more methodologically reserved is nurtured, for example, by an elementary particle physicist who attempts to explain the characteristics of chemical combinations, for example of alcohols, not entirely on the basis of the physical qualities of elementary particles. At least as a hypothesis, the assumption is plausible that macro-physics has an undeniable microphysical basis just as chemistry has a macro-physical, biology has a chemical, and psychology has a biological foundation. As a consequence, however, the hypothesis is in each case of a more complex, "higher," under-determined level, so that this higher level cannot be reduced without any remnant to the lower level.

In contrast, simple dualism (that is, the naive assumption that the mental world of humans is entirely independent and ontologically thoroughly distinct from the world of things) is not seriously defended by anyone. Even the "arch-dualist," Descartes, doesn't succumb to this assumption. This frequently scolded philosopher surely maintained that mind and body are two different substances; however, they function in two respects as a functional unity. On the one hand, Descartes assumed a correlation between the body and mind that from case to case is empirically determined, whereby they are entirely open to the appropriate investigation, even that of the new brain research. On the other hand, Descartes sees the mind "as complete in the whole body," even present "in every random part of the body" (Descartes 1642/1987, 59–60).

Just as macro-physical processes are under-determined microphysical processes and psychological processes are under-determined biological processes, one cannot expect purely methodologically to be able to eliminate the freedom of the will of complex actions on the basis of the neurophysiological explanation of atomic actions. Appropriately, eleven leading German neuroscientists present themselves far more cautiously in "Manifest" (Elger et al. 2004). Including Roth and Singer, they declare "that neuronal networks as highly dynamic, nonlinear systems" to be sure "adhere to simple natural laws," but they bring about "completely new characteristics" because of their complexity.

Of their three levels of objects, brain researchers "understand" ever more precisely not only the highest level, the function of the larger areas of the brain, but also the processes of the lower levels, those at the level of individual cells. They are able, thanks to computer developments and imaging procedures, to present their data in a media-compatible fashion. However, the occurrences at the middle level are largely closed off to them. The modest assessment of the "Manifest" can, therefore, serve as a further interim conclusion: "According to whatever rules the brain works; how it represents the world in a way that conflates immediate perception and earlier experience; how the brain experiences its internal activity as 'its' activity, and how it plans future actions, are all things that we don't even begin to understand. Even more: it is entirely unclear how one could research it on the basis of today's means. In this respect we find ourselves in certain respects still at the stage of hunters and gatherers" (33).

Philosophy subsequently adds and proposes a heterogeneity that is just as fundamental as it is insurmountable: Already when it comes to the more modest form of the freedom of the will, one is concerned with reasons, and, with the complete freedom of the will, one is even concerned with reasons of a special kind. In both cases, with respect to their kind of being, they are representations in consciousness and belong to the language of the philosophy of mind, not to brain research. For the philosophy of mind, they may indeed have the functions of internal causes that, in order to become effective as actions, bring about neuromotor causes. However, when it comes to freedom, neuronal correlates are not what are decisive but, rather, reasons themselves are what is decisive. Reasons, viewed ontologically, are not neuronal conditions but intellectual arguments. When it comes to contexts of action, they are, for example, possible answers to questions—placed in part beforehand, in part concomitantly, and in part subsequently; presently asked by the self, presently asked by others—who demand accountability. Whoever overlooks the difference and smuggles into the discussion of the brain concepts which, like "reason," come from the language of the mind makes a category mistake, and whoever does so consciously engages in intellectual deception.

20 The Criterion

20.1 Interim Conclusion

The decisive freedom for morals, personal freedom, consists in the freedom of an individual with respect to his willing, reflecting, and acting. It is not satisfied with a mere agency nor does it consist in an indeterminism, capriciousness, or in groundless behavior. Rather, it consists in a free agency that acts on the basis of reasons that one has chosen for oneself.

Already this "acting on the basis of reasons" is an ambitious condition. It says, first, that whatever is done or not done does not occur because of external constraint. From the beginning, then, the antonym to freedom is not determinism but necessity; more exactly: the antonym to freedom is necessity in the sense of an externally imposed necessity, since self-imposed necessity is compatible with freedom. In contrast to someone who falls because he was pushed, when it comes to freedom, one must oneself be the author of the event—in this way, one acts voluntarily.

A voluntary, unconstrained agency, however, is itself not sufficient. Whether or not one aids or harms someone else can be a matter of chance. An event is morally relevant only when, second, it is intentional. Intention, in this case the aid or the harm, must be, third, not arbitrary; it must follow from the "inwardness" of the action, from reasons.

One can view these reasons as causes. Something else, however, is decisive: the agent, fourth, takes the reasons to be his own; wherever they come from, they must become one's own reasons for action. The philosophical tradition says as well: one makes the matter a goal for oneself. In any event, it does not depend upon its origin but on self-possession, and by self-possession one does not mean simple possession (someone *has* a reason) but acknowledgment of the possession by the individual. One can speak here of an (action-generating) willing ("volition") of a second order (Frankfurt 1971). More important than the hierarchical

252

relationship, however (although not entirely absent in Frankfurt), is the reflective acknowledgment: one distances oneself from simple possession, and, out of the distancing, one resolves to take a position that some accept and others reject. There is no general compliance with but, rather, a selective embracing of the reason for one's action.

Whether it is one of acceptance or rejection, the response doesn't need to follow explicitly. One is not concerned here with some kind of notarized documentation that one presents as a (celebratory) declaration to others or for oneself. It is also not decisive whether or not the reasons followed are thoroughly considered, merely intuitive, or somewhere in between. What counts is the acceptance or rejection "in point of fact" as a response that results in effective action. Such a response occurs in several ways, for example, in terms of the kind of intention that one conceives, the orientation of reflection with respect to the action that one initiates, or with respect to the accompanying or subsequent feelings about the action, such as self-respect or shame.

Obviously, the manner of response, that is, the intentions, reflections, actions, and feelings, all hang together as a whole. They are distinguished from one another in terms of the form and intensity of their acceptance or rejection. What they all have in common, however, is that, through the experience of their being embraced, the simple conditions, which themselves can be external to the actor, are transformed into one's own, self-affirmed, reflectively practical reasons for action. This all amounts to an act of liberation; to be sure, a liberation that is personal and not social: one liberates oneself from the otherwise all-powerful determinism of nature, acts in consonance with personally selected, "one's own" reasons, and is thereby free in the fundamentally personal respect appropriate to morals.

The circumstances of one's internal world, not only the physiology of the brain, but also the psychology of pleasure and displeasure, and not least the circumstances of one's external, natural and social world, play a crucial role when it comes to this personal freedom. However, they are not what in the end determines that and how a person acts; rather, what is determinative are those reasons that the individual has made his own. It is precisely for this reason, that is, because they are practical and reflective reasons, that one can attribute them to the individual concerned: his action occurs out of his own will. It is only a freedom that extends on the basis of reasons beyond the mere freedom to act that one can call a freedom of the will in the strict sense.

In response to precipitous critics, it is worth repeating that, with this understanding, the will is not proposed to be some kind of quasi-empirical mental substance that is independent of experience. It depends rather on the person concerned, on his experiences, talents, interests, character, and, finally, life story. The will is so internally connected with "body and soul" that one, as it is expressed in the aphorism, "can't get outside of one's skin."

Even less are we concerned with a "starter paradigm." The will is, indeed, comparable to the starter of an engine to the extent that it is the condition for the actuation and not already the running motor itself. In contrast to a starter for an engine, however, it is not its own substance, a pre-motor that precedes the action and is some kind of external actuator component that sets into motion the main engine, the activity process. The expression "will" expresses far more a structural complication, the practical reflexivity of human action, which explodes linearity—as if there were some will followed by its actualization.

However, the affected individual is not yet morally free, but free only so far as his practical reflexive reasons reach. To the extent that these reflections are limited to the means for accomplishing a given end, one is free in a technical-personal sense. If these reasons extend to include ends that have as their aim one's personal well-being, then one is free in a pragmatic-personal sense. Freedom of the will in its fullest sense, truly moral freedom, is achieved, however, only with the readiness in a situation of conflict to put aside one's personal well-being for the sake of morals.

Philosophers like Kant speak here of the unconditional. A superficial critique takes the notion of an absolutely free will to be an absurdity. Such a will would be independent of the body and the character of a person, independent of his thoughts, perceptions, wishes, and memories. A will entirely unrelated to what constitutes a person would be entirely alien to that person and, therefore, actually improper for conceiving of personal, more precisely, moral freedom.

Practically speaking, "unconditional" means something very different from this. Reasons that limit the means to a given end or have as their primary end one's own well-being owe their ranking as a "reason" to a condition external to them, that is, they owe their ranking to the arbitrary goal or the natural governing end to which they are directed. In light of this precondition, reasons are "conditional." Consistently, a reason would be "unconditional" that was independent of such preconditions. Of course there are reasons that belong to the person concerned; the accusation is overhasty, however, that "unconditional" means independent from one's body and character. What remains undecided and still in need of clarification is merely whether "unconditional" in the sense of independence from preconditions still contains a possible determination where neither an arbitrary end, nor a personal primary end, nor other precepts are involved. It might appear at first glance that this is implausible. A second glance which sees that one can act morally contrary to one's own well-being calls into question the implausibility.

This reconstruction of personal and moral freedom breaks the constraints of the usual alternatives, either compatibility (compatibilism) or incompatibility (incompatibilism) of determinism and freedom. Superficially, compatibilism asserts that the freedom of action, even freedom of the will, is compatible with determinism. Compatibilism includes, however, the previously mentioned transformation of "deterministic" conditions, namely, those foreign conditions external to the subject, into those practical-reflexive reasons that are embraced by the subject. Paradoxically formulated: out of a deterministic determination arises a nondeterministic but, nonetheless, not indeterminate, determination. Because personal freedom arises out of a transformation and emancipation, no perspectival dualism occurs either in its Kantian form (the dualism of an experienced [phenomenal] world and one that is merely thought [noumenal]) or in the newer variation from Habermas 2004 (that one can consider the world of action in two ways—as deterministic or free). As soon as "determining" reasons take on a practical-reflexive character, they are, namely, an element of the experienced world and, simultaneously, have the character of freedom in the sense of personal freedom.

20.2 Concept, Criterion, Imperative

What criterion determines whether one has a moral basis for one's decision; what is the reliable benchmark for morals? Whereas the answer is controversial, the search for an answer as if from itself shows the way to its resolution: if the standard is to be convincing, it must emerge from the concern itself; the concept of morals is a necessary if perhaps not a sufficient criterion for the criterion. As a consequence, the normative ethical principle, the measurement of morals, is to be acquired out of its application, which one can in turn call meta-ethics: it is acquired by clarification of the concept of morals itself.

Because normative ethics, viewed methodologically, emerges out of this meta-ethics, one can assume substantive moral duties, but one must bracket the different contents, which are in part controversial, to which these duties are applied. For example, when one disregards the specific content of the moral duties not to lie or to kill, one encounters a formal similarity between them: these *prohibitions* are not merely valid in that happy situation in which there is no possibility of offense. For example, within one's normal circles, such as one's family, friends, and acquaintances, perhaps even with cooperative neighbors: here there is nothing threatening. However, a moral act occurs only in the case where one finds oneself in a less happy circumstance in which one readily wants to be dishonest or to be violent. The circumstance is similar to positive *obligations,* moral commands. The obligation to assist others doesn't apply just in that happy circumstance in which one does something good for a fellow human being out of an altruistic sentiment but, rather, categorically. Finally, both prohibitions and obligations are not mere means to accomplish something else, such as economic success, social prestige, or merely peace of mind in the face of the state power that can legally prosecute one, for example, in the case of the violation of a contract, the use of violence, or a neglected performance of first aid after an accident.

Moral commitments are valid, therefore, independent of personal moods, fortunate interpersonal relationships, and farther-reaching goals and intentions. With the very concept of morals, one is concerned with obligations that claim validity for themselves and as such. They are binding in the absolutely highest and unconditionally valid sense: in other words, they are categorical imperatives.

Already in Kant's ethics, however, the categorical imperative means far more than only a highest moral criterion. More fundamental than a mere standard of measurement, he first of all defines morals as "applicable" to beings who don't always and on their own acknowledge morals. He presents, then, a moral criterion only in a second respect. At that point, the categorical imperative, in terms of his meta-ethical or semantic meaning, is nothing but the concept of morals itself: the concept of obligations that, perhaps, in the case of their being in conflict with one another, are to be weighed against one another, but which can never be relativized in light of another, presumably higher, obligation.

A problem-solving ethics can hardly evade this argumentative sequence that begins with a concept of morals in order, then, to obtain a moral criterion out of this concept. As will be seen, this argument consists of three moments: (1) in terms of obligations, it is concerned with an imperative; (2) the concern of the obligations is life principles or maxims; and (3) their moral criterion lies in generalizability.

The first moment is trivial and, therefore, is often suppressed: the moral criterion is no measuring stick that is indifferent whether or not it is acknowledged, as if it is a thermometer that measures the warmth of a room without prescribing a temperature. The moral criterion is no "moralometer" that only indicates morals and leaves up to the agent whether or not he deigns to conduct himself appropriate to the prompt. As with every obligation, a moral obligation challenges one to an appropriate action. It is an imperative, so that the short version of a moral obligation says: "Act morally!" Because it depends upon an imputable participation on the part of the will, it says more precisely: "Act on the basis of a moral will!"

Because finite, incomplete rational beings like human beings do not act morally inevitably and on their own, morals are for them a "should" and not a state of "being." Regardless of the possibility of shaping oneself appropriate to the main features of an ordered life by means of *secondary* character behavior and a normative life-world, morals here have a *primary* prescriptive, imperative character. This can be shown by means of the supposed alternatives to a Kantian imperative ethic, that is, with Aristotle and Hegel.

Aristotle does not avoid imperative language; he employs, for example, the term *deon,* that which is compulsory and rationally necessary (e.g., *Nicomachean Ethics* 3.10.1115b12 and 1116a6–7, as well as 3.15.1196b16–18). Even Hegel, who prefers the strategy of avoiding such language, can only deny with difficulty the fact that not every institutional life-world and also not every individual is without hesitation moral. Incidentally, the character of an imperative is not bound to an explicit language of imperatives, to commands and prohibitions. It can be concealed, for example, in biblical parables, where it unquestionably comes into play: "Go and do likewise!" Even moral examples or models that one can give without any moral finger-pointing are life- or behavioral-forms that count as authentic or truly human without everyone actually acknowledging or following them. They have the nature of a challenge, even an imperative character.

Still today, one can hear the opinion that a moral imperative is precisely the opposite of freedom since it is an authoritative rule of law that, as in Franz Kafka's story *The Trial,* makes humanity powerless in the face of an extraneous and simultaneously inscrutable sovereign power. In truth, a moral imperative consists in a demand that isn't external but comes out of an internal, practical reflexivity. Certainly, an imperative prescribes, but it does so only on the basis of what a practical, rational being requires of itself. This prescription is manifest in the three levels of technical, pragmatic, and moral reason. In the case of the categorical imperative, the third level, it constitutes in a nutshell the self-reflection of a moral agent.

20.3 Maxims and the Ethics of Maxims

Whether technical, pragmatic, or moral, where one's reasons for action belong to the core element of a person, to his personal characteristics, those grounds of action constitute the complete reality of a practiced life principle, a lived maxim. Action takes on the character of willing in the emphatic sense when one lives according to maxims: one wants something, applies one's capacities toward accomplishing it, and doesn't allow other distractions to interfere. What is wished for is also no isolated wish to help someone here and now. Maxims represent life preferences with respect to the larger dimensions of one's actions, such as the readiness to help someone in need. They are fundamental principles in a double sense: not only the ultimate motivating force, but also a normative common ground among different actions.

Maxims, which follow imperatives as the second moment in the hierarchy of moral criteria, are even more frequently undervalued or even suppressed. Even professional moral philosophers often overlook the fact that the moral criterion of a strict ethic of the will doesn't follow just any reasons and rules but reasons or rules of a higher level, fundamental principles. What are well known are those maxims that arose in the critique of morals in the early modern age, for example those of La Rochefoucauld, whose reflections on humanity appeared precisely under the title *Maxims*. However, the label is much older; it appears already in Boethius's Latin commentary on Aristotle's logic. There, in the context of argumentative chains of those absolutely highest and supreme principles that are not only universal but also obviously valid, he acknowledges that such principles require no demonstration. On the contrary, they are capable of proving other principles. He is concerned here with those veritable principles Kant calls "first principles" ["Anfangsgründe"]; they are less principles *from* which one demonstrates than they are principles *with* which one demonstrates the validity of one's thought and actions.

Later, the label "maxim" is applied to nonlogical principles, which, still later, force their moral-practical meaning into the foreground. Already more than a generation before La Rochefoucauld, in his *Discourse on Method* Descartes called the principles of his provisional morals "maxims." The same label is used elsewhere to refer to social and behavioral rules and, then, to advice in the form of life wisdom acquired through experience. In reaction to the rapidly rising tide of affirmative literature, which was often devoted only to etiquette, La Rochefoucauld and subsequent French moralists with their critique of morals exposed the dominant socially acceptable rules of behavior and their accompanying encouragement of elevated self-estimation as hardly moral and often, in fact, as immoral. With their sharp humor and aphoristic brevity, these moralists are appreciated because of their frequently almost cynical style as ridiculers.

Within the framework of an ethic of the will, maxims refer to the absolutely highest and first principles of a normative chain of argumentation. As a consequence, maxims emphasize the normative quality of willing with its moral, immoral, or possibly even amoral character. First of all, they are something subjective: maxims are adhered to by someone; they are not cognitively but practically significant for this someone. More precisely, maxims are determinations of the will; that is, not schemas of order that an objective observer mandates for the agent, but determinations that the agent himself recognizes as his own and seeks to practice.

Second, maxims are practical rules, but they are not commonplace and relatively concrete but seemingly general rules. Practical principles, on the one hand, can govern an entire life, and, on the other hand, they can apply to a far broader range of life. Within the parameters of a life or a range of life, for example in cases of assistance to others, they can involve considerable differences. For example, someone needs financial, or another psychological, or a third surgical aid, and a fourth threatens suicide. Depending upon the type of situation, they confront others with a call to action that corresponds to issue-specific and far less general rules of action. A maxim disregards all descriptive differences and concentrates on the decisively normative aspect; in this case, one's readiness to help or, in the situation in which one refuses to help, one's hardheartedness. With respect to the rules of action for a specific situation (for example, when it comes to financial, psychological, or surgical aid, etc.), a normative principle of action, for example, the need to assist or hard-heartedness, mediates when it comes to regularly repetitious kinds of circumstances. The rules that emerge in such cases are concerned with the ever-changing conditions of life, that is, not simply with different types of situations, but also with differences in abilities on the part of the agent. Despite identical maxims, practical rules can turn out to be different as a consequence. A nonswimmer assists a drowning person differently than a trained lifeguard.

What is normatively common to maxims is their concern, thirdly, with the moment of action that is at one's own disposal. When it comes to moral praise or condemnation, the fact that in addition this normativity possesses an end- and not a means-character is decisive. Factually ("technically") good is someone who offers the right aid to the injured person; pragmatically good is someone who accepts money or some other reward for the offered assistance. Morally good, in contrast, is someone who attempts to help when there's not a hint of either a criminal punishment (because of failure to offer first aid) or any kind of reward.

Out of the complex collection of factors that come together in concrete action, a maxim highlights the decisively normative, ultimately determining basis of the action, that incentive for the evaluation of the possible options and, finally, for the action itself. Since a maxim is no merely momentary guiding factor but a character-shaping intention, it reflects an enduring orientation of the will. From the internal perspective of the will, such a maxim is called a "disposition"; from the perspective of observable behavior, an "attitude" or "demeanor."

Not every maxim is morally significant. Someone who carefully locks his bicycle in front of his house is only following the pragmatic maxim to protect his possessions. Here as in other circumstances, maxims determine the validity, the value or non-value, of everyday, relatively concrete rules. They are not concerned with the proverbial, disparaging moralizing that consists in an obstinate adherence to a rule established at some point in the past. What is decisive is the orientation toward standpoints of a second order that allow everyday rules of first-order experience to appear rational and make possible a generally well-considered, pragmatically or morally meaningful life conduct. Such deliberation of a second order elevates one's interest to include practical rationality. Everyday reasons for action are limited to narrowly delimited types of situations; maxims eliminate such limitations.

It is an unusual ethic whose criteria are concerned neither with merely individual actions nor with everyday rules of behavior but with life principles or maxims. As unusual as it is, it offers several advantages. To the extent that the maxims are independent of ever-changing life circumstances, they remain open, *first*, to the diversity of life situations. The person who in a normative sense follows maxims rather than rules of behavior rejects an inflexible, pedantic life. He engages varying challenges with an *esprit de finesse* that creatively engages each new situation in terms of an appropriate contextualization.

Because maxims concentrate on the normatively decisive point, the fundamental determination of the will, they aid, *second*, in understanding how human actions can be so varied yet nonetheless possess a common either moral or nonmoral quality: the trained lifeguard can save the drowning victim himself; in order to prevent a double drowning, the nonswimmer does best to call for help from others. A maxim-based ethic is able to counter two opposed misunderstandings of morals: not only that of an inflexible rule-based dogmatism but also an absolute ethical relativism. The latter concludes from the considerable differences in positive moral principles among cultures that there is no such thing as universal moral principles. A (morally significant) maxim is, namely, precisely the moment of identity, that of a moral or nonmoral commonality, which denies this relativism. The necessity in concrete action that requires mediation between a universal maxim and a concrete situation demands, in contrast to rule-based dogmatism, a contextualization appropriate to each circumstance. To do so successfully, in turn, requires empirical knowledge and a capacity for practical judgment.

In passing, one can neutralize the fear that an ethic of the will leads to an overmoralizing according to which the morals of each undertaking must be evaluated ever anew. The very sense of a moral philosophy that concentrates on its determining reasons for action, an ethic of maxims, is that its moral principle does not refer directly to individual acts but to maxims. To the degree that this concentration on maxims allows for the structuring of a life according to very formal principles, it permits leeway for both solid and proven kinds of behavior as well as a situation-sensitive capacity for judgment.

Moral maxims are called duties. An ethic of maxims amounts, therefore, to an ethics of duty (deontological ethics), however—*third* advantage—avoids the frequently maintained antithesis of a virtue ethics. The expression "virtue ethics" has, of course, many meanings because there are different kinds of virtue: namely, virtues of character and intellectual virtues, on the one hand, and, on the other hand, within the framework of the normative aspect of character virtues, primarily moral, secondarily pragmatic, and thirdly technical or functional virtues. The fundamental philosophical moral debate is concerned primarily with character virtues and in this respect with moral virtues. It is decisive for these that the moral principles determining the will fulfill the relevant conceptual moment of virtue, which consists in actions that recognize morals. It is not decisive for maxims that they are capable of linguistic formulation by the agent. Rather, they are norms in the life-practical sense that they in fact shape what one actually does or does not do. Furthermore, these norms or duties consist not in specific actions, nor even in fundamental rules, but, rather, in actually lived fundamental principles.

Supposedly, Kant is the primary representative of a non-virtue ethic. In point of fact, however, the second part of his systematic moral philosophy has precisely the title "Doctrine of Virtue" [part 2 of *The Metaphysics of Morals*]. In addition, he makes a distinction that allows him to intensify the concept of virtue even in terms of its normative aspect ("Doctrine of Virtue," "Introduction," part 14, note, 6:407). The model of virtue ethics in Aristotle is, indeed, not satisfied with simple proficiency (*habitus*) through repetitive action that Kant calls "habit" ["Angewohnheit"] because Aristotle insisted that virtues are combined with free will and with choice or decision-making (*Nicomachean Ethics* 3.7.1114b22–3.8.1115a3). As Kant explains, they don't occur simply "by means of oft-repeated actions." In order, however, to fulfill Kant's normative, higher concept, a "simultaneously general legislative capacity of the will" [*Begehrungsvermögen*] must be present which, as Kant continues, is determined "by means of the representation of a [moral] law in the action" that is "not the result of capriciousness but of the will" ("Doctrine of Virtue," 6:407). *Religion Within the Boundaries of Mere Reason* (part 1, 6:47) combines the intensification with an addendum that one likes to overlook. Empirical virtue or virtue as it is manifest in action is considered the "*firm resolve* in following one's duty [that] one accomplishes by habit" [emphasis by the author, Höffe]. In any case, there are elements necessary for the concept of virtue in an ethic of the will that are absent in Aristotle's ethic of teleological striving. Because Kant defines moral virtue by means of this more demanding element, he represents in fact an intensified concept of virtue in the moral sense.

The grandes dames of more recent virtue ethics, Ascombe and Foot, may indeed prefer as Aristotelians to privilege the master from Stageira and appeal in addition to the great Aristotelian of the Middle Ages, Thomas Aquinas. In point of fact, however, there is no simple confrontation between an Aristotelian virtue- and a Kantian duty-ethics but, rather, the more subtle alternative: Aristotle's ethics of teleological striving and happiness or Kant's autonomous virtue ethic. The latter in addition intensifies the concept of virtue.

There is also the fact that the lists of virtues from the two protagonists are not the same. The virtues that belong to the four examples from Kant's *Groundwork of the Metaphysics of Morals* could be called Kant's quartet of cardinal virtues. They consist of a kind of loyalty to one's own life (prohibition of suicide), honesty (prohibition against lying), the readiness to aid the needy (command to assistance), and attendance to the cultivation of one's talents (command to self-development). None of these virtues appears in Aristotle's list (*Nicomachean Ethics* 2.7). Instead, Aristotle's list is comprised of virtues such as courage, prudence, generosity, and justice, which are absent in Kant's quartet. Aristotle's virtue of truth or truthfulness (*alêtheia*) doesn't correspond to Kant's honesty because Aristotle's truthfulness doesn't forbid lying but boastfulness. However, when one turns from Kant's preparatory *Groundwork of the Metaphysics of Morals* to his systematic "Doctrine of Virtue," one discovers several commonalities with Aristotle. Kant mentions courage right in part 1 of the "Introduction"; in his discussion of the duty of charity, there is an echo of largesse and generosity; in the "social virtues," urbanity and friendliness. In the first part of his systematic moral philosophy, the "Doctrine of Right," there is a treatise on the objective demand for justice that, when freely acknowledged by a virtuous person, can become the virtue of justice.

Fourth, an ethic of maxims rejects the preconception that as a (supposed) alternative to an Aristotelian virtue ethics it leaves no room for judgment. In fact, this very capacity is required in an ethic of maxims. It occurs in three forms and plays, as a consequence, three roles (see Höffe 2001, chapter 3): first, an empirical-hermeneutical judgment seeks the appropriate, at first alternative, maxims for the various regions of action and spheres of life; for example, in emergencies the maxim of readiness to assist the injured or the opposite maxim, hard-heartedness. Second, the identified alternative maxims, those moral and immoral maxims applicable to the same region of action, are to be distinguished by means of a thought experiment of pure rational generalization (see the next section). Finally, a given situation, for example, a concrete emergency, is to be responded to in accordance with the standards of a morally perfect maxim; in the case of an emergency, the willingness to offer assistance. In doing so, one is not concerned with a mechanical subsumption or a logical derivation as is suggested by the popular notion of "application" ["Anwenden"]. Rather, there is a hermeneutical task to be performed that one can describe as reading the given situation in light of the maxim or as mediating the empirical factors with a normative factor, the maxim. Here the functional virtues of judgment are required: situational malleability, flexibility, and creativity.

A *fifth* advantage: the truly ultimate principles of the will are concerned with such general regions of action and spheres of life that occur not only in one's own culture but also at all places and at all times (such as to give one's word ["promise"], such as the reality of emergency situations demanding a response, such as the danger that one's body and soul, one's possessions, and one's good name ["reputation"] are damaged). One would have to demonstrate the claim in any specific sense, but a glance at other cultures makes it reasonable to assume that at least a significant number of regions of action have an anthropological rank. An ethic of maxims concerns itself with legitimate culture- and epoch-overlapping alternatives such as honesty or dishonesty or the willingness to assist in an emergency or indifference toward it. It is, therefore, not surprising that generalizable maxims like honesty and willingness to help are morally prized in (for all intents and purposes) all cultures. An ethic of maxims helps humanity to relativize many differences into subtle differences beneath which lie essential commonalities. In spite of cultural differences, commonalities dominate not only with respect to moral challenges but also in moral responses that allow one to speak of a general moral world heritage analogous to UNESCO's protections of cultural world heritage sites (see *Lesebuch* [Höffe 2007b]). The ethic of maxims offers an essential pillar of support for today's pressing intercultural discourse about ethics.

An ethic of maxims is important not only for the identity of a species, humanity, but also, *sixth,* for the identity of the individual. General principles that are to be properly applied to situations contextually prevent the fragmenting of the life of an individual into an inestimable variety of rules or a limitless number of specific actions. Instead, the parts of a biography are combined into a unified whole, into a life- and meaning-totality in which the test of generalization vets whether or not the parts are morally valid. As a consequence, one's moral character either as moral or immoral comes to expression in these maxims. It is not concrete rules of action but only maxims that allow qualifying someone as revengeful or magnanimous, as reckless or thoughtful, as selfish or upright, honest or courageous, in short, as moral or immoral.

The *seventh* advantage follows. An ethic of maxims is important not only for the assessment of persons but also for raising them. The inoculation with rules moves upbringing into the realm of training. Since maxims are open with respect to personal differences in temperament, abilities, and encountered situations, they allow for a free space that is indispensable for personal freedom and moral self-determination. Kant hits the nail on the head in one of his *Reflections* [*Reflectionen*]: "Character requires, first, that one generates maxims and then rules. However, rules that are not restricted by maxims are pedantic when they limit one's own self, and they are cantankerous and unsociable when they limit others. They are the crutch of the immature" (15:514–15, no. 1164).

Still a further, now *eighth*, argument speaks for an ethic of maxims: the reasons that a person offers do not have to be his true reasons. They can be only intermediate reasons behind which stand other, higher-ranking reasons that for their part can depend upon even higher-ranking reasons. In order to evaluate the moral quality of an action, then, one must each time pay attention to the ultimate reason, to the fundamental principles that justify the other more commonplace reasons.

Practical self-consciousness does not exclude what is known theoretically: because maxims are not necessarily on the surface of consciousness, one can deceive not only someone else but also oneself about them. Nevertheless, what is decisive are not explicitly or silently alleged [theoretical] reasons for one's actions but, rather, those on the basis of which one actually acts (or refrains from acting) and, in the case of the precise conditions of maxims, those that are the ultimate basis for one's actions.

Because those ultimate reasons that are most effective for acting are not always obvious, neither the agent, nor the victim of the action, nor any neutral observer can be counted on as an error-free authority for their determination. However, the danger of the self's or the other's deception as well as the danger of an erroneous attribution of the reasons for an action are significantly reduced when one abstracts the reasons from the character of a person, from his preferences, attitudes, and individual attributes; in short, from his personality. In such a case, the reasons for the action correlate not simply with those maintained or intended but with the actually practiced principles of the agent. The action has a certain determination because of these actually practiced principles: whoever "from the core of his being" is honest cannot do otherwise than not deceive; whoever is hard-hearted cannot be anything but immune to the suffering of others. Nonetheless, one cannot speak here of an absolute determination: the hard-hearted individual can be moved to do otherwise, and, in the case of repeatedly giving way to the suffering of others, he can even change his character. Just as well, someone who up to a certain point has always been responsive to suffering on the part of others can become hard-hearted.

20.4 Universalization

Because of their subjective character, maxims as such are indifferent to the opposition between moral and immoral. A further step, the third moment in the morals criterion, identifies the missing distinguishing characteristic. Once again, the clarification at a second, reflective and self-critical level becomes manifest. Whereas moralizers like La Rochefoucauld (with the motto "Our virtues are mostly only cloaked vices") are skeptical of true virtues, moral philosophers take up such unmasking criticism of morals into their own second-order critique of morals. Fully aware that there are cloaked vices but also that there are their opposite, true virtues, these moral philosophers seek a criterion that enables them to distinguish one from the other. Consequently, they are able to do what moral critics cannot; they can distinguish moral from immoral principles in the great variety of maxims. This criterion acts as an audit that maxims must undergo in order to establish themselves as moral; or it acts as a filter that permits the passage of the moral and blocks immoral maxims from flowing through. One can also compare the criterion with the chemical litmus test that dependably distinguishes an acid from an alkali.

A criterion emerges out of the concept of unconditional validity. Because this concept rejects any and all reduction of authority to personal particularities, moral principles, positively formulated, are in the strict sense above subjectivity and in this sense strictly universal, that is, not merely generally but universally valid. This third and final moment of a moral principle consists in the strict generalizability of the primary basis for one's action, in the universalization of maxims. Because the prototype for strict universality is found in law, especially natural law, one can speak here of a universal (natural) law or of a universal legislation. Those maxims that stand the test of universalization are moral; those that fail the test prove themselves to be immoral.

Even pre- and extra-moral maxims, for example, the principles to become by all means rich, famous, or powerful, are rules by which one acts in entirely different situations. They distinguish themselves by a universality, but in a normative respect they have a relative universality. The extra qualification "universal" in the criterion "universal law" maintains that a relative universality does not suffice. What is required is an escalation to the superlative, to that narrow and strict universality, universalization, whose model is given by natural law. The test examines, then, whether the subjective and relative universality of a maxim can be taken to be the strict universality of a natural law.

Strict universality can be tested at three levels. These begin on the other side of the merely momentarily and subjectively valid (level zero) and lead, from a still subjective but no longer merely momentary validity, that is, from a validity applicable to the entire life of an individual (level one), through an intersubjective, social totality (level two), to an absolute validity (level three). Only then does an initial, merely subjective maxim establish itself as an objective law that is of service for the determination of the will of any rational being capable of practical reflection.

Appropriate to the first level, the individual considers whether or not his momentarily valid reason is suited to be a principle on the basis of which he can act not merely now and then but which he can follow within the framework of an entire life: is the ground for his action suitable as a life principle, a maxim? Secondly, one tests whether or not the personally subjective maxim is adequate as a maxim for many, and especially whether it can serve as a principle for their social lives. For example, is it possible not only for the "perpetrator" of a dishonest promise but also for his victim to acknowledge "a right to dishonesty"? On the third level, one asks whether or not what has now been established as a socially competent life principle is valid for everyone in any culture and epoch, even for members of another biological species; in other words, for every conceivable "extraterrestrial" being, who likewise possesses the ability of practical reflection.

According to an all too frequent misunderstanding, universalization is understood to require the abandoning of every sense of individual personality. Such a demand looks like a plea for Zen Buddhism, which, according to the claim of some of its masters, challenges humanity to overcome all of its desires; ultimately, one should abandon one's "I." Doubtless, the life that leads to this goal, the "holy, eightfold path," contains moral grounds such as right speaking and right acting; in other words, it embodies a moral option. Nonetheless, it remains to be clarified whether someone who arrives at integrity by means of the eightfold path in fact forsakes his "I." In any event, the test of universalization does not require him to do so. It demands merely that one develop one's personality exclusively within the framework of universalizable, hence moral, maxims.

Even so, the fear that a strict universalization demands that one give up all particularities of tradition and history is laid to rest. The moral criterion demands no such "cultural revolution" that is contemptuous of tradition. However, it does offer a criterion in order to distinguish morally incompatible from morally compatible traditions.

20.5 Consequentialist or Discourse Ethics as Alternatives?

There are two popular alternatives to the ethics of the will: consequentialism and discourse ethics. Consequentialist ethics is represented in a form similar to Kant's ethics. Drawing on Kant's categorical imperative, moral philosophers like Marcus Singer 1961 and Richard M. Hare 1963 see the moral criterion in the universalization of actions: "One should undertake no action whose universal accomplishment has bad consequences." This principle only at first glance appears to be similar to Kant's criterion and the moral principle of universalization developed here. A more precise examination discovers two differences. Singer and Hare allow for the privileging of a consequence-oriented universalization; they defend, then, a consequentialist (or teleological ethic) that rejects the pure rational universalization proposed here. In addition, they refer neither to the will nor to maxims but rather to everyday actions.

Above all, the first distinction usually counts as an advantage because one likes to reproach duty ethics for its indifference to the consequences of actions and, therefore, its indifference to the well-being of concrete persons. The duty ethic defended here can neutralize this reproach with two complementary arguments. First, it allows for reflection about consequences, but only in a specific action-internal respect. Reflections concerning consequences are not only permitted but even absolutely necessary for the questions of for whom and what the demanded aid promises to accomplish. They are not permitted, in contrast, for the ultimate why, for the decisive motivating force. They are entirely excluded with respect to action-external reflections of the kind: "What do I gain by offering assistance?" Whoever only helps where there is a hint of a good reputation or financial benefit is motivated by hope for honor or payment. Ultimately, he doesn't act out of a willingness to help but for personal gain, perhaps even out of an addiction to praise or out of avarice. Duty ethics is therefore oriented toward consequences, but only in relationship to action-internal, not action-external, consequences.

Moral consciousness agrees. It does not call someone helpful who eases the distress of another only when it is advantageous for the agent, but only when the reward is already in the assisting itself. In this respect, the difference between morally correct and morally good becomes manifest (see chapter 22.3): whoever helps someone in need, no matter for what reason, acts morally correctly. Whoever helps without any other interest, therefore, whoever helps *with* sympathy but not *out* of sympathy, is morally good.

Now, one could consider reflections over action-internal consequences to be trivial because such reflections arise out of the concept of goal-oriented action itself. Duty ethics responds with its second argument: its reflection over consequences occurs within the framework of a maxim that is not concerned with an arbitrary goal but, rather, with precisely the goal erroneously taken to be the ostensible disregard for the well-being of concrete individuals. With the aid of the test of universalizability, duty ethics reveals that a maxim that is indifferent to indigence is not universalizable, and hence is immoral. At the same time, it demonstrates the alternative to indifference, the readiness to help, to be moral. The authoritative philosopher of duty ethics, Kant, declares the maxim of active well-being, the practical love of humanity, to be a duty of all persons to one another in his systematic moral philosophy, the "Doctrine of Virtue," in paragraphs 26–27. Already in the "Introduction" (parts 4 and 5.B), the ultimate goal of well-being consists in the happiness of other persons, and it is a goal that is simultaneously a duty.

There is a further argument that contradicts the usual contrast between consequentialist and duty ethics: the most influential form of consequentialism, utilitarianism, contains *à contre coeur* a moment of duty. This doesn't occur somewhere at a subordinate point but, rather, at a philosophically, morally decisive point, in the utilitarian principle itself. It maintains its claim to seek the well-being of all concerned to be correct or even good in itself or, in other words, to be absolutely binding. Thereby, this is declared a moral duty, a *deon*, that is comprehensive and at the same time fundamentally binding and both of these independently of considerations of consequences. Utilitarian duty is not only

valid when the agent views himself as accidentally in charitable high
spirits and experiences love, friendship, or compassion for all involved
in a situation in which he, in addition, has an abundance of time and
money. On the contrary, duty is taken to be independent of such motives
and circumstances and, consequently, to be unconditionally binding as
a categorical imperative. Silently, one even assumes that utilitarian duty
is, first, valid for one's entire life; second, that it is valid for society in
general; and third, that it is also valid for nonhuman, likewise morally capable beings. One maintains this duty to be in the strictest sense
universalizable.

The consequence is that teleological and deontological ethics don't
have to exclude one another. The question of whether or not the highest
moral principle occurs in the singular (utilitarianism) or in the plural
(the usual duty ethic) is here of secondary significance. More important
is that ethics is more meaningfully, even necessarily, deontological in
its foundation; and, in contrast, ethics is teleological with respect to
the "application" of principles to certain regions of life and concrete
situations. In doing so, a primarily deontological ethics allows only for
action-internal reflection, whereas a far-reaching teleological ethic also
allows for action-external reflection over consequences—although at the
price that it satisfies only morally correct and not morally good action.

The other alternative to the ethic of the will as developed here, discourse or consensus ethics, is popular above all in the German-speaking
world. Outside of professional moral philosophy circles, that is, among
social scientists and jurisprudence scholars, as well as in the educated
public, this alternative has achieved the status of the primary or standard theory that disputes those "incorrigible utilitarians." According to
discourse ethics, morals cannot be established without the requirement
of a possible interpersonal justification. An action is moral that maintains others could find it to be correct and could approve of it as good.

If one looks more closely at discourse ethics, two different forms,
viewed as ideal types, catch one's eye. Either a historical-factual discussion and cooperative reflection in the sense of real communication counts
as the highest normative criterion, or one sees this highest normative
criterion in a discourse that occurs under special conditions in the form
of ideal or idealized discourse. Philosophically serious moral theories belong entirely to the second group. Because such serious moral theories
are indebted to an explicit or silent critique of the theory of concrete discourse, we begin with it. To be sure, one thing is common to both theory

groups. Neither considers "discourse" in the sense of mere debate but rather as the debate over grounds or reasons, here over moral principles.

In opposition to concrete discourse as the highest criterion, experience confirms that not every conversation and cooperative reflection leads to a common understanding, a consensus. Even in the circumstance when the will is present to solve discursively a conflict over norms, the represented principles can be so radically different and those differences so deeply rooted that an agreement is factually impossible. Furthermore, the demand to act often creates such a pressure to decide that there is no time for a long discussion that might lead to universal agreement about common principles.

In addition, the agreement applies, initially, only to those involved. Even where everyone is invited to participate in the discussion, as with some African tribes or in Swiss canton decision-making, not everyone affected by the decision is included. As long as there are the mentally ill, invalids, and above all babies and small children, there will be groups who are incapable of directly expressing their own interests and beliefs.

The criticism extends further: concrete discourse is of no value for a highest moral principle even when, first, it achieves a consensus that, second, is achieved at the right time, and, third, all affected are involved in the process. For with respect to the amount of information available, the ability to process that information, and the intellectual capacity for study, or with respect to the capacity for concentration and perseverance as well as argumentational-rhetorical capacity, there is too great a difference among those involved for the actual agreement to be able to count in the minimal sense as rational, or for all involved to be taken equally into consideration in the achieved result. The best argument is not always victorious in a discursive deliberation.

In addition, concrete discourse is threatened not only by superficial distortions, by self-deception concerning one's own interests, by errors in grasping the situation, precipitous judgment, and emotional barriers but also by deep distortions, structural prejudices, ideological biases, or psychic illness. One might argue that even action in accordance with moral maxims is subject to these same dangers. However, discourse is supposed to serve the function of moral criterion here; it primarily wants to replace not maxims but the universalization test, but this test as a pure rational process is suspended in principle by these named dangers.

Finally, concrete discourse can be shaped by conscious deception, by lying and fraud, and by violence or the threat of it; that is, it can be shaped by elements that obviously contradict the task of establishing a moral basis for action.

Because of these and other difficulties, more careful discourse ethicists proceed not only on the basis of concrete but of ideal discourse. Not every naturally accomplished agreement counts, but only those that are arrived at under ideal conditions. These ideal conditions, admittedly, are determined differently. According to John Rawls's contract theory, the agreement is sought behind a veil of ignorance with respect to personal and socially marginal conditions. Jürgen Habermas proceeds on the basis of an ideal speech situation, dominance-free communication with a symmetry of multiple opportunities. Karl-Otto Apel's communicative ethic with its aporia of an unlimited communicative social context declares as the basis for ethical norms the recognition of all claims that others can raise—to the extent that these claims can be argumentatively justified. Finally, the constructive ethic of the "Erlangen school" declares that all affected by the outcome are to be considered participants in any deliberation, and they are to be guided by a communicative interest, that is, an interest in the resolution of conflicts.

The preconditions or the structural characteristics of discourse are to comply with these kinds of conditions. From the perspective of theoretical legitimation, they play the role of fundamental normative principles that must be fulfilled in advance in order for the discourse to serve as a moral criterion. The preconditions distinguish from the multitude of possible discourses the "true" from the "false" and declare only the true discourses, those that fulfill the established preconditions, to be the moral criterion. A critique, then, does not need to examine the specific individual preconditions because, independent of those preconditions, the theories are caught in a circle: for the self-designated task, the determination of a moral criterion, which is supposed to evaluate all fundamental principles with respect to their moral validity or invalidity, the theories presuppose in advance the validity of a portion of the principles that are supposed to be evaluated. Moral elements, for which above all a standard of measurement is sought, are already in play in the definition; specifically, the very standard of measurement to be employed as the precondition and structural characteristic to govern the moral adjudication is already assumed.

Even more: the theories do not depend only upon a circle. The defining elements of ideal discourse present, as well, those basic *fundamental* principles that constitute the objective, first objects of a philosophically moral justification. Explicitly or implicitly they maintain, namely, that the conversation partners' body and soul are inviolable; that one seeks agreement consciously and freely (i.e., without external coercion); that one in the process does not engage in lying or deception; and so on. The first task, then, does not consist in establishing a discourse under ideal conditions but in establishing a measurement for the determination of the preconditions for such a discourse.

Because discourse is valid as a moral criterion only under specific conditions, but those conditions no longer constitute the object but rather the presupposition of the discourse (its prejudices), moral justification must begin at a more radical level than discourse itself. It must begin with a conceptual analysis of morals, an analysis of the absolutely highest good, and on its basis obtain a standard of measurement for all morals. Then by means of this standard, it must determine the principles that work for an ideal discourse. Because protection of body and soul in contrast to violence, or honesty in contrast to lying and deception constitute generalizable principles, they rightly enter into the ideal discourse as pre-decisions or pre-judgments. Certainly, ideal discourse itself is no longer the highest moral principle. Rather, its ideal measurement, universalizability of the maxim, is the highest moral principle.

This alternative principle to discourse does not consist in a process of agreement among historical agents and victims in the sense of a process under either concrete or ideal conditions. Rather, it demands the engagement of a thought experiment in which the conditions of an ideal discourse in the first instance are legitimized: the highest criterion does not consist in either concrete or ideal discourse, but in a thought experiment capable of implementation by everyone. This is not some kind of marginal capacity, either. It is the very capacity that establishes the individual as a moral subject who, in spite of his intersubjective connectedness, is essentially himself and even alone responsible. The moral philosopher is obliged to provide a scholarly presentation of the criterion of universalization, but not the moral subject himself. The latter must, however, be capable of performing the basic task of following maxims that could be taken to be valid by everyone in the same particular life circumstance.

Because of their validity for everyone, maxims permit of intersubjective justification. What is the determining factor? It consists in a threefold nature. (1) In terms of a theoretical legitimation, priority is given to universalizability; it includes interpersonal justification as a (logical) consequence. (2) An ethic of universalizable maxims places weight on two levels: on the escalation from what is morally right to what is morally good (see chapter 22.3). (3) Universalizability of principles of the will, maxims, allows what discourse ethics as a rule rejects: duties of the individual to himself. (For a critique of discourse theories, see Höffe 1985, chapter 9; Höffe 1995b, chapters 12–13; and Höffe 2000a, chapters 8–9.)

21 The Universalizability Test: Two Examples

The universalizability test can be illuminated by two related examples that have been frequently discussed since Kant: a false promise, that is, a dishonestly made promise, and lying about a security deposit.

First, a preliminary remark: Kant distinguishes two levels of the universalizability test: not being able to think something as universalizable and not being able to be universalized. In both cases, the universalizability test is carried out on the basis of its opposite (*e contrario*) and, simultaneously, it is carried out purely rationally without concern for consequences and experience. Within the context of duties owed to others, the more strict test of not being able to think something as universalizable corresponds to the moral interest whose recognition human beings owe one another. This is the legal morality or justice that forbids, for example, murder, stealing, and fraud because they cannot be thought of as universal laws of nature without involving a contradiction. Moral philosophy also speaks of perfect duties and means two things by them: with respect to the kind of obligation (*modality*) it means being owed, and with respect to the *scope* it means a validity without exception. Consequently, duties occur as prohibitions: with the exception of extraordinary circumstances like self-defense, acts like murder, stealing, and fraud are not merely usually but always forbidden.

On the other, more modest level of not being able to want something to be universalizable, one finds moral virtue with its meritorious performance of more than is required. It demands, for example, a willingness to assist others and charity. One can imagine a natural condition in which finite rational beings, hence, beings also in need of assistance, never aid one another in emergencies. Given the knowledge that one could find oneself in such an emergency, no rational being could want that kind of natural condition. The consequent duties are called imperfect, once more, in both respects: with respect to *modality*, these duties do not belong to those morals one owes but to the meritorious more; and with respect to *scope*, they occur as commands that oblige humanity to an attitude of assistance to others without demanding that in every specific instance of need, one must alleviate the suffering.

The question of whether or not this distinction between perfect and imperfect duties, between legal duties and meritorious performance, is meaningful can be left undecided here. Both examples that are now to be discussed fall under the more strict criterion, that of not being able to think something as universalizable.

21.1 Promising

As often as Kant maintains that a false promise is not universalizable, he is just as sparing in his justification for the claim. In the *Groundwork of the Metaphysics of Morals*, the proof is only hinted at in a half-sentence: "because no one would believe what was promised him but would only laugh at all such expressions as vain pretenses" (4:422; "vain pretenses" means essentially "futile deception"). Because Kant doesn't develop the argument in detail, he contributed to the generation of much misunderstanding (for a more detailed discussion, see Höffe 2000b).

Should a false promise be incapable of being thought of as universalizable, it would have to contradict itself if made into a universal law (of nature). The contradiction in the universalizability, in our case, is found in the false promise itself, in the combination of "promise" with "false" (in the sense of "dishonest") and not first in auxiliary action-external consequences. Where does the contradiction lie? Whoever makes a promise involves himself in a personal obligation. In the case of a false promise, he makes a commitment with the intention of not holding to the obligation. As a consequence, he maintains a self-obligation that is simultaneously not a self-obligation.

In *Groundwork of the Metaphysics of Morals*, Kant examines the subset of false promises in which one is not somehow dishonest with oneself but lies to another; one is concerned here with the violation of a duty to someone else. A lie is made in a financial emergency with the goal of avoiding the financial catastrophe by means of the wealth of another. The situation is one of asset misappropriation by means of deception and with the intention of self-enrichment; in other words, with a simultaneous wrongful enrichment as well as claims fraud. (In the case where the asset injury is slight and the need exceptionally large, one might have a case of petty fraud [*Notbetrug*].) Kant doesn't just discuss whether or not there is a moral *right* to lie with his example of false promising. Should a false promise be able to be thought of as universalizable without involving contradiction, it would be morally acceptable, which would amount to a moral right that surely would be difficult to defend, that is, a right to dishonesty. Kant also questions concurrently whether or not one is permitted to overcome one's destitution by any means necessary, including fraud.

The confirmation that not all means are morally acceptable presupposes an argument (a prior semantic move) that designates trustworthiness as an element in the definition of promising. In doing so, empirical elements can appear without impairing the properly pure rational character of the universalizability test. On the contrary, the characteristic interplay (eventually) emerges of both experience-dependent conditions of application and experience-independent morality: That an individual can give his word (that is, can promise something) and that he is capable of being honest or dishonest involves a host of presuppositions that one knows for the most part from experience. The same is true for the benefit that promising is a social institution which offers all sides concerned interpersonal advantages by means of the coordination of one's own action with that of others. However, given the alternative between an "honest or dishonest" promise, the fact that the second option is immoral is capable of being determined, ultimately, entirely independent of experience, that is, purely rationally. Experience independence applies *primarily* to the grounds of the commitment involved in honesty; it applies *secondarily* to pre-philosophical moral consciousness in the form of the natural awareness of duty; and as a consequence, thirdly, it offers philosophical ethics a subsequent certainty when it comes to the test of universalizability.

The *prior semantic move* takes into consideration the circumstance that two defensible justification strategies are conceivable. The one already mentioned (that of an empirical-pragmatic universalization from Singer and Hare) shares with the other (the strictly rational justification) the insight that credibility belongs to a promise. The differences between the two justifications commence with the determination of the kind of identification between credibility and promising. According to a purely rational universalization, credibility belongs to "the concept of the action in itself" (*Groundwork of the Metaphysics of Morals*, 4:402) with which the destitute person seeks to solve his financial difficulties; in other words, credibility is an element of the very definition of "promising." According to its empirical-pragmatic opponent, credibility plays a role only when the additional question surfaces: why should one get mixed up with the institution of promising? The difference here between the purely rational and the empirically pragmatic strategy is: according to the first strategy, the abrogation of the promise is a consequence of false promising internal to the action; in the second strategy, the abrogation is a consequence external to the action.

Even more important is a further difference: with an empirical-pragmatic legitimation of a promise, one is concerned with credibility without qualification [*tout court*], whereas a purely rational legitimation is concerned merely with its subjective or personal aspect, honesty. In any event, the controversy doesn't just begin with the kind of universalization—empirical-pragmatic or purely rational—but already with the very concept of a promise.

Whoever seeks to alleviate his financial distress by means of a promise does not want, purely conceptually considered, a gift but a loan. Included in the notion of a loan is the readiness, purely conceptually considered, to pay back the loan at a later point. A loan is a commercial transaction based upon interaction, an exchange (hence, a reciprocal give-and-take) that can transpire only if the creditor and debtor each objectively in his own way are either solvent or stand ready to pay.

Of course, there are different ways to loan money. According to an alternative manner, now involving a "specific" conceptual element, a loan can occur on the basis of a promise or on collateral. In the latter, special case of exchange, the transaction involves a time lag, but not exclusively. Even in the case of a non-collateral loan, there is a simultaneity to the exchange, but it occurs on a different level. In the case of a non-collateral loan, based exclusively on a promise, no material security is involved; rather, one's collateral is one's word. The exchange should occur exclusively on the financial level of the exchange itself. The assumption of the loan involves the readiness that is formally declared in the promise: the readiness to repay the debt.

In the characteristic situation in which only one side gives and the other takes, the mere pronouncement ("I promise that p") has as its aim a twofold credibility. The first, "propositional credibility" (". . . that p"), extends to the content of the promise and indicates a double creditworthiness: objectively, according to the expected ability to repay, and subjectively, according to the date of repayment of the anticipated readiness to pay. Credibility is not decided, however, exclusively on the basis of creditworthiness but, also, on a second credibility, the "speech-pragmatic credibility" that the pronouncement "I promise that . . ." is meant honestly, that is, that it actually stands for the prior intention to comply with the promise.

Of the two sides to credibility, propositional creditworthiness and speech-pragmatic honesty, rational universalization is limited by the second side in a manner imperceptible to the empirical-pragmatic perspective. In order to be able to coordinate one's action with another on the basis of a promise, both forms of credibility are necessary, whereas with the empirical-pragmatic strategy, the precise ground for the loss of credibility is irrelevant. The question of whether or not persons generally underestimate future difficulties as a consequence of an intellectual deficiency with respect to calculating prospective resources and, nevertheless and in spite of the best of intentions, renege on many promises is for this legitimation strategy just as important as the other question: whether or not there is already a lack of good intention, precisely honesty. Of course, one could take the speech-pragmatic credibility of the debtor to be objectively foundational to a higher degree and give it preference over the empirical-pragmatic. Where a promise is not meant honestly, repayment doesn't occur despite creditworthiness. In many situations, however (with children, for example), the other side, creditworthiness, is more important.

In the strict sense, morality depends not only on the priority of, but exclusively on, honesty. This is because morality is concerned with actions for which human beings can be responsible. Honesty is not a future event—future events are only partially in our power—but honesty is something today that co-decides tomorrow: that "something" is our present intention. Precisely this side is what is emphasized by a promise when one leaves out propositional credibility and focuses exclusively on speech-pragmatic credibility. Whoever investigates neither whether or not the promise is capable of fulfillment nor whether the promise comes from a trustworthy or "forgetful" person, whoever merely asks whether the promise is honestly or dishonestly given, thematizes what is decisive, even exclusively relevant, for an ethics of the will with respect to the concept of a promise.

After honesty is determined to be the morally relevant element, one can turn to the *primary, rational moment* and, finally, reconstruct the contradiction. The motive for dishonesty is obvious: with the knowledge that one is incapable of repaying, the needy individual, nevertheless, wants to receive the money. A *first* reconstruction attempt that is still without the criterion of universalizability speaks against such dishonesty: This kind of exchange turns the loan into a gift although the money lender, according to the definition of lending rather than giving, is not willing to make a gift. The "conversion" of the loan into a gift occurs against his will and defrauds him of his assets; the dishonest promise turns into a theft. According to this reconstruction, false promising appears as a violation of duty. The argument, however, occurs without the concept of honesty; as a consequence, it doesn't touch the core of morality.

A *second* reconstruction attempt recognizes full well that, in the world in which we live, both options, not only honest but also dishonest promises, are real possibilities and both occur. Because the creditor cannot look "into the heart" of the debtor to determine his actual intention, there is always an uncertainty in any specific situation as to which of the two possibilities will occur. Whoever as a consequence balks at the risk rejects the acceptance of a mere word and never loans his money without collateral. Whoever, on the contrary, is open to risk takes his earnings in appropriate interest, otherwise places his hopes in honesty, and offers a loan without collateral. In the real world in any event, promises are not universally unreliable; trust in someone's mere word is a rational and by no means contradictory option.

Things are different when for promising—now with a universalizable test—a natural law of dishonesty obtains. In this hypothetically imagined world, no one who makes a promise takes seriously in any sense what he promises. What is promised in terms of the internal concept of speech-pragmatic credibility is neutralized by the law of dishonesty, and, to be sure, not just occasionally but in principle. Precisely here is where the contradiction surfaces with the attempt at universalization: the conceptually internal goal of pragmatic credibility is made impossible in principle by the establishment of a law of dishonesty, which amounts to a speech-pragmatic impossibility or, what is the same thing, a speech-pragmatic contradiction. In Kant's trenchant formulation: "It cannot hold with the universality of a law of nature that statements should be allowed as proof and yet be intentionally untrue" (*Critique of Practical Reason*, 5:44).

In the sense of a subset that occurs under the law, a petitioner cannot achieve his specific goal of escaping financial need by means of a promise. In a world governed by the law of dishonesty, the creditor *knows* that the pronouncement "I promise that . . ." has no meaning. The hope that one is dealing with an "honest prankster" is crushed, so that in fact one has the case of which Kant spoke in the *Groundwork of the Metaphysics of Morals:* "No one would believe what was promised to him but would only laugh at all such expressions as vain pretenses," namely, futile simulation (4:422). In a natural order where what occurs, in this case a speech act of promising, is combined with dishonesty, trust in a promise is not a rational option even for the risk-taking creditor. For this reason alone and not because of any additional empirical-pragmatic reflections, the general goal of finding a financial backer would be impossible. A fortiori, the specific goal of escaping financial need evaporates.

The question of whether or not the impossibility of a loan without collateral destroys important opportunities for an advantageous cooperation for all concerned and, thereby, harms general well-being is decided by an act-external, and therefore, relative to the concept of promise, empirical-pragmatic, specifically social-pragmatic (utilitarian) reflection. Strict abstract generalization, however, has no need of such reflection because it has achieved its proof already: promising is already banished as an injury to duty in such a hypothetical world.

A precise examination of the situation makes clear that an empirical-pragmatic reflection over the question of the moral acceptability of a false promise is not only unnecessary, but also leads to no contradiction. A world in which one cannot trust any promise because of disappointed expectations makes us all perhaps extremely uncomfortable; however, it is not logically impossible. It is not inconceivable even when one assumes the extreme case in which persons cease to communicate with one another because they frequently experience dishonesty; but such an extreme circumstance of noncommunication couldn't even exist if a world with disappointed expectations ultimately were to lead to a world without human beings, which would be absurd. A society that doesn't recognize the institution of promising is only absurd; whoever makes a false promise, in contrast, is immoral.

One could also formulate the contradiction as an anti-freeloader argument: the dishonest promiser expects others to be honest, which he himself is not ready to be. The petitioner, namely, can escape his distress only when his creditor treats him honestly, and he obtains neither a commitment from the creditor that is not serious nor a commitment that involves an exchange of counterfeit, hence worthless, money.

Were the absence of the other, propositional side of credibility generalized to a law, one would have, it appears, the same consequence: a loan without collateral ceases to be a rational option. In fact, the hope of repayment is fruitless in a hypothetical world in which the creditor knows that a promise is meant honestly but because of bankruptcy or forgetfulness never will be repaid. In this case the corresponding expectation is missing, but not because a maxim raised to a universal law is contradictory.

Now that we're at the end of these reconstruction options, we can examine the scope of *e contrario*–legitimated duty: the justified duty in our example is not limited to this special case, the case of honesty in money lending; it extends to honesty in general. Furthermore, the command to honesty is valid for all beings who are capable of giving their word and, as a consequence, are subject to the alternative to be "honest or dishonest." In agreement with our moral intuitions, Kant says that "the command 'thou shalt not lie' does not hold only for human beings, as if other rational beings did not have to heed it" (*Groundwork of the Metaphysic of Morals*, 4:389).

There are two opponents to an ethics of the will in the discussion of the permissibility of false promises. With the primary opponent, one quarrels at the level of the object, morality; with the "secondary" opponent, one argues at the meta-level, the theory of morality. Contrary to our primary opponent who claims exceptions out of self-interest, it will be shown that the exception, dishonesty in a circumstance of distress, is morally unacceptable because dishonesty does not allow itself to be taken to be a natural law. With the secondary opponent who defends an empirical-pragmatic generalization, one can agree with respect to the concept of promising: "to promise" means that "one's word is one's bond." One also agrees that the general goal of promising depends upon credibility and that dishonesty is its contrary. Where one disagrees is about the kind of knowledge by means of which one determines the contradiction. According to the rule-utilitarian question ("What does it mean for the general welfare when someone acts in this manner?"), there is an empirical, and moreover a (social-)pragmatic, knowledge; however, according to strict universalizability, one is concerned with a pre-empirical knowledge.

Whoever wants to know how he can obtain by fraud an unearned trust from a money lender needs "acumen" and "experience in the ways of the world." Furthermore, he needs experience in order to know whether or not he can extricate himself from a situation of distress with money or by some other means. In contrast, one doesn't need experience in order to know that a false promise contains two concept-internal but incompatible goals. For that reason, someone who wants to expose a false promise as illegitimate *can* take the path of empirical-pragmatic reflection. This detour, however, is superfluous; even more, it misses the essential point that the maxim of a false promise, taken as natural law, is *in itself* a contradiction. As a consequence, the ethical conflict over fundamentals between an empirical-pragmatic, especially (rule-)utilitarian ethic and a strictly rational ethic ends to the advantage of the rational ethic.

21.2 Security Deposit

The second example for the test of universalization has been known in philosophy since Plato (*Republic* 333b-d). Even Kant uses it (*Critique of Practical Reason*, section 4, note). However, it is in a certain respect criticized by Hegel (e.g., *Phenomenology*, "Reason as Lawgiver") in a manner that empowered generations of Hegelians to repudiate Kant's moral philosophy. Once again, we must examine generalization *e contrario*. One shows that a maxim which contradicts morality—in the case of a security deposit, the maxim of a greediness that seeks by all certain means to gain riches—is not capable of universalization.

We begin with the *preliminary semantic step:* since Roman law, a security deposit consists of a movable object turned over to someone for safekeeping. The legal act of transfer is called a *pactum depositi*, or custodial contract. It is distinguished from the object itself that has been turned over for custodial care. Because a custodial condition is unusual without a supporting document (a testament), one can imagine as an alternative the embezzlement of an unfavorable testament.

Next to be observed is that Kant doesn't discuss just any embezzlement of a security deposit, but solely that case in which greed is combined with cleverness. In the case where the "owner," as Kant calls him, "has died and there is no will," a "secure means" is provided for illegitimate personal enrichment. Only the special case is examined where there is no written testament and one is concerned merely with good faith. Hence, given the letter of deposit similar to a false promise in combination with a case of death, there is no possibility of the custodial giver himself reclaiming the security deposit.

Hegel correctly sees the security deposit as a case of ownership, but he accuses Kant of two faults. On the one hand, he proposes that Kant's thought experiment of generalization results only in a tautological conclusion: "If there is ownership, ownership must exist." On the other hand, Kant does not undertake the decisive task, "to *argue* that ownership must be"; instead, he presupposes this legal institution as already given. In opposition to this second argument, it is to be observed that Kant's argument does not presuppose the security deposit as actually already given, even if it should be found for all intents and purposes in all developed cultures. For his reasoning, the thought process is enough. As a matter of fact, it is sufficient that some means is conceivable that fulfills the condition of a "certain means in order to increase my wealth" that, in turn, can be contrary to morality. All that is presupposed is that there are morally compatible and incompatible means for the generation of wealth. Apart from that, Kant certainly provides a justification for ownership; however, he does so at a different point—in the "Doctrine of Right" [part 1 of *The Metaphysics of Morals*], whose "Private Right" constitutes to this day one of the most thoroughly reflective theories of ownership.

Kant rebuts in passing Hegel's first objection, as well. The test of universalizability does not amount to the banal pronouncement: "If there is ownership, ownership must exist." It shows rather that certain forms of wealth accumulation are immoral. Apart from that, the non-universalizability of a riskless fraud is only an intermediate argument. Ultimately, Kant attacks the belief that desire for happiness functions as a general practical law, and he rebuts this belief by means of the example of the passion of greediness.

In a remarkable text saturated with experience, the *Anthropology from a Pragmatic Point of View*, paragraphs 80–88, Kant undertakes a general critique of passions. He defines passions as inclinations that render inoperative one's sovereignty over oneself not merely temporarily but over an extended period of time, whereby they hinder reason from distinguishing among them and from comparing them. With passions ("a damaging cancer for pure practical reason"), an extreme "foolishness" becomes manifest in that one makes part of an appropriate goal the goal itself and in the process blocks other inclinations, with the consequence that together they squander all that matters for pre-moral humanity: happiness. Happiness is achieved, namely, not by the satisfaction of one imperialistic inclination but only by taking into consideration different (therefore, each for itself as limited) inclinations.

In the case of a disavowed security deposit, Kant criticizes greed as foolishness, but not pragmatically. To the contrary, he attacks a well-thought-out, and therefore hardly foolish, but thoroughly clever action: the denial of a non-traceable security deposit. Furthermore, he doesn't reject greed as a whole because he considers it to be an "entirely mindless" but still "not always morally reprehensible" passion. Greed is criticized only to the extent that it uses an immoral means, a (well-calculated) fraud, more precisely a concealment that harms another person and enriches oneself.

The *rational primary step* now shows that the denial of a non-traceable security deposit fails to satisfy the universalization test because, were it to be turned into a law, it "would annihilate itself." Self-annihilation corresponds to the stricter criterion of universalization, that of not being able to think something as universalizable. Because in the *Critique of Practical Reason* one also finds that, in the case of the universalization of fraud, there would be "no security deposits at all," one could maintain the argument to be oriented by consequences and social pragmatics: the consignment of a security deposit involves a socially binding rule of action, an institution, that is defined by means of advantages as well as commitments. Simultaneously, it creates expectations and enables an agreement between one's own action and that of another; as a consequence, it establishes a rule-governed coexistence, or, at the least, it makes such an existence easier. Denial of a security deposit undermines the credibility of this institution, and were everyone to conduct himself in such a fashion, no one would make security deposits. According to this interpretation, the institution of security deposits is destroyed by the universalization, and, with its destruction, also the possibility of a rational social life.

This consideration of consequences is correct, but it addresses neither Kant nor the actual problem. Examined in a consequentialist manner, it is, once again, indifferent from where the general depletion of trust comes: whether from an absent honesty or as a result that one occasionally as a consequence of an unanticipated difficulty is incapable of returning the security deposit despite one's best intentions. Whereas the second reason is harmless, Kant is only interested in the moral point of view, in the underlying determination of the will.

In opposition to the right to deny a security deposit is the fact that there would then "be no deposit," which is to be understood as a "self-annihilating" consequence. Whoever turns over an object for safekeeping is not making a gift but, rather, maintains his ownership: he only temporarily turns it over to another. For the recipient (the fiduciary), the object is not his own. In the case, then, where one denies a security deposit, one eliminates that moment in the transaction that is definitive. The foreign or alien object is destroyed in its essence; with the consequence that, as one confirms with the attempt at universalizability, the status of denial of the security deposit annihilates its very condition.

For an ethics of the will, what is genuinely moral manifests itself not in action but in the determination of the grounds for action. In this respect, the case of a security deposit is not concerned with whether or not one actually returns it; the consigned object could be destroyed by fire or could be lost by theft. What is decisive, rather, is the eventual denial, the fraud, and as their willful background, greed.

With the empirical-pragmatic interpretation, the self-annihilation doesn't occur. A world in which one no longer deposits items with others because of disappointed expectations and in which one, rather, hides all valuables under a mattress or buries them in one's garden may be disagreeable, but it is not inconceivable. One encounters the logical contradiction (that is, what is not able to be thought of as universalizable) and not, as Korsgaard (1996, 92) assumes, the practical contradiction, only when one puts aside the question of unfavorable or favorable consequences, and thus when one focuses solely on the maxim to increase one's wealth at all costs. With this maxim, fraud, theft, even predation, in other words, open violations of duty, are permitted as means to one's enrichment. All that is presupposed is that in the specific case the violation of duty proves to be a certain means to the end of enrichment, that is, the danger of being caught and punished is eliminated.

Why is this maxim that serves one's own happiness not universalizable? The maxim permits that others' property loses its decisive defining element, its otherness, and thus annihilates itself as others' property. Because safekeeping of someone else's possession includes, purely conceptually, the enduring ownership by the other, any attempt to deny the safekeeping combines two opposed actions that in the case of an attempted universalizability is contradictory: on the one hand, one acknowledges that the object is not one's own, since it is to be kept in safekeeping for another and was not received as a gift. On the other hand, in the event of a denial of the security deposit, one treats the object not as belonging to someone else but as one's own. Someone who accepts a security deposit with the intention of keeping it for himself makes a false, fraudulent promise. This fraudulent promise is based on the "in itself contradictory" maxim that one gives one's word ("I will hold the other's object in trust") and that one doesn't give one's word ("I won't hold the other's object in trust, but I will take it into *my* own possession"). The thought experiment of universalization illuminates this contradiction; one can imagine a single fraud; they occur often enough. One cannot think of a law in which the giving of one's word simultaneously means that one withholds one's word.

Within the framework of the general theme of the false promise, the example of the security deposit illuminates a particular case of a breach of contract that can occur only after the contract is closed. The recipient of the security deposit can take it in all honesty, namely, with the intention to return it, and only later become a thief with the occurrence of the advantageous circumstance that the owner dies without a will. The example of a security deposit also engages the question of whether or not in the case of a security deposit a theft is morally permissible. The presumed moral permission lies in the "in itself contradictory" maxim that one can acknowledge something as someone else's and simultaneously deny it is someone else's.

22 Reality

22.1 Two Thought Experiments

A thorough moral philosophy is not satisfied merely with a moral criterion and its exemplary application. The more demanding the morals advocated, the more pressing is the question of whether or not what is morally demanded is possible as well as realizable in fact. A philosophy based upon the autonomy of a free will is the most demanding. Therefore, it must answer the question of whether or not what it expects, that is, to live according to universalizable maxims, can actually be accomplished. Only after the various forms of doubt have been satisfied—doubts that arise from everyday experience, the specific sciences, and even on the basis of philosophical principles—will it be possible for a philosophy of autonomy to overcome the charge that it is perhaps astute but nonetheless a product of the ivory tower that is out of touch with the basic human condition.

According to a venerable principle of law that is shared by the Western world with other cultures (e.g., *Koran*, sura 7, verse 42), no one can be expected to do more than he is capable of doing (*ultra posse, nemo obligator*). Should the expectations of autonomous morals fundamentally overtax someone, he is exculpated from the obligation. However, he is not entirely free of the obligation. As a practical, rational being, he is challenged to pursue the possibilities of practical reason to the end and that means to the level of morals. The individual can find himself, nonetheless, in an inhuman, even tragic situation. He can be subject to two competing demands: on the one hand, that of a morally universalizable maxim; on the other, that of a human nature which recognizes the relevant demand but is incapable of fulfilling it.

What is to be investigated here is not the application question of whether or not there are persons in general or in particular situations

who are overtaxed by the unreasonable demands of a morals of autonomy. There is no serious doubt about this possibility. The investigation
of each particular case or type of circumstances, however, would extend
well beyond the parameters of a fundamental ethics. As an ethics of the
will, therefore, fundamental ethics undertakes only a preliminary task. It
resists the inclination of a purely performance-oriented ethics to either
under-challenge or over-challenge persons. If only performance counts,
then a good outcome counts to the benefit of the one involved even if not
so much he himself but, rather, fortunate circumstances brought about
the performance. Furthermore, an eventual failure is attributed to him when
he did everything humanly possible to accomplish a better outcome.

What will also not be discussed is the more fundamental question
of whether or not a specific kind of morals, for example, a strict altruism, is too much to be expected of people. In any case, morals do not
demand a strict altruism. They call for sympathy, readiness to help, and
benevolence, but not this further altruism, which expects the bracketing
of the self. Crucial for a fundamental ethics is the even more fundamental question of whether or not moral autonomy constitutes for rational
beings of the human kind a challenge that is foreign to lived reality,
perhaps even contradictory of lived reality: are rational beings who are
shaped by sensuous appetites capable of free will whatsoever, or is this
capacity a mere fiction?

In order to rebut a radical skepticism, we will undertake a thought
experiment (inspired by Kant). It begins by taking the side of the skeptic in assuming the fundamental moral overtaxing of humanity only to
then show that this assumption is by no means convincing. We begin,
cautiously, with a discussion of the more modest, pre-moral freedom.
Resuming the theme of chapter 19, we discuss it in terms of the natural scientist who himself doubts the reality of practical freedom: One
imagines a brain researcher—one could just as well imagine a journalist,
businessman, or politician—who experiences so much pressure in his
career that he is ready to engage in fraud. In light of such a temptation,
one can ask the ruthless achiever how he would act if he knew that he
would lose his position immediately were the fraud exposed and that he
would never again be able to pursue his career as a researcher, journalist,
businessman, or politician.

If we set aside the clinical case of an ingenious psychopath, the answer is obvious: a career as a scientist is aimed beyond one's discoveries
at the respect one has from colleagues and beyond them to the respect

one finds in one's circle of friends and even from the public. Apart from the curiosity that drives one's research, there is the hope that the career will one day bring a solid income if not a scientific prize, perhaps even self-respect. Whoever sees all of this (proverbially, "a golden future") clearly threatened, even the most ambitious person, will seek to control his ambition. Only a fool assumes that a professional guild can be taken to be a collection of fools not only temporarily but in perpetuity. As a consequence, we can reckon with pragmatic freedom (again, apart from difficult cases of illness) as a fact.

One can even set aside the goal of a promising future or one's personal general well-being and be satisfied with the desire for a scientific career and thereby discover a contradiction—admittedly, no logical but an empirical-pragmatic contradiction: because science lives from the repeatability of experiments and competition, one cannot count on the "lucky break" of a deposit without a testament or on fraudulence as a means to obtain security. As a consequence, the denial of fraud is not only advisable from the perspective of life wisdom but also from the most elementary knowledge of the profession in which one wishes to pursue a career: Whoever constructs his scientific career on the basis of fraudulent means thwarts with these means the very goal he wants to achieve. He succumbs to a serious technical error; he violates the technique of a research career.

On both sides, then, on the technical as well as the pragmatic side, freedom hints at a principle that can serve as the motto for the argument with the freedom-skepticism of the brain researcher: "Precisely rejection of this waywardness was the highest command that I imposed on myself; I, free ape, acquiesced to this yoke." As appropriate in a debate with a scientific researcher, the principle arises out of a fictitious "Report to an Academy," written by a linguistically gifted, admittedly nonprofessional scientist, Franz Kafka (1919/1971).

One recalls: the author and hero of the report is an ape that was taken captive by a hunting expedition from the Hagenbeck firm on the Gold Coast and transported back to Hamburg in a cage. This ape reports a short five years later how he first learned social customs, namely to shake hands and to spit—he travels with sailors—to smoke a pipe, and how to properly uncork a bottle of hard liquor. Very quickly, he acquires the rudiments of language and cries out: "Hello!" A bit later he achieves "the average education of a European."

More important to him than these skills is a personal accomplishment that qualifies as a "yoke," that is, the highly painstaking self-development

by means of which he reaches the status of a "free ape." Confronted
with the alternative at his arrival in Hamburg between the zoo or vaudeville, he chooses against the zoo, invests "all of his energy to get into
vaudeville," and to that end embraces a radical "abnegation of every kind
of self-will." Because of a scar from a bullet, he is called "Red Peter."
He becomes a free ape through two technical imperatives. Because both
are oriented toward relative well-being, they amount together to a pragmatic imperative.

Very elegantly, namely in passing and without any moral finger-
pointing, Kafka says: one who gets no further than solely pursuing one's
own well-being is no more than a free ape. Even when he belongs to
the species *Homo sapiens,* he is still far from being human in the full
sense. Red Peter himself seems to know this because he attributes to
the "Honorable Members of the Academy" an ape status that they possibly—the ape leaves the possibility open with a gentle "so far"—haven't
"left behind."

The first technical imperative takes the only truly live option under
consideration: "If you want any realistic chance of escaping from a caged
existence, then you must qualify for vaudeville since any other alternatives appear to be unrealistic." Because there was no chance to escape
on the Gold Coast, and in Hamburg the zoo alternative is "only a new
cage," the ape sees in vaudeville the only possible route to his well-
being and follows the pragmatic imperative: "If you want to achieve for
yourself a relatively superior well-being, you must submit yourself to the
thoroughly repressive rejection (the "yoke") of one's self-will." Already
at the pragmatic level, then, freedom demands a renunciation. Only
through exertion, by education, above all by one's own subordination
to the pragmatically commanded renunciation, that is, through self-
discipline, can one acquire true freedom.

This thought experiment doesn't directly follow a widely shared strategy in the debate over freedom that is itself ensnarled in hardly re-
solvable difficulties, that is, in aporias. This strategy attempts indirectly
to demonstrate that one could have acted differently. It depends upon
a threefold ability: that one contemplates alternative actions, considers these alternatives in terms of calculating their future advantages or
disadvantages, and in light of these calculations can counter conflicting inclinations. Parenthetically: Kafka is not concerned with the usual
education of a person but with the elementary education *to become* a
person; in this case, to become a free ape.

A second thought experiment concerned now with the reality of a completely moral freedom of the will takes us beyond the free ape to a free person. Once again, one imagines a researcher, but this time one who in the face of the same threat of losing his career is expected to circulate a lie about an, indeed, disliked but upright colleague. Should one ask the researcher whether or not he, no matter how great his joy in his profession and career, takes it to be possible to resist the expectation, the convincing answer might be: no one who is self-critically honest would risk guaranteeing that the researcher would actually refuse to lie. He would unquestionably acknowledge that the refusal to lie is morally commanded and also realistically possible. As a consequence, he maintains that full moral freedom is not merely conceivable, but is actually realizable, even in reality possible.

The brain researcher must now ask himself whether or not he can formulate a decisive (contrary) experiment, an *experimentum crucis,* for this freedom in the sense of a complete freedom of the will. The philosopher doesn't know. In light of the curiosity for knowledge given at birth, he remains curious, to be sure, but also skeptical. How can one unhinge the world of *should* on the basis of insights from the world of *being?* The mere assumption that one could eventually disprove empirically the (full) freedom of the will already appears to be logically impossible. As long as the *experimentum crucis* has not been found, the brain researcher conducts himself like the mountaineer who already takes the promised view of the mountain peak to be a fairy tale, although he has reached only a fore-summit and balks at the effort required to climb the summit itself.

At least preliminarily, one can correct the brain researchers: to the extent that they attribute to themselves ingenious experiments with deliberation, execution, and media-appropriate presentation, they are making claim to the lowest level of free will; in the widest sense, technical freedom. To the extent that they pursue their personal well-being and scientific careers together with honors and prizes for their experiments, they are taking into consideration an intermediate, pragmatic freedom. The same applies to the highest level, moral freedom: to the extent that researchers remain fundamentally honest, even in those situations where dishonesty would remain forever concealed as if beneath a magic cape, they engage moral freedom. Only when the brain researchers reject these self-attributions and, indeed, not merely in debates but in their very lives, only when they hold themselves responsible neither for the ingeniousness of their experiments nor for their positions as research professors, nor for the achievement of a scientific prize that they have won, nor, also, for the fact that they manage their institute fairly, only at that point must non–brain researchers fear—against which Kafka's "Report," however, makes one resistant—that the brain researchers have in their research eliminated freedom.

We can surely say that neural circuits define us without question, but not to the extent that we must cease to speak of education, responsibility, and freedom. A person does not have complete disposal of the brain (at best psychological, pharmacological, or surgical procedures do), nor does the brain direct the brain; rather, a person with a brain directs his life. This disposal over one's life, we can readily acknowledge, is within limits. However, because moral reason is not so closely bound to technical and pragmatic reason, the case of morals is not all so closely tied to these limits.

Were one to compare this second thought experiment with the results drawn from the first thought experiment, one discovers a tremendous advantage on the part of the second precisely because it is not dependent upon technical and pragmatic reason. One needs relatively a great deal in order to answer the first question: considerable knowledge of the world, creativity, and a rather high capacity for judgment. Hence, the ape decides against an attempted escape by springing into the water only after a careful analysis of the situation: how great is the distance to shore; with what kind of water currents must one calculate; how great is the chance that one can jump overboard without notice? Further, he must contemplate possibilities of action including difficult detours or escape routes. He must look well into the future and come to a circumspectly balanced conclusion. The case is similar with the researcher who is ready to engage in fraud: what arguments with which pretended data will result in making his otherwise hypercritical colleagues ready to accept the false claims? Finally, because only self-interest would hold him back from fraud, the scheme requires his intimate knowledge of the "mechanisms" of research and his research competitors.

In contrast, one can act on the honesty that is appealed to in the second thought experiment almost without knowledge of the world and without an empirical-pragmatic capacity for judgment. One need know only two things: that a lie is a lie and that no honest person constructs his future on the basis of a lie that harms his fellow human beings. One can therefore generalize: the cognitive effort required for a morals of autonomy is quite limited. The capacity for morals doesn't determine the amount of one's intelligence quotient: neither intellectuals nor scientists nor philosophers are in this respect superior to ordinary persons. The happy consequence: it is cognitively easier to be moral than it is to be happy. If one leaves (small) children, the mentally disabled, and psychopaths out of the equation, moral freedom is no illusion but something every person is capable of exercising.

22.2 A Prescriptive Fact

What kind of reality attests to these thought experiments? What was sought was a fact, the fact that invalidates the radical skepticism about morals. What was found was what one can name a real possibility, namely, the circumstance that one is able not only to refuse but also to avoid a lie. This real possibility is no normal fact. What it proposes is not that certain persons actually refuse to lie but, rather, that one is capable of judging, one even usually judges: confronted with the alternative "a career at the price of honor" or "honor at the price of a career," it is not only exceptional persons who say point-blank: even when the first option is more attractive to me, I know that it is false. I even demand not only of myself but also of others the rejection of the first option. Should I myself in fact place my career first, there must be justifiable grounds, but, nonetheless, I will experience shame. Even someone who fears succumbing to the first option will unequivocally condemn it, and not merely when he imagines himself to be the victim: a career that is based on the defamation of a (disliked) colleague is not acceptable.

The freedom manifest here contains the manner of existence that belongs to morals: the *should*. This is no mere should that remains ineffective in the world of *being*. It comes to light in a judging and being judged that includes a feeling of shame; therefore, this is a should manifest in lived reality. In the face of the alternative between a career at any price, even the price of dishonesty, and honesty at any price, including the price of sacrificing one's own career, unconditional career loss appears as a possible inclination, and unconditional honesty is declared to be a moral duty. At the same time, the closing argument will be made against the inclination and for the duty. Above all, one is not satisfied with a mere plea. Someone who makes such a choice expects with the first option a guilty conscience and that shame to which the commentary of a fraudulent insurance agent applies: "Sorrow elevates and tragedy enobles. But shame eats away at you and debases you—it consumes your eyes, it drinks your blood and it bends your back" (Lars Saabye Christensen, *The Half Brother*, 2004, 502). The second option brings respect, even veneration. However, it is combined with the addendum: simple respect can be earned by anyone; veneration, though, is earned only by someone who advocates the second option, but not out of an expectation of respect or the pursuit of a gain in prestige.

Having accomplished this reconstruction, one is directly aware of the reality of moral freedom in the form of a spontaneous judging and being judged. In the case of being judged, shame occurs that can in turn be "embarrassingly and openly" manifest in blushing. Some are able to repress or hinder this visible signal. However, in their brains real activity can occur that is combined with a sense of being morally uncomfortable. Only the proverbially hard-boiled person is immune to this emotion of shame.

One may not overlook that spontaneous judgment, including any of shame, is not the same as the (here only sketched) philosophical reconstruction. This proposed philosophical thought experiment does not pertain to moral consciousness itself but to the becoming conscious of moral consciousness. It either makes the skeptic aware of a phenomenon that he hasn't seen or hasn't taken into consideration, or it declares to him that (direct) moral consciousness possesses a consequence that wasn't clear to him.

Shame and, even more so, blushing and the aforementioned brain activity suggest that one considers moral freedom to be an everyday fact: a fact that allows itself to be demonstrated according to the model of scientific research, if only by means of the appropriate interpretations. The suggested kind of judgment does not exist, however, like other usual natural events because it depends upon an antecedently acknowledged recognition. This antecedent element neither occurs with necessity nor does it always happen. It is, rather, something that *should* happen. Behind the usual moral should is a second level of moral should that in terms of its systematic significance constitutes a level that is superior even to this usual first level.

A usual moral "should" consists in a challenge to act whose consequence is the previously discussed kind of moral judgment. The new, unusual moral "should" can be seen by means of a further thought experiment. It might well be that no one can escape his conscience forever. Such can be the case, though, only where one has a conscience in the first place.

Now imagine someone who wants to be morally conscience-free. He attempts so to wean himself from the prick of conscience that it can no longer arise. Should he be successful, he would be an amoral person in the strictest sense of the term. As a person who has become inaccessible to morals, he would be morally insensitive in the emotional sense, and in the cognitive sense he would be lacking any moral conviction. Immune to all remonstrance, he would be singled out by his moral deafness and blindness, which were they to be widely dispersed, would turn into moral barbarism. In opposition to these two forms of moral stupor, namely a complete deficiency not only of moral feeling but also of moral conviction, morals raise their veto. This occurs in the form of a moral *should* of a second order that says: moral stupor is not permissible; there should be moral receptivity; the former is morally prohibited, the latter morally commanded.

Morals are a fact only when a basic moral *should* is acknowledged. In contrast, someone who adheres to a moral emotionlessness and lack of moral conviction is excluded from the world of morals. Only someone who rejects this latter option and opens himself to moral commands and prohibitions enters into the moral world and finds himself exposed to the usual moral *should:* one is challenged by an obligation that one should fulfill and, in the case in which one doesn't, one experiences the prick of conscience and shame.

Entrance into the moral world involves, structurally speaking, a personal achievement that is subordinate to the moral command to bring about the moral world. As a consequence, morals are ultimately a fact [*Faktum*] in the original sense of the word. It is not simply given, or merely present (that would be a "datum" in the original sense), but something that needs to be done. (At the same time, the doing is nothing necessary in the sense of an assembling, in contrast to acting.) One can also speak of an actuality [*Tatsache*], namely a thing [*Sache*] that occurs by being done [*Tat*]. In addition, a (morally) commanded fact [*Faktum*] is present in a manner that one must formulate as a paradox: the moral world is a morally commanded actuality [*Tatsache*]. It consists of the ontologically special object of a prescriptive fact [*Faktum*]. The moral fact is nothing other than the moral self-development of a moral being for whom "to be a moral being" is a moral command.

One could maintain, to the contrary, that this argument is circular and therefore unacceptable. In fact, there are morals only when one subordinates oneself to a basic moral command, the commitment to be receptive to morals. This circular character comes through with the question of whether or not there is such a thing as moral freedom because the answer is: there is moral freedom simply when both sides, the individual and the social order, are working on the development of a fundamental moral receptivity. Why should they do so rather than dismantle and, finally, eliminate morals?

This question can be a more fundamental one than the popular: "Why should one be moral?" The prior question is directed not toward ontogenesis, the development of the individual, but in addition and primarily toward the phylogenic, the development of humanity: "Why should humanity develop the capacity for morals?" The accompanying question is: "Why should a moral capacity, once developed, be preserved?" This circumstance that the dual question of a moral *should* is itself an object of a moral *should* is appropriate, and it invalidates the charge of a circular argument: An entirely collective advantage, in other words, a socially pragmatic argument, can speak for morals. Ultimately, however, one can make an argument for or against morals not at a pre-moral level but only at the moral level itself. With respect to the question of why there should be a freedom at the third and highest, truly moral level, the answer can only be: a human being may not incorporate any brakes into the developmental possibilities of practical reason; as a being with freedom and reason he may not belittle himself.

One cannot in principle eliminate this belittling, to be sure. Humanity cannot so lightly forget the manner of judging described here, either. One can imagine only with difficulty how humanity is able to so effectively block the question with respect to practical principles that it not only frequently, but perhaps even as a rule, only rarely reaches the highest level of judgment. At the same time, what the methodological status of the moral fact specifies is also not unthinkable: morals do not occur in the world like minerals, plants, and animals. Rather, they must be created by persons and must always be created anew. A full freedom of the will is exclusively that which a *should* allows to be transformed into a *being:* an actuality [*Tatsache*] that should be.

This manner of existence rejects other points of view. The thought is rejected that morals exist in the form of moral values that occur as objective and eternal truths in a kingdom of the spirit for itself alone, independent from the moral subject, the human being. In contrast, moral objectivity, indeed, remains a given; it is even emphatically asserted. To that extent, a second position is also dismissed: that one-dimensional opponent to value ethics who reduces morals to mere conventions and, therefore, takes morals to be only historically and culturally valid. In contrast to such a strict ethical relativism, morals are time-transcending, transcultural, even independent of any species, in short: morals are absolutely, universally valid. Nonetheless, in contrast to a value ethic, morals can occur only thanks to the power of a basic recognition—more specifically: self-recognition, that is, thanks to the morally capable subject who contemplates reasons for what is right. Any mere show of values is, in contrast, entirely secondary.

The opinion that morals exist only because God wishes there to be inalterable moral obligations also opposes the necessity of the basic recognition defended here. A morals based upon recognition is no voluntary product of a divine will. Not least, a psychological altruism is rejected that bases moral action in a *feeling* for the well-being of others. Well-being is, to be sure, a self-evident constituent of morals, but not on the basis of a merely emotional apologia.

22.3 Morality as Escalation

There are three possibilities for the fulfillment of moral commandments. First, one ultimately does so out of self-interest, as in the case of businesses that, out of fear that they might lose customers or might be victims of fraud, treat even inexperienced customers fairly. Included in this first possible manner of conforming to moral principles are those who are moral out of fear of punishment or in expectation of a reward. Second, one can act on the basis of a direct inclination. For example, one gives aid out of sympathy, whether it be out of personal devotion to a friend or relative or whether out of a general empathy and goodwill, as in the British ethics of feeling. Finally, one can act in conformity with the moral command as such, independent of either self-interest or inclination.

Obviously, one is not already acting morally where one fulfills the expectation of the moral command on the basis of just any reason. Mere conformity with duty, called legalism, is not sufficient to establish a person's moral status. At stake with legalism here is not a positive juridical legality but a moral legalism. Merely to act in conformity with duty without taking the reasons for one's actions into consideration is, therefore, not yet unequivocally good. This meta-ethical criterion for morals, the unequivocally good, is only satisfied when one acts in accordance with what is morally right because it is morally right. Legalism (in the moral sense) escalates to morals when the morally right is pursued for itself and as such. Only when one acts on the basis of this escalation does one reach the highest level of morals, morality. That person possesses a moral disposition who makes this escalated morals the fundamental orientation of his life.

The fact that morals are not satisfied with mere dutiful conformity to moral principles is significant because it means that morals are not found at the level of observable behavior or its rules. In contrast to (moral) legalism, one cannot determine morals on the basis of the action itself but only by means of the determining ground, by what is willed. For this reason, the unequivocally good consists in universalizability, but not already with respect to what is actually done, but far earlier in terms of the establishment of the ultimately decisive rule, the maxim, governing what is done. Nevertheless, many attempt to conceive of morals solely in terms of the concept of norms, values, or procedural regulations. Such a definitional strategy applies, say, to a value ethics, utilitarianism, and an empirical-pragmatic variation of universalization as well as to discourse ethics. However, none of them reaches the level of morals in the strict sense. At best, they are satisfied with the morally right but not with the morally good, the good of the acting subject.

As a critique of this alternative and as an indirect confirmation of one's own position, one likes to accuse an ethics of morals of distorting morals into a subjectivity of good intentions. The charge against a mere ethics of intention conceals two different objections, although both are capable of rebuttal. On the one hand, someone who defends good intentions fosters a world of idle inwardness that is indifferent to every materialization, any real performance, in the real world. Marx and Engels take this attitude to correspond "entirely to the unconsciousness, dejection, and misery of the German bourgeoisie" who, because of their narrow-minded interests, "are incessantly exploited by the bourgeoisie of all other nations" (*The German Ideology*, part 3, section 1.6.A). On the other hand, an ethic of good intentions permits the baptism of every action as good and right. In the sense of the often misunderstood Augustinian saying: "*dilige et quod vis fac*" ("love and do what you will": *In epistulam Ioannis ad Parthos, tractatus decem*, part 7, section 8), restriction to mere intention appeals only to one's good conscience and lacks any objective standard.

As popular as this double critique is, it is grounded in misunderstanding. Intention consists in an attitude of willing that in turn is no mere wishing but includes the mobilization of all available means for the fulfillment of the intention. Neither a moral will nor the intentions of a life attitude are indifferent to their externalization in their social and political worlds. Rather than constituting a hereafter to reality, they are the ultimate determining ground of one's actions, to be sure with the crucial restriction: so far as the determining ground is within the power of the subject. The actual action can lag behind the intention because of physical, mental, economic, and other shortcomings. In the case of one's offering assistance to someone, it can come too late, too ineffectively, or even be wrong.

No one can avoid such a danger. Every action or nonaction occurs within the parameters of a field of forces that is dependent upon natural and social conditions independent of the will of the agent and not even entirely capable of surveyance. Furthermore, personal morals are concerned only with the range of responsibility of the subject, that is, with what is possible for him. As a consequence, the bare result, the objectively observable product, cannot be a standard of measurement for the morals of an individual, his morals. Personal morals are determinable not with the externalization, the perceptible action itself, but, rather, in the will at the base of the action. The alternative to a "mere ethic of intentions," a pure ethic of performance, takes humanity to be completely responsible for something, the actual outcome, for which it cannot be fully responsible. In a fundamental and consistent sense, a performance ethic is inhuman since it fails to recognize the fundamental human condition.

This critique of an ethic of morals overlooks to a great extent that legalism is no alternative to morals but is its necessary condition. John Steinbeck describes in his humorous novel *Tortilla Flat* (1935/1965, chapter 13) how likeable scoundrels help a family threatened by hunger. They "plundered the Hotel Monte's vegetable garden" and relished "a magnificent game of theft, free of the label of stealing, an offense that," described by Steinbeck with a wink, "was performed out of altruism. There's nothing that can impart a deeper satisfaction." Such an enjoyable act of illegality, however, cannot claim to be moral because the morally legal, grounded in one's accomplishment of constructive help, was in fact inconvenient for the scoundrels but not impossible.

Can there not be human beings who as honorable knights employ morally reprehensible means to accomplish the morally good? Does not literature from Robin Hood to Shen Teh in Bertolt Brecht's play *The Good Person of Szechwan* rest upon such a moral sentiment? The moral philosopher is no moralizer, who condemns every deviation from moral principles as immoral from the get-go. There is hardly any moral command that requires one to accept formidable oppression and exploitation without any resistance. In the event that all options have been exhausted, it could (!) be that, as a truly final option, one could take an action to be moral that would be considered immoral in normal circumstances; at least, it could be excusable. What is at stake is not illegality in spite of morals but (moral) legality itself: deviations from moral principles are defensible only when they conform to principles at a higher level that, for their part, satisfy the test of universalization.

Another objection maintains that an action can be unintentionally illegal. Surely, this is a real possibility, but it doesn't constitute an objection, since an ethic of the will embraces the restriction: insofar as the agent has the power to act legally. It doesn't deny either that one can unintentionally, and without even knowing it, injure someone and yet not be accused of inattention, thoughtlessness, carelessness, or some other responsible mistake. The event occurred unintentionally and also without even indirect guilt. For example, in an attempt to break one's fall, one can unintentionally and without it being one's fault cause another to fall and thereby break a bone. In an attempt to aid someone, including a morally legitimate act, one can actually cause the other harm. In both cases, one indeed violates a moral obligation, and actually the same one, the prohibition against harming others. One acts contrary to duty. However, the morally relevant concept of action includes a direct or indirect intention: it requires that one at least be able to be held responsible for having been inattentive or having committed some other fault.

Neither an unintentional injury that is not one's fault nor an unintentional harm is an action in the strict sense. One is, indeed, the free agent of what is intended: in the one case, the attempt to break one's fall, in the other, the intent of offering aid. However, when it comes to the consequent violation of duty, one is not a free agent but merely a simple cause, so that one best speaks in such a case of a quasi-violation of duty. The consequent injury is a violation of duty; however, since it is neither intended nor merely accepted indifferently, it is not attributable to the agent. One can speak of legality and morals only with respect to the intended aspect of the event, but not with respect to the completely unintentional part.

In other words, from the perspective of the total event, one can satisfy morality but nonetheless contradict moral duty; morals and legality are concerned with different aspects of the total event. Should the assistance occur from a moral disposition, it satisfies the legal condition with respect to assisting another that can escalate the disposition to morals. In contrast, an unintentional and also not indirectly blameworthy injury of another does not have the character of an action; it is not subject to the concepts of legality and morals. In short: one can hardly speak of morals with respect to an illegal act.

Contrary to Max Scheler's separation of a dispositional and a consequentialist ethic (1916/1980, part 1, chapter 3) and Max Weber's examination of an ethic of ultimate ends and an ethic of responsibility (*Politics as a Vocation*, 1919/1965, 46–47), legality and morals are also not concerned with two partly or completely exclusive orientations. Moral action does not compete with legality but, rather, intensifies its demands. For these demands, mere fulfillment of moral duty is not sufficient; one must go beyond fulfillment of the duty to the determining ground for one's action. Morals is no backsliding of legality but rather an escalation and exceeding of legality: complete moral action demands, first, that one act according to a moral command and, second, that one act only on that basis—because it is morally commanded. Not least, there is an objective criterion for the moral command, a strict universalization, which repudiates the charge of a merely internal, standardless intention.

22.4 A Moral Feeling: Respect

Like many of its competitors, an ethics of the will has an objective standard. The alternative to these objective standards is a subjective or personal criterion that as a rule is called an ethical or also a moral feeling (*sensus moralis*, "moral sense" or "moral sentiment"). In the classical formulation by Shaftesbury, Hutcheson, and Hume, one means an organ that is responsible for morals, which performs two services at once. It recognizes the morally good (serving as a criteriological or judicative achievement), and it stimulates one to act in accordance with the morally good (serving as a motivational or affective achievement). Both achievements, one assumes, occur directly and immediately. As a natural foundation, both are said to constitute an altruistic inclination: empathy for others, sym-pathy, and the inspired well-being that results. As an immediate insight, moral feeling is close to being a pre-empirical, solely rational intuition, a pure intuition that sanctions what is morally good. However, it can only get close. Any sanctioning as a consequence of feeling depends, namely, upon the uniqueness of the person concerned. Therefore, it cannot be certain of that strict [rational] universality that is characteristic of the universalization test for morals.

Nonetheless, one may not consider the ethics of feeling naive. As was already the case with Shaftesbury in 1711, so too with Hutcheson in 1725, ethical feeling consists in a feeling of a second order that reacts to feelings of the first order in terms of sanctioning or disapproval—depending on whether or not the first-order feelings motivate one to benevolent and generally useful actions.

In terms of what is perhaps the most sophisticated ethic of feeling, that of Adam Smith in 1774, the two components of sympathy, the affective and the criteriological, are supplemented by two further components. Because one cannot have direct experience of the feelings of others, sympathy cannot be a feeling that one contracts merely by being in the presence of another's emotions, like an infection by an emotional disease. It requires, in addition, a participatory imagination by means of which one can place oneself in the emotional state of the other. This third component reminds one of the productive fantasy of a novelist who, like Jules Verne, can travel to the moon without ever leaving France. Sympathetic imagination, however, should not create persons and narratives as does a novelist, but should so empathize with concrete human beings and their real relationships that one changes how one acts in one's own emotional world. One experiences others not only socially and not merely egocentrically, but one also acts differently whereby the "acting differently" involves one's "body and soul": one becomes a different person.

An effective social feeling such as empathy by itself runs the danger of being only partisanly active and acknowledging too much the suffering of persons close by and too little the suffering of those more distant. Adam Smith proposes a fourth component to avoid such a danger: the thought of the nonpartisan observer. This component allows the advancement of one's own well-being and that of one's friends only to the extent that it is compatible with the needs and interests of all others.

One comes close to a universalizability test in the ethics of feeling with this general compatibility. There remain, however, three differences that together militate against the ethics of feeling. The first difference can be formulated as an alternative interpretation: either one is concerned with the actual feeling of sympathy of a *particular* individual; then one cannot count on a *general* compatibility. Feelings are merely subjective and, further, they fluctuate (are "labile") in the same individual, which leads to a relativism that is difficult to reconcile with morals; or the decisive moment resides in the general compatibility; then what counts is not the actual *particular* feeling of sympathy, but the *general* compatibility. Similar to ideal discourse, sympathy has a normative demand that shoulders the load of a criterion and, as a consequence, is a prejudice, a normative presupposition.

A second difference to the ethics of feeling: the question of which needs and interests are reconcilable with generalization can be answered only from experience, which is not what is needed for a universalizability test. Because sympathy includes a normative demand in order to function as a moral principle, the judicative and affective capacities must be distinct. The moral philosophy defended in the present project substitutes for ethical feeling the internal attitude of the subject, that is, the ethical or moral disposition that wants as such what is morally required. What the moral requirement is, however, cannot be determined by a factual feeling either as empathy and benevolence or as a moral disposition; ultimately, the test of universalizability is solely determinative.

A third difference to the ethics of feeling: the nonpartisanship that occurs in sympathy doesn't just happen automatically. It requires an effort that raises the question for self-love: why should one transform self-love into a strict, nonpartisan empathy? Interest in empathy for others justifies only a limited, strategically applied empathy. One needs to develop it only to the extent that is required to generate an empathy in response. Because not the actual empathy but that which appears needful to others is what counts, all that is needed is a skillful pretending. The ethics of feeling cannot give an adequate answer to the question of why one should assume the moral standpoint of nonpartisanship.

These criticisms do not demand the complete rejection of moral feeling, but they do call for a new approach. Just as in the case of the criterion for morals, so also feelings must be determined exclusively by moral reason. This condition is satisfied where one permits oneself to be motivated by nothing other than a moral law. Hence, in the case of a conflict, one's own well-being is overruled by the moral law. In contrast to the, to be sure, higher-level but empirically driven feeling of the British ethics of feeling, moral law does not respond to empirically specific perceptions but to an empirically independent object, the moral law. As a consequence, it excludes all self-interest and its empirically determined feelings. In addition, because there is an independent standard for the moral law, it is relieved of the task of determining what is morally right. All that remains is the readiness to obey the self-selected moral law, that is, to obey that motivational power which escalates legality to morals.

In order for the truly moral feeling to displace the British ethics of feeling as described, it should be called respect—although admittedly not in the sense of attention or warning, but in the sense of appreciation and respectful acknowledgment. Further, morally unsurpassable appreciation is more precisely called moral respect. What is meant is that successful, free, and unequivocal consent out of the inner self that accompanies this only internally possible self-commitment to the moral. As an accompanying feeling, respect creates the connecting link between the purely rational moral determination and action in the actual world. Because of this bridge function, it is moral, and, therefore, purely rational and yet experienceable. Respect is the sensuous, experienceable perception of the acknowledgment of morals as practiced in life.

Respect is what establishes that only a moral inwardness (see chapter 5.4) is defensible: whoever in the strictest sense of willing, namely, in the manner of empowerment to act, is convinced that a certain action, rule, or maxim is moral acts for no other reason than this conviction. Whoever doesn't and acts out of a weakness of the will is wanting in terms of this complete recognition, this action-empowering conviction: he is lacking a moral will and moral respect.

One surely should not overestimate the motivational power which moral respect commands. Precedence must be given to the free acknowledgment of moral principles and their embodiment, the moral law. Moral respect can make it easier for the moral law to establish its place in the human will, but only in the sense of a feedback strategy that is self-reinforcing. Because precedence is due to autonomous acknowledgment of the moral law, respect can be neither the grounds for acknowledgment nor its cause. It is simply an accompanying feeling that doesn't evoke the recognition but does strengthen the influence of the moral law. What is objective with respect to the moral law corresponds to the subjective in terms of moral respect. However, the moral law itself is now taken not as a standard of measurement but as an ultimate motivating power.

When viewed phenomenologically, there are two sides to a moral motivation driven by nothing other than the moral law. Negatively viewed, this motivation subjects the natural longing for well-being to a humiliation: appetites and self-love (egoism) lose their right to be the

ultimate motivating power over action. Viewed positively, this motivation elevates to a purely practical reason that being which is capable of
acting according to self-selected grounds as a practical, rational being.
To that extent, moral respect contains a reflective moment: the self-
respect of a moral being in terms of its morals. With the feeling of respect, he experiences himself as essentially the same as all other morally
capable beings. Paradoxically formulated: moral respect is simultaneously subjective and intersubjective. Whereas in the case of desire for
well-being there are serious differences among persons, an individual, as
long as he feels respect by means of the self-obligation to the moral law,
is entirely equal to all other persons when it comes to this feeling.

There is also the alternative feeling. Someone who violates morals
experiences guilt that is, properly understood, not forced on one externally or authoritatively but is grounded morally: the individual rebukes
himself. In that case where the violation of the moral law is clear and
obvious, the rebuke escalates to the opposite of self-respect, that is, to
self-condemnation. One who lives with respect for morals and makes
it the cornerstone of one's character is in command of a moral ethos. A
moral ethos consists in the acquisition of the feeling of moral respect as
a fundamental life attitude.

What is this moral reality that emerges with the moral orientation
of life? The answer begins with a distinction among various levels of
reality. At the very null-level, one can speak of the morally illiterate
person, who recognizes neither theoretical nor practical morals. In both
respects, morals are for him entirely foreign. He is in the literal and
widest sense amoral because he doesn't merely deny moral expectations
as in the case of the anti-moralist but, rather, because of ignorance he is
not even open to the alternative of accepting or rejecting moral expectations. He doesn't know even vaguely what morals are, much less show
any tendency toward moral behavior.

At the *first* and weakest level, morals have an exclusively theoretical
and no practical existence. When it comes to the determinative practical
aspect, this level is only preliminary; however, in contrast to the morally
illiterate, it is more than nothing. The individual concerned knows, to
be sure, that there is such a thing as a moral *should,* but he relegates it
to a world other than his own; for himself and in his own life, he is in
an extreme sense "morally nonmusical." Nonetheless, to the morally illiterate, he does know about morals; he is not *theoretically* but practically
amoral: as a knowing subject, he is familiar with morals, but as an acting

agent, morals remain alien to him. Like the person who is not religious but, nonetheless, is familiar with the opinions and demands of religion without in any way accepting them, so, too, the theoretically moral person knows about moral obligations but doesn't feel himself in any way subject to them. The difference here is that between knowing and acknowledging. The moral world of *shoulds* is for him an exotic culture: a merely known but, with respect to life praxis, completely meaningless reality.

At the *second* level overall, but the first level in terms of the *practical,* reality extends to praxis. Unlike the lax adherent to a religion, one doesn't merely know the moral kind of *should* but feels himself subject to it—however, not in any strict sense. Instead of a mere self-awareness, one encounters here a first, though still weak, acknowledgment of personal moral obligation. However, in those circumstances where morals extend into the realm of self-interest, one quickly finds reasons why one can ignore the moral demand. One recognizes that morals constitute the highest level of obligation but does not take them with any real seriousness.

With the *third,* already fairly strong level of reality, morals are acknowledged to a large extent. In the event that one violates the moral law, one is aware that one should not have. One has a bad conscience. Perhaps one even experiences remorse, practices penance, and commits to improving one's behavior in the future.

At a *fourth,* even more robust reality, moral behavior becomes a solid habit, a personality trait called "virtue." This level of moral reality can be encouraged and made easier with the aid of institutions without for that reason acknowledging those institutions to be in possession of a logical, authoritative superiority.

At a still higher *fifth* level, one acknowledges moral obligations simply for the reason that they are moral obligations. At this level one acts out of pure and simple respect for what is moral.

Should morals lose at this highest level all sense of *should,* would that mean that they have been transformed entirely into *being*? For at least two reasons and in two respects, the answer is: "No!" On the one hand, respect for the moral law is not something that occurs naturally but is the *product of* a basic *should.* On the other hand, a sober understanding anchored in reality acknowledges that given the parameters of human life, namely, given the constant presence of conflicting appetites, respect for morals could achieve only with difficulty the status of an absolutely invulnerable reality. In both respects, morals preserve their *should* character. After all, thirdly, a virtuous person can make mistakes. One who takes morals seriously demands that his *should* cannot be ineffective in reality. However, he remains skeptical that the moral *should* could ever dissolve into reality (*being*) without remainder and difference.

22.5 Moral Grace

In another thought experiment, all three points of view emerge: not only the prescriptive fact but also the escalation of legality to morals, and finally the feeling of respect for morals. For the purposes of illustration, we imagine the dramatic situation that the two laws contradict one another: the moral law and that of one's own well-being. The much-discussed conflict between duty and inclination consists precisely in this contradiction.

By duty one does not mean just any capricious, even morally incompatible, perhaps even crassly immoral task. In contrast to a functional or even authoritarian concept, we mean here an exclusively moral duty. The other concept, inclination, characterizes the actually dominant, guiding aim of action in a person. As a mere guiding aim, it is indifferent to the moral question. Already for this reason, morals do not in principle forbid spiritual, mental, or physical indulgence including one's own well-being. Even Kant, who is often scolded for being rigoristic, speaks of a certain duty toward one's happiness ("Doctrine of Virtue" [part 2 of *The Metaphysics of Morals*], "Introduction," part 5.B., 6:388). A repertoire of positive inclinations that are partly natural and partly acquired through upbringing, such as a readiness to help and compassion, is not something to be repressed but, on the contrary, is to be encouraged.

A conflict with duty surfaces first with the question of scope. If inclinations count as the decisive authority, in other words, if inclinations exclusively possess the license to establish one's guiding aim, then compliance with the moral law is only occasional and coincidental. An agreement with the moral law without any exceptions is possible only where inclination surrenders its exclusivity and, in the case of a conflict with the moral law, hands the license over to morals. That duty *actually* is privileged is manifest where duty and inclination are in conflict and duty triumphs.

Our thought experiment of a conflict between duty and inclination is not governed by a false pathos that humanity is constantly confronted with the dramatic decision that it must incessantly choose against its inclinations and for duty. All that is said is the following: in order to understand, on the one hand, the full expectation of morals and in order to be able to determine, on the other hand, whether or not persons are not only legally right but also morally good, one must imagine such a conflict situation. Only with such a situation can the existential rigor of the moral imperative become clear, namely, the expectation that one unequivocally acknowledge the moral, and even accept a "humiliation" of one's inclinations.

Everyday awareness of morals concurs: it is one thing to do something out of pleasure; it is something else to do it because it is morally expected. Duty has little if anything to do with a life of pleasure that seeks only the satisfaction of inclinations. Duty has its own law, the moral law, whereas the law of inclinations, if one can even call it a law, is that of one's own well-being. Fulfillment of one's duty only when it is to one's advantage contradicts the very concept of duty; however, the consequence is not that duty must always be a bitter pill. Nonetheless, the assumption of a contradiction between duty and inclination evokes an incisive and simultaneously influential critique in the couplet: "Gladly, I serve my friends, but, unfortunately, I do so only with interest / Hence, I am often rankled, that I am not virtuous." The author of these lines, Friedrich Schiller, tries to overcome the conflict with the aid of the thought of a beautiful soul. This attempt fails as long as one takes it to be an alternative agenda to morals; it succeeds as soon as it for a moment emphasizes that the moral is not foreign to a beautiful soul even if it is often overlooked (for a closer analysis, see Höffe 2006d).

A beautiful soul elevates neither moral legality nor morals; in this respect there is no competition with moral excellence. Furthermore, other competencies like the art of living are not something to be added. When it comes to a beautiful soul, morals no longer struggle with an internal resistance, in contrast to a "morals with a darkened brow." This escalation to morals in harmony with sensuousness occurs in fact with pleasure; therefore, one can call it "beauty" or "moral grace." Whoever leads his life out of such grace, that is, out of a morally developed sensuousness (or a sensuously developed morals), is permitted to boast of a free and sovereign moral nature. He has become a maestro, a master of what it means to be a human being.

Only someone who assumes in the case of opposition between duty and inclination that ultimately duty is fulfilled out of an inner struggle against inclination deserves Schiller's reproach that the thought of duty can occur solely in accompaniment with a severity that shrinks back from all grace. The accusation, however, is as unjustified against Kant as it is unjustified against any other consistent ethic of duty. Only that person acts out of moral respect who makes respect of morals a part of his free behavior and therefore in "cheerful mind" adheres to the moral law. At the end of his lectures on *Anthropology from a Pragmatic Point of View,* Kant himself says: "The *cynic's purism* and the *anchorite's mortification of the flesh,* without social good living, are distorted forms of virtue which do not make virtue inviting"; rather—one reads in astonishment—"being forsaken by the graces, they can make no claim to humanity" (7:282).

Schiller and one of his philosophical mentors, Kant, are united in their praise of the graces, so that one could accept over and above their different formulations a complete, "beautiful harmony." The question of whether or not this harmony in fact obtains is determined by the content and kind of existence of moral grace. The answer, then, consists of an "in part, Yes!; in part, No!" The question deserves an initial "Yes!" because the question with respect to morals escalates the mere fulfillment of duty to a free internal commitment; it deserves a second "Yes!" because this fulfillment of duty by a "cheerful mind" broadens the laws for an improved humanity. Just before the quoted passage, Kant says: "Anything that promotes sociability . . . is a garment that dresses virtue to advantage." In opposition, though, the question demands a double "No!" First, when viewed with respect to content, an improved humanity doesn't enhance what is decisively human, morals. Second, methodologically, Schiller's moral feeling admits the role of an empirical moment of emotional approbation that excludes pure respect for the moral law.

Not least, the beautiful soul appears in Schiller to be a real possibility, which Kant doubts. His opposing reasons are not by any chance derived out of pessimism or misanthropy. They follow from the condition of application for the concept of duty: because the human as a being with a body and needs has appetites that can oppose morals, the moral law is no natural law to which he must necessarily adhere, but is an imperative that summons to compliance without one ever being entirely certain that one acknowledges it. The antonym to the moral disposition "in a struggle" is not the moral disposition "with ease" but the possession of a *complete* purity in the disposition. This occurs, however, only with that saintliness in the "ontological" sense for which not even a model behavior is sufficient, exemplified by the merciful Samaritan, Francis of Assisi, or Mother Teresa. It requires the pure intelligence of an angel or of a god, that is, of beings who are fundamentally different from humanity and whom Schiller hardly had in mind. As a consequence, one cannot exclude what the expression "in a struggle" means: the leftovers of pre-moral interests that lead into temptation. The possibility of temptation and, further, of seduction is something that no human being can escape.

22.6 Freedom in Institutions: Ethics

Another partial alternative to the notion of morality [*Moralität*] and moral respect [*moralische Achtung*] is found in Hegel's catchword, "ethical life" [*Sittlichkeit*]. As with Schiller's notion of the beautiful soul, here we expect no program of straight opposition to Kant, but we do, however, expect a supplementation. Perhaps Hegel's reflection even contains a thought that is not foreign to Kant but one that only receives more weight.

Hegel develops the notion of ethics with his characteristic dialectic. It allows the arrival at an ever more substantial form of free will, a concept shared with Kant. In the process, the fundamental conflict between duty and inclination recedes into the background to the advantage of an increasing content, an ever-richer freedom of the will. The first level in the three-step dialectic is that of (abstract) right. It can be formulated by the command to treat oneself as a person and to recognize all others as persons. In the institutions of this first, objective level, that is, property, contract, and penal law, the will is only externally free. At the next, subjective level of morals, the will is merely internally free. The synthesis of the two features, better: the achievement of the unity between the external and internal freedom is accomplished only at the third level, that of ethical life. Its institutions—again a threefold—are the family, the economy, and the work world that are called "bourgeois society," and a concrete state.

A philosophy of moral freedom is not searching for a general comparison and contrast between Kant and Hegel. Instead, it recalls something that much of the polemic against Kant inspired by Hegel overlooks: when it comes to the question of the existence of moral freedom and the prior question, how one is to think about them, the debate is not con-

cerned with social freedom. Even when the development of moral freedom is made easier by certain institutions, this circumstance establishes
only the right to a complementary, not an alternative, theory. As it is,
Kant's systematic ethic, *The Metaphysics of Morals*, begins with an ethic
of rights that treats all three of the institutions in Hegel's ethic. The
family plays, admittedly, a systematically more significant, and the economic and work world a far greater, role for Hegel. In contrast, Kant's
theory of the state has a dimension of international law and world citi-
zenship that is put aside too quickly by Hegel.

Hegel (or more carefully formulated, a dominant Hegel interpretation) acknowledges the Kantian concept of morals, which understands
the individual to be free as a person capable of the legislation of a moral
law and of its recognition. However, this person is free only in an abstract manner: indeed rigorously, but in the first place empty of content;
second, disinterested in all consequences; third, condemned to impo-
tence with respect to the shaping of the social world; and fourth, the
abstract person tends toward a terror of pure disposition.

These accusations have in fact already been rebutted; therefore, all
that is required is a short recollection. The circumstance that the uni-
versalizing principle refers to maxims—that is, to substantial principles,
and for which a fundamental ethic is not responsible for determining
their content—speaks against the supposed content-emptiness of Kant's
moral person. Instead of normative deliberations, a universal principle
requires descriptive, in part anthropological, in part historical-cultural
experience to which an ethic of maxims is itself expressly open. The universalizability test undertakes "only" a moral selection and dignification.

The dual accusation of an idle inwardness, that of a supposed disinterestedness in consequences and of a consequent powerlessness to
shape the [social] world, is countered by the concept of the will itself: a
mere wish is satisfied with a mere positive feeling in favor of a state of
affairs; it undertakes nothing to preserve or to bring about the state of
affairs; it remains in this respect indifferent. In contrast, the will is necessarily engaged; it is manifest by the application of one's own powers
and means, which, in the case of the moral disposition, leads to a fundamental attitude that governs one's life. In no fashion is morals, as it
sometimes is caricatured, imprisoned in an internal world. It is manifest
in actions that as such intervene in the social and natural worlds and,
as a consequence, shape them. (Hegel's frequently quoted and often
misunderstood sentence in the preface to the *Philosophy of Right:* "What

is rational is real; and what is real is rational" appropriately applies far more in opposition to the Romantics than it does to Kant; for Hegel's own understanding of the sentence, see the *Encyclopedia*, section 6.) If necessary, a moral will opposes a situation of injustice and is not satisfied with mere verbal protest but works toward a transformation of the circumstances. The source from which the transformation is initiated and from which it draws its power, however, is the will that, in turn, acts on the basis of moral principles.

22.7 Metaphysically Free Metaphysical

Two concepts essential for an ethics of the will, the autonomy of the will and pure practical reason, stand under suspicion that is politically deadly for philosophy: they are supposed to be metaphysical. Today, one is accustomed to label notions "metaphysical" that because of their age are worthy of honor but because of their lack of convincing power are taken to be long outdated.

It would be wise, then, to avoid such incriminating concepts, even to avoid an ethics of the will. Against such wisdom, however, speaks the fact that the expression "metaphysics" is equivocal and that a fundamental ethics cannot avoid two of its meanings. A fundamental ethics undertakes such a thorough investigation of its object that it is in an intentional respect a fundamental philosophy. Its object has a metaphysical character because, as the absolute good, it transcends nature (*physis*) and, therefore, goes *beyond* (*meta*) what is at home in nature (see chapter 3.5).

As is well known, the history of metaphysics commences with a critique of metaphysics. Aristotle's collection of philosophical essays that employs the title "metaphysics" for the first time presupposes a critique of the prior and archetypal metaphysics (Plato's doctrine of ideas). Aristotle's alternative, his substance ontology, has for its part a metaphysical character, but it plays no significant role in his ethics. That which matters to a great extent for the historical model of the [Aristotelian] eudaimonistic ethics of teleological aspiration applies completely to the systematically developed theory of part 2 of this present study. Themes like being as being and the absolutely highest being, God, are entirely absent.

Teleology is, indeed, indispensable for an ethics of aspiration; however, not the often criticized teleology of nature, but a teleology of action. Nevertheless, an ethics of aspiration fulfills the condition that one can call the formal kernel of metaphysics. Taken with respect to the practical world, it is a theory of ultimate reasons, a theory not only with respect to the highest object, happiness [eudaimonia], but also with respect to the whole because all aspiration-theoretical praxis is ultimately held together and encompassed by happiness [eudaimonia]. In the formal and still today hardly obsolete sense of a fundamental philosophy of praxis, a thorough ethics of aspiration has the status of a practical metaphysics. This leads to the paradoxical situation that a eudaimonistic ethics is metaphysical in a metaphysically free sense. It renounces every theoretical and every other metaphysic foreign to its object. It investigates its object, humanity's orientation toward goals, so thoroughly, namely, all the way to that goal beyond which no other can be thought, so that one can speak of a metaphysical character. Its metaphysical portion quantitatively considered, however, is extremely meager. Its investigation is limited in this study to a part of chapter 6, above all, chapter 6.2. The reason lies in the ultimately practical interest that ethics is no end in itself. Because it ultimately serves action, it investigates its "metaphysical" object, eudaimonia, in such a multifaceted and realistic fashion that it discusses a host of other, no longer metaphysical, and also not quasi-metaphysical, objects, namely, the moral (character) virtues and intellectual virtues of wisdom.

It looks no different with the ethics of the will. If one reserves the notion "metaphysics" for its traditional forms, its definitive Kantian form is non-metaphysical because it overrides all prior metaphysics. Nevertheless, the literal meaning of "meta-physics," the transcending of (natural) experience, necessarily is preserved insofar as one reflects at least in part in a non-empirical manner about fundamental questions. This observation applies to other attempts at foundational thinking. Habermas's theory of communicative reason, for example, consists in the attempt at a non-empirical theory of understanding-oriented action. Such an attempt belongs to the second, practical side of the alternative between an empirical and a pre-empirical, hence metaphysical, theory. The same applies to the third part of the present study. Its fundamental concepts, will, duty, categorical imperative, and moral respect, and also legality, morals, and moral grace, belong to a fundamental philosophy, but one of a practical, not a theoretical nature.

Why should one speak of metaphysics at all? The primary reason lies in the essence of the object. Since morals are independent of sensuous appetites, they already transcend with their very concept the kind of nature that is decisive here (not theoretical but practical sensuousness). It is not a philosophical discipline, ethics, that is first and foremost metaphysical, but its object, morals. This peculiarity begins with that notion common to an ethics of aspiration and an ethics of willing: the absolute good. The difference between an ethics of eudaimonia and an ethics of autonomy is not about metaphysics, and the difference is not genuinely of an ethical but of an action-theoretical nature. In terms of the notion of aspiration, what counts is an *insurmountable goal*, precisely eudaimonia; in terms of the notion of willing, what counts is an *indisputable origin*, autonomy.

Despite the difference between eudaimonia and autonomy, both kinds of ethics are related to metaphysics in a similar manner. Namely, both are metaphysical in a metaphysically free fashion. On the one hand, they consist in a genuinely practical, fundamental philosophy that is to a great extent independent of a theoretical, fundamental philosophy. On the other hand, their fundamental notion, for the one, eudaimonia, for the other, autonomy, has a definitely non-empirical, and to that extent a metaphysical, character.

Today one prefers, admittedly, a simpler, antimetaphysical ethics. However, a fundamental and simultaneously presuppositionless reflection runs into a complicated situation. Whether one is concerned with a theoretical-aspiration ethics of happiness or a theoretical-willing ethics of freedom, both require such a radical grounding that they have a metaphysical character in two respects: intentionally in terms of fundamental philosophy and thematically in terms of a non-empirical foundation. However, for both, neither theoretical philosophy nor a theological element is essential, so that they are in terms of normal understanding metaphysics-free; as a whole, however, they consist in a metaphysically free metaphysics.

23 Morally Evil

A moral philosophy is incomplete that doesn't devote at least rudimentary attention to the antonym of morally good, evil. For centuries this was taken for granted because the fundamental concepts of morality and ethics appeared as twins, as good and evil. Of course, one could fear that evil is a religious or theological concept and, hence, necessarily foreign to secular thought. In fact, though, the concept occurs not only in the Christian Middle Ages but also in pre-Christian antiquity and in secular modernity. It is not the concept of evil but doubtless its personification in the devil that one can label as genuinely religious, but even that is not accurate. Just as a secular philosophy seeks to conceive of a completely good person as a personified idea, as an ideal, so also can it conceive of a completely evil person as its personified contrary idea, as an anti-ideal, even as the devil.

In modernity—one could still argue—the concept of evil was tied to a philosophical direction that proceeded out of presuppositions that in the meantime have become problematic, possibly even theological remnants. It is not merely a philosophical movement concerned with the concept of evil, that of German idealism from Kant through Fichte to Hegel and Schelling, that one occasionally reproaches as a theological remnant. It surfaces as well, even if modified, with Thomas Hobbes in his ethical naturalism. In order to counter the suspicion that evil is merely a metaphysical concept, one is permitted to remember that it finds its place, for example, in the epoch between Hobbes and German idealism, not only in Leibniz's metaphysics but also in Rousseau's essentially metaphysic-free thought. Even Nietzsche acknowledges the antithesis, even though he prefers the conceptual pair good and bad rather than good and evil.

In response to the charge that the concept is tied to Western thought, one can counter with the assessment of a classical Buddhist Sanskrit poet. According to Bhartrhari, there are four kinds of human beings (see Liebich 1905, 271): the best help even when their own happiness is threatened. The inferior help when it won't hurt them in any fashion. Whoever harms others in order to establish his own advantage is demonic. Finally, there are those who harm others without there being even a hint of advantage to themselves; Bhartrhari calls them the nameless. Should the mentioned harm occur intentionally as an end in itself, it comes at least close to what deserves the label evil.

Although one finds the concept in many cultures and epochs, moral philosophy for more than two generations has had difficulties with it. In such influential forms as the analytic ethics of R. M. Hare and the discourse ethics of Jürgen Habermas, the concept of evil surfaces either not at all or with such insignificance that one is not wrong to have missed it. When it comes to the highest form of humanly responsible wickedness, evil, the twentieth century was overabundant; it was "destitute," in contrast, when it came to philosophical reflection over it. Although there are a few important contributions, namely from Paul Ricoeur 1960/1986, the "insignia" of a larger philosophical debate are missing: clarification of the concept, presentation of theses and antitheses, proposal of a "theory" and skepticism over it, and finally, the attention of specific sciences and their competent public treatment. To this extent, philosophy has lost the theme of evil.

Does one no longer want to believe in the difficult phenomenon? Or does contemporary moral philosophy no longer need the notion because it can conceive of the good without its antonym, evil, and, as secular ethics, must perhaps even consider that evil is only a religious phenomenon that restricts it to only theological discussion? Doubts are raised not only by such an explicitly religion-free moral philosophy as Hobbes's which nevertheless knows what is more than merely bad, evil. Above all, there occurs in much cultural phenomena that which is recognized by strictly secular philosophy to be a certifiably sane sadism, which can hardly be conceived without the concept of evil. Just as intentional compliance emerges out of a morally good will, so also an intentional contradiction arises from a morally bad will that can be called evil. Street talk has a good reason to preserve the notion. Even when it seldom applies it in conscious accusation, it unequivocally calls an action, a perspective, or an individual in the strictest sense of the term evil and understands thereby an abysmal wickedness and damnability. Someone counts as bad, for example, who follows his own well-being at the cost of the deserved happiness of another. Someone counts as evil, in contrast, who in full awareness inflicts suffering on another for his own pleasure (i.e., the certifiably sane sadist).

A thorough investigation of evil requires, of course, its own study. The fact, however, that one at this point rarely even attempts such a study does not justify entirely ignoring the theme. (On the analysis of the notion, see McGinn 1997; on evil as an aesthetic category, see Bohrer 2004; for an initial look in the literature and at today's most significant theorists, see Höffe 1995a.)

23.1 On the Concept

Many authors maintain that evil is not precise enough to comprehend. The vocabulary for the description of what is bad and evil is, to be sure, inexhaustible. Furthermore, the phenomena themselves are too disparate. In addition, evil shuns unambiguousness in order to better be able to avoid detection and to accomplish its business of reversal of the good.

In order to identify something as something, for example, in ethics to call an action or even an individual evil, one requires a preliminary concept. It commences with the delimitation of a moral concept from any other kind of evil. The concept's possible range of application is broad since it can apply to what is bad, to suffering, to misconduct, to what is appalling, and to almost all kinds of things adverse, sick, and fatal on up to guilt, vices, and sins. Moral philosophy emphasizes its delimitation over and against a "physical" concept. One with whom "evil plays" is not a victim of malice [*Bosheit*], but of badness and suffering. "Physical evil," the badness that extends from normal everyday adversity and extends over evil blows of fate up to the mortality of each person, applies to an unpleasantness independent of its origin. Evil in the moral sense, in contrast, applies to a responsible individual. Imputability and clear intent, then, are necessary, but they are not sufficient, conditions for a moral concept. Someone like Neiman (2002/2004, 267–68 in the German edition), who wants to eliminate such essential differences, is confronted with an implausible alternative: either nature is moralized, namely, has responsibility attributed to it, or the world of responsibility is naturalized, in which one equates evil with natural evil. Either alternative is devastating for morality.

Even in sociobiology, which involves the combining of behavioral research with evolutionary theory, one speaks of evil. One of the most prominent behavioral researchers, Konrad Lorenz 1974, takes evil to be an internal kind of aggression: the members of the same biological species fight with one another. He interprets this aggression as an instinct and assigns to it a positive meaning because it serves the preservation of life and of the species. In this case, evil is not attributed merely to persons, and not even additionally to our relatives, the primates. Countless other species, even those of the most simple kind as viewed evolutionarily, can be evil. However, does it make sense to call insects evil? Cautiously, Lorenz limits the concept to a "so-called evil" and acknowledges thereby that he's employing an aberrant concept. The widespread aggression found in nature counts as evil because it is destructive and life-annihilating. Because or to the extent that evil in this sense serves life, either in part for the survival of the individual or in part for collective survival, it deserves the mitigating etiquette "so-called." (See the newer sociobiological theory in Watson 1996.)

The moral philosopher weakens the concept of this "so-called" evil even more: an animal that uses force to drive off his sexual competitor or the wasp that stings are by no means evil in the strictly moral sense. According to recent primate research, it appears that the most basic level of evilness is foreign to humanity's closest relatives: confronted with the choice with respect to food that is unreachable either to assist a member of the same species in reaching it or to hinder it "in evil intent," chimpanzees behave with remarkable indifference. Half did absolutely nothing, and the other half divided equally into those who helped and those who hindered (Jensen, Hare, Call, and Tomasello 2006). In contrast, a human being is evil who harms another "diligently" (that is, who harms consciously and freely, and in addition, often with no inhibitory resistance). In marginal circumstances the notion sounds, admittedly, too pathetic; in grave circumstances, in contrast, it is not.

There are three levels to distinguish with respect to the negative side of free agency as there are with respect to the positive side: when something is bad in the technical and in the pragmatic sense, one calls it foolhardy. Evil has its place only with the third level, that of the moral sense of badness.

Skepticism with respect to the concept occurs not infrequently from a concern that evil will be trivialized. The concern may be justified when it comes to that determination of evil in the sense of deficiency that is frequently found in the philosophical tradition. In this sense, evil is related to the good as pure darkness is related to light; just as pure darkness consists in the absolute absence of light, so, too, evil consists in the absolute deficiency of the good. The conceptual presupposition of evil, free agency, speaks against this determination and introduces a by no means trivial concept. This concept constitutes, after that of free agency, a second conceptual element, that of the negation of the morally good, which beyond mere deficiency consists in the very reversal of the good, a perversion. However, even with these two conceptual elements, evil is by no means technically identified. Someone who as a free agent acts contrary to what is morally proper acts morally improperly but is not necessarily evil.

As in the case of compliance with the moral law, so also in its contradiction there are obviously two fundamental levels: one can either act in simple opposition to the moral law or consciously act contrary to it. Inversely to the escalation of moral legality to morality, the negative side begins with the basic level of simple immorality, mere lawlessness or what is contrary to legality. This can certainly be thought of as an ethics of aspiration in any number of ways, as Aristotle exemplarily documented (for a discussion of the specific concepts, see the articles "Akrasia" and "Kakia" in Höffe 2005): in steps to an escalated immorality, moral misconduct begins according to Aristotle with weakness (*malakia*) and extends over weakness of the will (*akrasia*) and self-indulgence (*akolasia*) up to wickedness or vice (*kakia*). On top of that, Aristotle speaks further of an animal brutality (*thêriotês*). In this latter case, the good is not intentionally vetoed, but, rather, is not even present.

Whoever acts irresolutely, uncontrolled, or even burdensomely indeed does a wrong thoroughly voluntarily. However, what is then missing is the intention of the second level on the part of someone who says: I know what is (morally) right; I am also capable of doing what is right; however, I don't want to; in contrast, I want nothing else than to act differently, that is, to act morally bad. As a consequence, within an ethics of teleological aspiration one can, indeed, conceive of the basic level of evil, opposition to a moral law, but hardly of evil in the complete sense of an intentional opposition to the morally good.

Both elements (the aspiration concept of acting and the principle of eudaimonia) raise difficulties. According to the concept of aspiration, every action reaches out for some good that stands within the horizon of fulfillment of all good, eudaimonia. Someone weak-willed or burdensome who acts badly remains someone, therefore, who desires a good, admittedly only a supposed good, but not something bad as such. Viewed objectively, he contradicts, to be sure, the ultimate goal, eudaimonia. However, he doesn't act in intentional opposition but under a special kind of illusion. He pursues only a supposed, not a true, happiness. Nevertheless, here there is no total rebellion against the morally good as understood in the aspiration-theoretical sense; it is simply that the characteristic intention of the second level is absent.

Revealingly, in a recapitulating passage, Aristotle provides as examples of bad action, indeed, avarice, ambition, and irascibility, even cruelty, not that which is the peculiar moment of evil, an unprovoked, sadistic cruelty, but cruelty out of revenge (*Rhetoric* 1.10.1368b 12–24). Even neo-Aristotelians like Anscombe 1981 and Foot 2002 speak about moral failure, namely vices, but not about evil. Because the escalation from simple immorality, mere contra-legality, to complete maliciousness in the sense of conscious and free opposition to the morally good is bound to intention at the second level, the escalated moral "contra" of contra-legality has a place only in an ethic of the will.

There are still differences of degree within actions of simple opposition to the moral. When it comes to a relatively insignificant moral offense, one doesn't speak of "evil" but of "injustice" or of the "(morally) bad"; however, one speaks of "evil" only when it comes to an especially glaring, cruel offense. This escalation within the fundamental level of the "objectively" immoral is strictly distinguished from the escalation of the second level, the immoral from the side of the subject. At this level, one is concerned with increasingly grievous acts that are perpetrated not only consciously but are even desired as such. One makes violation of the moral explicitly the goal, whereby the contrary of the morally good will is clearly present as the evil will, including an evil disposition, immorality in the strictest sense of anti-morality.

Perfect moral goodness consists in an unsurpassable positivity, a respect for the moral law that influences action; perfect evil, in contrast, consists in an unsurpassably escalated negativity. In the latter, one doesn't merely accept violation of the moral law but intends it. Such contempt for the moral does not merely cloud one's sense of the morally good. More transpires than the escalation from cloudiness to blindness with respect to the good. Here one knows what is morally good and acts, nevertheless, in opposition to it.

Opposition can be directed not only against specific actions, against moral violations, but also against the principles (maxims) on the basis of which one has done those actions. In terms of "particular evil" one is concerned only with a concrete action, hence, one is temporarily evil; with actions "as a rule" or "fundamentally evil" actions, willing evil is a basic disposition that has become a (moral) vice or an escalation of maliciousness to sinisterness. Not only this or that action but the individual himself is evil: the person concerned has a profoundly evil character.

The sinisterness of a person can be understood as a third and highest level of moral corruption. At the first level of moral weakness of the will or moral infirmity, one knows what is morally expected. One has a certain inclination to fulfill the expectation, but the inclination is not strong enough to withstand contrary inclinations: one acts contrary to one's better self in that one succumbs to temptations. At the second level, that of moral disingenuousness, one mixes good and bad maxims so that even in those circumstances where one acts morally, it all too often occurs on the basis of immoral motives: one is ready for moral action only to the extent that it serves one's long-term self-interest, that is, one's clear personal well-being.

Only when one has reached the third level, that of sinisterness, does one explicitly reject the moral; one acts consciously on the basis of morally reprehensible maxims. One does evil for the sake of evil; one has—at least, so it appears—a demonic will. (On recent discussions about the demonic will, see Ehni 2006, 231–41.) Even then, however, not every action needs to be immoral. Even when compatible with the moral, such an action can occur out of the accidental course of the world and not out of any transient recognition of morality. The sinisterness of complete evil can be limited to certain aspects of an individual's life, or it can extend to one's entire life orientation.

We can make a classificatory intermediate tally: leaving aside the lowest level, there are two fundamental classes of moral evaluation, each with two levels, which, together with the possibility of moral indifference, gives us altogether five main levels. The two fundamental classes of moral good and evil qualify not only actions (legality) but also the fundamental orientation or disposition (morality). Without determination of any specific content, these are mere concepts of orientation for moral or immoral contents. "Good" is what one does (legality) and should want (morality); "evil" is what one should not do (contra-legality) and not want (contra-morality).

What are the five main levels of moral evaluation? Proceeding from the positive to the negative, we begin with (1) morality. Here the moral command is not only satisfied, but also is adhered to exclusively because it is the morally right thing to do. It is followed (2) by (moral) legality: a consenting to what is moral on whatever grounds. (3) Moral indifference is where no moral obligation is solicited; the question of whether or not there is a moral obligation is ignored. (4) With moral illegality or the "objectively" evil or malicious action, the moral is intentionally rejected. (5) With immorality in the strict sense of anti-morality, which is the highest level of the immoral or maliciousness, the contradiction of the moral occurs on the basis of a fundamental defiant contempt for the moral that is extended to a life maxim.

23.2 On the Reality of Evil

Semantics alone is incapable of rehabilitating the concept of evil. It can establish differences; especially, it separates the bad in the physical sense, that is, evil experiences and suffering, from what is bad as a consequence of human responsibility. Within this framework, as was the case with the good, it distinguishes three levels, but now in the sense of a negative valuation: the level of the technical, that of the pragmatic, and the highest, moral level of bad that, given the case of an intentional rejection of morals, is called evil in the moral sense.

These differences, however, leave open the question of whether or not there is a corresponding reality to each level. With respect to the basic level of evil, the existence question is easily answered. Everyday experience is entirely familiar with glaring violations of the moral. At the second, primary level, however, methodological difficulties emerge. With escalated morality, everything depends upon the ultimate intention of the agent. This can be discerned by means of its "manifestation," as it were, in the world in the action itself. However, the intention remains something internal that allows no certainty when it comes to trying to establish what it really is. The same occurs when it comes to escalated immorality, sinisterness.

Whether or not one wants as such to act contrary to the moral can, indeed, be established by what is done; however, one can never establish for certain whether the violation was intended. To be sure, one can name principles for action, that is, maxims, and attribute them to concrete persons. Someone is evil who, for example, lives by means of deceit, shiftiness, and guile, who causes suffering and destruction that is especially obvious, such as plaguing a child, torturing people, or committing premeditated murder in a cruel fashion, and experiences pleasure in all such actions. In the face of such "free sadism" and unmitigated cruelty, one can judge the perpetrator to be evil. Another example is the most abominable form of lying and deception: one presents oneself as a friend and then seeks to cause harm to one's "friend"—once again, with the qualification that one takes pleasure in the deceptive game.

A phenomenology of evil reveals different forms—at least the following three: especially spectacular is the affective, "hot" evil, or the "senseless" cruelty of a stormy and nondeliberate force that occurs as a rampage or massacre. Either as an individual or group, the agent experiences a blood frenzy that can exceed all normal limits. The contrast to such "hot" evil is calculated, "cold" evil, for example, completely conscious and deliberate torture, which is fueled by the victim's fear and takes pleasure in the victim's suffering. In place of an unrestrained outrage, one has a well-planned and escalating dosage of intentional agony. A third form was named by Hannah Arendt 1963 as banal evil: the cruelties of so-called armchair strategists who, admittedly, know what they do, but who, absent an empathy-inspired imagination, have no grasp of what they are causing.

In Dostoevsky's novel *The Raw Youth* [*Der Jungling*] (1970, 68–69), we are told about a sixteen-year-old "who, as soon as he reached maturity and receives his inheritance, wants to realize as the greatest pleasure, the feeding of dogs with bread and meat as poor children die of starvation; and, while they have nothing with which to fire their furnaces, he wants to purchase an entire lumber yard, construct a huge pile of wood in an open field, and burn the wood without giving the poor a splinter." Whoever turns mockingly against morality, if not only by magniloquent words but also in actual life, must be called evil.

For centuries, from ancient Rome down to Leibniz, the Roman Caesars, Nero and Caligula, were portrayed as the models of evil. Other examples are taken from the horrible civil wars of early modernity and the "colonization" of North and South America. However, evil has not been limited to the West. In his novel *The Brothers Karamazov*, Dostoevsky describes the barbaric crimes perpetrated by the Turks in Bulgaria. They are supposed to have tossed babies into the air and impaled them on their bayonets, and what counted "as best" was to do so in the presence of the babies' mothers. The histories of China and Japan are, also, not free of possibly perfect barbarism.

The twentieth century escalated barbarism to the colossal, especially with respect to politically responsible barbarism. The millionfold murders by Hitler, Stalin, and Mao Zedong as well as the string-pullers responsible for much genocide have by no means faded from memory. The great and small tyrants, warlords, and the agents of innumerable terror attacks perpetuate a spirited, glaring contradiction to any non-controversial, interculturally acknowledged morality. Because the contradiction all too often occurred intentionally and in the largest of style, evil remains ever present in public life. To be sure, no one would dare to wager that it has significantly receded in personal lives.

Not infrequently, one draws the conclusion from the enduring presence of evil that one should doubt the strength of reason. One is familiar with this kind of doubt in the form of a defeatist cultural critique; astonishingly, it is expressed even by an academic philosopher: "What sense does it make to appeal to reason in the face of evil that defies all reason?" (Neiman 2004, 12). This all too global question, of course, is rhetorical. It should evoke a negative conclusion, but it is asked without undertaking the effort to differentiate the concept of reason, that is, to distinguish between practical and theoretical reason and within practical reason to set aside the technical from the pragmatic, to retain only moral reason, and finally, within moral reason to distinguish between legal and virtue reason. For the last two forms of reason, there are adequate criteria not only for the present project's position but also for Neiman's own Enlightenment philosophy.

That an organizer of massive public crimes, for example, Adolf Eichmann, who was responsible for the deportation of countless Jews, was no sadistic monster, unlike the expectations of many; that he was, rather, as Hannah Arendt describes, supposedly an exemplary father, a lover of animals, duty-conscious, and always civil, may not be unimportant for understanding his personality and may justify Arendt's concept of the "banality of evil." However, the decisive question for legal morality is concerned with two other things. First: did the individual violate a clear legal, moral command, in this case the command not to kill, without being able to invoke the excuse of personal self-defense or a war situation? Second: did the individual responsible for the violation act not simply as an agent, but as a free agent without the excuse of having acted under coercion, for example, out of fear for his own life? Should the answer in both cases turn out to be affirmative, one is clearly concerned with a moral illegality, that is, an "objective" evil.

How do things look from the subjective side? If the moral violation occurs again and again, over many years, and on a large scale, one can hardly speak merely of a moral weakness of the will, that is, of the weakest level of personal maliciousness. When it comes to repeated and eager perpetration of the violation, it appears, as well, that the second level, that of moral disingenuousness, is still too little, so that the accusation of the third level is not far off. Perhaps the agent was only a compliant perpetrator, but then, in any event, he was such "out of a self-imposed immaturity."

A fundamental ethic doesn't judge the individual person. It is concerned, rather, with the global question evoked by doubt about reason itself: moral reason can acquire a considerable validity by means of appropriate practice within legal systems both in persons and institutional practice. It preserves its *should* character, but this doesn't eliminate the moral violation that is as extreme as it is glaring, namely evil. In this respect, the oft-repeated question of whether or not we live in the best of all possible worlds can be set aside. In the world that we experience and know, which includes beings capable of acting on the basis of moral principles but not being forced out of necessity to do so, one can be expected to act morally, and one can even expect extraordinary examples of the same. Nevertheless, one can never eliminate the possibility of backsliding into barbarism.

23.3 Abolishing the Concept of Evil?

To the semantic preliminary question of how evil is to be understood conceptually, we added the further question of whether or not the very phenomenon of moral evil really occurs. Because the theme of evil is—almost—forgotten, there arises a third formulation in which, perhaps, one encounters the ultimate question with respect to moral philosophy: Would it be right to give up on the very idea of evil; isn't that ethics more compatible with humanity, even more humane, which renounces all (immoderately?) exaggerated fashions of condemnation? Or does an ethic not thereby mask, in the face of anxiety over an uncompromisingly hard-line condemnation, an important experience without which it cannot be true to its object, praxis in view of the highest possible level of evaluation? The reason for the masking might lie in a lack of that evaluative courage which conceives humanity's responsibility in all clarity and as a result acknowledges as not only conceivable but often enough also as real a highest standard of the bad (the immoral and the amoral) in addition to the highest standard of the good (the moral). Doesn't evil belong to the "drama of human freedom," so that inattention to it would amount not only to a moral-philosophical but also to an anthropological deficit? In short: what is gained by acknowledgment of the phenomenon of evil; what is lost by its denial?

A denial can occur in two ways: either one questions the very existence of evil, or one acknowledges its existence but sees no connection between it and human nature. If our sketch of indicators for the existential reality of evil is in any sense convincing, the first option involves at least a partial blindness, if not a too optimistic view of the world. For someone who is a victim of "unprovoked cruelty," this blindness appears to be cynical. The second option hardly touches the self-understanding of humanity. Should it be that humanity is by nature good, the responsibility for an "unprovoked cruelty" would be someone else: one's parents, teachers, one's milieu, or society at large. Even the most extremely immoral acts would be excusable.

The following dual strategy is more convincing: when it comes to the concrete question of whether or not a particular individual is evil, one draws, first, a positive conclusion only after careful reflection. Rather than succumb to the tendency to categorically play down all objectionable actions because one attributes their differences to a homogeneous concept of misbehavior, one acknowledges, second, qualitative differences. In particular one recognizes two escalations: with respect to the action itself, one discerns an escalation from simple through more grave up to extremely reprehensible misbehavior; and with respect to the motivations for the action, one discerns an escalation from negligent through willful up to premeditated and purposive misbehavior.

A further argument: someone who rejects the notion of evil silently supports the danger of a personal self-overestimation, or arrogance. Further, someone who believes that evil can be eliminated once and for all must answer to the charge (evoking Kant) of unbridled enthusiasm (*Schwärmerei*). Perhaps such a belief arises where one classifies evil simply as an "unresolved inhumanity" and, thereby, suggests that evil could be resolved at some point in the future. In contrast to these expectations, or if only out of hope, there is the possibility that lies in the very concept of freedom: that one acknowledges moral commands and, nonetheless, acts contrary to them. A person can, indeed, attribute moral action to a character trait, virtue. However, one will never achieve saintliness in any ontological sense, that is, one will never become an incorruptible person.

Human beings conscious of their natural propensity to evil, however, take into consideration the possibility that the propensity can flare up. Hence, they take precautions against it. For this reason, the initial merely moral-philosophical discourse about evil is expanded not only to a pedagogical but also to a legal-political discourse. Furthermore, the second dimension, the legal-political, involves both a domestic as well as an international discussion.

24 Autonomous Morality and the Art of Living

24.1 An Antithesis?

Theories of the art of living and autonomous morality are often taken to be antithetical in which case, surprisingly, both sides believe that each is superior to the other. A theory of the art of living asks what can be better than a good life; whereupon autonomous morality answers that it alone can determine what a good life is. Within this antithesis, one can distinguish two opinions; and, further, given these opinions, there are two possibilities for their reconciliation so that, in the end, four positions are conceivable.

1. In the strongest opposition thesis, the contradiction thesis, one maintains that the art of living and morality constitute an irreconcilable, absolute conflict because they are already fundamentally different conceptually, and thus in their guiding principles (happiness in the former; autonomy in the latter). This dual heterogeneity, not only conceptually but also in principle, is clearly manifest in concrete actions. Politically, happiness and morality are hostile to one another. It is one thing to seek one's well-being, which approves of immoral means; it is something else entirely to be moral, which forbids these means. The antithesis is insuperable: whoever wants to pursue a happy life must accept a strong dose of immorality, and whoever rejects the dosage cannot achieve happiness.

2. According to the weaker opposition thesis, the thesis of a dissonance that is capable of consonance, a successful life and morality fall apart not only with respect to their concept but also according to their principles. A dual heterogeneity is maintained; however, its consequences for, or application to, concrete life can be minimal. Because, for example,

an advantage acquired by immoral means can prove itself to be damaging over the long term, it appears that the conflict between happiness and morality is more of a moral-theoretical than it is of a moral-practical nature. In actual life there is no irreconcilable hostility but, rather, a limited competition, above all, with the possibility of coexistence.

3. According to the modest compatibility thesis, the thesis of an overlapping between happiness and morality, the art of living and morality can already intersect with respect to their concepts and principles, and in actual life this is frequently the case.

4. The more ambitious convergence thesis maintains, finally, that there is not merely a broad agreement but even an internal unity to our dialectic. To the extent that one properly understands each side, the art of living and morality collapse into one another: there is no art of living without morality and no morality without an art of living.

Which of these theses is correct does not depend merely upon concepts and principles but also upon an open and sober examination of life's realities. There can be no decision made with respect to the four theses independent of concepts, principles, and life experience. According to the concepts of our study, the art of living lies in the good life as the sense of well-being that, admittedly, includes a jolting dosage of interest in the well-being of others as well. One who discounts sympathy for others encounters resistance from them in one's pursuit of one's own well-being. More importantly, though, are those indispensable ingredients for the art of living like friendship, love, and respect for the interests of others that belong to reciprocal well-being. An examined self-interest does not pursue merely one's own interest, and the virtuous person won't always be, but indeed will mostly be, happy (see chapter 12.1).

Even where the art of living and morality are to a great degree in agreement, though, there remains an essential difference. Already the elementary level of autonomous morality, legality, demands the satisfaction of morality even in those cases where it contradicts a carefully considered self-interest. As is demonstrated by the antithesis between duty and appetites, there are conflict situations in which the contradiction thesis applies: either morality but with curtailment of one's own well-being, or one's own well-being at the price of morality (see chapter 22.4). The optimal level of morality even demands that what is moral consistently be recognized in itself from the beginning without concern for one's personal well-being.

Nevertheless, it remains possible to reconcile the art of living and autonomous morality. One can affirm the judgment by a theoretician of the art of living that there is nothing better than a good life—under the assumption that two things are accepted. First, one takes into consideration the polyvalence of the concept of the good that distinguishes among a technical, pragmatic, and a more than pragmatic, a truly moral sense of the good life. Second, one calls only that life good without qualification or restriction, hence, an absolutely good life as that which satisfies the highest, moral meaning of "good." As soon as one not only acknowledges this level but also accepts it as governing, the tension between the art of living and morality is eliminated. In accordance with thesis 4, that more ambitious thesis of convergence not as a mere "for the most part" but as a complete agreement, the contradiction between the art of living and morality turns out to be only apparent: at that point where one thinks the art of living through to the end, it is transformed into a theory of moral life.

This proposed solution is not wrong, but it overlooks a distinction in the concept of eudaimonia. An aspirational, theoretical superlative of the good splits itself into two meanings that in life can blend into one another, but not always or completely: eudaimonia is not only the highest, dominant, but also the most complete, inclusive, and integrative good. Only the first of these two notions of the good fulfills the moral life; the second does so only, at best, through happy circumstance. As a consequence, a morally good life is no sufficient condition for a totally good life, whereby the thesis of a not merely extensive but complete agreement between the art of living and morality, thesis 4, is invalid. The morally good life is, however, a necessary condition for the art of living because the second, inclusive concept of eudaimonia includes the first, more dominant concept: without a highest good, there is no absolute good so that the morally good life is indispensable for a good life as a whole. This brings us to the following preliminary conclusion.

Between the art of living and the moral there is no contradiction, not even an internal tension, so that both opposition theses, that of a pure and that of a limited discord, are wrong. Hence, theses 1 and 2 are excluded. Rather, one has a considerable overlapping so that at least thesis 3, the more modest compatibility thesis, is accurate. However, because the morally good life is only a necessary and not a sufficient condition for a good life as a whole, no more than modest compatibility is correct. Hence, thesis 4 is eliminated and only thesis 3 remains: between the moral and the art of living there is a far-reaching but no complete compatibility.

When it comes to their incompatibility, however, the moral takes precedence, but not so exclusively that it eliminates all rights to the art of living. To the extent, namely, that the moral can be implemented only at the expense of the art of living, there remains a deficit, that is, an incapacity. Only where the moral and happiness are in harmony does human life find its full and complete valuation. As a consequence, a philosophical ethics is not satisfied with a philosophy of morals. It recognizes happiness as an independent, admittedly subordinate principle. Whoever doesn't believe in an afterlife has only a single, this-sided life. In a this-sided life, he is concerned with both, with a moral integrity and a happy success, and he hopes, similarly, to achieve both. He who believes in an afterlife can, certainly, be more serene.

Contrary to first impressions, one can more likely satisfy an autonomous morality than the principle of happiness. Even a highly developed art of living, namely, cannot guarantee a full and complete happiness. Since the art of living is not in control of the flow of life, it cannot prevent either natural or social disappointments even when it is capable of protecting us against some power of others.

The morally good life is concerned with this capacity only as an aside within the framework of an indirect duty to fulfill one's personal happiness. This duty is established by the following: the individual knows that he is subject to moral temptation and is never certain that he can withstand the temptations. As a consequence and so far as it is within his power, he has the duty to prevent the very occurrence of temptation. However, situations involve a potential for moral temptation because of pain and suffering, failure and humiliation, and further, because of emergencies and many negative surprises. By contrast, factors like health and material advantage, a successful career, honor in the eyes of others, and a full social life can reduce the potential of temptation so that concern for them can assume a moral status. However, they are no end in themselves; above all, they cannot justify the application of any immoral means. Pursuit of them within the framework of the morally acceptable is not merely morally permitted but also indirectly commanded.

When it comes to the art of living, however, the situation is different. For it, the just-named factors constitute essential elements. They are not merely indirectly but directly commanded, so that here in the case of the art of living the aspirations extend beyond those of the moral. For its part, morality can assume elements of the art of living like the virtue of imperturbability and even strengthen them: with awareness that the good life ultimately depends upon moral self-respect, sub-moral incidents lose something of their power to threaten happiness.

24.2 Prudence, Benevolence, Inner Freedom

Before entirely leaving behind the two contradictory theses, thesis 1 and thesis 2, the question needs to be addressed of whether or not the opposition between the art of living and morals doesn't surface at another point. We will handle the question indirectly by examining, namely, whether or not typical building blocks of the eudaimonic art of living are recognized by autonomous morality, albeit, also transformed. We will be satisfied with three examples of eudaimonic character virtues: with the more self-concerned prudence, with the usually other-oriented benevolence, and with a comprehensive serenity, inner freedom.

The first example (eudaimonic prudence) contradicts the natural inclination to succumb to spontaneous feelings of pleasure and displeasure and to allow oneself in the final instance to be driven by emotion and passion. To that end, a dual (i.e., a negative and a positive) effort is necessary. The primarily negative side, that one must free one's spontaneous feelings of pleasure and displeasure from the danger of one-sidedly running riot, can by all means be called apathy or passionlessness. What is meant here is a *moral* countenance and not an emotional numbness. On the positive side, prudence is able so to coordinate the fragmented tugging of the appetites that a long-term successful and an enduringly good life is highly likely.

The art of living devoted to autonomous morality demands both the negative and the positive efforts of prudence. It also encourages curtailing the power of one's feelings of pleasure and displeasure without suppressing or supplanting them. As the conflict between duty and the appetites comes to a head, everything depends "only" on depriving pleasure-displeasure feelings of the right to the final decision, of turning the decision over to the right of (moral) duty, and the implementation of the decision by means of a cheerful disposition. Someone is prudent in the context of autonomous morality who doesn't simply suppress his appetites but reshapes them according to the standard of duty in order, finally, to exercise control over his morally trained appetites. An autonomous and completely prudent individual conducts his life with the moral grace of a beautiful soul.

The second example: within a eudaimonic art of living according to one of its primary proponents, Aristotle, benevolence consists in a good will (*eunoia*) that inclines toward even an unknown person's welfare without any opposition or other advantage. Because here the transition from wishing to doing is absent, it remains only a friendly attitude and affection, that is, an inclination toward well-being. The usual translation simply as "well-being" is, in contrast, misleading because to well-being belongs the notion of actively doing something within the parameters of one's own possibilities. The escalation that leads from wish to act belongs to friendship. As a gift without any gift in return, the Aristotelian inclination toward well-being appears—astonishingly for the principle of aspiring happiness—to extend into the dimension of the meritorious more. However, the accomplishment of more, this gift without a gift in return, is not strongly emphasized. Furthermore, it remains to that extent a particular virtue since one applies it, not exclusively but primarily, toward others whom one personally likes. The concept that one likes all humanity (that is, a general philanthropy) is foreign to Aristotle. It is enough to say with respect to the eudaimonistic inclination to well-being: whoever lives entirely without it, the curmudgeon, loses opportunities for a happy life (that is, he harms himself), whereas the one inclined toward the well-being of others enhances his chances for happiness.

The Christian command to love one's neighbor offers the possibility of deepening this intention of well-being toward others as well as extending it to all persons and, to that extent, to stretch it to a universal virtue. However, it is found only rudimentarily in the thought of the (Christian) Middle Ages. Only with an ethic of feeling grounded in sympathy does this inclination toward well-being become explicitly universal; in addition, it becomes here a virtue with effective power as an intention of well-being toward all rational beings. In addition, it gets disconnected from any religious background. For example, by assuming a concordance between self-love and a universal inclination toward the well-being for others, Hutcheson (*An Inquiry into the Original of Our Ideas of Beauty and Virtue*, 1:8) annuls any opposition between a eudaimonistic art of living and strict morality. As much as one might want this concordance, experience raises an objection. It doesn't doubt a frequent concordance, but it does doubt, to be sure, an invariable concordance. For example, the fraudulent administrator of a deposit can increase his wealth through morally impermissible but pragmatically certain means (see chapter 21.2). His own well-being demands a fraud that morality forbids.

A strictly moral ethic grounded in experience counts well-being as a duty owed by all persons toward one another. In order to satisfy the principle of justice with respect to equality, a strictly moral ethic extends this duty to one's own person: One is permitted and one should want and act to achieve even one's own well-being. However, this reflexive well-being directed toward the self is permitted only as long as one wants the well-being of all others as well.

In the case of a morally shaped art of living, the eudaimonic inclination toward well-being is escalated to a universal desire for well-being and, finally, in contrast to a self-negating altruism, includes one's own person. As distinct from optimism with respect to a natural compatibility between self-love and love for others, a moral art of living sees, however, that the compatibility does not always occur and therefore must frequently be sought. To that end, it establishes a criterion, that of the universalizable maxim: include in the circle of persons whose well-being you seek not only yourself but also all other persons.

The third example already finds its justification in a eudaimonistic art of living and preserves its place in an autonomous morality as well: inner freedom begins, for example, with the capacity neither to disdain widely held life goals such as subjective well-being, success in one's career, a high standard of living, or honor, nor to hold them as determinative for one's happiness. It proceeds onward out of the capacity to remain open to new experiences. Instead of deciding too quickly and too narrowly, it remains ready to always attempt something new. A host of other abilities play, in addition, a role: the capacity for a solitude that is not to be understood as loneliness; a capacity not to allow oneself to be consumed either by anxiety or cares; a capacity for an appropriate grief over a loss (for example, of a partner or child) without succumbing to depression; a capacity to see and enjoy the beauty of life; a capacity to take advantage of what happens to one; and especially, a capacity not to hold a grudge or to allow it to grow into hate. Properly, Nietzsche spoke of a power of forgetfulness, although supplemented by the contrary power, one's ability to be open to the future (*On the Genealogy of Morals*, 2.1).

Someone is inwardly free who is able to act naturally and to recover from an eventual lost naturalness; generally, someone who leads a relaxed life, free from unnecessary cares, and is even cheerful. The payment for all of these capacities: one does not succumb to the resigned life maxims of a brooding Karl Valentin: "I am happy that things are as they are because were I not happy, they would still be so." Inasmuch as one is able to engage creatively with the natural, social, and one's own "inner" world, one discovers and develops a maneuvering space for satisfying activities, and one fills this space in a powerful and rich manner.

Autonomous morality does not deny these eudaimonistic capacities their accolades. Within the framework of the duty to develop one's talents and with the addition of a further, if only indirect, duty to advance one's own well-being, it maintains that such recognition is even desirable. The moral perspective carries out a selection and evaluation while granting only a pre-moral rank to the role of cleverness; in fact, at the noble rank of morality this role is not extolled. The truly moral aspect remains, in contrast, simply indirectly commanded, and when it comes to a circumstance of conflict, it defers to the priority of direct duties.

24.3 Moral Education

Among the missing themes for many moral philosophers is that of moral education. This deficit is astonishing because already two paradigmatic Western moral philosophies, Aristotle's *Nicomachean Ethics* and Kant's *Critique of Practical Reason,* engage the topic. In the case of Aristotle, it occurs by the oft-repeated reference to continuous practice; for example, one becomes prudent by acting prudently and just by doing just actions. For his part, Kant devotes one of a total of three parts of his second critique to moral development. After the "Doctrine of the Elements of Pure Practical Reason" comes the "Analytic of Pure Practical Reason," which discusses not only how one philosophizes about morals but how one develops morally. In Kant's more systematic ethics, the "Doctrine of Virtue" [part 2 of *The Metaphysics of Morals*], the situation is no different: after "I. Doctrine of the Elements of Ethics" comes "II. Doctrine of the Methods of Ethics." The second parts in both texts are, admittedly, far shorter than the first parts. Thereby, philosophy here partially indicates that it only invokes a few fundamental thoughts. They are concerned, however, with both sides: with theoretical practice, dialectic, and its practical counterpart, ascetics (whereby "ascetic" is understood in the literal sense of a practice and not as mere self-denial).

More broadly understood, morals include not only the eudaimonistic art of living but also the generalizable maxims of morality. However, humanity does not enter the world already in possession of these respective proficiencies at birth, nor does it spontaneously develop them as with its biological growth. In the case of the individual person, this extremely dependent being, who enters the world with a thoroughly undeveloped brain, requires, in addition, a decisive moral development that occurs essentially after birth.

Much that is learned after birth commences with examples and emulation. Later, systematic learning processes are added that one can encourage by means of models from history and through literary narratives, so long as one doesn't employ "romantically" exorbitant or impossible paradigms. Much of what is to be learned, for example, walking and talking, is crucial for life and is learned by practically everyone. Other things, for example, the learning of a musical instrument, a foreign language, or mathematics and philosophical reflection, broaden one's opportunities in life and as a human being. Both the development of the art of living and of one's moral autonomy belong by definition to what is rather important for life; everyone is an addressee.

Whether intentional or in the course of things—because of deeply influential childhood impressions, moral development begins quite early. In this respect, one of the most influential texts of "philosophical" pedagogy, Rousseau's *Émile,* requires correction. According to this text, which is a mixture of treatise and novel, moral development begins only in the years from fifteen to twenty. Even if the relative completion, the development of a free respect for morals, occurs at this time, one can acquire the guiding theme "from self-love to love of neighbor" much earlier than Rousseau suggests. Strong impressions should be acquired earlier. Incidentally, Kant is right: "Even children are capable of discerning even the slightest taint of admixture of spurious incentives: for in their eyes the action then immediately loses all moral worth" (*Religion,* 6:48).

We have already addressed the question of how one learns to lead a successful life (see chapter 9.2). However, how does one learn autonomous morality? Much that applies to the development of the art of living remains valid for the development of autonomous morality; once again, one should not exaggerate their differences. What remains valid for both is the following: nothing depends upon either a socially, gender-, or culturally specific, but rather upon a generally human upbringing. Ultimately, it is not individual actions but one's fundamentally established character that matters. Because character constitutes a unity, one shouldn't fight against particular weaknesses but against their common root. One accomplishes more with praise and blame than with punishment. One achieves the benefits of encouragement best in the presence of others, but to avoid ridicule, one should engage in blame in private. One needs the capacity for temporary renunciation and self-control. One can link a natural sensitivity such as a sense of justice with compassion. According to recent research, children at the age of eighteen months have at their disposal a purely natural cooperativeness: in experiments, one apparently unintentionally drops a small object so that it lands beyond one's own reach. When the tester is unsuccessful at recovering the object on his own, 84 percent of all children help within ten seconds without a glance to them seeking help or any expression of a call for assistance.

What is new here over and against the art of living is the capacity in a conflict between duty and natural inclination to learn to subordinate one's inclination. Yet one can be deceived by one's inclinations. Nonetheless, whether or not one is actually prepared to set aside one's inclinations can be tested with a thought experiment that corresponds to the reality of moral freedom: for example, does one remain honest when it costs one something—even as much as a long-desired success in one's profession? In the case of a positive answer, one may say that one has performed a duty for the sake of the duty itself; that is, without having pursued any (financial, social, . . .) gain. The one gain that is allowed but, because of its special status, is best called a quasi-gain, is the gain of moral self-esteem. This gain emphasizes that the epitome of moral obligation, the moral law, constitutes its own motivation. In the case of autonomous morality, moral development aims at moral self-esteem and autonomous freedom.

The experiential sciences like pedagogy and empirical psychology investigate the conditions that influence moral development. The studies of Kohlberg are pathbreaking (recently 1995; also compare Garz, Oser, and Althof 1999; on teaching ethics in a pluralistic culture, see Höffe 2000a, chapter 16). Three moral-psychological principles proposed by Rawls (1972, section 75) are not drawn from empirical experience, but they are carefully reflective and thoroughly saturated with experience. However, the decisive moment, the moral moment, is not grounded in experience, so that the decisive principle, as well, cannot arise out of experience. Morality is what determines the crucial principle, and the empirical sciences derive the principle from moral philosophy. To be sure, neither morals nor their philosophy are the privilege of professional philosophers. Empirical scientists are also competent in moral philosophy, not as empirical scientists but rather because they are well grounded in generally human practical reason and even in the generally human ability to philosophize.

A fundamental ethics leaves to political ethics the question concerning those institutions that make moral development easier, and even facilitate it. Fundamental ethics itself contemplates how morals come to be anchored in an individual. There are three models taken to be ideal types that one can also apply in the sense of three levels: an authoritarian, an adaptively anchored, and finally an autonomous self-commitment. At the third level, one will find, in addition, a heretofore neglected (subordinate) gradation.

The first, authoritarian model one knows from Sigmund Freud. According to him, the feeling of guilt, including shame and a guilty conscience, has two origins that complement one another in the course of their development. First, the anxiety of a small child in the face of the external authority of his father or parents forces the suppression of the satisfaction of his appetites. Should the authority be internalized by the establishment of a superego, one is urged, in addition, to impose a self-punishment; however, even when the suppression is successful, one experiences a feeling of guilt for the original impulse. The second origin: culture shuts off any opposing aggression to it by means of an internalization so that the aggression is directed toward one's own self. This aggression is assumed, namely, by a part of the ego that as the superego stands in opposition to the remaining ego—we can name it the personal ego. As "conscience," it exercises the same strict readiness for aggression against the personal ego that the ego would rather satisfy by attacking others, strangers.

The fact that Freud's model contains not only insights but also oversimplifications is indisputable. From the standpoint of morals the linear hierarchy, for example, is questionable: the dual dominance of the superego and the id over the ego without the possibility of a corrective feedback. In conjunction with this arises a second misgiving. It questions the assumption that there is not only a tension but necessarily hostility between the culturally shaped superego and the epitome of demand on the part of the appetites, the id. In truth, when it comes to appetites and needs like hunger, thirst, and, for Freud, the all-dominant sexuality, one can distinguish two moments. The *formal* moment lies in the drive for immediate satisfaction; the *substantive* moment lies in what the drive seeks to achieve. What is hostile to culture is only the formal and not necessarily also the substantial moment. And in the case of a successful culture, what stands in opposition to constant momentary satisfaction is not at first this culture understood as an authority that is alien to the individual and hostile to his interests. As the reflections on hedonistic reason have shown, enduring personal well-being needs a correcting authority (chapter 11.2).

Freud's primary weakness consists in a missing distinction: that, when it comes to guilt, shame, and conscience, everything depends upon which specific kind. These occur, namely, not only in an authoritarian but also in an adaptive, and, finally, an autonomous form. To be sure, Freud doesn't exclusively present an authoritarian model. For example, when it comes to the maxims for therapy, "Where the id was, the ego should be" and the ego is "to be made stronger than the superego," Freud approaches the third, autonomous model (*Neue Folge der Vorlesungen zur Einführung in die Psychoanalyse,* 1933/1974, 516).

The second, adaptive, model is represented by the sociologist Talcott Parsons in 1964 and the psychoanalyst and social philosopher Erich Fromm in 1956. Parsons emphasizes the interaction between the superego and the personal ego. In addition, the third ego, that called by Freud the "id," the appetitive ego, is also constructed socially. For this reason, the appetitive ego and the superego do not confront one another in an irreconcilable hostility. Rather, they interpenetrate one another and create, as a consequence, a stable individual capable of mastering inner conflicts. What in the authoritarian model appears as externally determined and imposed upon the individual is viewed by the adaptive model as an unconstrained agreement. The ego does not act as the mediator between two enemies, the appetitive ego and the superego. In the assumption of social roles that serve the unfolding of personal needs, the ego brings, rather, the supposed enemies to a productive collaboration.

Even closer to the ego and more strongly determined by the personality is the third model of free self-determination. Its existence is not the consequence of wishful thinking but is confirmed, it appears, by empirical studies; for example by LOGIK, a long-term study of approximately two hundred representatively selected children and youths from four to seventeen years old (Nunner-Winkler 1998). Other questions with respect to the moral, theoretical interpretation of the conclusions of this study are shelved, such as the questionable interpretation of the guilt- and shame-feelings as expressions of an authoritarian motivational structure. One wrong interpretation, however, must be addressed so that *the* philosopher of autonomous morals, Kant, is not turned back into a proponent of authoritarian self-coercion. He elevates, rather, the demands of free self-determination to their complete potential. The internal judge that the individual experiences as conscience is no rigid superego for Kant but the voice of the moral ego that addresses the immoral ego with admonishments and warnings. Furthermore, he introduces an important distinction with the three consecutive, constructive developmental processes: that of cultivating, civilizing, and moralizing processes (e.g., *Idea of a Universal History in a Cosmopolitan Plan*, "7th Proposition").

We return to the LOGIK study. According to it, already at the age of four, for all intents and purposes, all children (98 percent) are convinced that one is not permitted to steal. At the latest between the ages of six and eight, most believe (85–95 percent) that one should share with and aid others. These conclusions demonstrate three things: first, how early a moral awareness occurs in childhood development; second, how extensively this moral awareness is shared by children, almost universally; and finally, how certain this consciousness is: these convictions are not developed over a phase of attempts and failures but occur very early "as a matter of fact." However, they don't fall out of the sky but are acquired, so it seems, by means of that collectively shared language game of one's "mother tongue."

When it comes to the recognition of morals in the strict sense, we have distinguished three levels (see chapter 22.4): the recognition of a neutral judger, that of a reflective judger (one demands of oneself recognition of morals and feels shame over any lack of recognition), and that full recognition of morals which is manifest in one's general living. All three levels are concerned not merely with an expected but also with a practiced autonomy. We call the first level a mere judicative (judging) autonomy; the second, the already reflexive (directed at oneself) autonomy; and the third, the complete, genuinely moral or biographical autonomy.

With respect to these three levels, moral psychology finds a clear development: when an injustice occurs, children younger than six employ as the usual expression of their feelings, "sad." This unusual expression for designating a moral circumstance could mean that one regrets the occurrence—the caused injustice that one actually doesn't want—but one doesn't yet experience it as morally wrong. Recognition at the second level of reflexive autonomy: that one "feels shame" surfaces first at the age of six to seven; that one has "a bad conscience" only between eight and nine; and both together only sporadically, by less than 10 percent of those asked. Knowledge of moral obligations—these conclusions demonstrate—is acquired by children very early. The wish to actually obey them develops only later as a second step in the learning process.

Empirical moral psychology usually overlooks that to this point the third level, complete moral recognition that is concerned with morals for the sake of morals, has not yet been reached. The reason could be methodological. According to the usual procedures of moral psychology, the questioning of test subjects or the confronting of test subjects with particular situations difficult to judge, it is not possible to determine the decisive point for complete autonomy. Because a discipline acknowledges only reluctantly that its procedures involve a fundamental epistemological limit, one is not surprised that one doesn't find in moral psychology this insight with respect to complete autonomy.

Complete autonomy demands that an individual in fact lives his life according to the standard of universal maxims; in addition, that the individual is so certain of this manner of living that he even, at that point where the sacrifice of his natural inclinations is required, performs the sacrifice for the sake of moral duty. In the sense of moral grace, a beautiful soul is not simply satisfied to make the sacrifice with a dark and cantankerous attitude. It is only when it occurs without any air of sacrifice and with internal cheerfulness, in which the sacrifice perhaps is no longer experienced as a sacrifice, that one is actually obeying morals for their own sake and one recognizes their inner value. Such a process is imperceptible in the judgment of children and in spontaneous action such as offering consolation and assistance. In order for this additional accomplishment to occur, one perhaps requires those greater dangers that occur only with puberty, and perhaps additionally even those that occur after one has left the protective environment of one's family and school.

The free recognition that characterizes autonomous morals cannot, ultimately, be learned through examples and imitation; neither by means of helpful or scary examples, nor by praise and blame or other sanctions. All of these forms of learning constitute perhaps a preliminary level, but they no longer function at the highest, moral level. No imitation is adequate for recognition of the moral law; a self-commitment out of moral insight cannot draw from foreign resources but only from one's own.

Does this mean that we must contradict the opinion defended since antiquity that justice is learned by being just, that prudence is acquired by means of prudent actions, and that one generally acquires a virtue by means of repetitive practice? By no means should one be permitted to assert the contradiction easily. It has often been confirmed by experience, for example, corroborated by psychology, that the best prevention consists in cultivating habits (in other words, the learning of a custom and behavior) to the point that the attitude could have the rank of a proven insight.

In fact, one doesn't have a contradiction here. The envisioned self-commitment out of moral insight is only completely achieved when it has become a free activity. Only that person who has stabilized the moral orientation of his appetites through practice possesses the capacity; nonetheless, the goal and kind of practice must yet be specified. If all we do is speak of practice, then the decisive question for morals has no adequately clear answer.

Obviously, the simplest kind of practice is insufficient for morals; this means that neither conditioned quasi-reflexive reactions, nor quasi-mechanical imitation of examples, nor actions evoked by threat of punishment, are adequate. The best that one can learn in these cases is what is morally right, but one cannot learn to act out of inner agreement, that is, to act morally good. There is a moral deficit when merely proper, duty-bound actions occur merely on the basis of (moral) legality, and this deficit can be overcome only when one has reached the level of morals. At this level, one acts according to the appropriate virtue from out of one's inner self, so that one doesn't act justly for any other reason than for the sake of justice itself.

A moral development that is concerned with the complete reality of morality does not contradict the ancient opinion. It undertakes, however, a specification that adds up to a much sharper standard: one is to cultivate not just any disposition, but a free one. Legality can be practiced; however, morality requires more. Someone who doesn't engage in fraud because he fears sanctions doesn't begin to practice that which leads over time to the virtues of honesty and justice in general. In contrast, someone who doesn't engage in fraud out of mere respect for the command against fraud practices honesty by repeatedly obeying the command at a truly moral rank; he makes a habit of free honesty.

This permits generalization: only the individual who himself acts honestly, righteously, cooperatively, and courageously, where he neither fears the consequences nor hopes for any advantage, only that individual acquires through repetitive action of this kind that virtue which satisfies the strict concept of morals. On the one hand, the moment of disposition, he obeys what is morally commanded and forbidden automatically. On the other hand, the moment of "free" disposition, it occurs in cheerfulness: out of the moral grace of a beautiful soul. One can only train oneself to be such a moral being; moral development is accomplished only in a self-development.

Is there an educational process that hinders evil? The answer is both "Yes!" and "No!" For persons whose development to the morally good commences early enough and who through repetitive practice acquire features of moral character, evil has as good as no chance. To be sure, the cautious qualification "as good as" is indispensable, yet it is supported by a consideration that belongs to the concept of a beautiful soul: by means of the intensification of the task (that is, with the development to morality) there follows a weakening of fulfillment, and for that reason no education to the morally good can avoid evil without exception. First, not everyone begins this development to moral goodness early enough; second, even with an opportune start, the development is not always successful. Above all, third, moral action can never achieve the certainty of an orientation insusceptible to temptation. Because a human being can be no pure rational being, the temptation is unavoidable. He is incessantly perfectible but never perfect.

25 Can Morality Make Us Happy?

A comprehensive moral philosophy asks the disturbing question: why should one be moral? The question is disturbing because the answer should be clear but nevertheless is difficult to give. Among the reasons for this is that one likes to exploit ambiguities about the kind of moral obligation and the nature of its recognition.

To begin with, one must distinguish between two groups of moral duties. With the more modest group, civic duty, also called justice, persons are required to respect one another. The answer here to the question of why one should be moral is: one should be moral because we owe it to each other. Persons have a right not to be murdered, not to have their possessions stolen, and not to be defrauded. As a consequence and to ensure the recognition of these rights, an order of civic law is required that provides sanctions for its violation. This leads to a second answer: one should be moral in order to avoid sanctions. The strongest forms of sanctions are the rules established by civic law itself. However, there are other kinds of civil sanctions to protect rights, especially imprisonment. In addition, there are informal social sanctions. They extend from tacit to explicit criticism to disfavor, contempt, and social ostracism.

Those duties that extend beyond civic duty (for example, responsibility for well-being) are not something that one owes to one's fellow human beings. The very concept of these duties involves a meritorious more, so that our first two answers to the question of why one should be moral are inadequate. One could point to a collective advantage: all involved are better off when more than a mere civic duty is followed. This answer forces the question in response: why should one serve collective well-being? One can answer *either* with the civic sanctions answer: in such a case, moral virtue would consist in a morality of owed obligations, a civic morality or minimal quasi-morals, but moral virtue would then lose its unequivocal obligation for its own sake. *Or* one declares service to the well-being of all a duty of virtue whereby, though, the question again surfaces: why should one fulfill such a virtue and be a morally virtuous person?

Personal escalation to morality is expected not only with respect to personal virtue but also with respect to civic duty. However, neither the escalation of objective justice to a personal deportment (justice as virtue) nor the escalation of objective well-*doing* to a personal well-*wishing* is a morally grounded expectation that one can have of one's fellow men. Why, then, should one nevertheless try? Pre-moral reasons, such as collective advantage, justify at best a meritorious more but not the escalation to morality, because collective advantage is sufficient only for moral legalism. The expectation that one pursues them for their own sake is not an escalation of collective advantage. Purely conceptually with respect to morality, this "for their own sake" eliminates every consideration of advantage—either collective or personal. Where collective advantage is omitted, there can remain personal advantage. However, because morals are to be acknowledged for their own sake, personal advantage is not something to be considered in addition to moral duty. What we seek is an extraordinary advantage, a presuppositionless advantage that consists in nothing but its recognition alone. Such an advantage is found in recognition of the moral law itself. This is the point where the individual achieves the status of an all-around moral person.

The response to the question of why one should be moral in the sense of morality (morals for its own sake) can only be: out of respect for oneself as a radical, that is, down to the roots, moral being. Ultimately, we are concerned here with nothing less, but also with nothing other, than a moral self-respect. This is no comparative and occasionally exaggerated self-respect in the sense cultivated by the lovable snob Mr. Warburton in his jungle residence (W. Somerset Maugham, "The Outstation"). Only such a one can be reproached with "You turn it into a matter of self-respect," as the friend of the materially spoiled author Gabriel Corte says when he rebels against a stuffy attic room after fleeing Paris (Irene Némirovsky, *Suite Française,* 2005, chapter 9). Instead of an exaggerated self-respect, here we have the more fundamental moral self-respect that is owed not, for example, to others but, above all, to oneself.

The "should" in the question of why one should be moral is, ultimately, a moral should, a moral duty. However, it is not as is usual a duty owed to others but a duty owed to oneself. Recent moral philosophy cultivates, admittedly, a fundamental skepticism about this moral should. If one doesn't from the beginning eliminate duties owed to oneself from the concept of morality but constructs first, as the highest level of being good, a neutral concept, then skepticism is not false. Skepticism may be appropriate against many claims for these kinds of duties owed to oneself; for example, a duty to develop one's talents thoroughly when it comes to a sweeping command for perfectionism.

The situation is different when it comes to the duty to escalate morals to morality (morals for its own sake). Only that person who constitutes himself as a moral being and conforms to morals not only for authoritarian and out of pragmatic reasons, only he who fulfills toward morality this particular duty of perfection, the duty to moral self-respect, will be properly awarded the dignity that comes with the capacity for morals. He achieves a fundamental personal contribution. In contrast, someone who violates duty degrades himself.

If one radically thinks through morals to the end, it is difficult to escape the duty owed to oneself. Once one acknowledges this dimension, it is easier to acknowledge other duties owed to the self. For example, the duty of self-respect quickly becomes clear: it is no error to claim that recognition of oneself as a legal individual, the basis of judicial self-respect, is required morally; that is, it is a moral demand not only to establish but also to claim one's relationship to other persons as legal persons. The first duty, the establishing, demands the development of a legal relationship to others and, as a consequence, the establishment of oneself as a legal individual—not merely a private individual. The second duty, the claiming of what is established, requires the defense of a legal status; for example, that one resist the threat of slavery or defend oneself against continued defamation (see Höffe 2002, chapter 3.5; and Höffe 2001, chapter 7.1).

The question of interests and motivations, "Why be a moral person?" involves a multistaged answer. Minimal interest says: one should be a moral person in order to live successfully with others; a medial interest says: in order to increase one's chances of a happy, successful, good life together with others. Once again, this escalated, medial interest calls for an interactive recognition of one another as privately and legally equal persons. The highest, optimal interest demands an even further escalation because it declares: one should be a moral person because one can; one can develop one's possibilities for being a good person and can be a genuinely moral person.

The first stage is minimal-pragmatic, the second optimal-pragmatic. At the third stage, the task of becoming a moral person is made a legal, moral duty to recognize one's interrelational duty to others. At a fourth, highest stage, it becomes only a duty to oneself. Here one cannot call for morality from others but only from oneself. However, one may not take this interest in moral self-respect to be too narrow. Here we encounter another reason why the art of living cannot dispense with a moral life. Only when one has combined the two is one able to maintain without overestimating oneself what everyone gladly does: "I am one of the few respectable persons whom I've met in life" (F. Scott Fitzgerald, *The Great Gatsby*, chapter 3, last paragraph).

Finite rational beings have two fundamental interests. As rational beings, they want to be moral; as finite, that is, as needy and not only physically but also emotionally vulnerable beings, they want to be happy. They remain rational as needy and vulnerable beings, so that only with difficulty can they be happy in an immoral manner. Morals and their escalation to morality warrant, in contrast, the moral feeling of self-respect. In turn, moral self-respect instigates within the vicissitudes of activities and experiences that unity and simultaneous meaningfulness without which no one can find enduring happiness. Self-respect creates a self-satisfaction, even a delight in one's existence, that makes a considerable contribution to one's well-being independent of experiences of all kinds. As a founding father of Western moral philosophy, Socrates, says: being good and well-being constitute a unity.

Perfect happiness, however, is not reached in this way. Whoever remains unsuccessful with his life plans or is afflicted with horrible experiences loses neither his moral self-respect nor the well-being that comes from it; nevertheless, he can be seriously affected with respect to his total life condition. These life and perceived circumstances—in spite of moral self-respect and a limited happiness—can be neither existentially eliminated nor philosophically argued away. Morality functions, indeed, in the natural and social world, and it does advance real happiness. However, the world is not so constructed that a morally proportional happiness always occurs. Morality can guarantee neither for the particular, moral person, nor for a group, nor for a society those constitutive elements of happiness: preservation of life and enhancement of life, high spirits and enjoyment of life. Morality alone can only bring a certain measure of, but no perfect, happiness.

Faith offers an alternative either as a religious faith or as a faith of moral reason. Faith presupposes an omnipotent, omniscient, and perfectly just God who assures us that there will be a balancing out of good and evil, admittedly not in this world, but in a next. In addition, it presupposes an immortal soul that is allowed to experience the resolution of the other world. However, what remains for him who doesn't share this faith, which according to Kant is a rationally justified hope; what remains for him who assumes neither a compensatory God nor an immortal soul subject to divine judgment? What happens when not only with a few but in many parts of the world there is an atheism that at least silently holds that God is dead?

In the Indian national epic, the *Mahabharata,* one reads in the "Adyâa": "The consequence of duty is in both cases happiness, not only in this but in the next life" (*Lesebuch* [Höffe 2007b], no. 27). Not a few adherents to religious and secular, rational faith indeed maintain the opinion that without the hope of the promise that is derived from the existence of God and an immortal soul, one must take the world for hopeless and must declare morality to be massive foolishness. This opinion, however, is not convincing; it isn't even close to the case. The fact that in a world in which, even when created by God, not God but the totality of natural and social laws are what reign, that, in the this-worldly temporal dimension, things are difficult for the righteous and the scoundrel thrives—all this is indisputable. Certainly, even in the example of the extremely shaken victim of fate, Job, there is a transformation of unhappiness into happiness—but already in this world. Not only the Old Testament text but also Joseph Roth's novel *Job* culminates in an elevated happiness, that of the blessed. Beyond religion, however, there is little ground to orient oneself after the manner of the history of Job. What happened to Job can occur, unquestionably, which justifies the repeating of the story, but it doesn't constitute the rule: neither with respect to the first part in which a righteous person is a victim of the most devastating conceivable catastrophe, nor the second part in which in the end the miracle of an even greater happiness is awarded. Just as little is it the rule that someone, as in Roth's novel, loses his wife and children and, through the return of a son thought to be dead, finds absolute joy again in his life.

The threat that there could be a loss of happiness: that the righteous will be unhappy, and the reprobate, to the contrary, happy, is not written into a world order without God. Whoever doesn't share the hope that the righteous at the end of the day and in the next life will be definitively happy doesn't need to fear the certain loss of happiness. The fear of a definitive loss of happiness does not justify a disrespect for morals. To the contrary, pragmatic individual and social arguments speak in favor of morals so that these can increase in the world over the course of time. To be sure, this presupposes that quite a few persons conduct their lives according to pragmatic arguments. The upright will always encourage this implementation; as the model for others, it makes worthwhile the emulation of the highest form of morals, morality.

Not only in terms of personal interest but also in terms of interest in a collective happiness, there are good arguments for morals. In some particular cases, happiness may contradict morals, but it holds no absolute veto. The circumstance that self-respect out of adherence to morality contributes to the experience of happiness speaks, of course, in favor of morality. Happiness doesn't even vote for an "epicurean" compromise of morality, that is, for a reining in of morals for the sake of the enjoyment of life. Contrary to those erroneous interpretations, morals are hostile neither to life nor to pleasure. Morals only relativize life and pleasure in that they remove from them their license as the ultimate motivating power in life. Furthermore, the delight, including well-being, that comes from adherence to morality is unachievable by compromised morals, so that complete happiness by means of an epicurean compromise is impossible.

Nevertheless, the following is valid: ultimately, the desire for happiness on the part of humanity doesn't speak for morality but for humanity's interest to be at ease with oneself as a moral being. Whoever understands the question, "Why should one be moral?" in the strict sense; whoever is not satisfied to know why one often, but why one consistently should will to be moral for the sake of morals themselves; for this person one can respond only by encouraging interest in moral self-respect and moral caring and stressing one's exclusively personal responsibility for losing them. It may be that for many other things one can place the responsibility on others and other things, one's fellow beings and circumstances; however, the responsibility for self-respect is something for which the individual alone is accountable.

We come to the following conclusion: even when moral reason bestows no successful, complete life and all-around happiness without the cooperation of fate, neither does moral reason jeopardize happiness, either. Happiness is not even to be expected without moral reason. Independent of this circumstance, however, humanity owes to nothing and to no one else but itself the task of being truly moral. It is in this sense but otherwise than its author meant that Adorno's expression applies: there is nothing proper in a false life (*Minima Moralia*, part 1, ephorism 18): whoever lives as a moral person on the basis of pre-moral grounds will live morally correctly; however, he is not a truly moral person simply because he does what is morally right for merely pre-moral reasons.

4. *Animal Morabile*

44, "Our energy surplus . . .": The German sentence ends ". . . zu Ehr*sucht*, Herrsch*sucht* und Hab*sucht* im wörtlichen Sinn von Sucht." The English words "ambition, dominance, and avarice" do not have the common stem "Sucht," which literally means "addiction," so that the etymological connection is lost in the English.

6. The Happiness of Aspiration

75, "Divided" in *Divided Heaven:* The German word here is "geteilte," which can be translated both as "shared" and as "divided."

7. The Art of Living

85, "It seeks existential meaning": The word "existentiell" is distinguished from "existential." The latter is concerned with universal structural components of life engagement, while the former is concerned with the specific experiences of individuals.

12. Can Virtue Make Us Happy?

165, [Ver-arbeiten] . . . [*Trauerarbeit*]: The German terms here are built on the verb "arbeiten," which means "to work." They allow an emphasis on action and not mere passive endurance of the misfortune concerned.]

15. Locating Moral Freedom

189, "Free Churches": a term applied in the German-speaking world to organized churches that are separate from the official state churches (i.e., the Lutheran and the Roman Catholic churches). The term may also apply to reform movements within the official state church.

Foundational Works by Otfried Höffe

1985. *Strategien der Humanität: Zur Ethik öffentlicher Entscheidungsprozesse.* Frankfurt am Main: Suhrkamp.

1988. "Naturrecht ohne naturalistischen Fehlschluß: Ein rechtsethisches Programm." In *Den Staat braucht selbst ein Volk von Teufeln: Philosophische Versuche zur Rechts- und Staatsethik,* by O. Höffe, 24–55. Stuttgart: Reclam.

1990. "Universalistische Ethik und Urteilskraft: Ein aristotelischer Blick auf Kant." *Zeitschrift für philosophische Forschung,* 44:537–63.

1995a. "Ein Thema wiedergewinnen: Kant über das Böse." In *F. W. J. Schelling, Über das Wesen der menschlichen Freiheit* (Klassiker Auslegen, vol. 3), ed. O. Höffe and A. Pieper, revised 2001, chap. 4, 11–34. Berlin: Pieper.

1995b. *Kategoriale Rechtsprinzipien: Ein Kontrapunkt der Moderne,* 3rd ed. Frankfurt am Main: Suhrkamp.

1997. "'Tugend' (Neuzeit)." With C. Rapp. In *Historisches Wörterbuch der Philosophie,* vol. 10, ed. G. Ritter and K. Gründer, 1554–70. Basel: Schwabe.

2000a. *Ethik und Politik: Grundmodelle und-probleme der praktischen Philosophie,* 5th ed. Frankfurt am Main: Suhrkamp.

2000b. "Kants nichtempirische Verallgemeinerung: Zum Rechtsbeispiel des Verspreches." In *Grundlegung zur Metaphysik der Sitten: Ein kooperativer Kommentar,* 3rd ed., by O. Höffe, 206–33. Frankfurt am Main: Klostermann.

2000c. *Moral als Preis der Moderne: Ein Versuch über Wissenschaft, Technik und Umwelt,* 4th ed. Frankfurt am Main: Suhrkamp.

2001. *"Königliche Völker": Zu Kants kosmopolitischer Rechts-und Friedenstheorie.* Frankfurt am Main: Suhrkamp.

2002. *Demokratie im Zeitalter der Globalisierung,* rev. ed. Munich: C. H. Beck.

2004. *Kants Kritik der reinen Vernunft: Die Grundlegung der modernen Philosophie,* 4th ed. Munich: C. H. Beck.

2005. *Aristoteles-Lexikon,* ed. O. Höffe. Stuttgart: Kröner.

2006a. *Aristoteles,* 3rd ed. Munich: C. H. Beck. English: *Aristotle,* trans. C. Salazar. Albany: SUNY Press, 2003.

2006b. "Ethik als praktische Philosophie: Methodische Überlegungen (I 1, 1094 a 22–1095 a 13)." In *Aristoteles: Nikomachische Ethik* (Klassiker Auslegen, vol. 2), 2nd ed., ed. O. Höffe, 13–38. Berlin: Akademie Verlag.

2006c. "Freiheit und kategorischer Imperativ: Kants Moralphilosophie auf dem Prüfstand der Hirnforschung." In *Kant lebt: Sieben Reden und ein Kolloquium zum 200: Todestag des Aufklärers,* ed. B. Recki, S. Meyer, and I. Ahl, 79–101. Paderborn: Mentis.

2006d. "'Gerne dien ich den Freunden, doch tue ich es leider mit Neigung/Und so wurmt es mir oft, daß ich nicht tugendhaft bin': Überwindet Schillers Gedanke der schönen Seele Kants Gegensatz von Pflicht und Neigung?" *Zeitschrift für philosophische Forschung,* 60:1–20.

2007a. "Ethik als praktische Philosophie—Aristoteles." In *Ethik—Wissenschaft oder Lebenskunst? Modelle der Normenbegründung von der Antike bis zur Frühen Neuzeit,* ed. S. Ebbersmeyer and E. Keßler. Münster: Lit.

2007b. *Lesebuch zur Ethik: Philosophische Texte von der Antike bis zur Gegenwart.* Munich: C. H. Beck.

2008. *Praktische Philosophie: Das Modell des Aristoteles,* 3rd ed. Berlin: Akademie Verlag.

Works Cited

Although English titles are provided for them (e.g., *Critique of Practical Reason*), Kant's works are cited by volume and page number of *Gesammelte Schriften,* the Royal Prussian Academy of Sciences standard edition of Kant's writings.

Adorno, T. W. 1951. *Minima Moralia: Reflexionen aus dem beschädigten Leben.* Berlin. English: *Minima Moralia: Reflections from Damaged Life,* trans. E. F. N. Jephcott. Frankfurt am Main: Suhrkamp, 1974.

Annas, J. 1993. *The Morality of Happiness.* New York and Oxford: Oxford University Press.

Anscombe, G. E. M. 1958. "Modern Moral Philosophy." *Philosophy* 33:1–9.

———. 1963. *Intention,* 2nd ed. Ithaca, N.Y.: Cornell University Press.

———. 1981. *The Collected Papers,* vol. 3, *Ethics, Religion and Politics.* Minneapolis: University of Minnesota Press.

Arendt, H. 1963. *Eichmann in Jerusalem: A Report on the Banality of Evil.* New York: Viking.

Aristotle. 1968. *The Basic Works of Aristotle.* New York: Random House.

Augustine. 1993. *On Free Choice of the Will,* trans. T. Williams. Indianapolis: Hackett.

———. 1977. *In epistulam Ioannis ad Parthos, tractatus decem.* In J. P. Migne, *Patrologia Latina,* vol. 35, *Aurelius Augustinus III,* 2. Supp. Paris, 2062.

Bellebaum, A., ed. 1994. *Vom Guten Leben: Glücksvorstellungen in Hochkulturen.* Berlin: Akademie Verlag.

Bentham, J. 1789/1948. *An Introduction to the Principles of Morals and Legislation.* New York: Hafner.

Bittner, R. 2001. *Doing Things for Reasons.* Oxford: Oxford University Press.

Bohrer, K. H. 2004. *Imagination des Bösen: Zur Begründung einer ästhetischen Kategorie.* Munich and Vienna: Carl Hanser Verlag.

Bollnow, O. F. 1958. *Wesen und Wandel der Tugenden.* Frankfurt am Main: Ullstein Taschenbücher.

Bormann, F.-J., and C. Schröer, eds. 2004. *Abwägende Vernunft: Praktische Rationalität in historischer, systematischer und religionsphilosophischer Perspektive.* Berlin: De Gruyter.

Brachtendorf, J. 2006. "Einleitung." In *Augustinus: Opera. Werke,* vol. 9, ed. J. Brachtendorf, 7–72. Paderborn: Ferdinand Schöningh-Verlag.

Brink, D. O. 1989. *Moral Realism and the Foundation of Ethics.* Cambridge, Eng.: Cambridge University Press.

Broome, J. 1995. *Weighing Goods: Equality, Uncertainty, and Time.* Oxford: Basil Blackwell.

Claussen, J. H. 2005. *Glück und Gegenglück: Philosophische und theologische Variationen über einen alltäglichen Begriff.* Tübingen: Mohr Siebeck.

Conze, W., et al. 1975. "Freiheit." In *Geschichtliche Grundbegriffe, Historisches Lexikon zur politisch-sozialen Sprache in Deutschland,* ed. O. Brunner, W. Conze, and R. Koselleck, 2:495–542. Stuttgart: Klett-Cotta.

Crisp, R., and M. Slote, eds. 1997. *Virtue Ethics.* Oxford: Oxford University Press.

Damasio, A. R. 1999. *The Feeling of What Happens: Body and Emotion in the Making of Consciousness.* New York: Harcourt Brace.

Davidson, D. 1980. *Essays on Actions and Events.* Oxford: Clarendon.

Descartes, R. 1637/1996. *Discourse on Method.* New Haven: Yale University Press.

———. 1642/1987. *Meditations on First Philosophy,* trans. J. Cottingham. Cambridge, Eng.: Cambridge University Press.

Diamond, J. M. 1992. *The Third Chimpanzee: The Evolution and Future of the Human Animal.* New York: HarperCollins.

Diener, E., D. Kahneman, and N. Schwarz, eds. 1999. *Well-Being: The Foundation of Hedonic Psychology.* New York: Russell Sage Foundation.

Diener, E., and E. M. Suh, eds. 2000. *Culture and Subjective Well-Being: Well-Being and Quality of Life.* Cambridge, Mass.: MIT Press.

Ehni, H.-J. 2006. *Das moralisch Böse: Überlegungen nach Kant und Ricoeur.* Freiburg and Munich: Alber.

Eibl-Eibesfeldt, I. 2004. *Die Biologie des menschlichen Verhaltens: Grundriß der Humanethologie,* 3rd ed. Munich: Piper.

Elger, C. E., et al. 2004. "Das Manifest: Elf führende Neurowissenschaftler über Gegenwart und Zukunft der Hirnforschung." *Gehirn & Geist,* 6:30–37.

Epicurus. 1940. "Epicurus to Menoeceus," trans. C. Bailey. In *The Stoic and Epicurean Philosophers,* 30–33. New York: Modern Library.

———. 1960. *Philosophie der Freude: Eine Auswahl aus seinen Schriften,* ed. J. Mewaldt. Stuttgart: Kröner.

Foot, P. 2001. *Natural Goodness.* Oxford: Oxford University Press. German: *Die Natur des Guten,* trans. M. Reuter. Frankfurt am Main: Suhrkamp, 2004.

———. 2002. *Virtues and Vices and Other Essays in Moral Philosophy,* 2nd ed. Oxford: Basil Blackwell.

Foucault, M. 1971. "Nietzsche, la généalogie, l'histoire." In *Hommage à Jean Hyppolite,* ed. S. Bachelard, 145–72. Paris: Presses Universitaires de France. German: "Nietzsche, die Genealogie, die Historie," in *Von der Subversion des Wissens,* ed. W. Seitert, 83–109. Frankfurt am Main: Fischer, 1974.

———. 1984. *Histoire de la sexualité,* vol. 2, *L'usage des plaisirs.* Paris: Gallimard. German: *Sexualität und Wahrheit,* vol. 2, *Der Gebrauch der Lüste,* trans. U. Raulff and W. Seitter. Frankfurt am Main: Suhrkamp, 1986.

Frankfurt, H. G. 1971. "Freedom of the Will and the Concept of a Person." *Journal of Philosophy,* 68:5–20. German: "Willensfreiheit und der Begriff der Person," in *Freiheit und Selbstbestimmung: Ausgewählte Texte von Harry G. Frankfurt,* ed. M. Betzler, 65–83. Berlin: Akademie Verlag, 2001.

———. 2004. *The Reasons of Love.* Princeton: Princeton University Press.

French, P., T. E. Uehling, and H. K. Wettstein, eds. 1988. *Midwest Studies in Philosophy,* vol. 13, *Ethical Theory: Character and Virtue.* Notre Dame: University of Notre Dame Press.

Freud, S. 1920/2003. *Beyond the Pleasure Principle.* New York: Penguin Books.

———. 1933/1974. *Neue Folge der Vorlesungen zur Einführung in die Psychoanalyse.* Vienna: Psychoanalytischer Verlag. In *Studienausgabe,* vol. 1, ed. A. Mitscherlich, A. Richards, and J. Strachey, 447–608. Frankfurt am Main: Fischer.

———. 1961. *Civilization and Its Discontents,* trans. J. Strachey. New York: Norton.

Fromm, E. 1956. *The Sane Society.* London: Routledge. German: *Wege aus einer kranken Gesellschaft: Eine sozialpsychologische Untersuchung,* 3rd ed., trans. L. Mickel and E. Mickel. Munich: Deutscher Taschenbuch-Verlag, 2003.

Garz, D., A. Oser, and W. Althof, eds. 1999. *Moralisches Urteil und Handeln.* Frankfurt am Main: Suhrkamp.

Geyer, C., ed. 2005. *Hirnforschung und Willensfreiheit: Zur Deutung der neuesten Experimente,* 4th ed. Frankfurt am Main: Suhrkamp.

Gläser, P. 2005. *Zurechnung bei Thomas von Aquin: Eine historisch-synthetische Untersuchung mit Bezug auf das aktuelle deutsche Strafrecht.* Freiburg and Munich: Alber.

Guardini, R. 1963. *Tugenden, Meditationen über Gestalten sittlichen Lebens.* In *Werke,* vol. 5, ed. F. Henrich, 4th ed. Mainz: Matthias-Grünewald, 1992.

Habermas, J. 2004. "Freiheit und Determinismus." *Deutsche Zeitschrift für Philosophie,* 52:871–90.

Hampe, H., and R. Schnepf, eds. 2006. *Baruch de Spinoza: Ethik in geometrischer Ordnung dargestellt,* Klassiker Auslegen, vol. 31. Berlin: Akademie Verlag.

Hare, R. M. 1963. *Freedom and Reason.* Oxford: Clarendon.

Hartmann, N. 1926. *Ethik.* Berlin: Walter de Gruyter.

Hegel, G. W. F. 1807/1977. *Phenomenology of Spirit,* trans. A. V. Miller. Oxford: Oxford University Press.

———. 1821/1967. *Philosophy of Right,* trans. T. M. Knox. London: Oxford University Press.

———. 1827/1990. *Encyclopedia of the Philosophical Sciences in Outline and Critical Writings,* trans. S. A. Taubneck. New York: Continuum.

Herodotus. 1992. *The Histories,* trans. W. Blanco. New York: Norton.

Herskovits, M. J. 1972. *Cultural Relativism: Perspectives in Cultural Pluralism.* New York: Random House.

Hildebrand, D. von. 1933. *Sittliche Grundhaltungen.* Mainz: Matthias-Grünewalt Verlag.

Hobbes, T. 1651/1996. *Leviathan.* Cambridge, Eng.: Cambridge University Press.

Holbach, P.-H. T. d'. 1770/1970. *The System of Nature.* New York: Burt Franklin. German edition: *System der Natur,* trans. F.-G. Voigt. Frankfurt am Main: Suhrkamp, 1978.

Horn, C. 1998. *Antike Lebenskunst: Glück und Moral von Sokrates bis zu den Neuplatonikern.* Munich: C. H. Beck.

Hume, D. 1739/1987. *A Treatise of Human Nature.* Oxford: Clarendon.

———. 1748/1962. *An Enquiry Concerning Human Understanding.* New York: Collier Books.

———. 1776/1988. "My Own Life." In *An Enquiry Concerning Human Understanding.* LaSalle: Open Court.

Hutcheson, F. 1725/1990. *An Inquiry into the Original of Our Ideas of Beauty and Virtue.* In *Collected Works,* vol. 1. Hildesheim: Olms.

Illies, C. 2006. *Philosophische Anthropologie im biologischen Zeitalter: Zur Konvergenz von Moral und Natur.* Frankfurt am Main: Suhrkamp.

Jankélévitch, V. 1968. *Traité de vertus.* Mouton: Bordas.

Jensen, K., B. Hare, J. Call, and M. Tomasello. 2006. *What's In It for Me? Self-Regard Precludes Altruism and Spite in Chimpanzees.* Proceedings of the Royal Society of London, Series B–Biological Sciences, Online Publication.

Kant, I. 1900–. *Gesammelte Schriften.* Königlich Preußische Akademie der Wissenschaften, Berlin.

———. 1927. *Idea of a Universal History in a Cosmopolitan Plan.* Hanover: Sociological Press.

———. 1991. *Groundwork of the Metaphysics of Morals,* trans. M. Gregor. Cambridge, Eng.: Cambridge University Press.

———. 1996. *The Metaphysics of Morals,* ed. M. Gregor. Cambridge, Eng.: Cambridge University Press.

———. 1997. *Critique of Practical Reason,* ed. M. Gregor. Cambridge, Eng.: Cambridge University Press.

————. 1998. *Religion Within the Boundaries of Mere Reason,* trans. A. Wood. Cambridge, Eng.: Cambridge University Press.

————. 1999. *Critique of Pure Reason.* Cambridge, Eng.: Cambridge University Press.

————. 2007. *Anthropology from a Pragmatic Point of View,* trans. R. B. Louden. In *Anthropology, History, and Education,* 227–429. Cambridge, Eng.: Cambridge University Press.

Kersting, W., ed. 2005. *Klugheit.* Weilerswist: Velbrück Wissenschaft.

Kierkegaard, S. 1843/1988. *Either/Or,* parts 1 and 2, trans. H. V. Hong and E. H. Hong. Princeton: Princeton University Press.

————. 1846/1992. *Concluding Unscientific Postscript,* vols. 1 and 2, trans. H. V. Hong and E. H. Hong. Princeton: Princeton University Press.

Kleist, H. von. 1799. "Aufsatz, den sichern Weg des Glücks zu finden und ungestört—auch unter den größten Drangsälen des Lebens—ihn zu genießen!" In *Sämtliche Werke,* ed. C. Grützmacher, 867–79.

Köchy, K., and D. Stederoth, eds. 2006. *Willensfreiheit als interdisziplinäres Problem.* Freiburg and Munich: Karl Alber.

Kohlberg, L. 1995. *Die Psychologie der Moralentwicklung,* ed. W. Althof. Frankfurt am Main: Suhrkamp.

Korsgaard, C. M. 1996. "Kant's Formula of Universal Law." In *Creating the Kingdom of Ends,* 77–105. Cambridge: Cambridge University Press.

Lackner, K., and K. Kühl. 2004. *Strafgesetzbuch: Mit Erläuterungen,* 25th ed. Munich: C. H. Beck.

Ladd, J. 1985. *Ethical Relativism,* 2nd ed. Lanham: University Press of America.

La Rochefoucauld, F. de. 1664/2007. *Reflections, or Sentences and Moral Maxims.* East Sussex: Gardners Books.

Layard, R. 2005. *Happiness: Lessons from a New Science.* London: Allen Lane.

Libet, B. 2004. *Mind Time: The Temporal Factor in Consciousness.* Cambridge, Mass.: Harvard University Press.

Liebich, B. 1905. *Sanskrit-Lesebuch.* Leipzig: Lesebuchverlag.

Lorenz, K. 1974. *Das sogenannte Böse: Zur Naturgeschichte der Aggression.* Vienna: Borotha-Schoeler.

Luhmann, N. 1988. *Paradigm Lost: Die ethische Reflexion der Moral. Festvortrag anläßlich der Verleihung des Hegel-Preises der Landeshauptstadt Stuttgart am 23. November 1988 im Neuen Schloß Stuttgart.* Frankfurt am Main: Suhrkamp.

MacIntyre, A. C. 1981. *After Virtue: A Study in Moral Theory.* Notre Dame: University of Notre Dame Press.

Maistre, J. de. 1814/1974. *Considerations on France,* trans. R. A. Lebrun. Montreal: McGill-Queen's University Press.

Marcuse, H. 1938/1965. "Zur Kritik des Hedonismus." In *Kultur und Gesellschaft,* 1: 128–68 and 1:177–78.

Markowitsch, H. J., and H. Welzer. 2005. *Das autobiographische Gedächtnis: Hirnorganische Grundlagen und biosoziale Entwicklung.* Stuttgart: Klett-Cotta.

Marquard, O. 1986. "Zur Diätik der Sinnerwartungen: Philosophische Bemer-kungen." In *Apologie des Zufälligen: Philosophische Studien*, 33–53. Stutt-gart: Reclam.

Marx, K., and F. Engels. 1845/1846/1972. *The German Ideology*. New York: International.

McGinn, C. 1997. *Ethics, Evil, and Fiction*. Oxford: Clarendon.

Metzinger, T. 2004. *Subjekt und Selbstmodell: Die Perspektivität phänomenalen Bewußtseins vor dem Hintergrund einer naturalistischen Theorie mentaler Repräsentation*, 3rd ed. Paderborn: Schöningh.

Meuter, N. 2006. *Anthropologie des Ausdrucks: Die Expressivität des Menschen zwischen Natur und Kultur*. Munich: Fink.

Mill, J. S. 1861/1949. *Utilitarianism*. Oxford: Blackwell.

Montaigne, M. de. 1588/1958. *Complete Essays*. Stanford: Stanford University Press.

Moore, G. E. 1903/1995. *Principia Ethica*. Oxford: Oxford University Press.

More, T. 1516/1975. *Utopia*. New York: Norton.

Neiman, S. 2002. *Evil in Modern Thought: An Alternative History of Philosophy*. Princeton: Princeton University Press. German: *Das Böse denken: Eine andere Geschichte der Philosophie*, trans. C. Goldmann. Frankfurt am Main: Suhrkamp, 2004.

Nietzsche, F. 1967. *On the Genealogy of Morals*, trans. W. Kaufmann and R. J. Hollingdale. New York: Vintage Books.

———. 1967–77. *Kritische Studienausgabe*, ed. G. Colli and M. Montinari, 15 vols. Berlin: Walter de Gruyter.

———. 1974. *The Gay Science: With a Prelude in Rhymes and an Appendix of Songs*, trans. W. Kaufmann. New York: Vintage Books.

———. 1982. *Daybreak*, trans. R. J. Hollingdale, Cambridge, Eng.: Cambridge University Press.

———. 1995. *Thus Spoke Zarathustra: A Book for All and None*, trans. W. Kauf-mann. New York: Modern Library.

———. 1996. *Human, All Too Human*, trans. R. J. Hollingdale. Cambridge, Eng.: Cambridge University Press.

———. 1998. *Beyond Good and Evil*. Oxford: Oxford University Press.

———. 2005. *The Antichrist, Ecce Homo, Twilight of the Gods*, trans. J. Norman. Cambridge, Eng.: Cambridge University Press.

Nivison, D. S. 2003. "De (Te): Virtue or Power." In *Encyclopedia of Chinese Phi-losophy*, ed. A. S. Cua. New York: Routledge.

Nunner-Winkler, G. 1998. "Zum Verständnis von Moral-Entwicklungen in der Kindheit." In *Entwicklung im Kindesalter*, ed. F. E. Weinert, 133–52. Weinheim: Beltz.

Parsons, T. 1964. *Social Structure and Personality*. London: Free Press.

Pascal, B. 1669/1965. *Pensées: Thoughts on Religion and Other Subjects*. New York: Washington Square.

Paul, A. 1998. *Von Affen und Menschen: Verhaltensbiologie der Primaten*. Darm-stadt: Wissenschaftliche Buchgesellschaft.

Perler, D., and M. Wild, eds. 2005. *Der Geist der Tiere: Philosophische Texte zu einer aktuellen Diskussion.* Frankfurt am Main: Suhrkamp.

Pfeifer, K. 1989. *Actions and Other Events: The Unifier-Multiplier Controversy.* New York: P. Lang.

Pieper, A. 2003. *Glückssache: Die Kunst, gut zu leben,* 2nd ed. Munich: Deutscher Taschenbuch Verlag.

Planck, M. 1934/1949. "Vom Wesen der Willensfreiheit." In *Wege zur physikalischen Erkenntnis: Reden und Vorträge,* 5th ed. Leipzig: S. Hirzel.

Plato. 1997. *Complete Works.* Indianapolis: Hackett.

Prinz, W. 1996. "Freiheit oder Wissenschaft?" In *Freiheit des Entscheidens und Handelns,* ed. M. von Cranach and K. Foppa, 87–103. Heidelberg: Asanger.

Raaflaub, K. 1985. *Die Entdeckung der Freiheit: Zur historischen Semantik und Gesellschaftsgeschichte eines politischen Grundbegriffes der Griechen.* Munich: C. H. Beck.

Rawls, J. 1972. *A Theory of Justice.* Cambridge, Mass.: Harvard University Press.

Ricoeur, P. 1960/1967. *The Symbolism of Evil,* trans. E. Buchanan. New York: Harper and Row.

———. 1960/1986. *Fallible Man,* trans. W. J. Lowe. New York: Fordham University Press.

Rippe, K. P. 1993. *Ethischer Relativismus: Seine Grenzen—seine Geltung.* Paderborn: Schöningh.

Rippe, K. P., and P. Schaber, eds. 1998. *Tugendethik.* Stuttgart: Reclam.

Roth, G. 2003a. *Aus Sicht des Gehirns.* Frankfurt am Main: Suhrkamp.

———. 2003b. *Fühlen, Denken, Handeln: Wie das Gehirn unser Verhalten steuert,* rev. ed. Frankfurt am Main: Suhrkamp.

Rousseau, J.-J. 1979. *Émile; or, On Education.* New York: Basic Books.

Ryle, G. 1950. *The Concept of Mind.* London: Hutchinson's University Library.

Sartre, J.-P. 1963. *Existentialism and Humanism,* trans. P. Mairet. London: Methuen.

Scarano, N. 2001. *Moralische Überzeugungen: Grundlinien einer antirealistischen Theorie der Moral.* Paderborn: Mentis.

Schaber, P. 1997. *Moralischer Realismus.* Freiburg and Munich: Alber.

Scheler, Max. 1913/1972. "Zur Rehabilitierung der Tugend." In *Gesammelte Werke,* 5th ed., vol. 3, *Vom Umsturz der Werte, Abhandlungen und Aufsätze,* ed. Maria Scheler, 1–31. Bern: Bouvier.

———. 1913/1973. *Zur Phänomenologie der Sympathiegefühle von Liebe und Haß.* In *Gesammelte Werke,* vol. 7, *Wesen und Formen der Sympathie, Die deutsche Philosophie der Gegenwart,* ed. M. S. Frings, 1–258. Bern: Bouvier.

———. 1916/1980: *Der Formalismus in der Ethik und die materile Wertethik,* in *Gesammelte Werke,* 6th ed., vol. 2, ed. M. Scheler. Bern: Bouvier.

———. 1985. *Formalism in Ethics and Non-Formal Ethics of Values: A New Attempt Toward the Foundation of an Ethical Personalism.* Evanston: Northwestern University Press.

Schick, K. 2005. *Otto Dix: Hommage à Martha.* Ostfildern: Hatje Cantz Verlag.

Schönburg, A. von. 2005. *Die Kunst des stilvollen Verarmens: Wie man ohne sein Geld reich wird.* Berlin: Rowohlt.

Schopenhauer, A. 1839/1986. *Preisschrift über die Freiheit des Willens.* In *Sämtliche Werke,* vol. 3, ed. W. von Löhneysen, 521–631. Frankfurt am Main: Insel Verlag.

———. 1840/1986. *Preisschrift über die Grundlage der Moral.* In *Sämtliche Werke,* vol. 3, ed. W. von Löhneysen, 632–816. Frankfurt am Main: Insel Verlag.

Searle, J. R. 1969. *Speech Acts.* Cambridge, Eng.: Cambridge University Press.

Seel, M. 1999. *Versuch über die Form des Glücks: Studien zur Ethik,* 2nd ed. Frankfurt am Main: Suhrkamp.

Seneca, L. A. 2004a. *Letters from a Stoic: Epistulae morales ad Lucilium.* London: Penguin.

———. 2004b. *On the Shortness of Life.* London: Penguin.

Shaftesbury, A. A. C. 1711/2001. *An Inquiry Concerning Virtue or Merit.* In *Characteristicks of Men, Manners, Opinions, Times.* Indianapolis: Liberty Fund.

Shen, V. 2003. "Zhenren (Chen-jen): The True Authentic Person." In *Encyclopedia of Chinese Philosophy,* ed. A. S. Cua, 872–74. New York: Routledge.

Singer, G. M. 1961. *Generalization in Ethics.* New York: Knopf.

Singer, W. 2004. "Keiner kann anders, als er ist: Verschaltungen legen uns fest: Wir sollten aufhören, von Freiheit zu reden." In *Hirnforschung und Willensfreiheit: Zur Deutung der neuesten Experimente,* ed. C. Geyer, 30–65. Frankfurt am Main: Suhrkamp.

Smith, A. 1774. *The Theory of Moral Sentiments.* London, Strahan.

Solomon, R. C., ed. 2004. *Thinking About Feeling: Contemporary Philosophers on Emotion.* Oxford: Oxford University Press.

Spaemann, R. 1993. *Glück und Wohlwollen: Versuch über Ethik,* 3rd ed. Stuttgart: Klett-Cotta.

Spinoza, B. de. 1677/1982. *The Ethics and Selected Letters,* trans. S. Shirley. Indianapolis: Hackett.

Staudinger, U. M., J. Smith, and P. B. Baltes, eds. 1994. *Handbuch zur Erfassung von weisheitsbezogenem Wissen.* Berlin: Max-Planck-Institut für Bildungsforschung.

Stevenson, C. L. 1944. *Ethics and Language.* New Haven: Yale University Press.

Sumner, L. W. 1996. *Welfare, Happiness, and Ethics.* Oxford: Clarendon.

Tomasello, M. 1999. *The Cultural Origins of Human Cognition.* Cambridge, Mass.: Harvard University Press.

Tugendhat, E. 2006. "Das Problem einer autonomen Moral." In *Ernst Tugendhats Ethik: Einwände und Erwiderungen,* ed. N. Scarano and M. Suárez. Munich: C. H. Beck.

Usener, H. 1887/1966. *Epicurea,* 2nd ed. Stuttgart: Teubner.

Waal, F. de. 1996: *Good Natured: The Origins of Right and Wrong in Humans and Other Animals.* Cambridge, Mass.: Harvard University Press.

———. 2005. *Our Inner Ape: A Leading Primatologist Explains Why We Are Who We Are.* New York: Riverhead Books.

Wassermann, C. 2002. *Die Macht der Emotionen: Wie Gefühle unser Denken und Handeln beeinflussen.* Darmstadt: Wissenschaftliche Buchgesellschaft.

Watson, L. 1996. *Dark Nature: A Natural History of Evil.* New York: Harper-Collins.

Weber, M. 1919/1965. *Politics as a Vocation,* trans. H. H. Gerth and C. Wright Mills. Philadelphia: Fortress.

Williams, B. 1985. *Ethics and the Limits of Philosophy.* Cambridge, Mass.: Harvard University Press.

Wittgenstein, L. 1914/1916/1961. *Notebooks 1914–1916* (*Tagebücher 1914–1916*), trans. G. E. M. Anscombe. New York: Harper & Brothers.

———. 1922/1961. *Tractatus Logico-Philosophicus.* New York: Humanities.

———. 1958. *Philosophical Investigations,* trans. G. E. M. Anscombe. New York: Macmillan.

Literary Works

Barnes, Julian, 1992. *The Porcupine.* Toronto: Random House.

Beaumarchais, Pierre Augustin Caron de. 1964. *The Marriage of Figaro.* Baltimore: Penguin Books.

Benn, Gottfried. 1956. *Einsamer nie.* Stuttgart: Klett-Cotta.

Blatter, Silvio. 2004. *Zwölf Sekunden Stille.* Frankfurt am Main: Frankfurter Verlagsanstalt.

Brecht, Bertolt. 1993. *The Good Person of Szechwan.* New York: Arcade.

Camus, Albert. 1975. *The Myth of Sisyphus and Other Essays,* trans. Justin O'Brien. New York: Knopf.

Christensen, Lars Saabye. 2004. *The Half Brother,* trans. Kenneth Steven. New York: Arcade.

Conrad, Joseph. 1903/1922. *Youth.* Garden City: Doubleday.

Dante. 2008. *The Divine Comedy.* Oxford: Oxford University Press.

Doerr, Anthony. 2004. *About Grace.* New York: Scribner. German: *Winklers Traum vom Wasser.* Munich: C. H. Beck, 2005.

Dostoevsky, Fyodor. 1970. *A Raw Youth.* New York: Macmillan.

———. 1995. *The Brothers Karamazov.* New York: Barnes & Noble.

Dürrenmatt, Friedrich. 1956. *The Visit: A Tragi-Comedy,* trans. Patrick Bowles. New York: Grove.

Fitzgerald, F. Scott. 1995. *The Great Gatsby.* New York: Scribner.

Frisch, Max. 1951. *Graf Öderland.* Berlin: Suhrkamp.

Goethe, J. W. von. 1993. *Egmont.* In *Plays,* ed. Frank G. Ryder. New York: Continuum.

———. 2008. *Gedichte: Studienausgabe.* Ditzingen: Reclam.

Hafiz. 2004. *Die Ghaselen des Hafiz,* trans. Joachim Wohlleben. Würzburg: Königshausen & Neumann.

Hawthorne, Nathaniel. 1982. "Egoism; or, The Bosom-Serpent." In *Tales and Sketches*. New York: Library of America.

Homer. 2009. *Iliad*. New York: Knopf.

Kafka, Franz. 1919/1971. "A Report to an Academy." In *The Complete Stories*, 250–62. New York: Schocken Books.

———. 1999. *The Trial*. New York: Random House.

Márquez, Gabriel García. 1986. *The Story of a Shipwrecked Sailor*. New York: Knopf.

Maugham, W. Somerset. 1965. *Of Human Bondage*. New York: Modern Library.

———. 1977. "The Outstation." In *W. Somerset Maugham Collected Short Stories*, 338–65. New York: Penguin Books.

McEwan, Ian. 2002. *Atonement*. New York: Nan A. Talese/Doubleday.

Mercier, Pascal. 2008. *Night Train to Lisbon*. New York: Grove.

Milton, John. 1969. *Paradise Lost; Paradise Regained; and Samson Agonistes*. Garden City: International Collectors Library.

Molière. 2000. *The Misanthrope and Other Plays*. London: Penguin.

Morrison, Toni. 2003. *Love*. New York: Knopf.

Nadolny, Sten. 1987. *The Discovery of Slowness*, trans. Ralph Freedman. New York: Viking Penguin.

Némírovsky, Irene. 2005. *Suite Française*, trans. Sandra Smith. New York: Knopf.

Ott, Karl-Heinz. 2007. *Endlich Stille*. Hamburg: Hoffman and Campe.

Racine, Jean. 2001. *Phedra*. London: Nick Hern Books.

Roth, Joseph. 1931. *Job: The Story of a Simple Man*. New York: Viking.

Shakespeare, William. 1927. *Venus and Adonis*. New Haven: Yale University Press.

Steinbeck, John. 1935/1965. *Tortilla Flat*. In *The Short Novels of John Steinbeck*, 1–133. New York: Viking.

Timm, Uwe. 2003. *Rot*, 2nd ed. Cologne: Kiepenheuer & Witsch.

Wolf, Christa. 1965. *Divided Heaven*, trans. Joan Becker. Berlin: Seven Seas Books.

Yourcenar, Marguerite. 1957. *Coup de grâce*, trans. Grace Frick. New York: Farrar, Straus and Cudahy.

Zweig, Stefan. 1987. *Ben Jonsons "Volpone" und andere Nachdichtungen und Übertragungen für das Theater*. Frankfurt am Main: Fischer.

NAME INDEX

Artists, writers of works of fiction, and fictional characters are *italicized.*

Achilles, 242
Adorno, T. W., 85, 350
Alceste, 100
Althof, W., 338
Annas, J., 86
Anscombe, G. E. M., 58, 120, 321
Antigone, 153
Apel, K.-O., 272
Arendt, H., 324–25
Aristotle, 3, 11, 14, 21, 28–29,
    37–38, 62, 69, 74, 78, 80, 86,
    91, 93, 96, 98, 101, 121, 123,
    125–26, 131, 141, 144, 156–57,
    160–64, 167, 171, 176–78, 180,
    183–84, 209, 237, 245, 257–58,
    262–63, 313, 320–21, 334, 336
Augustine, Saint, 141, 225

Baltes, P. B., 84
Barnes, J., 18
Beaumarchais, P. A. C. de, 160
Beckett, S., 143
Bellebaum, A., 73
Benn, G., 97
Bentham, J., 3, 146, 148, 150, 152
Bhartrhari, 317
Bieri, P., 231
Bittner, R., 59–60
Blatter, S., 190
Boëthius, 258
Bohrer, K.-H., 318
Bollnow, O. F., 120
Bormann, F.-J., 155
Briest, E., 153
Brink, D. O., 52

Briony, 206
Broome, J., 148
Buddenbrook, T., 153
Buddha, 78, 96

Caligula, 324
Call, J., 319
Callicles, 35
Camus, A., 34, 88
Christensen, L. S., 295
Claussen, J. H., 86
Cleobulus, 96
Conrad, J., 164
Conze, W., 191
Corte, G., 346
Crisp, R., 121

Damasio, A. R., 240
Damon, 243
Dante Alighieri, 209
Darwin, C., 240
Davidson, D., 59, 204, 232
Descartes, R., 225, 241, 249–50,
    259
Diamond, J. M., 39
Diener, E., 87, 98
Dix, O., 105
Doerr, A., 140, 164
Don Juan, 97, 220
Dostoevsky, F., 25, 324
Dürrenmatt, F., 125

Eibl-Eibesfeldt, I., 39
Eichmann, A., 325
Elger, C. E., 250

365

syllogism, 54–59
sympathy, 26, 35, 47, 143–44, 153, 217, 269, 289, 303–4, 330, 334

thankfulness, 173
theft, 234, 246, 280, 286–87, 300
theology, 225
thesis of dissonance, 329
tolerance, 42, 164, 166, 222
torture, 15, 164, 169, 324
tradition, 1, 35, 88, 128, 155, 210, 268
transcendental, 80, 232, 234

universalism, 128
universality, 33, 66, 125, 127–28, 266–67, 303
universalizability, *see also* generalization, 227, 269, 273–87, 299, 303–4, 312
utilitarianism, *see also* ethics (consequentialist), 3, 15, 18, 34, 66, 81, 98, 146, 150, 180, 269–70, 299
utopia, 75–76, 85, 174

vice, 118, 128, 132, 143, 160, 209, 266, 318, 320–22
virtue, 2, 13, 43, 59, 74, 83, 117–31, 140, 156, 158, 262–63, 307, 333; duty of, 20, 346; eudaimonistic, 126, 128, 131, 137, 159, 172, 181; intellectual, 66, 118, 131,

155, 262, 314; moral, 20, 66, 117–19, 124–28, 131–32, 150, 153–57, 159, 167–68, 178, 262, 275, 345; primary, 120, 124, 171
voluntariness, 48–51, 54, 61, 199–200, 232, 243, 252, 262, 273, 319–20

weakness of the will, 58, 68, 209, 305, 320, 322, 326
wealth, 66, 74, 95–96, 107–8, 127, 130, 141, 154, 190, 212, 276, 284
welfare, general, 80, 282
well-being, *see also* self-interest, egoism, 1, 2, 13, 18–20, 30–39, 56–57, 76, 87, 112, 134, 144–45, 149, 154, 158, 161, 168, 171–76, 178, 180–81, 211–14, 226, 229, 243, 254–55, 268–69, 281, 290–92, 302–6, 322, 329–30, 334–36, 340, 345–47, 350; others', 171–75, 178
why one should be moral, 297, 345–47, 350
will, 50, 211–17, 230, 241–43, 253–54, 299–300, 311–15
wisdom, 1, 6, 66, 74, 84, 88, 131, 145–57, 313–14; life, 2, 84–85, 117–21, 128, 131, 154–57, 159, 163, 169, 178, 181, 290; literature, 91, 95, 101, 142, 240; popular, 143; practical, 156

Otfried Höffe is a professor of philosophy and director of the research area of political philosophy at the University of Tübingen, Germany. His other works include *Kant's "Critique of Pure Reason," Immanuel Kant, Aristotle,* and *Kant's Cosmopolitan Theory of Law and Peace.*

Douglas R. McGaughey is a professor of religious studies at Willamette University in Salem, Oregon.

Aaron Bunch is an assistant professor of philosophy at Washington State University.